# ActionScript®

*Your visual blueprint™ for creating interactive projects in Flash® CS4 Professional*

## by Rob Huddleston

WILEY

Wiley Publishing, Inc.

ActionScript®: Your visual blueprint™ for creating interactive projects in Flash® CS4 Professional

Published by
**Wiley Publishing, Inc.**
10475 Crosspoint Boulevard
Indianapolis, IN 46256

www.wiley.com

Published simultaneously in Canada

*Library of Congress Control Number:* 2009928479

ISBN: 978-0-470-48194-3  41379677   9/09

Manufactured in the United States of America

10 9 8 7 6 5 4 3 2 1

## Trademark Acknowledgments

## Contact Us

For general information on our other products and services, please contact our Customer Care Department within the United States at (877)762-2974, outside the United States at (317)572-3993, or fax (317)572-4002.

For technical support, please visit www.wiley.com/techsupport.

Perhaps the most famous of all monuments to love, the Taj Mahal is also among the world's most recognizable structures. Built by Emperor Shah Jahan in the 17th century, the white marble edifice fulfilled his pledge to his dying queen, Mumtaz Mahal, to build for her a mausoleum unlike any the world had seen before. Designed by Persian architect Ustad Ahmad Lahori, the magnificent domed structure is resplendent with intricate pierce-work carvings, gemstone inlays, and ornate sculpture. It remains a wonder of the world more than 350 years after its completion.

Discover more of India's wonders in *Frommer's India,* 3rd Edition, available wherever books are sold and at www.frommers. com.

# PRAISE FOR VISUAL BOOKS...

"This is absolutely the best computer-related book I have ever bought. Thank you so much for this fantastic text. Simply the best computer book series I have ever seen. I will look for, recommend, and purchase more of the same."

—David E. Prince (NeoNome.com)

"I have several of your Visual books and they are the best I have ever used."

—Stanley Clark (Crawfordville, FL)

"I just want to let you know that I really enjoy all your books. I'm a strong visual learner. You really know how to get people addicted to learning! I'm a very satisfied Visual customer. Keep up the excellent work!"

—Helen Lee (Calgary, Alberta, Canada)

"I have several books from the Visual series and have always found them to be valuable resources."

—Stephen P. Miller (Ballston Spa, NY)

"This book is PERFECT for me — it's highly visual and gets right to the point. What I like most about it is that each page presents a new task that you can try verbatim or, alternatively, take the ideas and build your own examples. Also, this book isn't bogged down with trying to 'tell all' — it gets right to the point. This is an EXCELLENT, EXCELLENT, EXCELLENT book and I look forward to purchasing other books in the series."

—Tom Dierickx (Malta, IL)

"I have quite a few of your Visual books and have been very pleased with all of them. I love the way the lessons are presented!"

—Mary Jane Newman (Yorba Linda, CA)

"I am an avid fan of your Visual books. If I need to learn anything, I just buy one of your books and learn the topic in no time. Wonders! I have even trained my friends to give me Visual books as gifts."

—Illona Bergstrom (Aventura, FL)

"I just had to let you and your company know how great I think your books are. I just purchased my third Visual book (my first two are dog-eared now!) and, once again, your product has surpassed my expectations. The expertise, thought, and effort that go into each book are obvious, and I sincerely appreciate your efforts."

—Tracey Moore (Memphis, TN)

"Compliments to the chef!! Your books are extraordinary! Or, simply put, extra-ordinary, meaning way above the rest! THANK YOU THANK YOU THANK YOU! I buy them for friends, family, and colleagues."

—Christine J. Manfrin (Castle Rock, CO)

"I write to extend my thanks and appreciation for your books. They are clear, easy to follow, and straight to the point. Keep up the good work! I bought several of your books and they are just right! No regrets! I will always buy your books because they are the best."

—Seward Kollie (Dakar, Senegal)

"I am an avid purchaser and reader of the Visual series, and they are the greatest computer books I've seen. Thank you very much for the hard work, effort, and dedication that you put into this series."

—Alex Diaz (Las Vegas, NV)

# Credits

Senior Acquisitions Editor
Jody Lefevere

Project Editor
Dana Rhodes Lesh

Technical Editor
Paul Geyer

Copy Editor
Dana Rhodes Lesh

Editorial Director
Robyn Siesky

Editorial Manager
Cricket Krengel

Business Manager
Amy Knies

Senior Marketing Manager
Sandy Smith

Vice President and Executive
Group Publisher
Richard Swadley

Vice President and Executive Publisher
Barry Pruett

Project Coordinator
Katie Crocker

Graphics and Production Specialists
Ana Carrillo

Quality Control Technician
David Faust

Proofreading and Indexing
Toni Settle
Ty Koontz

Media Development Project Manager
Laura Moss

Media Development Assistant
Project Manager
Jenny Swisher

Layout
Andrea Hornberger
Jennifer Mayberry

Screen Artists
Ana Carillo
Ronald Terry

Cover Illustrator
David Gregory

## About the Author

**Rob Huddleston** has been developing Web pages and applications since 1994 and has been an instructor since 1999, teaching Web and graphic design to thousands of students. His clients have included the U.S. Bureau of Land Management; the U.S. Patent and Trademark Office; the States of California and Nevada and many other federal, city, and county agencies; the U.S. Army and Air Force; Fortune 500 companies such as AT&T, Bank of America, Wells Fargo, Safeway, and Coca-Cola; software companies including Adobe, Oracle, Intuit, and Autodesk; the University of California; San Francisco State University; the University of Southern California; and hundreds of small businesses and nonprofit agencies. Rob is an Adobe Certified Instructor, Certified Expert, and Certified Developer, serves as an Adobe User Group Manager, has been named as an Adobe Community Expert for his volunteer work answering user questions on online forums, and also helps users as an expert moderator on Adobe's Community Help system. Rob lives in Northern California with his wife and two children.

Rob is the author of *XML: Your visual blueprint for building expert Web sites with XML, CSS, XHTML, and XSLT*; *HTML, XHTML, and CSS: Your visual blueprint for designing effective Web pages*; and *Master VISUALLY Dreamweaver CS4 and Flash CS4 Professional,* all published by Wiley. You can visit Rob's blog at www.robhuddleston.com or follow him on Twitter: @robhuddles.

## Author's Acknowledgments

There can be no doubt that I would never be able to take on, much less complete, a project like this without the love and support of my wife, Kelley, and the love and understanding from my kids, Jessica and Xander. Thank you all for everything.

Thanks are also due to Dana Lesh for another fantastic round of editing. You're an absolute pleasure to work with, and I look forward to our next project together. Finally, thanks to Paul Geyer for keeping me honest as the technical editor.

# TABLE OF CONTENTS

# TABLE OF CONTENTS

# TABLE OF CONTENTS

# HOW TO USE THIS VISUAL BLUEPRINT BOOK

*ActionScript: Your visual blueprint for creating interactive projects in Flash CS4 Professional* uses clear, descriptive examples to show you how to use the ActionScript language to add interactivity to your Flash projects. If you are already familiar with ActionScript, you can use this book as a quick reference for many scripting tasks.

## Who Needs This Book

This book is for the experienced computer user who wants to find out more about ActionScript. It is also for more experienced ActionScript users who want to expand their knowledge of the different features that ActionScript has to offer.

## Book Organization

*ActionScript: Your visual blueprint for creating interactive projects in Flash CS4 Professional* has 20 chapters and 3 appendixes.

Chapter 1, "Introducing ActionScript," explains the basic workings of Flash CS4 Professional and Flash Player. It then gets you started in creating new projects and opening the Actions panel, in which you will be writing your code.

Chapter 2, "Introducing the Basic Syntax of ActionScript," shows how to create variables, work with strings, create and work with arrays and generic objects, add constants and comments to your code, and test your movie.

Chapter 3, "Controlling Objects on the Stage," shows how you can use ActionScript to manipulate MovieClips and buttons that you draw in Flash.

Chapter 4, "Working with Nonvisual Classes," introduces the Math and Date classes in ActionScript and demonstrates how to use them to perform tasks such as generating random numbers and calculating time between dates.

Chapter 5, "Writing Functions," shows how to write and call functions, how to pass arguments to functions, and how to return values from them.

Chapter 6, "Creating Custom Classes," shows how you can create your own classes to organize your code. It shows how to create packages and class files, define class properties and methods, create constructors, and use getters and setters. It also shows how to use a custom class automatically in projects.

Chapter 7, "Using Events," covers the ActionScript event model. You will learn how to add and remove event listeners, call events, define events within custom classes, and use event targets.

Chapter 8, "Controlling the Timeline in Code," shows how to start and stop movies, start and stop MovieClips, work with the display list, and add sprites and MovieClips through code.

Chapter 9, "Working with Text," covers the use of text fields in ActionScript. You will learn how to create dynamic and input text fields, both visually and through code, and how to capture and process the text entered by users.

Chapter 10, "Formatting Text," shows how to use the TextFormat object to apply formatting to dynamic and input text fields.

Chapter 11, "Making Decisions in Code," covers the use of conditional statements, including if, if/else, if/else if, and switch.

Chapter 12, "Looping over Code," shows how to use for and while loops to execute blocks of code repeatedly.

Chapter 13, "Animating in Code," teaches how to use the EnterFrame and Timer events to make objects move. This chapter also shows how to add easing, allow users to drag and drop items, and animate in 3D.

Chapter 14, "Adding Keyboard Controls," shows how you can have your code capture keyboard input from your users.

Chapter 15, "Working with Sound," shows how to add sound and music files to your movie and use ActionScript to control the sound.

Chapter 16, "Working with Video," covers the process of encoding video for Flash, adding it to your movies, and using ActionScript to control it and to add closed captioning.

Chapter 17, "Working with Data," shows how you can use ActionScript to read, write, and load XML data into your movies.

Chapter 18, "Exchanging Data with a Server," teaches how to download and install the software necessary to set up a local testing server using either PHP or Adobe ColdFusion, how to create XML files in either language, and how to use ActionScript to read server-based data and use it in Flash movies.

Chapter 19, "Drawing Vectors in Code," shows how to use ActionScript to draw shapes and add solid and gradient fills, entirely through code.

Chapter 20, "Working with AIR," covers the Adobe Integrated Runtime and shows how you can create standalone desktop applications in Flash.

Appendix A, "ActionScript Class Reference," contains a complete reference of the classes built into the ActionScript language that are applicable to Flash.

Appendix B, "ActionScript Operators," shows the operators that can be used in ActionScript expressions.

Appendix C, "Supported HTML Tags," shows the tags from HTML that can be used to format text fields.

## What You Need to Use This Book

In order to complete the steps in this book, you will need a copy of Flash CS4 Professional. It can be purchased individually or as part of one of the Creative Suite 4 editions. You can also download a 30-day trial of Flash at www.adobe.com/products/flash.

### Windows Requirements

The minimum recommended system requirements for Flash CS4 Professional in Windows are as follows:

- 1GHz or faster processor
- Microsoft Windows XP with Service Pack 2 (Service Pack 3 recommended) or Windows Vista Home Premium, Business, Ultimate, or Enterprise with Service Pack 1 (certified for 32-bit Windows XP and Windows Vista)
- 1GB of RAM
- 3.5GB of available hard disk space for installation; additional free space required during installation (cannot install on Flash-based storage devices)
- 1,024 x 768 display (1,280 x 800 recommended) with 16-bit video card
- DVD-ROM drive
- QuickTime 7.1.2 software required for multimedia features

### Mac Requirements

The minimum recommended requirements for Flash CS4 Professional on the Macintosh are as follows:

- PowerPC G5 or multicore Intel processor
- Mac OS X v10.4.11 – 10.5.4
- 1GB of RAM
- 4GB of available hard disk space for installation; additional free space required during installation (cannot install on a volume that uses a case-sensitive file system or on Flash-based storage devices)
- 1,024 x 768 display (1,280 x 800 recommended) with 16-bit video card
- DVD-ROM drive
- QuickTime 7.1.2 software required for multimedia features

In addition, some of the tasks in the book use Adobe Dreamweaver CS4, which is also available separately or as part of the Creative Suite packages. A 30-day trial of Dreamweaver is available at www.adobe.com/products/dreamweaver.

To complete the steps in Chapter 18, you will need an active Internet connection in order to download the required software, and you will need administrative privileges on your computer to install the programs. Detailed instructions on downloading and installing the files are contained in the chapter.

## The Conventions in This Book

A number of styles have been used throughout *ActionScript: Your visual blueprint for creating interactive projects in Flash CS4 Professional* to designate different types of information.

`Courier Font`

Indicates the use of ActionScript code such as tags or attributes, scripting language code such as statements, operators, or functions, and code such as objects, methods, or properties.

**Bold**

Indicates information that you must type.

*Italics*

Indicates a new term.

### Apply It

An Apply It section takes the code from the preceding task one step further. Apply It sections allow you to take full advantage of ActionScript code.

### Extra

An Extra section provides additional information about the preceding task. Extra sections contain the inside information to make working with ActionScript easier and more efficient.

### What's on the Web Site

The accompanying Web site contains the sample files for the book that you can use to work with *ActionScript: Your visual blueprint for creating interactive projects in Flash CS4 Professional.* Go to www.wiley.com/WileyCDA/WileyTitle/productCd-0470481943.html and click Downloads.

### Operating System Difference

Flash CS4 Professional has been designed by Adobe to work, as much as possible, the same on both Macintosh and Windows-based machines. The only differences between the two are those related to the operating system itself — for example, the File Open and Save As dialog boxes. All Flash movies in Flash Player and all projects in AIR run in precisely the same way on both operating systems, so there is no difference in the code that you need to write. With only minor exceptions, all the screenshots in the book were taken on a computer running Windows Vista, but the differences between Vista and older versions of Windows and between Vista and Macintosh, with regards to what is shown in the book, are so minor that they should not present any problems.

# Introducing Flash

**A**dobe Flash is the industry-standard application for creating animation and playing video on Web sites. It is fairly easy to learn when you are first getting started but has many powerful features that enable advanced developers to create full Web sites, interactive games, or almost anything else they need.

Flash was originally developed under the name *FutureSplash*. At the time, it was a simple tool for creating animation. Macromedia purchased it in 1997 and changed the name to *Flash*. Flash was the primary motivation for Adobe to purchase Macromedia in late 2006.

## The Flash Platform

Today, Adobe markets a series of products under the Flash Platform. All of these products can work together to develop Flash-based applications for a variety of delivery systems. The Flash Platform's two primary applications are Flash CS4 Professional and Flash Player, but the Flash Platform also contains the Flex 3 platform, several server-based products including the Flash Media Server, and Flash Lite.

### Flash CS4 Professional

Flash CS4 Professional is the primary integrated development environment (IDE) for developing Flash movies. When you think of "learning Flash" or "using Flash," this refers to learning or using Flash Professional, and it is the application that is discussed throughout this book. Unless stated otherwise, any further references in the text to *Flash* should be assumed to mean Flash CS4 Professional.

### Flash Player

Flash Player is the free application used to view Flash movies. Regardless of the tool used to create a Flash movie, your users actually view and interact with it through Flash Player. Flash Player is the single most-installed software, with current estimates putting it on more than 99 percent of computers worldwide.

As of the release of Flash CS4 Professional, Adobe has also released Flash Player 10. Flash Player has enjoyed record-breaking adoption rates, with previous versions averaging six million downloads per day.

### The Flex Platform

Flex offers a more developer-centric environment than Flash. Flex is an open-source platform that enables developers to create visual layouts in an XML-derived markup language called *MXML* and to add interactivity and back-end connectivity through ActionScript 3.0. Regardless, Flex applications are viewed by the user through Flash Player, and unless the site specifies it, there is no real way to look at a Flash-based site and know whether it was created in Flash Professional or Flex.

#### FLEX BUILDER

The Flex platform is open source and can be downloaded from the Adobe Open Source Web site, http://opensource.adobe.com. Although Flex applications can be created in any text editor, Adobe has developed an IDE to assist in the creation of Flex applications called *Flex Builder*. Built on the open-source Eclipse toolset, Flex Builder is available for purchase from Adobe's Web site.

#### FLASH CATALYST

In late 2007, Adobe announced that it had begun development of a new application in the Flex platform. This tool, at the time code-named *Thermo,* would enable designers to take visual compositions, created in applications such as Adobe Photoshop, and easily convert them to Flex applications. In November 2008 at Adobe MAX, the company's annual developer's conference, Adobe announced that the product would be officially named *Flash Catalyst* and that the product would be released sometime in late 2009 or early 2010.

## The Flash Platform *(continued)*

### Flash Media Server

Flash Media Server enables you to deploy streaming media such as video through Flash Player. Flash Media Server works as an intermediary between a Web server and the browser to deliver the content seamlessly. Any Flash video can be deployed to a Flash Media Server.

### Flash Lite

Flash Lite is a version of Flash Player designed specifically for cell phones and other mobile devices. Many new cell phones allow their users to play games created in Flash and deployed to Flash Lite; some new phones even use Flash for all the menus and other interface elements. You can test Flash applications in Flash Lite using the tool Device Central, which is included with Flash Professional.

## Vector Art

Flash uses vector art to create graphics. Traditional graphics applications and formats such as JPG and GIF are known as *raster* or *bitmap* art. These images are made up of pixels. If you think of your computer screen as a large sheet of graph paper, each square of the graph represents a pixel. By filling in each square with a color, you can create full-color images.

However, raster images are dependent on the resolution at which they were created. In order to double the size of the image, each colored pixel needs to expand to fill four squares, or pixels; quadrupling the size of the image forces each pixel to fill eight pixels, and so on. Eventually, these ever-expanding squares will be noticeable in the image, causing the file to become *pixelated*. In addition, each of these size increases has a proportional impact on file size: Doubling the pixel dimensions of an image roughly quadruples the file size. It is therefore impossible to resize a raster-based image without affecting the file size and quality.

Vector programs take a radically different approach. Rather than fill in squares, you create vector art by defining points and then having the program use mathematical algorithms to calculate a line or path between the points. The path can be either straight or curved, and the space between the points can be filled with color. In a vector image, resizing is accomplished by moving the two points either farther apart or closer together and having the program recalculate the math. Therefore, you can freely resize vector images without affecting either the file size or the quality of the image.

Most graphics programs today lean toward being either vector-based, such as Adobe Illustrator, or raster-based, such as Adobe Photoshop. Both, however, contain tools to work in the other methodology. Photoshop, for example, contains a set of vector-based tools, whereas Illustrator contains some tools for editing raster graphics. Flash, on the other hand, is purely vector-based, and you will not find any raster manipulation tools in it. Although you can import raster graphics into a Flash movie, and those graphics can be animated, you cannot edit the graphic without first converting it to vector format. The only exception is that raster graphics can be resized in Flash, but as they are raster images, they become pixelated if resized too much.

## Creative Suite 4

Flash CS4 Professional is marketed as a part of Creative Suite 4. The suite includes a series of integrated applications that provide a set of tools designers and developers can use to create Web, video, and print applications. Adobe currently offers four main editions of CS4 and includes Flash in each of them.

# Understanding Flash Player 10

The most important application in the Flash Platform is Flash Player. With the release of Flash CS4 Professional in late 2008, Adobe also released Flash Player 10. At the time of this writing, Flash Player 10 was too new to be included in studies, but according to a June 2008 study, Flash Player 9 was on 97.7 percent of computers in the United States, Europe, and Asia, whereas Flash Player 8 was on 98 percent of computers in similar regions.

## Downloading and Installing Flash Player

Even though the overwhelming majority of computer users worldwide have Flash Player installed on their machines, you may still encounter users who, for a variety of reasons, do not have the player installed or have an older version that will not support ActionScript 3.0. Fortunately, this issue is generally very easy to handle. Your users can manually visit Adobe's Web site at www.adobe.com and click the Get Adobe Flash Player button. Alternatively, you can include code in your HTML document that will detect the lack of the player or an outdated version and automatically prompt the user to install the Flash Player. If you create your HTML document using Adobe Dreamweaver CS4, this functionality is included automatically in the code that is added to the page when you insert a Flash movie.

## Flash Player Versions

At the time of this writing, Flash Player 10 is the most current version. Released in late 2008 alongside Flash CS4 Professional, Player 10 was designed to use several new features of Flash, including the ability to render 3D graphics and effects. However, most users today still have Flash Player 9 installed. Almost all the techniques used in this book will work correctly for users on either version 9 or 10, but ActionScript 3.0 is not supported on earlier versions at all. In the cases when Player 10 will be required for your users, it will be pointed out, but if Player 10 enjoys the same adoption rate as past versions, it should only take a year or so for it to become the dominant version on the Internet. Flash Player is available in Windows, Macintosh, and Linux versions.

You can view a detailed report on the current rate of adoption of Flash Player on Adobe's Web page at www.adobe.com/products/player_census/flashplayer/. The site includes data based on the version, locations of users, operating systems, and more.

## Flash Player Debug Version

The "normal" version of Flash Player does not include the ability to debug troublesome ActionScript code. However, Adobe has developed a special Debug version of the Player with this added capability. You can download the latest version of the Debug Player at www.adobe.com/support/flashplayer/downloads.html.

## Standalone Projector

Although the majority of Flash content is delivered through a Web browser, there may be times when you want to allow your users to save a copy of the movie to their hard drive and play it back whenever they choose, even offline. In Flash CS4 Professional, you have the option of publishing your movie to a standalone projector, which is a file that contains Flash Player and the content of your movie.

## File System Access Restrictions

For security purposes, Flash Player has very little access to the local file system of your users' computers. Likewise, it cannot generally access their hardware such as printers. If you need to create an application with full local file system and hardware access, you will want to create an application using Adobe Integrated Runtime (AIR) instead. See Chapter 20 for more details on creating AIR applications.

## Server-Side File and Scripting Access

Flash is a client-side technology. Flash Player is an application that runs on your user's machines, not on your Web server. However, Flash Player does have the capability of communicating with the Web server from which the Flash movie was sent via normal HTTP calls — the same as the browser. Flash can request external assets such as images, other Flash movies, sound files, video, and text files and then, through ActionScript 3.0, use that content in the current movie as it plays. See Chapters 17 and 18 for information on accessing and using server-side content in your Flash movies.

Flash Player cannot, under normal circumstances, request data or external access from any server other than the one that delivered the movie. Several techniques exist to work around this issue, which are covered in Chapter 18.

## The ActionScript Virtual Machine

ActionScript executes in Flash Player via the ActionScript Virtual Machine, or AVM. Traditionally, one of the most difficult aspects of creating and maintaining Web sites is the need to test your HTML and XHTML pages on multiple browsers and across multiple platforms, including Windows and Macintosh. Developers creating content in the Flash Platform are freed from this worry, as the AVM will ensure that all content running in Flash Player will work in precisely the same way, regardless of the operating system the users employ or the browsers through which they accessed the page.

With the release of Flash Player 9, Adobe completely rebuilt the AVM, primarily to include support for ActionScript 3.0. Flash Player 9 and 10, and presumably future versions, all include both AVM versions 1 and 2. When the player encounters a file that relies on ActionScript 3.0, it uses AVM version 2; when it renders a file using ActionScript 1.0 or 2.0, it falls back to AVM 1. This is in fact one of the primary reasons why Flash designers should consider switching to ActionScript 3.0: AVM 2 is far more efficient than AVM 1, meaning that similar movies will run faster and smoother if written in ActionScript 3.0 than they will if written in ActionScript 2.0. However, it is also the reason why movies that rely on ActionScript 3.0 require that the end user have at least Flash Player 9.

# Introducing ActionScript 3.0

You can add interactivity to your Flash movies using ActionScript. By adding interactivity, you can allow users to interact with a movie, triggering an immediate change in the movie. For example, a user may click a button to activate another movie clip or jump to a Web page, or you may set up a movie to stop when it reaches a certain frame. Interactivity can be as simple as a button click or key press or as complex as an e-commerce site or an online videogame.

## What Is ActionScript?

*ActionScript* is an object-oriented programming language based on scripts. *Scripts* are simply short statements that tell Flash what to do. ActionScript statements are composed of code based on the ActionScript language. When you assemble several statements, you create a script. You can control parts of the script by specifying parameters. For example, you can write a script that tells Flash to go to and play a particular frame in your movie. When assigning this action, you set the parameter for the action by designating a particular frame in your movie.

With ActionScript, you can write instructions that tell Flash to respond to mouse clicks and key presses a user might perform while viewing a movie, or you can request information from the user and have your Flash movie respond to the information the user provides. You can also use ActionScript to animate objects in your movie, and you can combine statements to produce sophisticated interactive elements for your movies.

## ActionScript Versions

As a Flash developer, you can choose to work in any of the three versions of ActionScript: 1.0, 2.0, or 3.0. ActionScript 3.0 is the newest version and has been thoroughly redesigned to support today's growing Web design needs. ActionScript 3.0 is based on ECMAScript — which is the same standard JavaScript is based on — and works best for users familiar with object-oriented programming. ActionScript 3.0 executes much faster than previous versions and is designed to allow developers to create highly complex Flash files.

ActionScript 2.0 is simpler than 3.0, but it is slower to execute in Flash Player. ActionScript 1.0 is the simplest form of ActionScript and is not as commonly used today. Flash Player 9 supports all three versions of ActionScript.

Because of its many advantages and increased functionality, this book focuses on using ActionScript 3.0 to build interactivity. To run movies created with ActionScript 3.0, your users must use Flash Player 9 or later.

## Assigning ActionScript Versions

When you start a new file in Flash, you have the option of choosing which version of ActionScript to base the file on. The Welcome Page and the New Document dialog box list both ActionScript 3.0 and ActionScript 2.0. You can also use the Publish Settings dialog box to change which version of ActionScript is associated with the file. You can assign only one version of ActionScript to a file.

## Using ActionScript in Flash

Unless you are writing scripts in an ActionScript text file, all ActionScript 3.0 instructions are attached to keyframes in your movie. As such, it is good practice to manage ActionScripts by placing them in one easy-to-locate place in your movie. You should create a new layer and place all ActionScript in the first keyframe of the new layer. After you establish a location for your scripts, you can open the Actions panel and start adding ActionScript. Most developers make this layer the top-most layer in the Timeline to make it easy to find.

The Actions panel is where you can add ActionScript to your movie. The panel includes a text editor for adding and editing script, a toolbox of common scripting codes, and a navigator area for viewing what scripts are assigned to what items in a movie. The Actions panel even offers a Script Assist mode to help you add actions without having to know a lot about writing scripts. However, if you are an experienced developer, you may prefer to use the special authoring environment for writing your code. You can write your own scripts separately from your Flash movies in an external Script window. You can use the external Script window to write ActionScript, Flash Communication, or Flash JavaScript files. See the Flash Help files to learn more about using the Script window.

If your Flash projects require form elements and user interface controls, such as check boxes, radio buttons, and list boxes, you can use components. Components are prebuilt, complex movie clips. Although prebuilt, components still require you to add some ActionScript coding of your own. Components are available in ActionScript versions 2.0 and 3.0.

## Other ActionScript Editors

Although this book focuses entirely on using Flash CS4 Professional to edit ActionScript, there are other editing tools available for working in the language. If you have not yet upgraded to Flash CS4, you can add and edit ActionScript 3.0 in Flash CS3 Professional, although any version of Flash before that will not have support for ActionScript 3.0.

You can add ActionScript 3.0 to Flash movies only in Flash, but as will be discussed in later chapters, there will be many occasions in which you will need to create ActionScript 3.0 in completely separate files. Because ActionScript 3.0 is composed only of text, you can in fact use any text editor. However, a plain text editor such as Notepad on Windows or TextPad on Macintosh will allow you to enter the code, but it will not provide any code coloring or code completion to help in your development.

Adobe currently has two applications on the market that support ActionScript 3.0 and provide a better development environment than a plain-text editor. One is Dreamweaver CS4. You can create a new ActionScript 3.0 file from Dreamweaver's New File dialog box, and the program will provide code coloring and limited code completion.

Even more powerful is Flex Builder 3. Because Flex applications rely heavily on ActionScript 3.0, Flex Builder 3 provides a powerful development environment for ActionScript 3.0. Its code completion for ActionScript 3.0 is far superior to Dreamweaver's and, at times, even surpasses that provided by Flash.

# Create a New Flash Movie

**Y**ou can begin working in Flash and ActionScript 3.0 very easily by creating a new, blank file. You can add assets to the file, commonly referred to as a *movie,* and control those assets through ActionScript 3.0.

In Windows Vista, you can launch Flash CS4 Professional from the Start menu. In the All Programs menu, you should see a folder labeled based on the edition of the Creative Suite that you purchased. In that folder, you will find a shortcut to Flash that you can click to launch the program. If you use a Macintosh computer, you should find Flash on the Dock after it has been installed, and you can simply click it to open Flash.

When Flash first opens, you will be presented with a Start screen that provides the ability to create one of several different types of files. In order to use ActionScript 3.0 in creating a Flash movie, your first option is to create a Flash File (ActionScript 3.0). You can also use ActionScript 3.0 if you select Flash File (Adobe AIR); AIR will be discussed in detail in Chapter 20. It is also possible to create a document that contains nothing but ActionScript code by clicking the ActionScript File option. See Chapter 6 for a discussion on when you might need to do this.

## Create a New Flash Movie

**Note:** *These steps show how to open Flash in Windows Vista. If you own a Macintosh computer, click Flash on the Dock and skip to step **5**.*

① Click Start.

② Click All Programs.

③ Click the edition of Creative Suite that you own.

**Note:** *The Creative Suite Master Collection is shown in this example.*

④ Click Adobe Flash CS4 Professional.

Flash opens and
displays the Start
screen.

⑤ Click Flash File
(ActionScript 3.0).

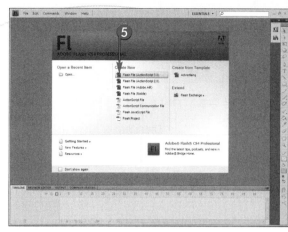

A new, blank
document opens.

## Extra

If you already have another document or movie open in Flash and want to create a new file, you can also click
File → New. The New Document dialog box that appears will present you with the same options that appear on the
Start screen, along with two additional choices for creating a Flash Slide Presentation, which allows you to use Flash
to create a PowerPoint-like document, and a Flash Form Application for creating movies that rely on user input.
Although both of these documents can use ActionScript 3.0, neither are covered in this book.

Flash CS4 Professional uses many of the same keyboard shortcuts as other applications when performing similar
tasks. Therefore, you can also press Ctrl + F (⌘ + F) to open the New Document dialog box. The dialog box,
regardless of how you open it, will default to the document type you created last or to Flash File (ActionScript 3.0)
if you are just getting started, so in most cases you can simply open it and then press Enter on your keyboard to
create the required document.

# Using the Actions Panel

You can use the Actions panel to write, format, and edit the ActionScript that you include in your FLA file, or authoring file. There are three parts to the Actions panel: the Actions toolbox, the Script Navigator, and the Script pane.

The Actions toolbox contains a list of ActionScript statements. The two top options — Top Level and Language Elements — contain commonly used statements such as variable declarations, looping statements, and the like. The remaining categories in the toolbox are organized based on how Flash Player internally accesses them. ActionScript 3.0 is an object-oriented language, which means in part that it relies on classes. These classes are organized into packages, based on their functionality. Chapter 2 discusses these concepts in detail, but for now, you should just understand that the list of categories that you see in the toolbox represent these

packages of classes. After you become more familiar with the language, you will be able to find script elements you need to add to your code by digging into these packages. When you find what you need, you can simply double-click to have that code added to the Script pane.

The Script Navigator provides a hierarchical listing of all the movie clips, buttons, and frames in your document that have scripts associated with them. You can click an element to view the associated ActionScript in the Script pane.

You use the Script pane to type and edit your scripts. The Script pane is a full-featured editor that helps you format your code. It has a toolbar that provides buttons that enable you to add script, find and replace text, insert a target path, check syntax, show code hints, debug your code, and turn on Script Assist.

## OPEN THE ACTIONS PANEL

**①** Click the frame to which you want to add ActionScript.

**②** Click Window.

**③** Click Actions.

You can also press F9 to quickly display the Actions panel or click the Edit ActionScript button in the Properties panel.

The Actions panel opens.

● The Actions toolbox lists categories, subcategories, and ActionScript code.

● You can use the Script pane to add and edit scripts.

● The Script Navigator pane lists all the elements by level in your movie, with the current selection at the top.

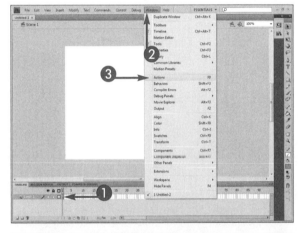

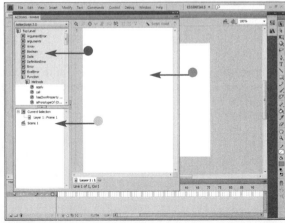

- You can drag the splitter bar, or border, to change the size of the Actions toolbox and Script pane.

- You can click the name of the object for which you want to see any associated code.

- You can click the Panel menu to view a context menu of related commands.

- You can use the tool buttons to work with scripts that you add to the Script pane.

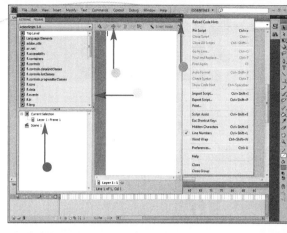

## USING THE ACTIONS TOOLBOX

④ Click a class category to see associated subcategories or codes.

- You can click a subcategory to see a list of codes.

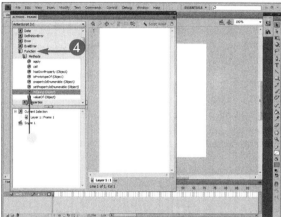

## Extra

Often, you will need the Actions panel to be as large as you can get it to provide the largest possible area for typing. When you need to view the Flash Stage, you can click the panel's title bar or click the panel's Minimize button to quickly minimize the panel. You can drag the title bar to move the panel around the screen. You can click the title bar again or click the Maximize button to maximize the panel. Also, if you drag the panel by the Actions – Frame tab to one of the edges of the screen, the panel will dock in that location.

The panel contains a set of additional features that make working in code easier. Just above the Script pane, you will find a set buttons that you can use to access much of this functionality. You can simply position your mouse cursor over any of these buttons to see a ToolTip that will indicate the button's functionality. You will also find a button in the top-right corner of the panel that provides a menu with even more features.

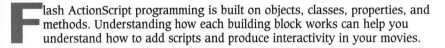

# Understanding
# Object-Oriented Programming

Flash ActionScript programming is built on objects, classes, properties, and methods. Understanding how each building block works can help you understand how to add scripts and produce interactivity in your movies.

## Understanding Objects and Classes

*Object-oriented programming,* or OOP, is a very common programming paradigm, used by most modern languages. In OOP, programmers organize code into objects that mimic real-world concepts, such as shopping carts, or encapsulate specific business models, such as a process to add a new customer to a database. As ActionScript 3.0 is an object-oriented programming language, understanding the basic terminology and concepts of OOP are vital to your success in using it.

As OOP is designed to mimic real-world situations, it can be helpful to think of a real-world analogy to apply to the terms. The following examples compare OOP concepts to the design and construction of a new housing community:

The main building block in OOP is a *class.* A class defines an object but does not represent an actual instance of the object. Before you can start using objects, you have to create them as a class. In the housing analogy, a new community cannot be built out of thin air. Before any construction can begin, the developers must plan out, or in a sense, define, each model of house they plan to build. To do this, they have a set of blueprints drawn up, one for each house model. These blueprints can be thought of as classes. You cannot actually live in a blueprint, just as you cannot actually use a class in a program; rather, each provides the definition for the actual objects.

*Objects* are *instances* of classes. Just as you must build a house based on a blueprint before you can live in it, you must also work with an instance of a class in order to use it. When

you create an instance of a class, you are creating an object, an actual "thing" that you can use in the program. When you create an instance of a class in OOP, you *instantiate* it.

If you have ever placed an instance of a movie clip or a button on the Stage in Flash, you have used objects. In fact, when you convert artwork in Flash to a symbol, you are actually creating a class; when you drag the symbol to the Stage, you are creating an instance of that class — an object.

The Button class in Flash is unique in that instances of it can be created only visually on the Stage. MovieClips, dynamic TextFields, and components are examples of classes that you can instantiate either visually on the Stage or through code. The remaining classes, of which there are several dozen, can be instantiated only through code.

In addition to the predefined classes, you can create your own. As mentioned earlier, you are actually creating a new class every time you create a new symbol. Specific business-logic needs or processes, such as a shopping cart in an e-commerce application, also need to be defined as custom classes. Creating custom classes is beyond the scope of this chapter but is an important topic for further exploration once you understand the basics of ActionScript.

Classes in ActionScript are organized into *packages.* Each class is defined in its own ActionScript file, and a package is nothing more than a folder that contains a group of related classes.

## Understanding Properties and Methods

A real-world object has properties — the things that make up the object. For example, a house can be defined by its square footage, the number of bedrooms and bathrooms it contains, the direction it faces, its color, and many other attributes. In OOP, these attributes are known as *properties.* Properties can be seen as the "nouns" of an object. Just as you would describe your house by these types of properties listed, you can describe a MovieClip by its shape, its color, its transparency or alpha, and its location on the Stage.

If you live in a modern housing subdivision, you are aware that your community contains only three or four models of houses. These were created from the sets of blueprints commissioned by the developer. Each instance of a particular model of home shares a group of common properties, such as the square footage and number of rooms. However, each house is also unique from the others in the neighborhood. Although you may live in the same model of home as your neighbor, your house is most likely a different color or may be located on a different side of the street. Certainly, your house has a unique address.

Instances of objects in ActionScript also share many properties while having other unique properties. You can create as many instances of a particular MovieClip as you like on the Stage. Each instance shares the same basic shape as each other instance. However, you can position each instance in a different place on the Stage, so their x and y properties are different. You can scale each instance in order to set different scaleX and scaleY properties.

In addition to defining objects through properties, you also want to do things to properties. In your home, you can enter and exit, cook dinner, sleep, watch TV, and work on the computer. Similarly, you need to be able to add and remove products from a shoppingCart class that you define for your e-commerce application. MovieClips can be animated on the Stage. The actions that you can perform to objects are known as *methods.* Just as properties can be seen as the "nouns" of an object, methods can be seen as the "verbs" of an object.

Most of the time, all instances of an object use a common set of methods. Although it is possible to define custom methods for individual instances of an object, doing so is beyond the scope of this book.

## Static Classes

Before continuing, it is important to understand a special type of class in ActionScript. These classes, known as *static classes,* cannot be instantiated. Instead, you can simply access their properties and methods directly. Static classes are used for cases in which having individual instances does not make logical sense. One example of a static class is Math. The Math class contains a set of properties that define mathematical constants, such as pi, and a set of methods to perform mathematical calculations, such as sine. Although it makes sense that you can have

more than one instance of a MovieClip on the Stage and thus need instantiation to control each one separately, it also makes no sense to need to instantiate the Math class: Pi is always pi, and so you do not need a separate instance. Other examples of static classes include Stage, as you cannot have more than one Stage in a movie; Mouse, because you cannot use more than one pointer device at a time on most computers; and Keyboard, as the same applies to keyboards.

# Understanding
# ActionScript Syntax Rules

**L**ike spoken languages, ActionScript has rules of punctuation and grammar that you must follow, and these rules compose the syntax of the scripting language.

## Using Semicolons

Each ActionScript statement ends in a semicolon. A statement is generally a single line of code. For example, a statement that declares a variable may look like this:

```
var myVar:String = "Hello World";
```

Although the details of declaring variables are discussed in the following section, "Create a Variable," you should note that the line is a single statement and thus ends in a semicolon.

## Whitespace

ActionScript is, for the most part, whitespace-insensitive, which simply means that it does not usually matter whether or not you have spaces in your code. As an example, the function declaration to the right could be written with the opening curly brace at the end of the first line or on a separate line as shown. Many developers prefer to put it on the first line, whereas many others prefer to have it on its own line — the choice is yours. The code also executes properly if you do not indent the line of code within the curly braces; however, ensuring that your code is readable saves untold amounts of time when debugging, so it is always recommended that you use whitespace to make your code easy to read. One important exception to this rule is that variable and function names cannot contain spaces.

## Dot Syntax

ActionScript uses *dot syntax* to separate an object name from a property, function, or method. For example, you would set the scaleX property for an instance called myButton by writing myButton.scaleX. The specifics of this concept are explained in later chapters.

## Using Curly Braces and Parentheses

Sometimes, ActionScript code is too complex to be expressed in a single statement. In these cases, you create a code block. A code block begins with a line that defines the block and then the code that will execute. The executable code is enclosed within curly braces. For example, a function declaration is written as a code block:

```
function myFunction():void
{
    return true;
}
```

You should always be careful that you close any curly brace you open. Unbalanced braces cause the script to return an error, but the error message often gives you the wrong line number. It is a good habit to always add both the opening and closing curly braces at the same time and then go back and add the code between them.

The same rules apply to the use of parentheses: You must always be sure to close any parentheses that you open. Parentheses are used to call functions and group mathematical operations.

## Case Sensitivity

ActionScript is case-sensitive. If you declare a variable with all lowercase letters, you must always use all lowercase letters to refer to that variable.

Functions, variables, keywords, properties, and methods built into ActionScript are always expressed with *camel casing,* whereby multiword names begin with a lowercase letter and then use an uppercase letter for the first letter of each additional word. As an example, the property that allows you to scale an object is scaleX — note that the $X$ is uppercase. Classes in ActionScript are all defined using Pascal casing, which follows the same concept as camel casing except that the first letter is also capitalized, such as MovieClip. So that the code you write matches the code built into the language, you should follow this same technique in your code: Use Pascal casing for custom classes you define and camel casing for everything else. You can choose to rely on a different scheme if you prefer; the only truly important factor is that you remain consistent throughout your code.

# Create a Variable

**V**ariables allow you to store information to use later in your script. For example, you can store a customer's name as a variable or the score a player has earned in a game.

In ActionScript, variables are declared using the `var` keyword, followed by the variable name. The name should be descriptive for easy reference. The variable name must begin with a letter and can contain only letters, numbers, and underscores. The variable name is case-sensitive throughout your script, so you should be consistent in what case you use. Most ActionScript developers rely on a camel casing for their variables, as described in the preceding section. It is not required that you use camel case, but as it is the casing used for built-in

variables in the language, using it will ensure that your variable names and those used by the program are consistent and thus easier to remember.

You should always declare a data type for the variable you are creating. You declare the data type by setting it after a colon, which follows the variable name. If the variable contains words or phrases or other alphanumeric characters, you should set the data type to `String`. If the data is numeric, you typically use the `Number` data type. A more thorough discussion of data types in ActionScript is in the following section, "Understanding Data Types."

You can give a variable a value when you create it by typing an equal sign and the value. String values must be quoted; numeric values must not be quoted.

## Create a Variable

1 If necessary, create a new Flash file.

2 If necessary, open the Actions panel.

**Note:** See Chapter 1 for details on creating new files and opening the Actions panel.

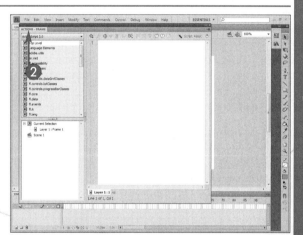

3 Type `var` and then the variable name, such as `pictureName`.

4 Type a colon.

A list of data types appears.

5 Type the variable type that you want, such as `String`.

**Note:** You can also press Enter (Return) when the code hints select the type that you want.

6 Type an equals sign.

7 Type a value.

8 Type a semicolon.

The variable is created.

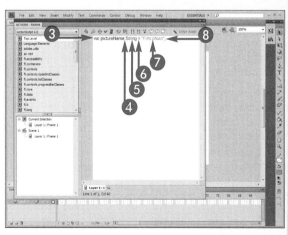

# Understanding Data Types

**A**ctionScript 3.0 is what is known as a "strongly typed" language, which is simply a way of saying that it understands and recognizes data types and that it forces you to declare these types and use them consistently through your application.

## Types of Data

Programming languages, databases, and other computer programs typically need to be able to distinguish pieces of information based on what kind of data they contain. If the type of data is not declared or understood, computers will often make mistakes. For example, in Microsoft Windows, if you have a series of files that begin with numeric characters, they will often be sorted incorrectly, with a file named 1.gif being followed by 10.gif, rather than 2.gif. This is because Windows treats all files types as being made up of strings of characters rather than containing numbers. In this method,

each letter is alphabetized individually, so therefore, it makes sense that all files that begin with a 1 come before any files that begin with a 2.

Issues such as these can be solved through data types. If we have the ability to specifically inform the program that a particular piece of data will always contain purely numeric characters, then it will treat them numerically and can correctly sort them, as well as perform math on the data and other functions.

## Data Types in ActionScript 3.0

Data types in ActionScript 3.0 are roughly grouped into three categories: fundamental, simple, and complex.

### Fundamental Data Types

ActionScript 3.0 defines three basic or fundamental data types: Null, void, and Object. The Null type can have only a single value — null — and means that a particular variable has no value. Note that having no value or being null is not the same as a zero or an empty string, as both of them actually contain *some* value.

Like Null, void has only a single possible value: undefined. You will most often encounter this type when working with functions that do not return a value, a topic that is discussed in detail in Chapter 5.

The Object type includes all instances of every class but is most often used as a generic type. You will see many instances of relying on the generic Object type as you work through this book.

In addition to these types, ActionScript 3.0 recognizes every class — both those defined in ActionScript 3.0 and those that you define yourself — as a data type. Therefore, as shown later in the subsection "Declaring Data Types," you can set a variable to be of type String, which is in essence creating the variable as an instance of the String class.

### Simple Data Types

A single variable can utilize a simple data type. The simple types in ActionScript 3.0 are String, Boolean, Number, int, and uint. Strings are units of characters, such as words or sentences. Strings can contain any type of character, including letters, numbers, and whitespace characters.

The Boolean data type is named for early physicist George Boole and represents true and false values. As with other programming languages, ActionScript 3.0 defines true with the literal word true, as well as any nonzero number, any nonempty string, and any nonnull value.

The Number data type can be used for any purely numeric data. The type contains a set of subtypes to better define the number. For example, you can use the int type for numbers that will contain only integers or whole numbers, whereas uint is for unsigned or positive numbers.

### Complex Data Types

Sometimes, you will need variables that store more than one piece of distinct data. This can be done through a complex data type. One common example of a complex data type is an Array, which is covered in later sections of this chapter.

## Declaring Data Types

You declare data types in ActionScript 3.0 when you declare variables by typing a colon after the variable name and then the data type. Most, but not all, data types in ActionScript 3.0 are actually classes and will thus begin with a capital letter. For example, say that you wanted to create a variable called `firstName` and declare that it be data typed as a `String`. To accomplish this, you would write

```
var firstName:String;
```

## Untyped Values

In certain situations, you may need to define a value that can be of any data type. It is possible to simply leave off the data type in this case:

```
var myData;
```

However, when you or other developers look back over your code, it may not be possible to tell if this variable was left untyped intentionally or if it was simply done in error. Therefore, whenever you use an untyped variable intentionally, you should denote this with an asterisk, as in

```
var myData:*;
```

Both examples above function in precisely the same way. Note that this should be done only when absolutely necessary. Variables that are given specific data types can contain only data that is appropriate to that type, and many coding errors can be handled easily due to the debugging messages that will be returned if you, for instance, attempt to put a number into a `String` variable. Untyped variables will not generate these errors and will often lead to problems that are much more difficult to troubleshoot.

## Casting Values

It is possible to convert a variable that had been previously declared as one type to another through a process called *casting*. To cast a variable to a new type, you write the new type and then include the variable in parentheses after the type:

```
var member:String = "Mal";
Boolean(member);
```

In this example, a variable called `member` is defined as a `String` and given the value `"Mal"`. Then, the variable is cast as a `Boolean` type.

Note that casting will not always succeed. In the above example, the code will execute correctly, resulting in `member` having a value of true because any nonempty string is considered true when cast as a `Boolean`. However, this code cannot as easily be cast as a `Number`:

```
var member:String = "Mal";
Number(member);
```

In this case, `member` would now contain the value NaN, or Not a Number, as nonempty, nonnumeric strings cannot be cast to a `Number`. Note that the reverse will always succeed because `String`s can always contain numbers:

```
var score:Number = 1500;
String(score);
```

# Test Your Flash Movie

In order to effectively test your ActionScript, you will need to test your movie in Flash Player. You can do this at any point by following the steps here.

If you are an experienced Flash designer, you may be familiar with simply pressing the Enter key to test animations directly in the Flash-authoring environment. Although this does indeed work for basic animation, many elements of your movie will not be shown, such as animation that may be contained within MovieClips. Further, it will not preview ActionScript, which can be previewed only directly within Flash Player.

If your ActionScript code contains errors, the Compiler Errors panel will appear and display an error message that specifies on which line the error exists, a description

of the error, and the offending code. You can then close the player, fix the error, and test the page again. If multiple errors appear when you test the movie, you should fix them one at a time, testing after each error is fixed, as often a single mistake in the code can result in multiple error messages. If your movie contains trace actions, they will appear in the Output panel. Trace actions are discussed later in this chapter in the section "Trace Variables."

When adding ActionScript to your project, you will most often have the ActionScript panel open. You can test your movie at any time, including when the panel is open. You can also test your movie without needing to save it.

## Test Your Flash Movie

① Click Control.

② Click Test Movie.

You can also press Ctrl + Enter or ⌘ + Return.

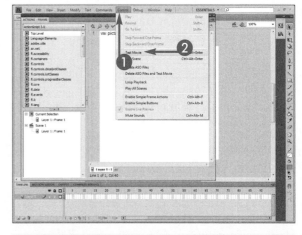

Flash Player opens and plays the movie.

**Note:** *In this example, nothing has been added to the movie, so nothing is displayed when the movie plays.*

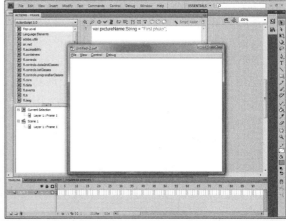

# Concatenate Strings

O ne of the most common data types for simple variables is `String`, which is used to store pieces of text. Depending on how you plan to use the text, you may need to combine multiple strings together into new variables. The process of combining strings is known as *concatenation*.

ActionScript uses the plus symbol (+) to concatenate strings. For example, if you declare a string variable for a user's first name and another for his last name, you could combine them into a single variable to use his full name:

```
var fullName:String = firstName +
  lastName;
```

Note, however, that if the user's first name is Mal and his last name Reynolds, the preceding code would result in a full name of MalReynolds — without the space. Quite often, you will need to add literal characters, such as spaces, to the string when you concatenate, which you can do by including them in quotation marks:

```
var fullName:String = firstName + " " +
  lastName;
```

Both of the preceding examples show concatenation in a variable declaration. You can concatenate any time you use strings, including when the string is used as an argument in a function or being set as a property of an object.

## Concatenate Strings

**1** Create a string variable and add a value.

**2** Create another string variable and add a value.

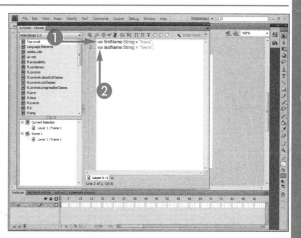

**3** Create a third string variable.

**4** As its value, reference the variable created in step **1**, add a plus sign, and the variable created in step **2**.

**5** Add any literal characters needed.

The concatenated variable is created.

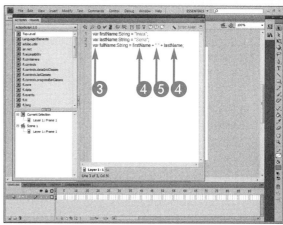

# Trace Variables

nfortunately, not all of your code will work correctly the first time that you write it. Typographical errors such as mistyping a variable name or forgetting a semicolon at the end of a line are all too common in coding, but fortunately, Flash Player will generate error dialog boxes when these occur.

Much more difficult to debug are what are known as *logical errors.* A logical error is when your code is syntactically correct but contains a mistake in the script that causes it to run incorrectly. For example, you may think that a variable is set to one value when in fact it is set to another. When you try to test for the value you believe exists, you get an unexpected result.

Fortunately, ActionScript contains a `trace` command that enables you to test the values of any variables you need. When you trace a variable, its value appears in the Output panel when you play the movie in Flash Player. You can trace variables, literal values, and other data to test to be sure that their values are what you expect.

`trace` is a global function. It is available throughout your code, so you can use it at any time. Always write `trace` in lowercase letters. Always place the value you will be tracing within a set of parentheses. If you are tracing a string, it must be in double quotes; if tracing the value of a variable or object or the value of a number, you will not use quotes.

## Trace Variables

**Note:** *You need to open the Actions panel to complete the following steps. See Chapter 1 for more details.*

1. Create a variable.

2. Assign the variable a value.

**Note:** *See the section "Create a Variable" for information on creating variables.*

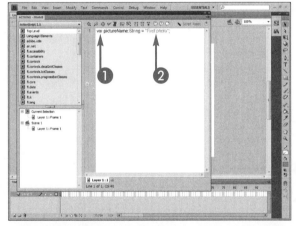

3. Type `trace`.

4. Type a parenthesis.

5. Type the name of the variable you created in step **1**.

6. Close the parentheses and type a semicolon.

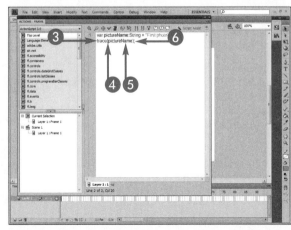

**7** Click Control.

**8** Click Test Movie.

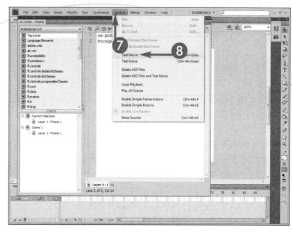

The movie opens in Flash Player.

● The Output panel opens, displaying the value of the variable.

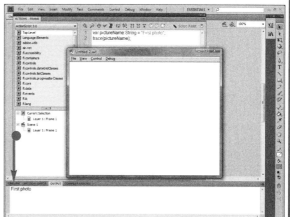

---

## Extra

Although tracing is an important debugging tool, you would not want a final movie to contain the `trace` statements, as they would confuse your user. You will most likely simply delete the `trace` statements after you have debugged your code or comment them out, but you can also tell Flash not to export `trace` commands when you publish the movie. If you click File ➔ Publish Settings and then click the Flash tab, you will see an Omit Trace Actions option. Simply check this option before publishing to have your trace actions ignored for your final output.

Although you will almost always trace the value of a variable, you can have the `trace` command display a literal value by placing the value in quotes inside the command's parentheses:

```
trace("This will be displayed");
```

# Create an Array

**A**ctionScript contains two built-in data types that allow you to store multiple values in a single variable. The simpler of the two is an `Array`. The more complex option, a generic `Object`, is discussed later in this chapter in the section "Create a Generic Object."

An array is simply a variable that can hold more than one piece of information. There are several different ways to create arrays. The most formal is to call the `Array` *constructor*:

```
var crewMembers:Array = new Array();
```

`Array` stores its values in indexes, which count from zero. You can populate the array, or add values to it, by repeatedly calling the array and the next index number, which is referenced in square brackets:

```
crewMembers[0] = "Mal";
crewMembers[1] = "Zoe";
```

A single array can contain values of different data types. Therefore, a single array could contain strings, numbers, other arrays, or other object types.

## Create an Array

① Type `var`.

② Type a name for the array that you want to create.

③ Type a colon and `Array`.

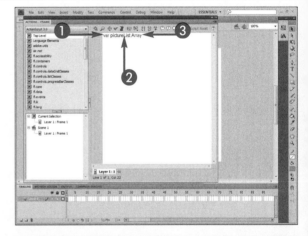

④ Type an equals sign.

⑤ Type `new`.

⑥ Type `Array();`

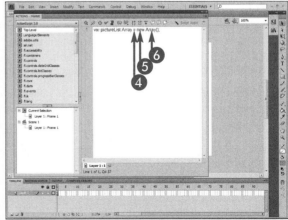

**7** Type the name of the array that you created.

**8** Type a left square bracket, a zero, and a right square bracket.

**9** Type an equals sign.

**10** Type a value.

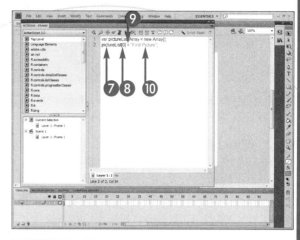

**11** Repeat steps **7** to **10** to add additional items to the array.

The array is created.

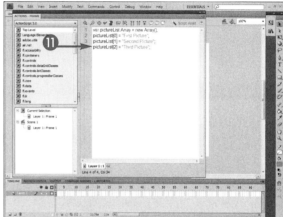

---

## Apply It

A more efficient method of creating arrays is to include the values that you want to add to your array within the parentheses on the constructor line:

```
var crewMembers:Array = new Array("Mal", "Zoe", "Wash", "Jayne", "Kaylee", "Simon", "River",
  "Book", "Inara");
```

You can shorten this even further by leaving off the `new Array` and placing the values within square brackets:

```
var crewMembers:Array = ["Mal", "Zoe", "Wash", "Jayne", "Kaylee", "Simon", "River", "Book",
  "Inara"];
```

Each of these methods creates the same array, so the one you choose is ultimately personal preference.

# Add and Remove Elements from an Array

The items in an array are technically referred to as *elements*. After you have initially populated the array, you can add new elements to it or remove existing elements.

You can add a new element to an array by calling one of two methods of the array: `push()` and `unshift()`. The `push()` method adds an element to the end of the array, whereas `unshift()` adds it to the beginning. For example, if you had an array that contained the values `"Serenity"`, `"Star Wars"`, and `"Requiem for a Dream"`, you could add a new element, `"Juno"`, to it via `push()`:

```
movieArray.push("Juno");
```

In this example, `"Juno"` would become the last element; if you added it via `unshift()`, it would be the first element. Note that although the placement of the new element varies, the code for adding it is essentially the same:

```
movieArray.unshift("Juno");
```

The matching methods to remove elements from an array are `pop()` and `shift()`. Whereas `push()` adds an element to the end of an array, `pop()` removes the last element; while `unshift()` adds a new element to the beginning, `shift()` removes it. Using the same example, calling `pop()` on the original array would remove `"Juno"`, leaving `"Serenity"`, `"Star Wars"`, and `"Requiem for a Dream"`, while `shift()` would remove `"Serenity"` and leave the other three.

## Add and Remove Elements from an Array

### ADD AN ELEMENT TO AN ARRAY

① Create an array.

**Note:** *See the preceding section for details on creating an array.*

② Type the name of the array, a period, and `push`.

③ Type a left parenthesis, a new value, a right parenthesis, and a semicolon.

**Note:** *If the value being added is a string, be sure to enclose it in quotes.*

④ Type `trace`, a left parenthesis, the name of the array, a right parenthesis, and a semicolon.

⑤ Press Ctrl + Enter to test the movie.

Flash Player runs the movie. The Output panel appears and displays the array.

● The element that you added in steps **2** and **3** appears at the end of the array.

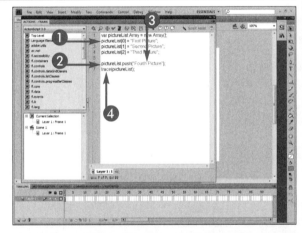

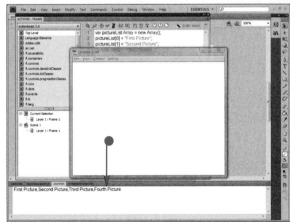

## REMOVE AN ELEMENT FROM AN ARRAY

**1** Type the name of the array, a period, `pop()`, and a semicolon.

**2** Type `trace`, a left parenthesis, the name of the array, a right parenthesis, and a semicolon.

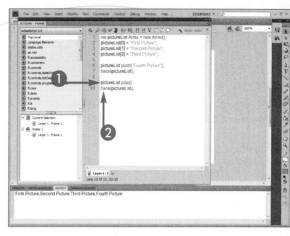

**3** Press Ctrl + Enter to test the movie.

Flash Player runs the movie. The Output panel appears and displays the array.

● The previous final element, which you removed in step **1**, is no longer included in the array.

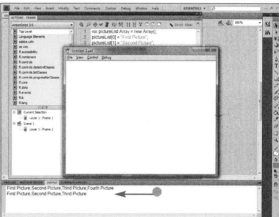

---

### Extra

If you think that keeping the four methods straight may be difficult, do not worry: You are not alone. In particular, many developers find it difficult to remember whether `shift()` or `unshift()` adds or removes an element. Generally, however, you will need to add items to an array much more often than you need to remove them, and as the exact order of the elements in an array rarely matters, you will more likely use `push()` than any of the other methods.

Most often, when you do remove elements from an array, you will be doing so to put the element into a variable. You can do this by simply assigning the `pop()` method call to a variable with the correct data type:

```
var individualMember:String = crewMembers.pop();
```

You can remove all the elements from an array, one at a time, by looping over the array and calling `pop()` repeatedly. Looping over arrays is discussed in Chapter 12.

# Create an Array in an Array

Sometimes, a more complicated data structure is necessary than can be achieved in either a simple variable or an array. If you need to relate multiple groups of data, you can store arrays within arrays. An array that contains one or more other arrays is known as a *multidimensional* array.

Although ActionScript arrays can technically contain many dimensions, you will rarely need one with more than two. A two-dimensional array can be seen sort of as a spreadsheet, where the outer array represents the

columns and the inner array the rows. For example, if you had an array that represented player ID numbers in a game, you could store an array within each element of that array that contained each player's score.

Arrays within arrays are constructed by creating the first, outer array and then creating a new array within each element of that array:

```
var players:Array = new Array();
players[0] = new Array();
players[0][0] = 4324;
```

## Create an Array in an Array

① Create an array.

**Note:** *See the section "Create an Array" for details.*

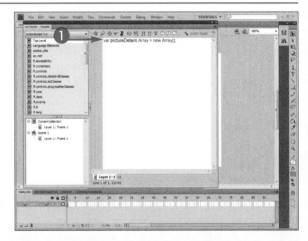

② Create a new array in the first element of the array that you created in step **1**.

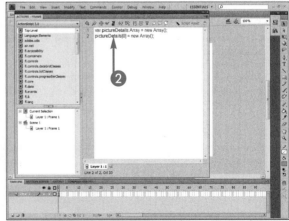

③ Populate the first element of the inner array with data.

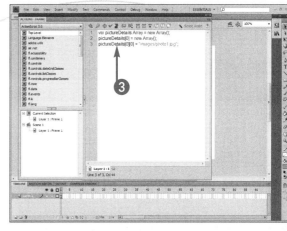

④ Repeat steps **2** to **3** to add additional elements to the array.

The array within an array is created.

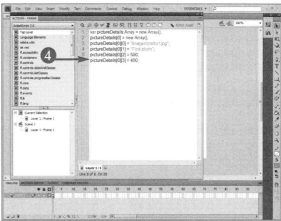

You can reference elements of the inner array by referencing the index number of each of the arrays. Therefore, given the following array:

```
var players:Array = new Array();
players[0] = new Array();
players[0][0] = 4324;
players[0][1] = 5545;
players[1][0] = 2234;
players[1][1] = 7685;
```

You could trace the first player's second score by typing:

```
trace(players[0][1]);
```

# Create a
# Generic Object

Many times, complex data can be expressed as either an array or an array of arrays. However, although an array enables you to store multiple pieces of data, you cannot create a logical association between the index — the number used to represent the element of the array — and the value. Depending on the nature of the data you are trying to store, this may be fine, but it may cause problems as well.

For example, say that you had a game and needed to keep track of the player name, her score, and her current level within the game. You could store this as an array, but you would need to remember that you placed the player name as element 0, her score as element 1, and her level as element 2. In this simple example, that would not be difficult, but imagine if you had many dozens of

data points. It would quickly become difficult to remember which element contained which piece of data.

In those instances when you need to maintain a relationship between the values in a data store and the indices by which you refer to them, you can use a generic `Object`. Like an array, generic objects allow you to store multiple values in a single object. But unlike arrays, a generic object is going to contain specific names, called *properties,* to associate with the values.

You create generic objects in much the same way as you create arrays. The only difference is that with an object, you create the property/value pairs for the data using dot notation, with the object name followed by the property name, an equals sign, and the value.

## Create a Generic Object

① Type `var` and a variable name for the object.

② Type a colon, `Object`, and an equals sign.

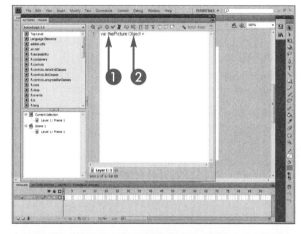

③ Type `new Object();`.

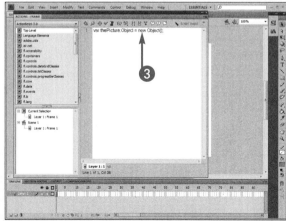

④ Type the name of the object that you created in step **1**.

⑤ Type a period and a property name.

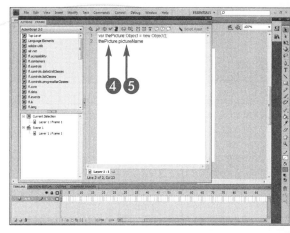

⑥ Type an equals sign and a value.

⑦ Repeat steps **4** to **6** to add additional properties to the object.

The generic object is created.

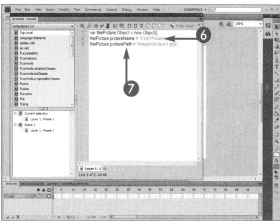

## Apply It

Both arrays and objects can contain data with varying data types. In an array, this is legal, where we are storing both strings and numbers:

```
var rawData:Array = new Array("Serenity", 2005, 150000000, "Great movie");
```

For objects, the same is allowed:

```
var rawData:Object = new Object();
rawData.movieName = "Serenity";
rawData.releaseYear = 2005;
rawData.gross = 150000000;
rawData.review = "Great movie";
```

# Add Constants

Variables, by definition, contain code that will possibly change over the course of the execution of a movie. In a quiz application, for instance, you will need to constantly update the user's score based on how he or she does in the quiz. However, you may encounter situations in which you want to create a *constant*: a named reference to something whose value cannot change as the movie runs.

You can create a constant by using the `const` keyword. The standard practice among ActionScript developers is to use all capital letters for the name of the constant, to more easily distinguish it from a variable. In fact, the language already contains a series of constants, all of which are written this way.

After you assign a value to a constant, you cannot assign another value to it later in your code; doing so will result in an error. Constants are often used to represent static values or settings within a movie. They are particularly useful when a numeric value is required but would be more difficult to remember than a string value. Using the preceding quiz example, you may have a predetermined, set value for the passing grade, but remembering that passing is, say, 73%, could be difficult, so you could instead assign a constant of `PASSING_SCORE`:

```
const PASSING_SCORE = 73;
```

Although the same could be accomplished with a variable, a constant is safer as you cannot inadvertently have a line of code that alters the value later in your script.

## Add Constants

① Type `const`.

② Type a name for the constant.

③ Type an equals sign and a value.

④ Type `trace(`.

⑤ Type the name of the constant, a closing parenthesis, and a semicolon.

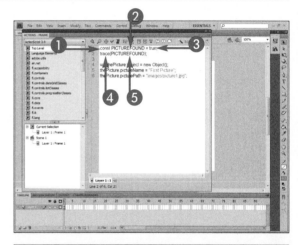

⑥ Press Ctrl + Enter.

The movie plays in Flash Player.

● The value of the constant is displayed in the Output window.

# Add Comments to Your Code

**C**omments are notes you place in your code that are ignored by Flash Player when the movie runs. You can use comments to document your code.

You should get in the habit of adding comments liberally throughout your code. Many developers add a comment block at the top of their script that states the purpose of the document, who wrote it, and a history of its revisions. You should add a comment above any code block whose functionality might not be clear from reading the code itself. You can also help keep track of closing curly braces on complex code blocks such as functions and conditional statements by adding a comment to the closing brace denoting what exactly it closes.

You can add a comment in a single line by beginning the comment with two slashes. Any text after the slashes is ignored:

```
var adminStatus:Boolean = true; //used to show
  extra functionality to admins
```

You can have a comment span multiple lines by beginning the comment with a slash and an asterisk and ending it with an asterisk and a slash; the text between the sets of symbols is ignored:

```
/* Code created on 12/4/08.
Revised 1/15/09 */
```

## Add Comments to Your Code

### INSERT A SINGLE-LINE COMMENT

① Type a line of code.

② Type two slashes.

③ Type a comment.

The comment is added to the line.

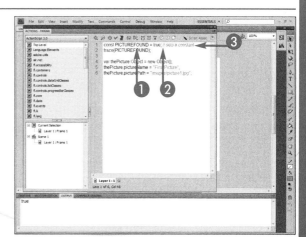

### INSERT A MULTILINE COMMENT

① Type a slash and an asterisk.

② Type a comment.

**Note:** *You can have the comment span more than one line.*

③ Type an asterisk and a slash.

The comment is added to the script.

# Understanding Coding Best Practices

**A**lthough poorly written, disorganized, or sloppy code will often work and "get the job done," following some accepted coding best practices will enable you to work more quickly, make future edits of your code easier, simplify debugging, and enable others to collaborate on your projects.

## Plan and Organize Your Code

Extra time you spend planning your code before you begin typing anything will pay dividends later. Think about what your code needs to accomplish and what the best ways might be to achieve that goal.

Keep your code organized. Group all variable declarations at the top of your code so that they are easy to find for reference later. Group other similar code blocks, such as functions or event handlers, together to make them easy to locate when you need to edit them later. If you are setting a series of properties on an object, place all the code to do so together in a single block. The more organized you keep your code, the easier it will be to maintain.

## Be Consistent

As mentioned earlier, ActionScript is case-sensitive. You can use any casing scheme that you want for variables, but as you must always type a variable using the same case as you did when you declared it, always being consistent in your casing will make it easier to be sure that you are typing variable names correctly.

The same consistency should apply in the names you use. Do not, for instance, have a variable to capture the first name of a user called `fname` while having another variable for the last name called `lastname`. Either is legal and will work, but the point is that they should either both use a single initial for the first word or both spell it out. You can use underscores in names as well, so `first_name` is also legal, but again, it should only be used if other variables will follow the same pattern and be `last_name` and `street_address`.

## Immediately Add Closing Parentheses and Curly Braces

Code blocks such as functions, discussed in Chapter 5, and conditional statements, discussed in Chapter 11, require the use of curly braces to denote their code. When you write these statements, get in the habit of adding the closing curly brace at the same time as you add the opening one. In other words, type the skeleton of the function first:

```
function sampleFunction(){
}
```

Then go back and add the necessary code between the braces. Doing this will ensure that you do not forget to add the closing brace after entering the code for the function.

The same should apply when you add parentheses. Parentheses are used when creating and calling functions and when writing complex mathematical operations. Often, you will have nested sets of parentheses, so it is easy to lose track of how many closing parentheses you need at the end of an expression. If you add each closing parenthesis as you add its opening partner, you will not have to worry about not having the correct number of closing parentheses at the end.

## Add Whitespace

ActionScript is whitespace insensitive, so you can improve the readability of your code by adding whitespace. Take for example this block of code, which takes two strings and concatenates them together but uses a minimal amount of whitespace:

```
var firstName:String = "Inara";
var lastName:String = "Serra";
function concatNames(str1:String,
  str2:String):String{return firstName + " "
  lastName;}
```

Compare the preceding to this code, which is spaced out better:

```
var firstName:String = "Inara";
var lastName:String = "Serra";
function concatNames(str1:String,
  str2:String):String{
          return firstName + " " lastName;
}
```

The results of running each block will be the same, but editing or debugging the second block would be much easier because the whitespace makes it more readable.

## Document the Code with Comments

Liberally commenting your code will help explain the purpose of code blocks to yourself and other developers who may need to edit the script in the future. Any block or line of code that is not immediately clear from reading it should have explanatory comments.

## Use Descriptive Names

Always use descriptive names in your code. Avoid vague, generic, or potentially confusing names. For example, store numbers in variables named `numberToAdd` or `playerScore` rather than `x` or `y`. Descriptive names are easier to remember and make your code clearer in general: You can tell or at least guess at the purpose of a variable `numberToAdd` or `firstName`, whereas a variable `x` could represent just about anything.

Functions should be named following the *verbNoun* convention and be given names that describe their purpose. In other words, if you have a function that will add a series of numbers, calling it `addNumbers` follows the *verbNoun* convention and makes the function's purpose clear at a glance.

# Draw Shapes in Flash

You can use shapes to create drawings, buttons, and other graphic objects in Flash. Flash includes a wide variety of drawing tools, including a pencil, pen, and line tool to draw lines or, as they are called in Flash, *strokes,* and a brush tool to draw *fills,* or colored areas between strokes. For more uniform shapes, such as circles, ovals, squares, rectangles, and polygons, you can use the shape tools.

Flash offers five different shape tools: Rectangle, Oval, Rectangle Primitive, Oval Primitive, and PolyStar, all of which share space on the Tools panel. The Rectangle tool can create square or rectangular shapes, and the Oval tool can create oval or circular shapes.

Objects that you draw with the Oval, Rectangle, and PolyStar tools consist of a stroke and a fill. Flash contains two drawing models. When you use the Merge Drawing model, the stroke and fill are separate objects, so if you move the stroke, for example, the fill remains in place on the Stage. Also, objects drawn on the same layer will interact with one another; if you move a shape on top of another shape and then move it away, the shape you are moving will cut itself out of the shape you moved it over. In the Object Drawing model, shapes are automatically grouped, so the fill and stroke will act as a single shape, and multiple shapes on the same layer will not interact.

You can use the PolyStar tool to draw multisided shapes (polygons) or stars. With any shape tool you select, the Property Inspector displays related options for fine-tuning the shape, such as controlling the corner radius and line style.

## Draw Shapes in Flash

### DRAW A STROKED SHAPE

1. Click the shape tool of your choice.

- Click Rectangle Tool to draw a square or rectangle.

- Click Oval Tool to draw an oval.

- Click Rectangle Primitive Tool to draw a rectangle with a combined stroke and fill.

- Click Oval Primitive Tool to draw an oval with a combined stroke and fill.

- Click PolyStar Tool to draw a polygon.

**Note:** *Flash always displays the button for the last shape tool you used.*

2. Click the Stroke Color button.

3. Select a color.

4. Click the Fill Color button.

5. Click the No Color button.

6. Click and drag to draw the shape you want.

**Note:** *To draw a perfect circle or square, press and hold Shift as you draw the shape.*

Flash creates the shape.

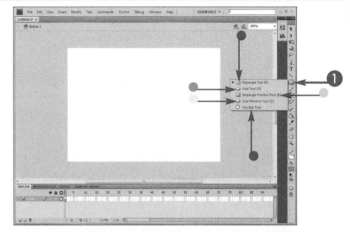

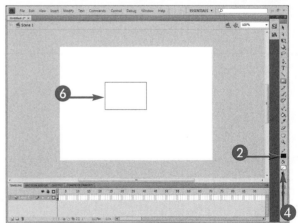

## DRAW A FILLED SHAPE

① Click the shape tool of your choice.

② Click the Fill Color button.

The Fill Color palette opens.

③ Click a fill color.

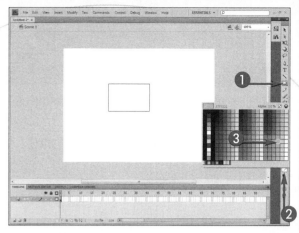

④ Click and drag to draw the shape.

**Note:** *To draw a perfect circle or square, press and hold Shift as you draw the shape.*

⑤ Release the mouse button.

Flash creates the filled shape.

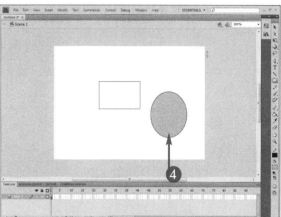

---

### Extra

You can use the Rectangle Settings or Oval Settings dialog box to create rectangles and ovals of a preset size. In the Rectangle Settings dialog box, you can also specify a corner radius to draw rectangles with rounded corners. To open the Rectangle or Oval Settings dialog box, click the Rectangle or Oval tool and then press Alt + click (or press Option + click) the Stage. The Settings dialog box appears. Type the width, height, and, if applicable, the radius. When you click OK, Flash places the oval or rectangle at the location you clicked on the Stage.

The Rectangle Primitive tool draws a rectangle with small dots in the corners. Using the Selection tool, you can drag any of these dots to create a rectangle with rounded corners. The Oval Primitive tool creates an oval with similar dots; dragging them allows you to create an oval with a missing section, something that will sort of resemble the classic arcade game character Pac-Man.

You can get much more detailed information on using the drawing tools in Flash in the book *Master VISUALLY Dreamweaver CS4 and Flash CS4 Professional,* published by Wiley.

# Introducing Symbols

In Flash, a *symbol* is a reusable element that you can store in the Flash library. You can repeatedly reuse a symbol throughout your movie by inserting an instance of the symbol in the frame in which you want it to appear. An *instance* is simply a copy of the original symbol. Drawings you create using the tools in Flash, text, and imported graphics can all be converted to a symbol.

## Flash Symbols

The primary purpose of using symbols in Flash is animation, but you also need symbols if you want to control objects on the Stage through ActionScript: You must convert shapes and imported objects to symbols if you want them to be seen or controlled through ActionScript.

Animating objects through ActionScript is covered in Chapter 13. Animating through traditional techniques such as tweening is beyond the scope of this book.

## Editing Symbols

All instances of a symbol are copies of the object in the library. Each instance is linked back to the original, so any changes made to the original are applied to all instances. There are certain edits that can be made to individual instances, such as their position on the Stage, their scale, and their rotation. However, more complex edits, such as changing the shapes that make up the symbol, must be made to the actual symbol.

You can either edit symbols in place, where you still have a visual reference to other objects on the Stage, or you can edit them individually on their own Stage.

## Storing Movie Elements

Every file that you create in Flash has a library that stores elements you want to reuse in your project. You can manage these elements from the Library panel by organizing them into related folders, much like organizing files on the hard drive of your computer.

You can open, close, expand, and collapse the Library panel as you work with various symbols and instances in your document. The Library panel lists the symbols alphabetically. You can drag symbols from the panel and drop them onto the Stage to use in a frame. You can also add and delete symbols as needed.

## Types of Symbols

You can reuse symbols to create animation in your Flash movies. Every time you reuse a symbol, you must specify how you want the symbol to behave. Flash classifies symbols into three types: graphics, buttons, or MovieClips.

### Graphic Symbols

You can create graphic symbols using the Flash drawing tools or by importing graphics from other programs to use in Flash. You can make graphic symbols as simple as a basic shape or as complex as a highly detailed drawing. You can also turn text into graphic symbols that you can manipulate and animate in your movies.

Graphic symbols have their own Timeline that closely resembles the Timeline of the main movie. However, the graphic symbol's Timeline is synchronized with the movie's Timeline, so while a graphic symbol can contain its own animation, that animation cannot play independently of the movie.

Most importantly, graphic symbols cannot be given instance names and thus cannot be controlled through ActionScript. You can use graphic symbols inside other symbols as visual building blocks, but you cannot rely on them as your primary type of symbol if you plan to use ActionScript.

### Button Symbols

You can add interactivity to your movie through buttons. Like graphic symbols, buttons have their own Timeline. However, the button's Timeline is very different from that of the movie and the other symbol types, as it contains only four special frames, which enable you to create effects when the user mouses over the button or clicks it.

You can create a button by drawing shapes on the Stage or importing graphics and then converting them to a symbol, or you can draw shapes or import graphics directly into the button. You can also use other symbols, such as graphics or MovieClips, within buttons.

Buttons are one of the two types of symbols you can control through ActionScript. To work with buttons, you need to add an event listener to the button and then write an event handler to describe what should happen when the button is clicked. Events are covered in Chapter 7.

### MovieClip Symbols

By far the most powerful symbol type is the MovieClip. Like graphic symbols, MovieClips have their own Timeline, which looks like the main movie's Timeline. However, unlike graphics, the Timeline of a MovieClip is independent of the main movie's Timeline; a MovieClip can also contain its own animation that is independent of the main movie's animation.

MovieClips can be created by converting existing drawings or imported graphics to a symbol or by drawing or importing graphics directly onto the MovieClip's Timeline. You can also use graphic symbols, buttons, or other MovieClips within a MovieClip. MovieClips can also be created through ActionScript code.

MovieClips are controlled through ActionScript. In fact, the majority of the symbols that you use in a script-driven movie will be MovieClips. You can even create MovieClips directly in code, without drawing anything on the Stage. The rest of this chapter, and most of the following chapters, will deal with working with MovieClips.

# Create a Symbol

**M**ost of the elements that you plan to use in your movies will be symbols. Most of the symbols you create in a movie in which you will rely on scripting will be `MovieClip`s, but you can also use `Button`s to provide clickable objects for your user.

You can convert existing objects on your Stage to a symbol by following the steps below or by using the keyboard shortcut F8. Any items on the Stage can be converted to a symbol. You can nest symbols within symbols, so you can for example use a button within a `MovieClip` or a `MovieClip` within another `MovieClip`.

When you convert an item, a dialog box appears that enables you to name the symbol, select the symbol type, and set the registration point. The *registration point* is a reference marker on the symbol. It is used for setting the

location of the symbol on the Stage and is the point from which references to the size and location of the symbol will be relative when changing those properties in script.

You can also create an empty symbol. When you do this, Flash opens the symbol in its editing mode, with a new, blank copy of the Stage and the symbol's Timeline visible. The crosshair marker in the center of the symbol's Stage represents its registration point. You can use Flash's drawing tools, import graphics, or insert other symbols onto the symbol's Stage.

Every symbol contains its own Timeline. The Timeline of a `MovieClip` looks exactly like the Timeline of the movie, while buttons have a special Timeline that contains only four frames. All symbols can be made of multiple layers.

## Create a Symbol

### CONVERT TO A SYMBOL

1 Select one or more shapes on the Stage.

**Note:** *See "Draw Shapes in Flash" for information on the drawing tools.*

2 Click Modify.

3 Click Convert to Symbol.

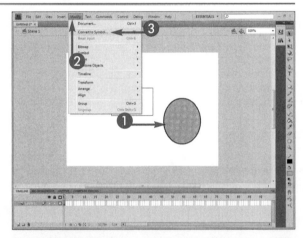

The Convert to Symbol dialog box appears.

4 Type a name for the symbol.

5 Click here and select a symbol type.

6 Click OK.

The object is converted to a symbol.

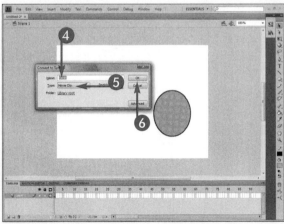

## CREATE A NEW SYMBOL

**1** Click Insert.

**2** Click New Symbol.

The Create New Symbol dialog box appears.

**3** Type a name for the symbol.

**4** Click here and select a symbol type.

**5** Click OK.

Flash changes to the symbol-editing mode.

**6** Create the symbol content.

**Note:** *You can draw with the drawing tools or import a graphic by clicking File → Import.*

**7** Click the scene name to exit symbol-edit mode.

The symbol is created.

**Note:** *You can also click Edit → Edit Document to return to the main Timeline.*

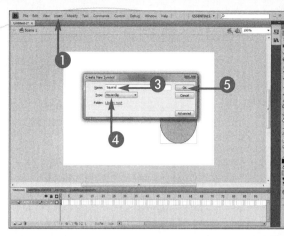

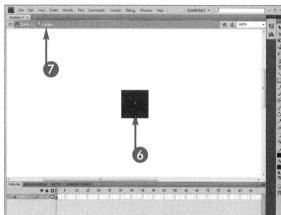

---

## Extra

When you create a symbol, it is stored in the library. You can access the Library panel by clicking Window → Library. By default, the Library panel is docked with the Properties panel on the right side of the screen. In the library, you can organize your symbols into folders by clicking the New Folder button at the bottom of the panel and then dragging the symbols into the folder.

There are no specific rules for naming symbols; however, Flash developers have established a set of best practices, or guidelines, for symbol names. First and foremost, the symbol name should be descriptive of its purpose. You should be able to glance at the library and, from the name alone, be able to determine how and why you would use the symbol. Second, the symbol name should begin with a capital letter. This is due to how symbols are treated in ActionScript; see Chapter 6 for more information. Third, most Flash designers and developers prefer to not use spaces in their symbol names.

# Insert and Name an Instance

When you create a symbol, you are actually creating a custom class within the ActionScript code underlying your movie. In object-oriented programming, you need to create an *instance* of a class in order to use it. See Chapter 2 for more details on object-oriented programming terminology and concepts.

You can create an instance of a symbol by simply dragging it from the Library panel to the Stage. You can have as many instances of a single symbol as you want at any given time in your movie. In order for ActionScript to be able to reference these instances, however, you must provide them with an instance name. This name in essence becomes a variable name by which you can reference the instance of the symbol in your code. Each instance must have a unique name.

You can type the name of the instance into the Properties panel. The instance name should follow the guidelines outlined in Chapter 2 for naming variables: They need to begin with a letter, and contain only letters, numbers, and underscores. Your instance names need to follow your variable casing scheme; most developers prefer camel casing.

Instance names for `MovieClip`s can be constructed by starting with an `mc` prefix, then adding the name of the symbol itself, and then an identifying number. In other words, instances of a `Box` symbol might be called `mcBox1` and `mcBox2`. Buttons are usually named with a `btn` prefix, followed by a descriptive name based on the button's purpose in the movie, such as `btnHomePage`.

## Insert and Name an Instance

① Click the Library panel.

The library opens.

② Click the symbol that you want to use.

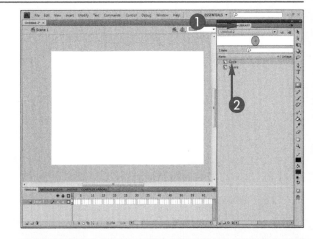

③ Drag the symbol from the library onto the Stage.

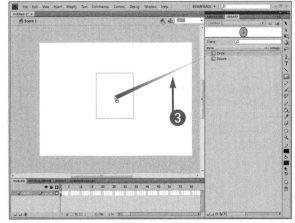

● An instance of the symbol appears on the Stage.

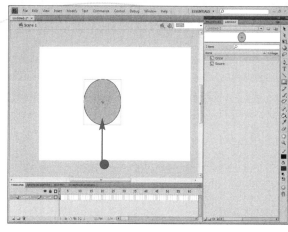

④ Click the Properties panel.

The Properties panel opens.

⑤ Click in the Instance Name box.

⑥ Type a name for the instance.

The instance name is assigned.

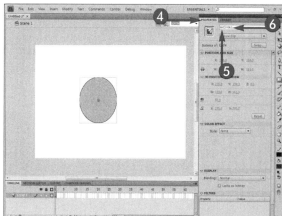

# Set Instance Properties Using the Properties Panel

A symbol is a class in ActionScript. Like any other class, it has a series of properties that define it. Some properties of the symbol are static and cannot be changed for individual instances, whereas others can. You can set most of these properties of symbol instances visually using the Properties panel in Flash. By default, the panel appears on the right side of the screen in the Flash window. You must select an instance by clicking it with the Selection tool before you can set its properties. The selection tool is the black arrow at the top of the Tools panel.

Most of the settings on the panel can be adjusted by "scrubbing" their values, or dragging over them with the mouse button held down. Dragging to the left decreases the value, and dragging to the right increases it. You can

also click directly on the current value, which will make it an editable text box so that you can type values in directly.

The Properties panel is divided into four sections. The first allows you to set the x and y coordinates, which determine the location of the symbol on the Stage. The top-left corner of the Stage is the zero point for both. You can also adjust the width and height of an instance; an icon to the left of the width setting allows you to adjust either relative to the other to maintain the symbol's original proportions.

You can adjust the colors using the settings in the Color Effect section and blend the instance with its background using the Display section. Filters enable you to apply effects such as drop shadows, bevels, or glows.

① Insert an instance of a symbol on the Stage.

**Note:** *See the preceding section, "Insert and Name an Instance," for details.*

② Click Properties.

The Properties panel opens.

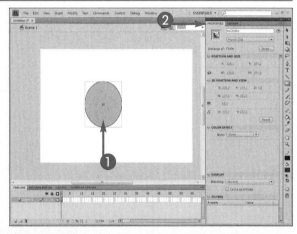

③ Click and drag to scrub the value of X.

The instance moves to a new location on the stage.

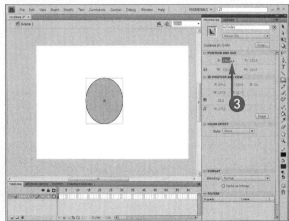

④ Click the value next to Y.

⑤ Type a new value.

The instance moves to a new location on the stage.

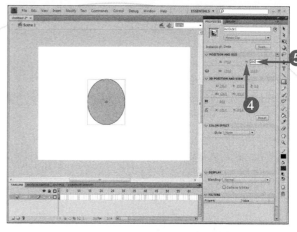

⑥ Click the Lock Width and Height Values Together icon.

⑦ Change the value of the width, either by scrubbing or typing a value.

The width changes, and the height adjusts accordingly.

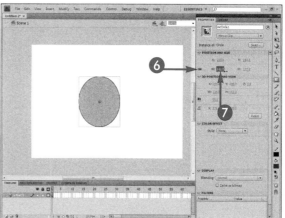

## Extra

In the Color Effect section of the Properties panel, you can choose to change the color of the instance in one of four ways. First, you can change the brightness, which allows you to make the entire shape of the instance either lighter or darker. Second, you can apply a new tint, in which you will select a new color that will be mixed, based on a percentage you select, with the original colors. Third, you can change the alpha of the instance, which is its transparency: 0% is completely transparent, whereas 100% is completely opaque. Fourth, you can choose to apply an advanced effect, which is simply a method that combines the ability to set the tint and the alpha together. You must make these changes as a whole on the symbol; you cannot apply them to an individual portion of the symbol without editing the symbol itself.

The x and y coordinates of an instance refer to the registration point of the instance. This point is established when you create the symbol.

# Set Instance Properties in Code

In addition to setting properties using the Properties panel, you can set them in code through ActionScript. You can change any of the properties that are available through the panel, plus many more. Some properties, such as x, y, width, and height require only a single line each to change; others, such as colors, require much more code. Setting the color of a shape in code is discussed in Chapter 19.

In order to set the properties of an instance in code, you must have given it an instance name. See the earlier section "Insert and Name an Instance" for details on how to do this.

In the Actions panel, you can type the name of the instance, a dot, and the name of the property that you want to set. Then, type an equals sign and the new value.

For example, you can set the x and y locations of an instance of a `MovieClip` named `mcBox1` like this:

```
mcBox1.x = 15;
mcBox1.y = 30;
```

As you set properties, you will need to be sure that the value you provide is the correct data type for that property. Properties such as x, y, width, and height logically take numbers, whereas others may take strings or, at times, even other object references or constants. If you are unsure about the allowed values for a property, you can easily find them by looking the property up either in the Flash help file or in Adobe's online ActionScript documentation at http://livedocs.adobe.com/flash/9.0/ActionScriptLangRefV3.

## Set Instance Properties in Code

① Apply an instance name to an instance on the Stage.

**Note:** See the section "Insert and Name an Instance" for details.

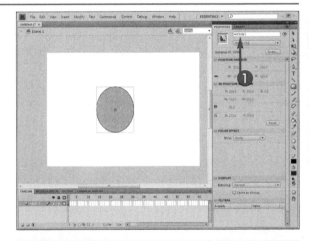

② Click the current frame.

③ Open the Actions panel.

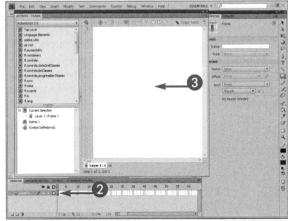

④ Type the name of the instance from step **1**, followed by a period.

⑤ Type a property that you want to change and an equals sign.

⑥ Type a new value and a semicolon.

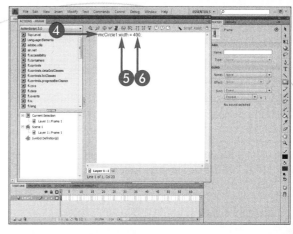

⑦ Repeat steps **4** to **6** for each additional property.

The new properties are set on the instance.

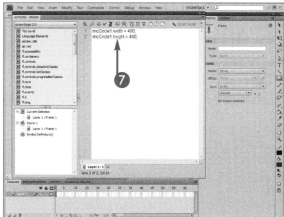

## Extra

You cannot see the properties applied through ActionScript until you actually play the movie. The Stage within Flash will continue to show the instance with only those properties that are set on the Properties panel. This is because ActionScript executes only at runtime, and it plays within Flash Player, not the Flash-authoring tool.

Oddly, although the settings for the Alpha value on the Properties panel scale from 0% to 100%, in ActionScript the values range from 0 to 1. Therefore, if you want to make an instance semitransparent in script, you would apply a value of, say, .5, whereas in the panel, you would set it to 50%. This is the only case where the panel uses a different set of values from the script.

# Perform Simple Mathematical Operations

You can perform basic mathematical operations in ActionScript by simply entering the formula that you want as the value of an expression. You can perform addition, subtraction, multiplication, and division. The symbols for each are the standard symbols used throughout the computer world: + for addition, - for subtraction, * for multiplication, and / for division. ActionScript also supports the modulus operator, %, which returns the remainder in a division problem.

ActionScript also follows the normal order of operations for math. If you are going to combine addition, subtraction, multiplication, and division into a single expression, the multiplication will occur first from left to right, followed by division, followed by addition and subtraction. You can group portions of the expression together with parentheses to force a different operating order, as parenthetical expressions will be evaluated first. In other words, 4+3*3 equals 13, as you first multiply 3*3 and then add 4, whereas (4+3)*3 equals 21: You add 4 and 3 and then multiply the result by 3. Be careful when creating complex formulae that you include the correct number of closing parentheses.

Mathematical expressions can be used as the values of variables, as the values of properties, or anywhere else a numeric value is allowed.

You can use the `trace` command to output the result of an expression to a window. See Chapter 2 for details on using `trace`. You can also create visual objects on the Stage, such as a text field, and place the result of the calculation in the text field. Using text in ActionScript is covered in Chapter 9.

## Perform Simple Mathematical Operations

① Type var theResult:
Number =.

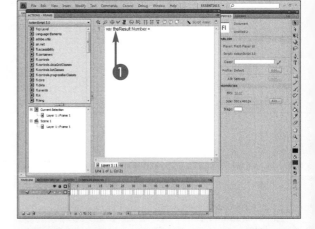

② Type a mathematical expression followed by a semicolon.

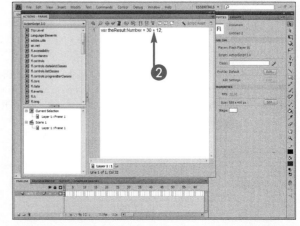

**③** Type `trace (theResult);`.

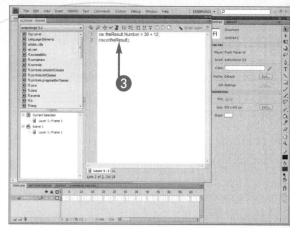

**④** Press Ctrl + Enter (⌘ + Enter on Mac).

The movie runs in Flash Player.

● The Output window appears, displaying the value of `theResult`.

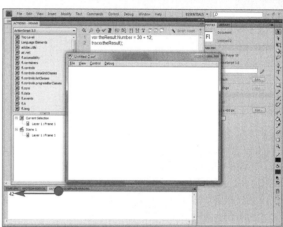

---

## Extra

Take care when creating expressions that you do not attempt to divide a number by zero, which is illegal and will cause a runtime error. If you are accepting input from a user for the values to be used in a division problem, you will need to validate it to be sure that it is not zero.

Some confusion may arise due to the fact that ActionScript uses the plus sign both for addition and concatenation, but the language will not confuse the two, as addition can only be performed on numbers and concatenation on strings. However, if you place a number in a string by putting it in quotes, it will concatenate. For example, this code results in sum equaling 9:

```
var sum = 4+5;
```

And this code results in sum as 45:

```
var sum = "4" + "5";
```

# Perform Complex Mathematical Operations with the Math Class

**B**uttons and `MovieClips` exist visually within your project, but most of the classes in ActionScript are nonvisual: They perform the background processing necessary to make your movie function but do not actually display anything onscreen. The `Math` class is an example of this. You need to use the `Math` class in order to perform any but the most rudimentary mathematical operations, but all it does is perform the math — it is not responsible for actually displaying the results of the calculations.

`Math` is a *static* class. Static classes are those that do not need to be instantiated in order to work. You have to create an instance of a `MovieClip` to work with it because a single `MovieClip` can have many instances

available at once. We need not create an instance of `Math` because logically, you cannot have more than one idea of `Math` around at a time: Math is just math. Therefore, you can simply use any of the properties and methods of `Math` by directly referencing the class itself.

The class contains a set of constants that represent common mathematical constants, such as pi:

```
var pi:Number = Math.PI;
```

Other constants include the square root of 2 or the natural logarithm of 2 and of 10. The `Math` class also contains a set of methods to perform calculations such as rounding numbers.

## Perform Complex Mathematical Operations with the Math Class

① Type the mathematical operation that you need, such as `var: sin20:Number = Math.sin(20);`.

② Trace the value of the variable, such as `trace(sin20);` in this example.

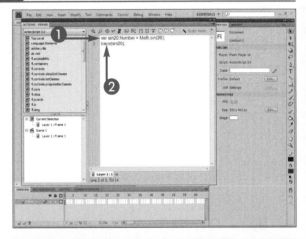

③ Press Ctrl + Enter (⌘ + Enter on Mac).

The movie runs in Flash Player.

● The Output window appears, displaying the result — in this example, the value of `sin20`.

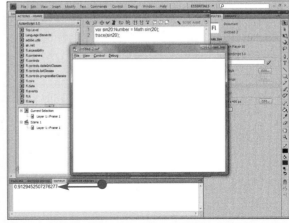

**4** Close Flash Player.

**5** Type another operation, such as
```
var
round:Number =
Math.
round(99/5);.
```

**6** Trace the value of the variable, such as
```
trace(round);
```
in this example.

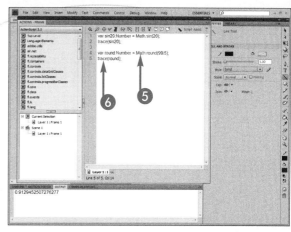

**7** Press Ctrl + Enter (⌘ + Enter on Mac).

The movie runs in Flash Player.

● The Output window appears, displaying the result — in this example, the value of `round`.

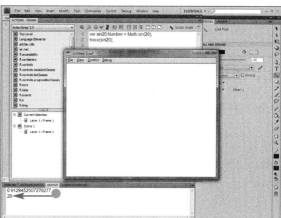

## Extra

The `Math` class has no properties. Because the values of things such as pi are never-changing, they are stored inside the class as constants. Following the accepted coding best practice, the names of the constants are in all capital letters, so if you want to get the value of pi, you would write `Math.PI`.

You cannot set the number of decimal places used by the `round()` method: It always rounds to the nearest integer.

A complete list of the properties and methods of the `Math` class can be found online in the official ActionScript documentation, known as `ASDocs`. The `ASDocs` entry for `Math` can be accessed at http://livedocs.adobe.com/flash/9.0/ActionScriptLangRefV3/Math.html; scroll down the page to see a list of the methods and constants. You can click the name of any method or constant to skip down further on the page and read its description.

# Generate Random Numbers

You can use the `random()` method of the `Math` class to generate a random number between 0 and 1. If you need a random number that falls within a particular range, simply multiply the result of `Math.random()` by the required number for the range, as in the following:

```
Math.random() * 255
```

This gives you a random number between 0 and 254.99999. You can force the result to be a whole number of passing it to the `round()` method:

```
Math.round(Math.random() * 255)
```

This returns a whole number between 0 and 255. You can create a number within a range of positive to negative numbers by multiplying the result of the `random()` call by twice the maximum positive value and then subtracting half from the entire result:

```
Math.round(Math.random() * 510) - 255
```

This results in -255 to 255.

## Generate Random Numbers

① Type a variable to be set to a random number, such as `var randomNumber:Number = Math.random();`.

② Round the number, such as `var randomInteger:Number = Math.round(Math.random());` in this example.

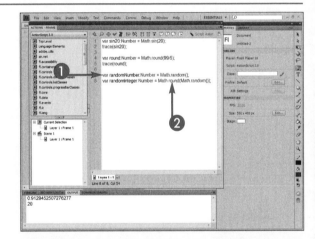

③ Type a variable to set to a random number within a range, such as `var randomPosRange:Number = Math.round(Math.random() * 255);`.

④ Type a variable to be set to a random number within a negative to positive range, such as `var randomRange:Number = Math.round(Math.random() *510) - 255;`.

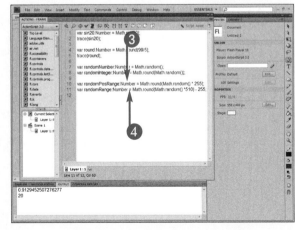

⑤ Trace the value of the first variable, such as `trace(random Number);`.

⑥ Trace the second variable, such as `trace(random Integer);`.

⑦ Trace the third variable, such as `trace(random PosRange);`.

⑧ Trace the fourth variable, such as `trace(random Range);`.

⑨ Press Ctrl + Enter (⌘ + Enter on Mac).

The movie runs in Flash Player.

● The Output window appears, displaying the values.

⑩ While still in Flash Player, press Ctrl + Enter (⌘ + Enter on Mac) again to see new numbers.

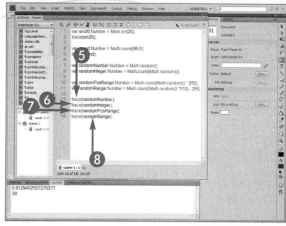

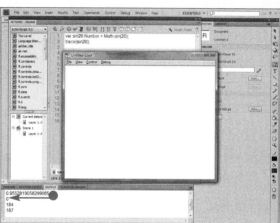

---

A practical application of a random number generator is to use it to place a `MovieClip` at a random location on the Stage by simply placing the result of a call to `Math.random()` as the value of the X property and another as the value of Y. To ensure that the `MovieClip` does not appear off-stage, force the result into the range between zero and the width of the Stage for X and the height of the Stage for Y:

```
var xPosition:Number = Math.round(Math.random() * 550);
var yPosition:Number = Math.round(Math.random() * 400);
mcBox1.x = xPosition;
mcBox1.y = yPosition;
```

When you test the movie, you can repeatedly press Ctrl + Enter (⌘ + Enter) and see the `MovieClip` "jump" to a different location. Chapter 13 discusses how to cause `MovieClip`s to move around the Stage randomly during an animation.

# Create Instances of the Date Class

nother nonvisual class in ActionScript that you will find useful is `Date`. The `Date` class serves two purposes: It can read the current date and time from the user's system, or it can be used to set a specific date and time.

Unlike `Math`, `Date` is not a static class: You may need one instance of the class to read the local time and another to set a specific time, so you need to create an instance in order to use it. You create instances of the `Date` class by declaring a variable and then using the `new` keyword to call the constructor of the class:

```
var today:Date = new Date();
```

The class contains a set of methods to get dates — that is, to read the local file system date and time. For example, to get the current year with the instance named above, you would write `today.getFullYear();`.

If you want to set a date in your movie, you pass the date that you want to set to the constructor:

```
var birthDate:Date = new Date(1971, 10, 18);
```

---

## Create Instances of the Date Class

### GET THE DAY OF THE WEEK

**1** Type `var today: Date =`.

**2** Type `new Date();`.

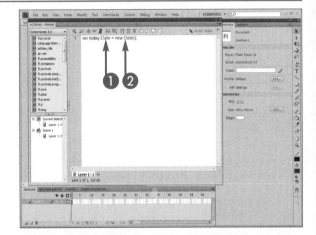

**3** Type `var weekDay = today.getDay();`.

The current day of the week is stored in a variable.

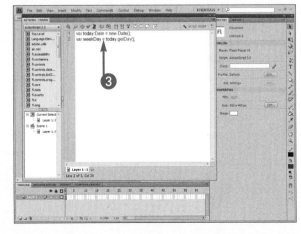

## SET YOUR BIRTHDATE

**④** Type `var birth Date:Date =`.

**⑤** Type `new Date(`*year, month, day*`);`.

***Note:*** *Use the year, month, and day you were born.*

**⑥** Type `var birthYear = birthDate. getFull Year();`.

**⑦** Type `trace (weekDay);`.

**⑧** Type `trace (birthYear);`.

**⑨** Press Ctrl + Enter (⌘ + Enter).

Flash Player runs the movie.

● The values of the variables are displayed in the Output window.

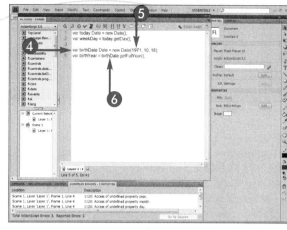

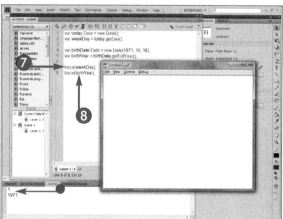

# Perform Math on Dates

You can perform mathematical operations on dates using the instances of the `Date` class that you create. You can add or subtract a given number of seconds, minutes, hours, days, weeks, or years to a given date. You can also add or subtract dates from one another to calculate the time elapsed between the dates.

You cannot simply perform math on instances of the `Date` class directly, as those instances are objects, and math can only be performed on numbers. However, instances of the `Date` class contain a `time` property, which represents the number of milliseconds that have elapsed since midnight on January 1, 1970. By adding or subtracting this time property from two given instances of `Date`, you can calculate the milliseconds that have occurred between those two dates.

After you have calculated this number, you can use simple mathematical expressions to convert it to a more usable number. If you want the number of days between two dates, you could create two instances of `Date`, one for the first date and another for the second and then divide the number by 1,000 to get the seconds. Divide that by 60 for the minutes, 60 for the hours, and 24 to arrive at the number of days. You may want to use the `Math.round()` method to round the result to a whole number of days. See the earlier section "Perform Complex Mathematical Operations with the Math Class" for details on using `Math.round()`.

## Perform Math on Dates

① Create a variable for the first date, such as `var today:Date = new Date(year, month, day);`.

**Note:** *You can use the current year, month, and day.*

② Create a variable for the second date, such as `var christmas:Date = new Date(year, 13, 25);`.

**Note:** *Again, you can use the current year.*

③ Create a variable that represents the first day, such as `var todayTime:Number = today.time;`.

④ Create a variable that represents the later day, such as `var christmas Time:Number = christmas.time;`.

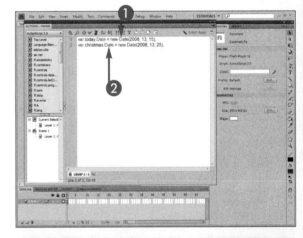

⑤ Create a variable to hold the number of milliseconds between the first day and the second day, such as `var millisLeft:Number = christmasTime – todayTime;`.

⑥ Create a variable that rounds the days between to a whole number, such as `var daysLeft:Number = Math.round();`.

⑦ Within the parentheses in step **6**, place the variable that you created in step **5** and the time calculators needed, such as `millisLeft/1000/60/60/24`.

⑧ Trace the value that you need for your movie, such as `trace(daysLeft);`.

⑨ Press Ctrl + Enter (⌘ + Enter).

Flash Player runs the movie.

● The result of the calculation is displayed in the Output window.

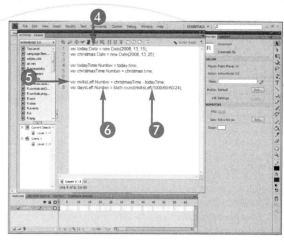

It may seem odd that the `time` property of the `Date` class returns the milliseconds since January 1, 1970. This date is known as the *UNIX Epoch*. The problem with calculating math on dates is, of course, that nothing related to dates or times uses any standard units: There are 60 seconds in a minute, but 24 hours in a day, and varying numbers of days per month. Although most people could probably calculate the number of days between today and an event later in the year, such as their birthday, they would really need to think about it, working through each month and making sure to add the right number of days. The problem is even more complicated when calculating over multiple years, thanks to the fact that there are not 365 days in a year, but rather 365.242199 days — hence the need for leap years.

All of this complexity is solved by using the UNIX Epoch to calculate dates instead. By converting all dates to a simple number — the milliseconds since a particular date — all the math becomes easy for the computer. The actual determination of that epoch occurring on January 1, 1970, was somewhat arbitrary.

# Write a Function

A *function* is nothing more than a reusable block of code. Functions are primarily designed to let you save development time. Rather than rewrite and retest similar code over and over, you can encapsulate the code into a function and then simply call it whenever you need its capabilities.

ActionScript includes a set of *global functions* to perform certain common tasks. Global functions are written into the core ActionScript code and can be accessed directly in your code.

One global function — `trace` — is covered in Chapter 2. Another common global function is `stop`, which is discussed in Chapter 8.

Most often, you will need some functionality that is specific to your project. In these cases, you will need to write your own function. Any code can be encapsulated into a function, and any time you are finding that you need to reuse code you already wrote, you should consider making it a function.

Functions begin with a signature line. This line begins with the `function` keyword and then defines the function by providing its name, determining what portions of the code can call it, what information may need to be passed to it, and what type of data it will return. This section looks at the first two parts: the name and access modifier. The following sections discuss passing data to functions and returning data from them.

The name of the function can be any valid variable name. Common practice is to use the form *verbNoun* for your function name, so a function that multiplied two numbers might be named `multiplyNumbers`.

## Write a Function

1. Type `function`.

2. Type a name for the function.

3. Type a set of parentheses.

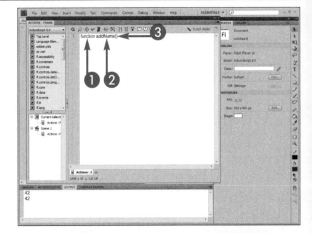

4. Type an opening curly brace.

5. Press Enter twice.

6. Type a closing curly brace.

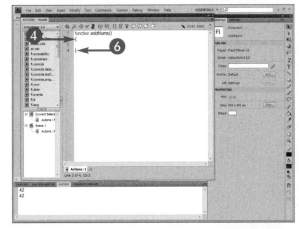

⑦ Click the line between the curly braces.

⑧ Type the code to be performed by the function.

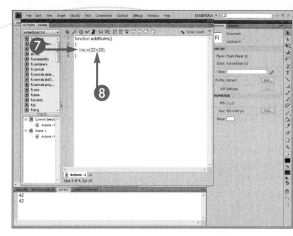

In this example, the function will trace the value of a variable.

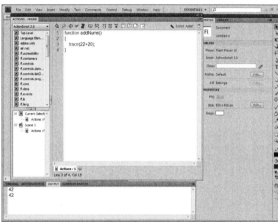

## Extra

Beginning developers often struggle with determining exactly when they should use a function and when they should not. As a general rule, functions should be used anytime you have a set of code that may need to be used more than once in your application. Certainly, anytime you find yourself copying and pasting a block of code and then making only minor modifications to make the code work in a new scenario, you should instead write a function to perform the task. This may not be faster initially than copy and paste, but over time it will save you a lot of development time. Imagine that you had the same block copied four or five times in your script but then needed to change a key element of that code block. Rather than have to change all five instances, you can make the change the one time in the function and be sure that the rest will work.

# Call a Function

In order to use a function's code, you need to call it. That is, you need to tell ActionScript to process the code within the function.

You call a function that you write in exactly the same way you call any of ActionScript's global functions: You type the name of the function and a set of parentheses. Functions can be called anywhere an ActionScript expression is allowed, so you can call them as their own line of code, as the value of a variable, or even from within other functions. How and where you call a function depend on its purpose. Simple functions, such as the one that is used in this example, can generally only be called on their own line. Later in this chapter, functions that return values are discussed; these functions will need to

be called as the value of a variable, as you will need to store and process the value being returned.

Functions will be executed as if they were written on the line where they are called. However, they can actually be written anywhere. A common practice is to have function definitions grouped together at the top of your script to make them easy to find when you need to edit them, but this is not a requirement. The important thing is that your code be organized: As long as you can find the code when you need it, then any organizational structure will work. Consider, however, that other developers may later need to work with your code as well, so be sure to include comments to explain your organizational structure to them.

## Call a Function

① Create a function.

**Note:** See the previous section, "Write a Function," for details.

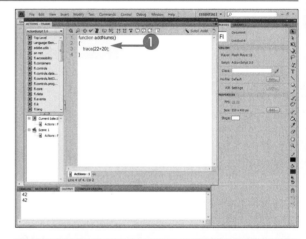

② After the function code, type the name of the function followed by a set of parentheses and a semicolon.

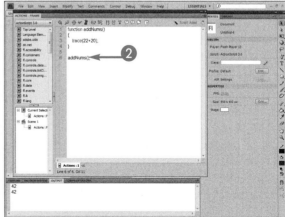

③ To call the function again, on a new line, type the name of the function, a set of parentheses, and a semicolon again.

**Note:** *Functions can be called as many times as needed in your code.*

④ Press Ctrl + Enter (⌘ + Enter on a Mac).

The movie opens in Flash Player.

● The result of the `trace()` statement from the function in this example is shown twice in the Output window.

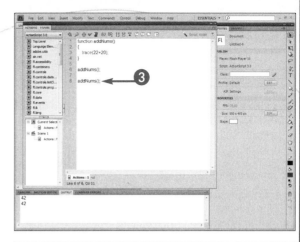

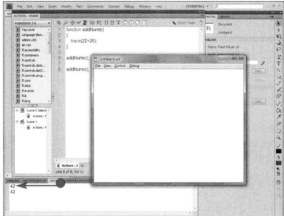

## Extra

Take care to ensure that each function that you write performs only a single task. Many beginning developers want to start encapsulating all their code into single, huge functions that try to do everything. It is better instead to write a series of shorter functions, each having their own specific purpose.

In particular, you should not have a function that is responsible both for calculating a value of something and for generating the display of that value. It is far better to have one function that calculates the value and then either have the main script create the display or have a second, separate function handle it. Which of the latter options you choose depends on whether you have other parts of the code that need the same display result — in which case you should use a function.

# Pass Data to Functions

Variables created within functions are said to be *local* to the function; that is, the rest of the script cannot read or write those values. Variables created outside of functions are said to be *global,* meaning that they can be accessed from anywhere, both inside and outside of functions.

However, it is never a good idea to have a function directly manipulate a variable that is created outside of it. You can quickly become confused as to when a variable is going to be manipulated and what its value may end up being. Instead, functions should always be independent of the code that calls them. In other words, functions should only ever work with their own data.

There are many times, though, that you will need a function to manipulate a variable from outside in the script. In these cases, you should pass the variable directly to the function in the form of an *argument.* You pass arguments in the parentheses in the signature line and then use them as variables through the function. You should declare the data type of each argument and be sure that the data being passed to the function is of the right type. This way, your script will return an error if you attempt to pass the wrong kind of data, rather than execute incorrectly.

When you call the function, you can pass the arguments within the parentheses after the function name. The arguments can be literal values, variables, or instances of objects, depending on the types of data the function can accept.

## Pass Data to Functions

**1** Type `function`, followed by the name of the function and parentheses, such as `addNums()`.

**2** Within the parentheses in step **1**, type the arguments that you want to pass, such as `numToAdd1:Number, numToAdd2:Number`.

**3** After the parentheses, type an opening curly brace.

**4** Press Enter twice and type a closing curly brace.

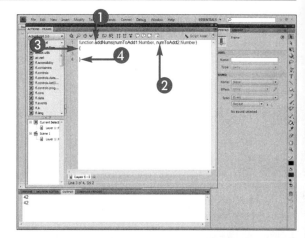

**5** Within the curly braces, use the first of the arguments as you need to, such as `var num1:Number = numToAdd1;`.

**6** Use the second of the arguments as you need to, such as `var num2:Number = numToAdd2;`.

**7** Create a variable to use the variables together, such as `var sum:Number = num1 + num2;`.

**8** Trace the ultimate result, such as `trace(sum);`.

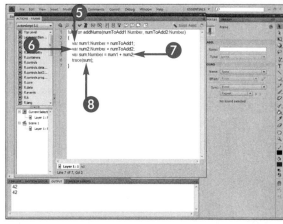

⑨ Below the closing curly brace, type the first code line that you want to perform outside the function, such as `var firstNum:Number = 10;`.

⑩ Continue your code that will require the function, such as `var secondNum: Number =32;`.

⑪ Put your function to work, such as `addNums (firstNum, secondNum);`.

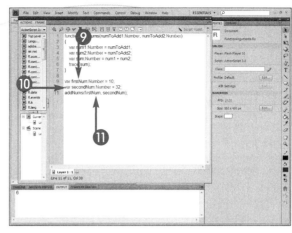

⑫ Press Ctrl + Enter (⌘ + Enter on a Mac).

Flash Player runs the movie.

● In this example, the result of the calculation from the formula is displayed in the Output window.

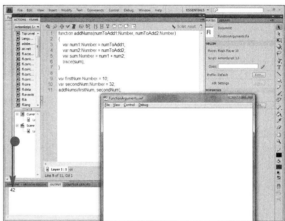

## Apply It

Normally, when you call a function, you need to pass the arguments to the function in the exact order in which they are listed in the function's signature. In the example in the steps in this section, `firstNum` is passed to the function as `numToAdd1` and `secondNum` as `numToAdd2`. However, it is possible to pass arguments by named reference instead:

```
addNums(numToAdd1 = firstNum, numToAdd2 = secondNum);
```

You can make arguments to functions optional by providing a default value within the signature line:

```
private function addNums(numToAdd1:Number, numToAdd2:Number, numToAdd3:Number = 0)
```

If you do this, the default value will be used for the argument whenever another value is not passed to the function. Optional arguments must always be given in the signature after any required values — those not given default values.

# Return a Value from a Function

A s discussed in the section "Pass Data to Functions," variables created within a function's code block are local to the function; that is, they are not accessible outside the function. However, many times, you will need to have the function perform its tasks and create some variable that needs to be used by the remainder of your script.

You can accomplish this task by having the function *return* a value. The actual process for doing this is simple: As the last line of your function, write the keyword `return` followed by the variable to be sent out of the function.

In order to use a function with a return value, you need to call the function as the value of a variable. This variable will then contain the value from the function, which can then be used like any other variable in your script. For example, if a function called `getCopyrightDate` returned a string with the date, you would call it as follows:

```
var copyright:String = getCopyrightDate();
```

Functions can return any data type, including simple types, such as `String`, `Number`, and `Boolean`, or even complex types, such as arrays, objects, or your own custom classes. The type of data being returned from the function should be declared in its signature line, after the parentheses for the arguments. You will need to ensure that the data being returned matches this type, or a runtime error will occur.

## Return a Value from a Function

① Define your function, such as
`function addNums`
`(numToAdd1:Number,`
`numToAdd2:Number)` in this
example.

② After the closing parenthesis,
type a colon and type of data to
be returned, such as `Number`.

③ Type an opening curly brace,
press Enter twice, and type a
closing curly brace.

④ Between the braces, type the
functionality that you want, such
as `var sum:Number =`
`numToAdd1 + numToAdd2;`.

⑤ Return the value that you need,
such as `return sum;`.

⑥ After the closing brace, type
the first code line that you
want to perform outside the
function, such as `var`
`num1:Number = 4;`.

⑦ Continue your code that will
require the function, such as
`var num2:Number = 2;`.

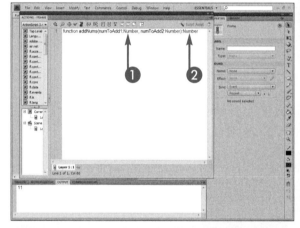

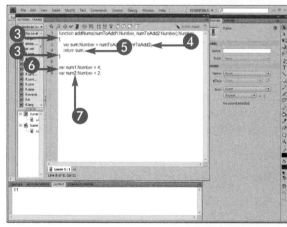

⑧ Complete your required script, such as `var total:Number = addNums(num1, num2);`.

⑨ Trace the value that you need, such as `trace(total);`.

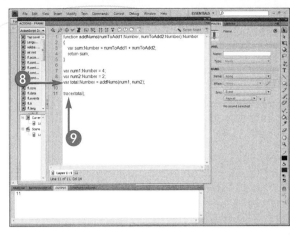

⑩ Press Ctrl + Enter (⌘ + Enter on a Mac).

The movie runs in Flash Player.

● The value returned from the function is displayed in the Output window.

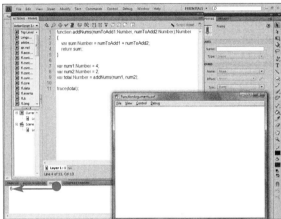

---

## Apply It

It would be possible to rewrite the function from the example in the steps in this section using a single line of code:

```
var sum:Number = numToAdd1 + numToAdd2;
```

However, expressly adding the numbers in a separate line of code makes the code more readable and easier to edit.

You cannot place any code after the `return` statement in a function other than closing curly braces. Doing so will generate a runtime error. The only exception to this is if the return is within an `if-else` conditional statement, which is covered in Chapter 11, although you will see at that time that it does not actually violate this rule.

# Create a Package

In object-oriented programming, a *package* is a container for a group of related classes. In real terms, a package is simply the folder on your computer that contains your class files. The packages you use for your Flash projects should be created in the same folder as the other files for your project; normally, the top-level package will be in the same directory as the FLA file. By convention, package names should begin with a lowercase letter and then contain mixed case after that.

Many classes exist in ActionScript, and the possibility exists that you could create a custom class with the same name as one of the built-in classes. In this situation, a name conflict will occur, resulting in an error when you attempt to publish the file. However, you do not need to memorize the names of all the classes in ActionScript, as name conflicts can be avoided through the use of packages. The technical name of a class includes its package name, so if you create a custom class called `PhotoGallery` and place it in a package called `bradyStudios`, then the name of the class is technically `bradyStudios.PhotoGallery`. As the name of the package is obviously not something that would be built into Flash, there would not be a name conflict even if ActionScript contained a built-in class called `PhotoGallery`.

You do not need to do anything special in setting up a package. In fact, you do not even do it within Flash: Simply use your normal operating system tools for creating the folder or folders you need.

## Create a Package

### CREATE A PACKAGE IN WINDOWS

**1** Open Windows Explorer.

**2** Navigate to the folder in which you are storing your FLA document.

**3** Right-click in the folder.

**4** Click New.

**5** Click Folder.

**6** Type a name for the folder.

**7** Press Enter.

The package is created.

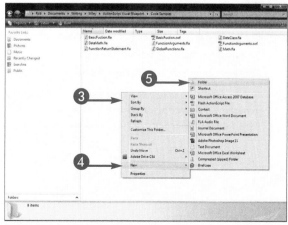

## CREATE A PACKAGE ON MACINTOSH

1 Open the Finder.

2 Navigate to the folder in which you are storing your FLA document.

3 Click File.

4 Click New Folder.

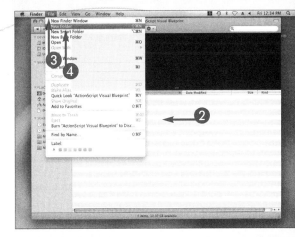

5 Click the folder.

6 Type a name for the folder.

The package is created.

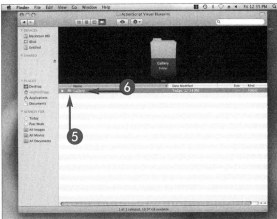

---

In order to guarantee the uniqueness of class names, developers have long used a process of reversing their domain name in packages. Therefore, a developer working on a site at www.bradyStudios.com would create a package com.bradyStudios.www. Because your domain name is guaranteed to be unique, so too is your package, and thus you need not worry about name conflicts with your classes.

Understand, however, that folder names cannot contain dots. In this example, you would not have a folder called com.bradyStudios.www. Rather, you would have a top-level folder called com, which would contain a folder bradyStudios, which in turn would contain a www folder.

Note that you are in no way required to use this structure. It was simply developed as a way to free you from ever having to worry about name conflicts. Even if you get code from another developer, if she follows the same structure, then her classes would be in a different package, so if you and she both had classes with the same name, there would be no conflict.

# Create a New ActionScript File

**E**verything that happens in ActionScript happens through classes. When you build a Flash movie visually in Flash CS4 Professional and then publish the movie to an SWF, Flash actually builds a series of ActionScript classes and compiles those into the SWF file. Each of your symbols becomes a class. In fact, the Stage itself is a class. Although relying on the default classes in ActionScript, such as Stage and MovieClip, can be useful in many cases, in many more cases you will need to create your own classes.

Each class that you create will reside in its own ActionScript file. An ActionScript file is simply a text file that contains ActionScript code. Although ActionScript files can be created in any text editor, creating them

in Flash provides for code hinting, code coloring, and context-sensitive help.

You can create a new ActionScript file in several ways. If you do not have any files open, you should see the Start screen, which will contain a link to create a new ActionScript file, as shown in Chapter 1. If you do have a file open, you can create a new blank document by following the steps in this section. Unlike normal FLA files, the ActionScript file will open in the Actions panel, but the panel will appear full-screen. ActionScript files do not have a Stage or Timeline, and you can only type code.

The file needs to be saved with an .as extension; although if you are creating it in Flash, the extension will be added automatically. Also, you should save your class files into a package to avoid naming conflicts.

## Create a New ActionScript File

### CREATE THE FILE

1. Click File.

2. Click New.

The New Document dialog box appears.

3. Click ActionScript File.

4. Click OK.

The new file is created.

## SAVE THE FILE TO A PACKAGE

1 Click File.

2 Click Save As.

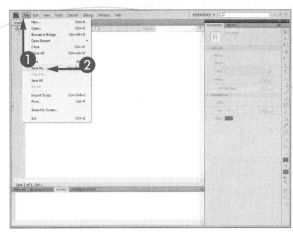

The Save As dialog box opens.

3 Navigate to the package into which you will save the class.

**Note:** *See the preceding section, "Create a Package," for more information.*

4 Type a name for the class.

**Note:** *Your class name should always begin with a capital letter.*

● Flash automatically gives the file an .as extension.

5 Click Save.

The file is saved.

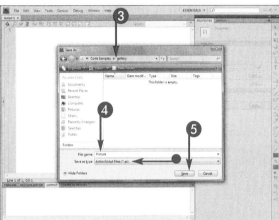

---

### Apply It

You can enter any ActionScript into an external file. Although the examples in this chapter show using the external file for custom classes, you can in fact copy any of the code from an FLA and place it in an external ActionScript file. That file can then be imported back into the document using an `import` statement that references the file:

```
import "actionscript/myfunctions.as";
```

# Create a Custom Class Skeleton

Before you begin coding your custom class, it can help to begin by creating the skeleton of the file that you plan to use. All custom classes follow the same basic structure, so you will quickly get used to the code that you need to add.

The first line of the code declares the package that will contain the class. Remember, a package is nothing more than a folder on your hard drive, and you should group similar classes together in a folder. See the earlier section "Create a Package" for more information. If the file is saved in the same folder as the FLA that will use it, you can simply type `package;` to declare that this class does not belong to any particular package. Otherwise, you will type the `package` keyword followed by the package

name. Either way, the package declaration will be followed by a pair of curly braces.

Within these braces, you will declare the class name itself by providing an access modifier, followed by the `class` keyword, and then the name of the class. The modifier defines what other code can create instances of the class. The most common modifier is `public`, which means that code from just about anywhere can instantiate the class. Other modifiers are discussed later in this chapter.

After the modifier and name, you will enter another pair of curly braces. Inside these braces will be all the code for the class. When you save the file, you need to be sure that the filename matches the name of the class declared in the code.

## Create a Custom Class Skeleton

① In a new ActionScript file, type `package` followed by the name of the package that will contain the class.

② Type an opening and closing curly brace.

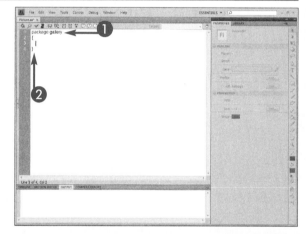

③ On a line between the curly braces, type a modifier, followed by `class`, and then the name of the class, such as `public class Picture`.

④ Type a pair of opening and closing curly braces.

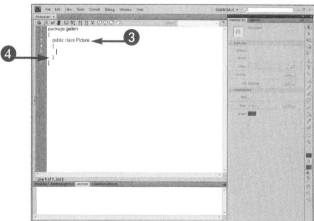

⑤ Click File.

⑥ Click Save.

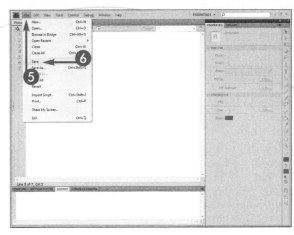

The file is saved, and the class is created.

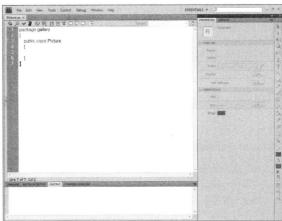

---

### Extra

Normally, filenames in Windows are not case sensitive, so the operating system sees the files Photo.as and photo.as as the same. However, in ActionScript, the filename for the class definition file must exactly match the name provided in the signature line of the class, including case. Therefore, if the file is saved as Photo.as, with a capital *P*, then the signature line of the class must be

```
public class Photo
```

It does not matter if you type the class signature line before saving the file or if you save the blank file first and then type the line — just be sure that they match. Keep in mind that all built-in classes in ActionScript begin with capital letters, and it is strongly recommended that you maintain the same convention in your custom classes.

# Define Properties of the Class

C lasses can contain *properties* and *methods*. Properties are the "nouns" of the class — the things that are used to define it. Methods are explored in detail later in this chapter.

A property of a class is in fact nothing more than a variable that is defined within the class. Properties are defined almost exactly as variables in other parts of the script by using the `var` keyword and a name. The only difference is that properties should also include an access modifier in their declaration. Most properties have their access modifier set to `public` or `private`. Public properties are those that can be read and set from outside of the class, whereas private properties can be accessed only by methods and other properties within the class.

For example, if you have a property `firstName` in a custom class and you want to be able to set the name from your main movie's script, then the property would need to be public.

As variables, property names must follow all the same rules as variable names: They must begin with a letter or underscore and can contain only letters, numbers, and underscores. As with normal variables, you should also declare a data type for each property. See Chapter 2 for a discussion on ActionScript data types and their use. You can set a value for a property when you create it or have the value set later in the code for the class. Public properties may also have values set by the code that instantiates the class.

## Define Properties of the Class

1 Open a custom class file or create a new one.

**Note:** See "Create a New ActionScript File" and "Create a Custom Class Skeleton" earlier in this chapter for information on creating new class files.

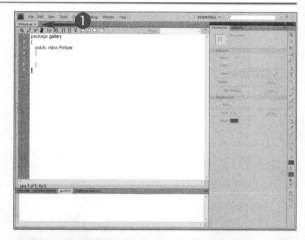

2 After the curly brace that follows the class signature line, type the first property of the class, such as `public var photoName:String;`.

3 Type the second property of the class, such as `public var photoPath:String;`.

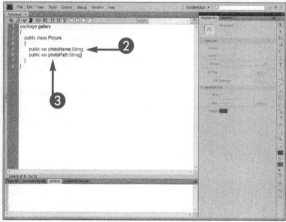

④ Type the third property of the class, such as `public var photoWidth: Number;`.

⑤ Type any other properties that you want, such as `public var photoHeight:Number;`.

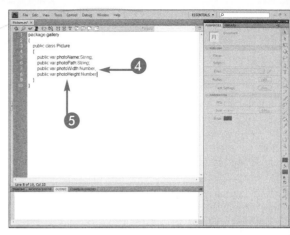

⑥ Click File.

⑦ Click Save.

The file is saved, and the new properties are added to the class.

## Extra

Besides `public` and `private`, there are several other access modifiers. You can also set properties as `internal`, in which case they are available only to other code within this class and to other classes within the same package. Internal is actually the default modifier in ActionScript, which is part of the reason why it is important to always set it: Properties defined without a modifier will not be settable to your movie unless you expressly set the modifier to `public`.

Programmers familiar with other languages, particularly Java, may prefer to set all properties to private and then use a series of functions to access them. This technique, called *getters and setters,* works in ActionScript as well and is covered later in this chapter in the section "Get and Set Class Properties."

# Create a Constructor

Whenever you instantiate a class in your Flash movie, ActionScript automatically calls a special method within the class called a constructor. A *constructor* is in fact nothing more than a function defined in the class that has the same name as the class.

Constructors are used to initialize the class. You may need to perform calculations on the properties of the class, call other functions within the class, or maybe even instantiate another class. Any and all of these can be done with the constructor.

The constructor is written almost exactly like a normal function. You begin with an access modifier, although constructors must always have their modifier set to `public`, which makes logical sense as by definition,

the constructor is a function that will be called from somewhere else — the code that is instantiating the class.

Following the access modifier, you write the keyword `function`, followed by the name of the class and a set of parentheses. You can have the constructor take arguments or not depending on what is needed by the class.

You are not required to write a constructor. If there is nothing specific that needs to be done when the class is instantiated, you can simply ignore the constructor. ActionScript will automatically create an empty constructor when a class without one is instantiated.

Constructors cannot include a return statement. The function actually returns an instance of the class, but you do not need to specify this. Also, the constructor signature line will not have a return data type.

## Create a Constructor

① Open a custom class file or create a new one.

**Note:** See "Create a New ActionScript File" and "Create a Custom Class Skeleton" earlier in this chapter for information on creating new class files.

● If you are defining properties of the class, they should be written before the constructor.

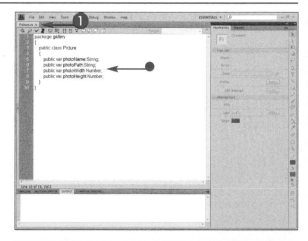

② Type `public function` followed by the name of the class and a set of parentheses, `Picture()` in this example.

③ Type an opening curly brace.

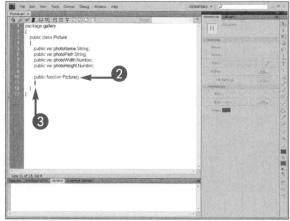

4 Press Enter twice.

5 Type a closing curly brace.

6 Click File.

7 Click Save.

The class is saved with the constructor.

## Extra

There is no way to prevent the constructor from being called when the class is instantiated. If there is code that you want to execute from within the class only in certain situations, then you should write that as a specific method within the class. This gives you the ability to control when the code is executed, as you would need to expressly call the method. Class methods are discussed in the next section, "Define a Method."

Even though ActionScript will automatically create an empty constructor, many developers consider it a best practice to create an empty constructor in your code rather than rely on ActionScript to do it for you. An empty constructor is simply one that contains no code within its curly braces.

# Define a Method

**M**ethods can be seen as the "verbs" of a class — the things that the class can actually do. As an example, the built-in `Math` class contains the `random()` method, which generates and returns a random number.

Your custom classes can contain methods as well. Just as a property is actually nothing more than a variable in the class, a method is in fact nothing more than a function in a class. As with normal functions, your methods should have a name in the form of *verbNoun*. Methods can take arguments and can return values.

You use an access modifier to define what code can call a method. A `public` method can be called either by other code within the class or by code outside of the class — for example, by the movie that instantiates the class.

A `private` method can be called only by other methods within the class. A method set to `internal` can be called by other code in the class or by other classes in the same package. Most if not all of your methods will be set to either `public` or `private`.

You create a method in the same way that you create a normal function. Begin with an access modifier, followed by the function keyword, the name of the method, and a set of parentheses. If the method will take arguments, declare those, along with appropriate data types, within the parentheses. After the closing parenthesis, type a colon and an appropriate return type for the method. Then type a pair of curly braces and within the braces any code that will be executed by the method.

## Define a Method

① Open a custom class file or create a new one.

**Note:** *See "Create a New ActionScript File" and "Create a Custom Class Skeleton" earlier in this chapter for information on creating new class files.*

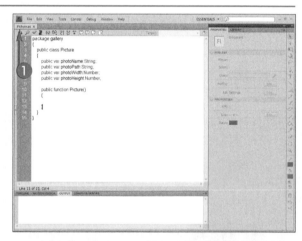

② Begin your method definition, such as `public function scaleImage()`.

③ Declare any needed arguments within the parentheses, such as `xScale:Number, yScale:Number`.

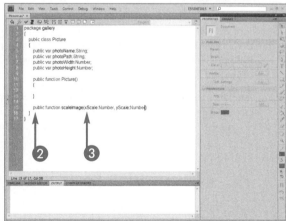

④ After the closing parenthesis, type a colon and the return type, such as `:void`.

⑤ Type a pair of curly braces.

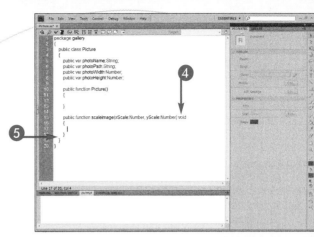

⑥ Between the curly braces, type the first line of code that will be executed by the method, such as `photoWidth *= xScale;`.

⑦ Type any other needed lines of code, such as `photoHeight *= yScale;`.

⑧ Click File → Save.

The class is saved, and the method is added to it.

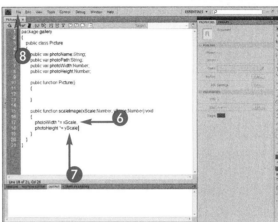

## Extra

The example in the steps in this section multiplies the values of the width of the photo by the `xScale` being passed into the method. Note that the class properties are directly available to the method of the class. As class properties, their access modifiers do not matter: You can call either `public` or `private` properties from anywhere within the class.

The code also uses a shortcut to perform the math. The `*=` operator tells ActionScript to take the current value of the variable on the left side of the operator and multiply it by the variable on the right. In other words, `photoWidth *= xScale` is the same as `photoWidth = photoWidth * xScale`. You can use this shortcut operator with any of the basic mathematical operators, as in `+=`, `-=`, and `/=`.

# Extend
# a Class

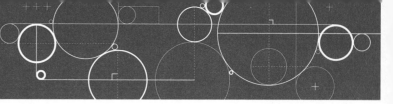

Sometimes, you will need to create a custom class that will derive some or all of its properties and methods from another class. The example in this section creates a thumbnail class to display photos. The basic properties of the thumbnail are the same as those of the photo: the name, file location, and so on. In fact, the only difference between the thumbnail and the photo is its size. Therefore, rather than re-create all the details contained in the `Picture` class, you can instead create a subclass. This way, `Thumbnails` can inherit the properties of `Picture` but also have its own properties, such as its smaller size.

Chapter 8 presents another example of this process. In that case, you will learn how to create visual elements on the Stage through code by creating a subclass of `MovieClip`.

Creating a subclass is known as *extending a class;* you are taking a current class and extending it into a new class. The class being extended is known as a *superclass.*

When you create a subclass, you need to import the superclass by providing its fully qualified name — that is, its name and package. You then add the keyword `extends` and the superclass name to the signature line of the subclass. Properties and methods of the superclass are available to the subclass via the `super()` method. If you are extending one of the built-in ActionScript classes, you can look up its fully qualified name either in the Flash help file or in the official ActionScript documentation online.

## Extend a Class

① Create a new ActionScript file.

**Note:** *See the section "Create a New ActionScript File" for details.*

② Declare the package that will contain the class, such as `package gallery`.

③ Type a pair of curly braces.

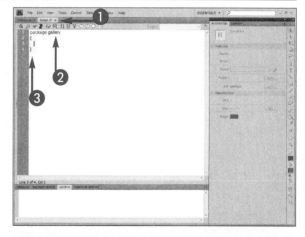

④ Between the curly braces, type the line to import the superclass, such as `import gallery. Picture;`.

⑤ Type the signature line of the subclass, such as `public class Thumbnails extends Picture`, and a pair of curly braces.

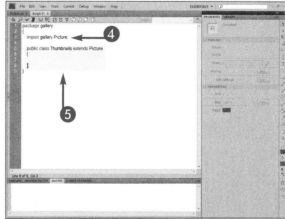

**6** Between the curly braces, create the properties for the subclass.

**Note:** *See the section "Define Properties of the Class" for details.*

**7** Create any methods of the subclass.

**Note:** *See the section "Define a Method" for details.*

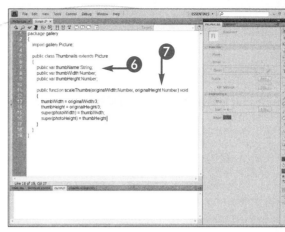

**8** Click File.

**9** Click Save As.

The Save As dialog box opens.

**10** Navigate to the appropriate directory.

**11** Type the name of the subclass, Thumbnails in this example.

**12** Click Save.

In this example, the `Picture` class is extended by the new `Thumbnails` class.

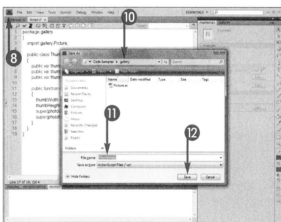

---

## Extra

Although it will make sense most of the time to place a subclass in the same package as its superclass, this is not required. Because the superclass is explicitly imported into the subclass and you must provide a fully qualified name for the superclass, the two can be in completely different packages if you prefer.

Any class, including those built into ActionScript, can be extended. In fact, when you create a symbol on the Stage, you are actually extending the `MovieClip` or `SimpleButton` class. While for convenience, we refer to symbols as "MovieClips" or "Buttons," they are actually their own classes, subclasses of the `MovieClip` or `SimpleButton` class.

# Using a Custom Class

After you have finished writing the code for your custom class, you can use it in your movie. There are several approaches to implementing custom classes. You can redefine the movie itself to be an instance of your class, which is covered in the next section, "Define a Document Class." You can also create an instance of the class in your ActionScript code by importing it and then calling its constructor with the `new` keyword:

```
import pictures.Picture;
var myPicture:Picture = new Picture();
```

This code creates an instance of `Picture` called `myPicture`. It assumes that the constructor of the class does not take arguments; if it did, you would need to provide those arguments inside the parentheses.

After the class has been instantiated, you can read or set values of its properties or call its methods using dot notation, such as `myPicture.photoWidth = 300` or `myPicture.scalePhoto(2,2)`. Keep in mind that only public properties and methods can be called this way. If you attempt to read or write a private property or to call a private method, you will get an error.

You must import your custom class, using its fully qualified name, including its package, in order to instantiate it in your code.

---

## Using a Custom Class

**1** Either open an existing Flash movie or create a new one.

**Note:** *See Chapter 1 for details on opening and creating movies.*

**2** Click Window → Actions to open the Actions panel.

You can also press F9.

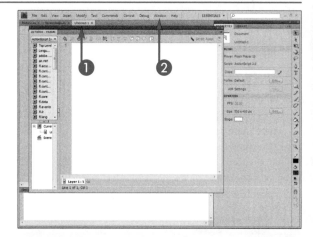

**3** Type a line to import your custom class, such as `import gallery.Picture;`.

**4** Call the class's constructor, such as `var myPicture:Picture = new Picture();`.

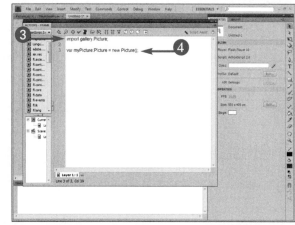

5️⃣ Set the value of the class's first property, such as `myPicture.photoName = "My First Photo";`.

6️⃣ Set the values of any other needed properties, such as `myPicture.photoPath = "assets/firstphoto.jpg";`.

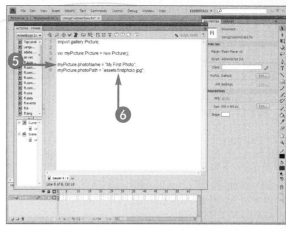

7️⃣ Press Ctrl + Enter.

The movie opens in Flash Player. In this example, the movie is blank; you are testing it to be sure that no errors occur when you run it. If any errors occur, return to your code to fix them.

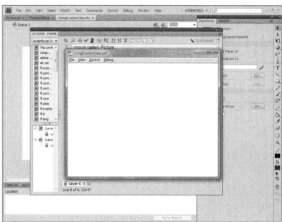

---

## Apply It

You can create as many instances of a class as you need by simply using the `new` keyword to call its constructor repeatedly. You need to import the class only once, regardless of how many instances you create:

```
import photos.Photo;
var myPhoto1:Photo = new Photo();
var myPhoto2:Photo = new Photo();
var myPhoto3:Photo = new Photo();
```

Each instance could then be dealt with independently:

```
myPhoto1.photoName = "My first photo";
myPhoto2.photoName = "My second photo";
myPhoto3.photoName = "My third photo";
```

# Define a Document Class

**B**y default, Flash movies are instances of the `Timeline` class, which is in turn a subclass of `MovieClip`. This is why you can do most of the things to the Timeline that you can do to a `MovieClip`; however, as with all subclasses, `Timeline` does have a few differences.

There may be times when it will be more efficient to base your movie off of another class instead. This new custom class for the movie is called a *document class.* For example, you may create a custom class that automatically instantiates a certain number of child classes. In the case of a photo gallery application, you could have a document class that imported the `Picture` and `Thumbnails` classes and generated a certain number

of instances of each, which would save you from having to do that yourself in the movie.

If you want the movie to continue to act as a regular movie — if you are creating a document class to add functionality, rather than remove it — then you need to be sure that the document class extends the `MovieClip` class. See the section "Extend a Class" earlier in this chapter for details. If you base your document on a class that does not extend `MovieClip`, you will lose the Timeline and the ability to animate within your project, and you may encounter other errors as you move through your project, so you should do this only after carefully testing the implications.

## Define a Document Class

**1** Create a new ActionScript file.

***Note:*** *See the section "Create a New ActionScript File" for details.*

**2** Declare the package that will contain the class.

***Note:*** *In this example, the class will be placed in the main document folder, so there is no package name.*

**3** Type a pair of curly braces.

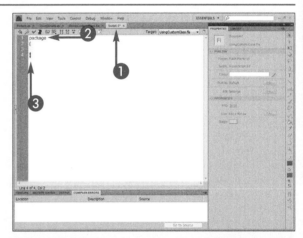

**4** Between the curly braces, type the line to import the superclass, such as `import flash.display. MovieClip;`.

**5** Import any additional classes that may be required.

**6** Type the signature line of the document class, such as `public class Gallery extends MovieClip`, and a pair of curly braces.

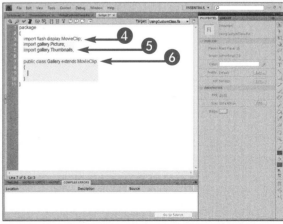

**7** Between the curly braces, create the properties for the document class.

***Note:*** *See the section "Define Properties of the Class" for details.*

**8** Create any methods of the document class.

***Note:*** *See the section "Define a Method" for details.*

**9** Save the file, using the name of the class as the filename.

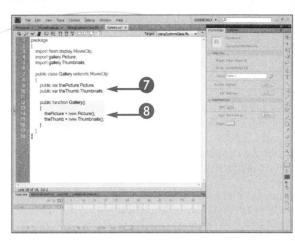

**10** Open the Flash movie to which you want to apply the document class.

**11** Click Properties.

The Properties panel opens.

**12** Type the name of the document class — Gallery in this example.

The document class is applied to the movie.

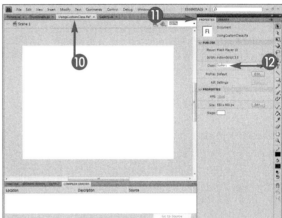

---

## Extra

In the example in the steps in this section, the document class will require three imported classes: the MovieClip that it is extending and the custom Picture and Thumbnails classes, instances of which will be created by the constructor. Note that each of these classes must be imported to be used: Picture and Thumbnails from the gallery package and MovieClip from its package in flash.display.

Although you will know the locations of your custom classes, finding the package that contains any of the built-in classes can be more challenging. The easiest way to find these packages is to simply use a search engine such as Google. If you search for "ActionScript 3 MovieClip" using Google, the first or second link of the results will likely be to the official Adobe documentation for the class, which will list the package. In fact, the package will likely be visible in the description on the search engine's page, so you may not even have to click the link to get the information that you need.

# Get and Set Class Properties

xperienced programmers with backgrounds in object-oriented languages such as Java have long practiced a technique whereby they declare all properties of a class as `private` and then use a special set of functions to either get the value of the property or set it. These *getters* and *setters* allow the developers to change the name of the property without having to worry about changing all references to it throughout their code: The property's name will be referenced only by the appropriate getter and setter within the class. Therefore, code that uses this technique tends to be easier to maintain.

To use this technique, you simply need to change the access modifier on each property from `public` to `private`. Then, to allow the value of the property to be set, you can write a method for the property, called set*Property*, where *Property* is the name of the

property to be set. The method will take as an argument the value to be set to the property and will return an instance of the property with the correct data type. A getter works the same way: Create a method called get*Property*, which returns an instance of the property.

For example, a method to set a `fileName` property might look like this:

```
public function setFileName(fileName:String):
String
{
    this.fileName = fileName;
}
```

Note here that although the properties are set to `private`, the methods must be set to `public`, as they will be called from outside of the class.

## Get and Set Class Properties

① Open a custom class file that contains properties.

**Note:** *See the sections "Create a Custom Class Skeleton" and "Define Properties of the Class" for details.*

② Change the access modifier on each `public` property to `private`.

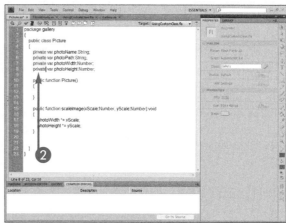

③ Below the properties, begin the method to set the first property value, such as `public function setPhotoName(newName: String):String`.

④ Add a set of curly braces.

⑤ Between the curly braces, set the value of the property, such as `photoName = newName;`.

⑥ Return the value, such as `return photoName;`.

⑦ Repeat steps **3** to **6** for each additional property.

⑧ Below the setters, begin the method to get the first property value, such as `public function getPhotoName():String`.

⑨ Add a set of curly braces.

⑩ Between the braces, return the value, such as `return photoName;`.

⑪ Repeat steps **8** to **10** for each additional property.

⑫ Click File → Save.

The file is saved and now uses getters and setters.

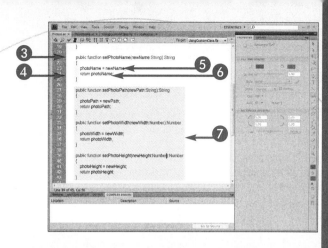

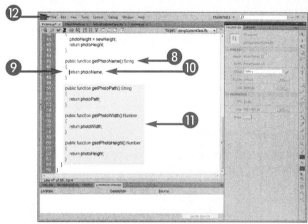

## Apply It

To use getters and setters, you will simply call the appropriate method instead of the property. In the example of the `Picture` class used in the example shown here, the `photoName` property was before set using

```
myPhoto1.photoName = "My first photo"
```

Now, you would call the setter:

```
myPhoto1.setPhotoName("My first photo");.
```

The `photoName` property would be retrieved using the same logic, so to create a local variable in the movie equal to the name, instead of this:

```
private var firstPhotoName = myPhoto1.photoName;
```

You would now type

```
var firstPhotoName = myPhoto1.getPhotoName():
```

# Add a Static Property to a Class

Occasionally, you may need to create a property within your custom class that can be called without specifically creating an instance of the method. These are properties that will not change or be affected by individual instances, and they are known as *static* properties.

For example, in a photo gallery application, you may have a standard copyright notice that you want to append to every photo. If you assume for the sake of the example that each photo will have the exact same copyright message, it would make sense to set the text as a static property of the class. You set a static property by adding the static keyword in the property's definition:

```
public static var copyright:String = "Photo
   copyright Brady Studios.";
```

You can then use the property by directly calling the class, instead of an instance. Using this example, if this is defined in a class called Photo, you could display the copyright notice in a text field named txtCopyright by simply typing

```
txtCopyright.text = Photo.copyright;
```

Text fields are discussed in more detail in Chapter 9.

---

Add a Static Property to a Class

① Open a custom class file.

**Note:** *See the section "Create a Custom Class Skeleton" for details.*

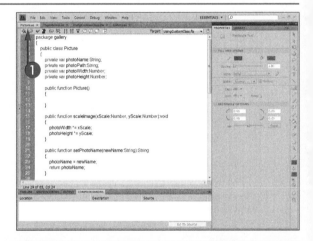

② Before the constructor, type public static var.

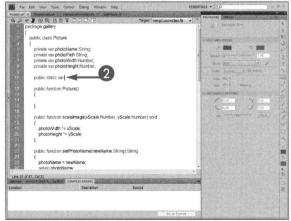

**3** Type a name for the property.

**4** Type a colon and the appropriate data type.

**5** Type an equals sign and a value.

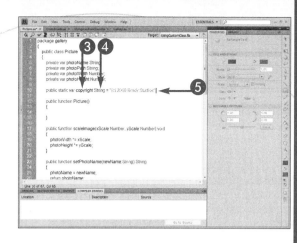

**6** Click File.

**7** Click Save.

The class file is saved, and the static property is added to the class.

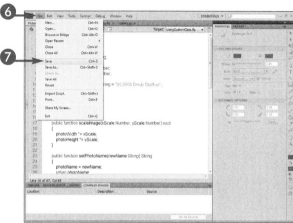

## Extra

By definition, static properties are those that do not change from one instance to the next. Taking the example shown here, if each photo needed a separate copyright notice, then you would need to add the notice as a regular property of the class and if needed, create a getter and setter for it.

You can also create static methods. As with static properties, you simply add the `static` keyword to the function definition:

```
public static function getCompanyName():String
```

Static functions and methods are designed to be directly called outside of the class itself, so they will always have their access modifier set to `public`.

# Create an Event Handler

**A**ctionScript is an event-driven language. This means that in order for anything to occur in your script, an event must be triggered by Flash Player. Events can be triggered by the system or by the user. Examples of system events include an external file finishing being loaded or the play head entering a frame. User-triggered events include the user moving his or her mouse, clicking the mouse button, or pressing a key on the keyboard.

You need two pieces in your code to deal with events: an event handler and an event listener. An *event handler* is nothing more than a function that describes what will occur when the event is triggered. Event handlers can calculate a total, increase a user's score, submit information to a Web server, restart a movie, or almost

anything else you need it to do. *Event listeners* allow you to register an event with a particular object in your movie. Listeners will be covered in the following sections.

All event handlers take a single argument, a reference to the event. As with all function arguments, you can give it any name that you want, although event and e are the two most common. The argument should be data-typed based on the type of event, so if the event will be triggered by the user clicking the mouse, you would use a type MouseEvent.

Event handlers can never return data, which makes sense if you consider that they are not being called by a line in the code that could continue processing but are instead being triggered by some action. Therefore, a handler's return type will always be void.

## Create an Event Handler

① Type function.

② Type a name for the event handler.

③ Type a pair of parentheses.

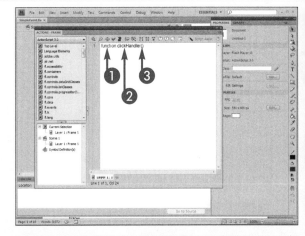

④ Within the parentheses, type event.

⑤ Type a colon.

⑥ Type an appropriate event type.

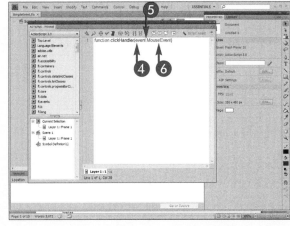

**7** After the closing parenthesis, type a colon.

**8** Type void.

**9** Type a pair of curly braces.

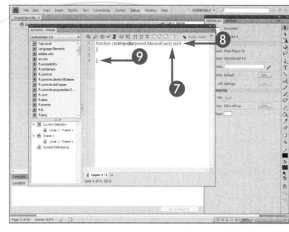

**10** Within the curly braces, type the code to be executed by the event.

The event is created. In order to trigger the event, you will need to create an event listener, which is covered in the next two sections.

## Extra

The ActionScript Event class provides a superclass for all the event types. Although it is possible to use the generic Event class for all events, it is better to rely on one of the 34 more specific subclasses of Event, as they provide more detailed properties and methods for the events. For example, MouseEvent is a subclass to use for all events involving mouse actions, including clicks, double-clicks, drags, and mouse movements. Unlike the Event class, MouseEvent includes specific properties to, among other things, detect the exact location of the mouse pointer. The KeyboardEvent class contains a property that allows you to detect which key was pressed, enabling you to respond to events differently depending on the key. Keyboard events are covered in Chapter 14.

You cannot pass other arguments to the event handler. However, it is possible to access details of the object being clicked through the event's target property, which will be discussed later in this chapter in the section "Using the Target Property."

# Call an Event from a Button

**E**vent handlers define the actions that you want to take when an event occurs, but like all functions, they must be called. An *event listener* enables you to specify the object and the event that will call the handler.

You can register an object with a handler by calling the addEventListener method. The method takes two arguments: the event that will provide the trigger and the handler to be called. The event could use the generic Event class, which can handle any event, but it is better to use a specific subclass of Event, such as MouseEvent. Most of these subclasses have defined constants for certain common events, so for instance, you can use MouseEvent.CLICK to call a handler when the user clicks the mouse button. The KeyboardEvent class likewise

defines constants for most of the keys on the keyboard so that it can respond accordingly.

The name of the handler for the event is provided as the second argument of the function. Even though the handler is a function, you will always call it without the set of parentheses normally used when calling functions, as you cannot pass any arguments to the function. An example of calling the addEventListener on a button might look like this, in which an event handler gotoHome is called:

```
btHomeButton.addEventListener(MouseEvent.
  CLICK, gotoHome);
```

After the event listener has been added to the object and the event handler written, the object simply waits for the event to occur. When it does, the object calls the specified handler, which assumes processing at that point and performs whatever actions are required of it.

## Call an Event from a Button

**①** On the Stage, create a button.

**②** Give the instance of the button a name.

**Note:** *See Chapter 3 for details on creating buttons and naming instances.*

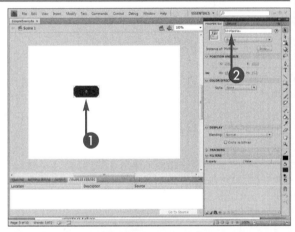

**③** Open the Actions Panel.

**Note:** *See Chapter 1 for details on opening the panel.*

**④** Create an event handler.

**Note:** *For details, see the preceding section, "Create an Event Handler."*

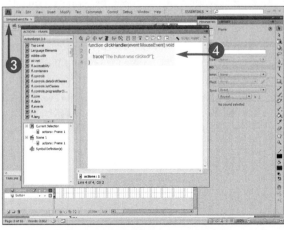

**⑤** Outside of the function, type the name of instance created in step **2** followed by a period.

**⑥** Type `addEventListener` and a set of parentheses and a semicolon.

**⑦** Within the parentheses, type `MouseEvent.CLICK` and a comma.

**⑧** Type the name of the handler created in step **4**.

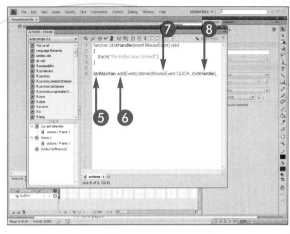

**⑨** Press Ctrl + Enter.

The movie plays in Flash Player.

**⑩** Click the button.

The event is triggered, and the event handler's code runs.

● In this example, the text from the `trace` statement is displayed in the Output panel.

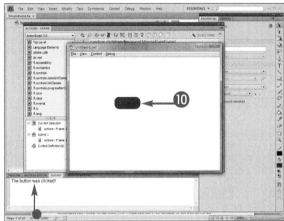

---

## Extra

If you have a button nested within a `MovieClip`, the user will actually be clicking both objects simultaneously. Most of the time, you will add the event listener to the button. As the `MovieClip` would not have a listener for that event, it would ignore it. However, it is possible to have a listener attached to the `MovieClip` as well. If the clip's listener called the same handler as the button's, the handler would be called twice: once by the button and then a second time by the clip. You could, though, have the clip call a different handler, which would execute immediately following the button. In theory, there is no real limit to this effect, so if you had a button within a `MovieClip` that is itself nested within another `MovieClip`, each of the three objects could call event handlers. This process is known in ActionScript as "event bubbling" — the event "bubbles" up through the various objects, and each can be used to handle it if needed.

# Define Events in a Custom Class

When you create a custom class, you have the opportunity to add an event listener and handler to the class itself, freeing you from having to repeatedly add the event code to individual instances. For example, say you were creating a complex application, and throughout various phases of the application, you wanted to provide a button that linked to a help resource. You could simply create a button symbol and place an instance of the symbol on the Stage whenever you needed it. However, you would then need to be sure to name each instance of the "help" button and then go into your code each time and add an event listener to that specific instance:

```
btHelp.addEventListener(MouseEvent.CLICK,
    helpHandler);
```

You could instead create a custom class that represented the button, and then you could add the event listener and handler within the code for the class itself. That way, the event would become a built-in part of the class and would be automatically applied to each instance, without you having to even think about it. You could then be assured that anytime you added an instance of the button, it would be able to automatically link to the help resource.

The process for doing this is simple: Just add the event handler within the class file and then call the `addEventListener` method to the class within its constructor. Remember that you can reference the class itself with the `this` keyword. As the event listener is being added in the constructor, it will be added to each instance as it is created.

## Define Events in a Custom Class

1 Create a custom class.

**Note:** *See Chapter 6 for details on creating custom classes.*

2 Within the constructor for the class, type `this` and a period.

3 Type `addEventListener` and a set of parentheses.

4 Within the parentheses, type the event, a comma, and the handler name, such as `MouseEvent.CLICK, showText`.

5 Type a semicolon at the end of the line.

6 At the top of the code, import any necessary superclass, such as `import flash. events.MouseEvent;`.

7 Create the event handler.

**Note:** *See the section "Create an Event Handler."*

8 Save the class file.

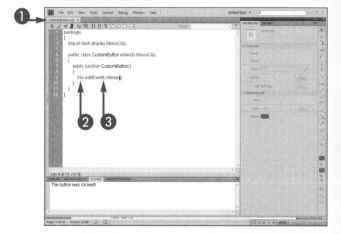

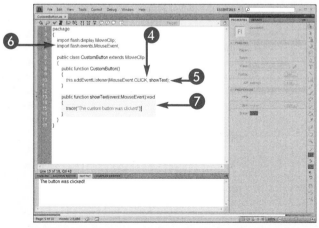

⑨ Open a Flash movie or create a new one.

⑩ Create a `MovieClip`.

⑪ Define the `MovieClip` as being an instance of the custom class created in step **1**.

**Note:** See Chapter 6 for details on creating `MovieClip`s as instances of custom classes.

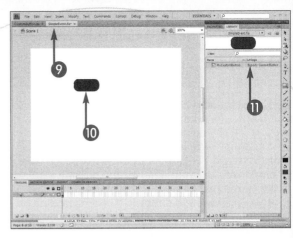

⑫ Press Ctrl + Enter to test the movie.

The movie plays.

⑬ Trigger the event — in this example, click the `MovieClip`.

The event is called.

● In this example, text from a `trace` statement is displayed in the Output panel.

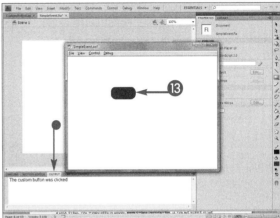

## Extra

You need to be sure to import the appropriate event class into your custom class code, just as you need to do any other time you are using any of the built-in ActionScript classes within your custom class. All event classes are in the `flash.events` package, so for example, if you want to add a click event, you would need to import `flash. events.MouseEvent`. If you are unsure of the package to import, you can simply search for the event class in a search engine such as Google. One of the first few results will invariably be the official ActionScript documentation for the event, which will display the package name.

Adding an event listener to a custom class does not prevent you from adding other listeners to an instance of the class. You might have a listener and handler for a click event defined in the class but then allow a particular instance of the class to be dragged and thus need to listen for the drag event on that instance. You could even in theory have two separate handlers for the same event: one in the class and the other on the instance. In this scenario, both handlers would be called, with the class handler called first, followed by the instance's.

# Remove Event Listeners

In certain situations, you may need to remove an event listener from an object. For example, you may have a game in which you want to allow your user to click an object only once and then have the object be either removed from the game or disabled. You may have a Flash-based Web site with a navigation bar and want to disable the button that links to the current state of the movie. Or you may want to disable a button on a form if you have written form validation code and need to prevent the user from trying to submit the form again until he or she fixes the errors.

You can remove an event listener from an event by calling the removeEventListener method. As with addEventListener, this method takes two arguments: the type of event and the handler being removed:

```
myClip.removeEventListener(MouseEvent.CLICK,
  handleClick);
```

After an event listener has been removed, the object will no longer respond to the event, but you can easily restore the listener by simply calling addEventListener on the instance again. Often, an event listener will be removed by the handler itself, so a handler responding to a click event might remove the listener to itself to prevent the same click event from triggering again.

Be careful to ensure that the event and the handler in the removeEventListener call are identical to those given in the corresponding addEventListener call. Otherwise, an event other than the one you expected may be removed, causing either an error or, more likely, unexpected behavior within your project. In the example shown here, an event handler on a button will, as part of handling the event, remove the listener so that the button can be clicked only once.

## Remove Event LIsteners

① Create an event handler.

**Note:** See the section "Create an Event Handler" earlier in this chapter for details.

② Outside the event handler code, create an event listener.

**Note:** See the section "Call an Event from a Button" earlier in this chapter for details.

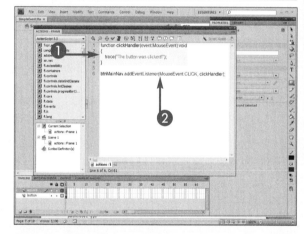

③ Within the event handler code, type the name of object that you used to call the event and a period.

④ Type removeEventListener and a set of parentheses.

⑤ Within the parentheses, type the event type, such as MouseEvent.CLICK, and a comma.

⑥ Type the name of the handler.

⑦ Type a semicolon at the end of the line.

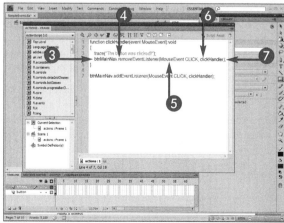

8. On the Stage, create a symbol.

9. Name the instance, using the name that you used in the code in steps **2** and **3**.

**Note:** *See Chapter 3 for details on creating symbols and naming instances.*

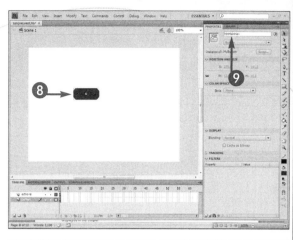

10. Press Ctrl + Enter.

    The movie plays.

11. Trigger the event — in this example, click the symbol on the Stage.

    The event triggers.

• In this example, text is displayed in the Output panel.

12. Trigger the event again.

    Nothing happens because the event handler removed the listener, preventing the handler from being called again.

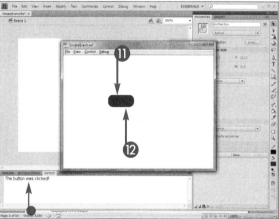

## Extra

It is a good idea to remove event listeners whenever you no longer need them. A considerable amount of programmatic overhead is consumed by event listeners, so having listeners still active in your code long after their purpose has been rendered moot is simply a waste of resources. As an example, if you have a navigation system that contains multiple levels of links but allows only the top level and a single sublevel to be clicked at any time, then you would want to remove the event listeners from the other sublevels to prevent them from consuming the additional resources when you do not want them active anyway.

This problem is particularly troublesome in game applications. In a typical shooting game, you would presumably have targets as instances of a custom class. They would each have an event listener attached. When a target is "destroyed" and removed from the game, its event listener would remain, consuming resources no longer needed.

# Using the Target Property

The addEventListener method requires that you call an event handler as a simple string, using just the function's name. It does not provide a method whereby you can call it as a function name and pass arguments to it. Most of the time, this will not pose a problem. If you simply need to perform an action when a button is clicked, there really is no other information that needs to be sent.

However, there are certain situations in which you may need to at least determine which item was clicked. For example, if you had a calculator and provided a button for each of the basic mathematical operators but wanted to handle the calculation with a single event handler, you would need to determine which of the four buttons was clicked.

The Event class provides a target property for this exact situation. The target contains a reference to the object that triggered the event. In turn, it contains a series of properties to identify the object. For example, you can determine the name of the instance of the object using event.target.name, assuming that the event argument being passed to the function is called event.

Other properties of the object being clicked may be available through target. For example, the location of a clicked MovieClip would be accessible through event.target.x and event.target.y, and the text property of a text field can be accessed in a handler with event.target.text. You can also set writable properties, so you could have a handler rotate a MovieClip with event.target.rotation += 45, which would set the rotation to the current rotation plus 45 degrees, causing the clip to rotate 45 degrees each time it was clicked.

## Using the Target Property

① Type an event handler, such as function clickHandler(event: MouseEvent):void.

② Type a set of curly braces.

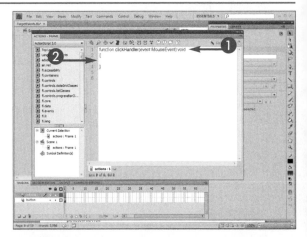

③ Within the curly braces, use target to get the property that you need, such as trace(event. target.name);.

④ Outside the function, create an event listener to call this handler.

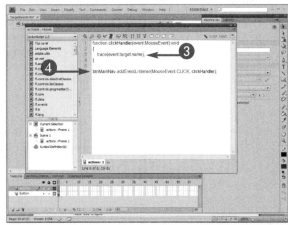

**5** On the Stage, create an instance of a symbol.

**6** Name the instance, using the same name that you provided in the event listener in step **4**.

**Note:** See Chapter 3 for details on creating symbols and naming instances.

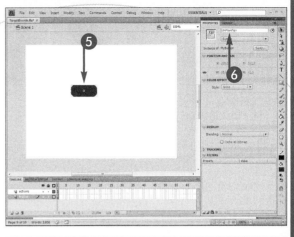

**7** Press Ctrl + Enter.

The movie plays.

**8** Trigger the event — in this example, click the symbol.

The event handler triggers.

● In this example, the name of the instance appears in the Output panel.

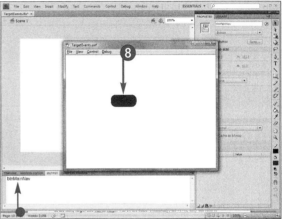

# Stop a Movie

Flash animates movies in much the same way film creates the illusion of motion onscreen. In both cases, a static image is displayed in a frame. The image is then changed slightly in the next frame, and then again in the next, and so on. When the frames are played back in quick succession, our eyes and brains are fooled into believing that we are seeing motion, thanks to something known as *persistence of vision.*

In Flash, this change in images over frames is controlled on the Timeline, a panel in the Flash interface. The Timeline panel shows each of the frames in the movie — Flash movies can contain up to 16,000 frames. Flash Player runs through the frames in the movie at the movie's frame rate. In Flash CS4 Professional, the default frame rate is 20 frames per second, but this can be changed if needed. As Flash Player proceeds through the frames, a play head indicates the current frame.

You can add *keyframes,* which are special containers in which you can change the position, color, transparency, size, or any other property of objects on the Stage. You can use ActionScript to control the play head. By default, Flash Player loops all movies, so when it reaches the end of a movie, it automatically rewinds the movie and then begins playing it again.

You can use the `stop()` global method in ActionScript to prevent this behavior by simply adding the method to the keyframe on which you want to end the movie. A *global method* is one that is available throughout your ActionScript code and does not require you to instantiate or even specify an associated object.

## Stop a Movie

### CREATE AN OBJECT THAT MOVES

① Draw an object on the Stage using any of the drawing tools in Flash.

② Click the Selection tool and double-click the object that you drew.

③ Press F8 on your keyboard.

   The Convert to Symbol dialog box appears.

④ Name the symbol, set the type to `MovieClip`, and click OK.

⑤ Right-click the symbol.

⑥ Click Create Motion Tween.

   Flash adds a motion tween to the Timeline.

⑦ Drag the symbol to a new location on the Stage.

### STOP THE MOVIE

⑧ Click the New Layer button.

⑨ Right-click in the frame on which you want to stop — in this example, frame 20.

⑩ Click Insert Keyframe.

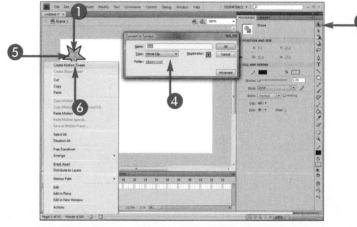

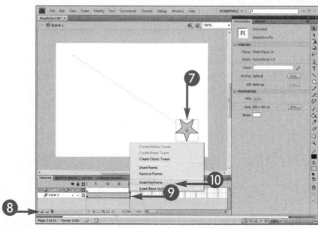

⑪ Open the Actions Panel.

**Note:** *See Chapter 1 for details on opening the panel.*

⑫ Type stop();.

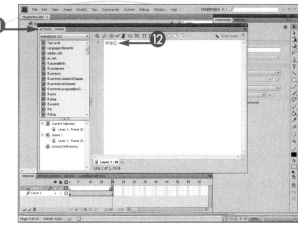

⑬ Press Ctrl + Enter.

The movie plays in Flash Player. The animation plays once and then stops.

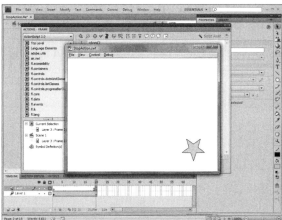

## Extra

After the play head has been stopped, you can programmatically start it again using the play() global method. Like stop(), play() takes no arguments, as there is no other information it needs: It simply begins at the current location of the play head and proceeds from there.

Motion tweens are the most common type of Timeline-based animation in Flash. In creating a motion tween, you simply define the starting and ending states of the symbol to be animated and then have Flash worry about the frames in between those. Motion tweens can only be done on symbols and text fields.

However, two other types of animation are possible — shape tweens and frame-by-frame animation. *Shape tweens* are similar to motion tweens, in that you need to draw only the beginning and ending states, but shape tweens can be performed only on drawn shapes, not symbols or text. *Frame-by-frame animation* is the third and most time-consuming method, whereby you must set up each frame individually. More details on animating in Flash can be found in *Master VISUALLY Dreamweaver CS4 and Flash CS4 Professional,* published by Wiley.

# Go to a Specific Frame in a Movie

Y ou can use ActionScript to cause the play head to jump to a specific frame in a movie. Once there, the play head can either continue to play from that point or stop, depending on whether you are calling the gotoAndPlay() or gotoAndStop() global method.

Both methods take a single argument, which is the frame to which the play head should jump when the method is called. You can specify the frame using either its number or an arbitrary label. You can add the label in Flash by selecting the frame on the Timeline and then entering the label on the Properties panel. Only keyframes can be labeled. The label is referenced in the gotoAndPlay() and gotoAndStop() methods as a string, so it can contain special characters such as spaces without causing

problems. However, as with everything else in ActionScript, the label is case-sensitive, so be sure to be consistent when labeling frames.

Often, going to a specific frame is used to provide navigation within a movie. You may have a navigation button that takes a user to a different section of a project or allows him or her to move forward or backward through a presentation. If you stop a movie at the end, you might provide a button on the last frame that returns to the beginning and replays the movie.

Providing navigation like this gives your users more control over their experience within your project. Instead of a passive viewing of the project, they can feel like they are controlling the action.

## Go to a Specific Frame in a Movie

### STOP A MOVIE WITH A MOTION TWEEN

1 Create a movie with a motion tween.

2 In the last frame, stop the movie.

**Note:** *See the preceding section, "Stop a Movie," for details on creating motion tweens and adding stop actions.*

### ADD A BUTTON THAT REWINDS THE MOVIE AND PLAYS IT AGAIN

3 Click the New Layer button.

4 Right-click in the last frame of the new layer.

5 Click Insert Keyframe.

You can also press F6 on your keyboard to add a keyframe.

6 Create a button.

**Note:** *See Chapter 3 for details on creating buttons.*

7 Name the button something like btnRewind.

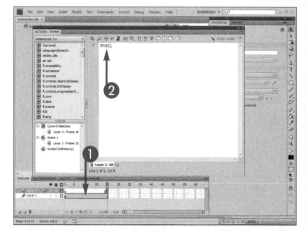

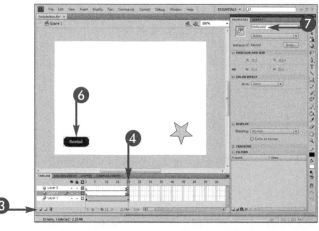

⑧ On the layer in which you added the stop action, click in the last frame.

⑨ Open the Actions panel.

⑩ Below the `stop()` action, type the button name, a period, and `addEventListener (MouseEvent.CLICK, rewind);`.

⑪ Type `function rewind (event:MouseEvent):void` and a set of curly braces.

⑫ Within the braces, type `gotoAndPlay(1);`.

⑬ Press Ctrl + Enter.

The movie plays. When it reaches the end of the animation, it stops, and the button appears.

⑭ Click the button.

The movie rewinds and plays again.

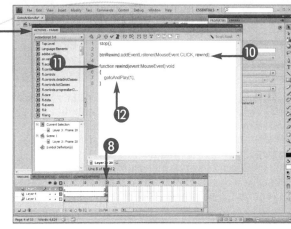

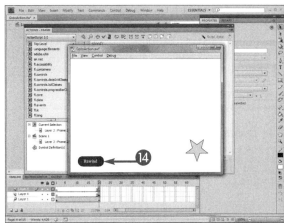

## Extra

In general, it is always a best practice to label frames and reference the label rather than reference frames by number. The problem with numeric references, beyond the obvious that they are harder to remember, is that the number may change if you add or delete frames before the one you are referencing, causing the action to go to the wrong frame. For example, the last frame in your movie might be frame 160, but if you later edit the movie and add 10 more frames, an action calling `gotoAndStop(160)` will now jump to a stop 10 frames before the end. In contrast, if you labeled the final frame "end," `gotoAndStop("end")` would work regardless of the additional frames.

An additional benefit of labeling frames is that labels will appear in the Timeline itself. If important points in your animation are labeled, you will be able to merely look at the Timeline and understand when those moments occur rather than have to manually move through the movie to find them. Labels should be placed in keyframes on their own layer, although many Flash developers combine the layer for the actions with the one for layers. The important point is keeping both separated from your visual elements.

# Add Code to a MovieClip's Timeline

**M**ovieClips, like all symbols, have their own Timeline. The Timeline looks exactly like the movie's. You can add layers to the clip's Timeline and animate objects on the Stage within the clip. What makes a MovieClip unique, however, is that its Timeline is independent from that of the movie. Therefore, if you stop a movie, any animation within a clip will continue to play. You must stop the clip directly to get its animation to stop.

Because the MovieClip's Timeline functions exactly like the movie's, you can add frames to the clip and, in turn, add ActionScript to those frames. Therefore, a MovieClip can contain its own set of ActionScript code, which will execute independently from the movie's code. Although it is not a best practice, it is legal to have variables of the same name exist in both the movie's code and a clip's

code; as the two execute independently of one another, they will not be in conflict.

Keep in mind, however, that you can and almost certainly will have multiple instances of a single symbol on the Stage. Any code that is written on the Timeline of a clip will be executed by each instance of the clip, although each will execute independently of the others. Generally, you will want to add code to a clip's Timeline only when you need code that will execute for every instance of the clip; code that should more logically be associated with individual instances should be placed on the Timeline of the movie itself.

In order to add code to the Timeline of a MovieClip, you need to edit the symbol. You can either double-click an instance of the symbol to enter editing mode or right-click the symbol in the library and select Edit.

## Add Code to a MovieClip's Timeline

① Create an instance of a MovieClip on the Stage.

**Note:** *See Chapter 3 for details on creating* MovieClip*s.*

② Double-click the instance on the Stage.

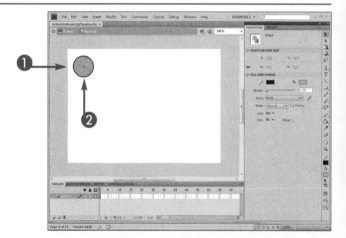

Flash opens the symbol in editing mode.

③ Click the New Layer button.

④ Click the first frame of the new layer.

⑤ Open the Actions panel.

**Note:** *See Chapter 1 for details on the Actions panel.*

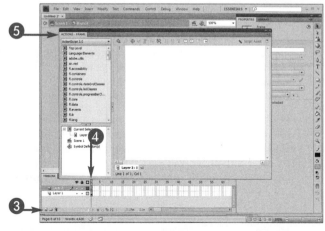

⑥ Type the code that you want to add, such as `var sampleText:String = "Hello world";`.

⑦ Trace any values as needed, such as `trace(sampleText);`.

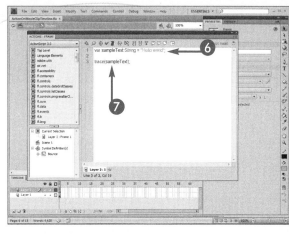

⑧ Press Ctrl + Enter.

The movie plays, and the code from the `MovieClip` executes.

● In this example, the sample text is displayed in the Output panel.

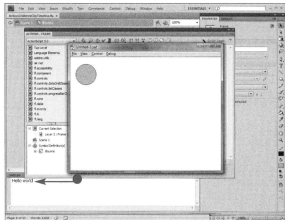

## Extra

The earlier statement that the Timeline of a `MovieClip` looks and functions like the main movie's Timeline is actually misleading. In fact, the opposite is technically true: The main movie's Timeline is what looks and feels like a `MovieClip`'s because in point of fact, the main movie is actually nothing more than a special instance of a `MovieClip`. Keeping this in mind, there are few if any restrictions on the code you place within the Timeline of a `MovieClip`: In general, any code that can be added to the main Timeline can be added to a clip, and vice versa. Keep in mind as well that all symbols can contain other symbols, so the `MovieClip`'s Timeline can contain code that will control nested `MovieClips` or buttons.

You can also add code directly to the Timeline of a button. As with `MovieClips`, a button's Timeline is independent from the movie's. As discussed in Chapter 3, buttons have a unique Timeline that contains only four frames, but this does not prevent you from adding code to the Timeline. Although it is possible to also add script to the Timeline of a graphic symbol, remember that a graphic's Timeline is synchronized with the movie's and thus does not execute independently.

# Control a MovieClip from the Main Timeline

A dding code directly to the Timeline of a `MovieClip` can be useful when you have code that needs to execute with every instance of the symbol. More often, however, you are likely to need to write code that will affect only a single instance. For example, if you wanted every instance of a `MovieClip` to rotate when it was clicked, you could add the necessary code to the clip itself; if instead you wanted only certain instances to rotate when clicked, you would write the needed code on the main Timeline, where you can specifically target individual instances.

Any property or method of the clip can be called from the Timeline by referencing the clip's instance name and then the property of method that you want to use, separated by a dot. For example, if you had an instance of a clip named `mcBounce1` and you wanted to stop the clip from the main Timeline, you could write

```
mcBounce1.stop();
```

You can use this technique not only to control clips' Timelines by starting, stopping, or jumping to specific frames, but also to set the properties of clips, such as their position on the Stage or their size. If the clip is an instance of a custom class, you can use the same technique to set any properties or call any methods of the class.

## Control a MovieClip from the Main Timeline

① Create an instance of a
`MovieClip` on the Stage.

**Note:** *See Chapter 3 for details on creating* `MovieClip`*s.*

② Name the instance of the symbol something like
`mcSquare1`.

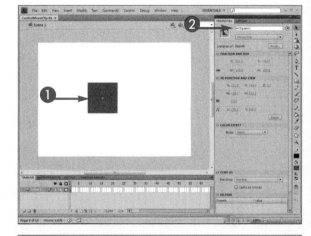

③ Click the New Layer button.

④ Click the first frame of the new layer.

⑤ Open the Actions panel.

**Note:** *See Chapter 1 for details on the panel.*

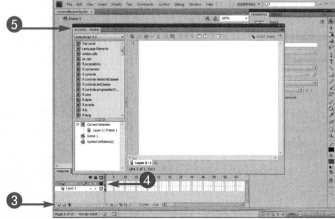

**6** Add the first line of code to control the clip, such as `mcSquare1.x = 50;`.

**7** Add your second line of code, such as `mcSquare1.y = 50;`.

**8** Add any more needed code, such as `mcSquare1.rotation = 45;`.

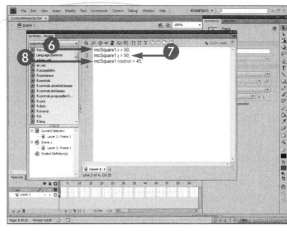

**9** Press Ctrl + Enter.

The movie plays.

● In this example, the properties set in the code are applied to the clip, specifying the position and rotation.

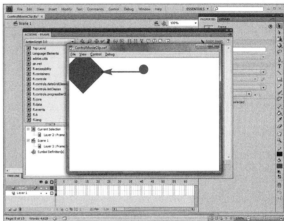

## Extra

Instances of symbols can only be called from the Timeline in the same frame in which they are created — or any frame after that. If you try to reference an instance of a symbol on a frame before it is created, a runtime error will occur. For example, you cannot add an event listener to a clip in frame 1 if that clip does not get added to the Stage until frame 20. In order to add the listener, you need to either add it in frame 20 or declare the clip as a variable in frame 1 so that a reference to it exists. You can declare an instance of a symbol as a variable in the same way that you declare other variables, being careful to use the correct data type:

```
var mcSquare1:MovieClip;
```

# Work with the Stage in Code

In Flash CS4 Professional, as with all prior versions of Flash, the Stage represents the area where you can draw and place objects to have them visible at runtime. ActionScript 3.0 also has a Stage class, which is a container for all the objects on the *display list,* or everything currently visible in Flash Player. Technically, the two are not implementations of the same thing, but for practical purposes, you can think of them in much the same light.

An instance of the Stage class, called `stage`, is automatically created when a movie loads in Flash Player. The instance contains several useful properties and

methods that you can leverage in your code. For example, `stage.stageWidth` and `stage.stageHeight` can be used to determine the width and height of the Stage or to position other instances relative to that width and height. Therefore, an instance named `mcSquare1` could be centered on the Stage by setting its x property to one half the width of the Stage and its y property to one half the height:

```
mcSquare1.x = stage.stageWidth/2;
mcSquare1.y = stage.stageHeight/2;
```

In the example shown here, a `MovieClip` will be placed in the center of the Stage, and then four more clips will be precisely placed relative to the first.

---

## Work with the Stage in Code

### PLACE INSTANCES ON THE STAGE

1. Create instances of a `MovieClip` on the Stage.

*Note: This example shows placing five instances.*

2. Name the instances of the symbol.

*Note: This example uses the names `mcSquare1` through `mcSquare5`.*

### POSITION THE INSTANCES ON THE STAGE USING CODE

3. Click the New Layer button.

4. Click the first frame of the new layer.

5. Open the Actions panel.

6. Set the position of the first instance, such as
```
mcSquare1.x = stage.stageWidth/2;
mcSquare1.y = stage.stageHeight/2;
```

7. Set the position of the second instance, such as
```
mcSquare2.x = mcSquare1.x +
(mcSquare1.width + 5);
mcSquare2.y = mcSquare1.y;
```

8. Set the position of the third instance, such as
```
mcSquare3.x = mcSquare1.x -
(mcSquare1.width + 5);
mcSquare3.y = mcSquare1.y;
```

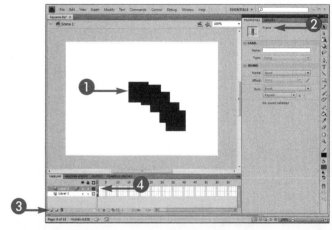

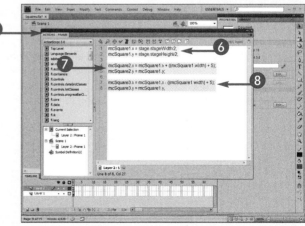

⑨ Set the position of the fourth
instance, such as
```
mcSquare4.x =
mcSquare1.x;
mcSquare4.y =
mcSquare1.y +
(mcSquare1.height + 5);
```

⑩ Set the position of any more
instances, such as
```
mcSquare5.x =
mcSquare1.x;
mcSquare5.y =
mcSquare1.y +
(mcSquare1.height + 5);
```

⑪ Press Ctrl + Enter.

The movie plays.

● In this example, the five squares
are displayed in a grid, centered
on the Stage.

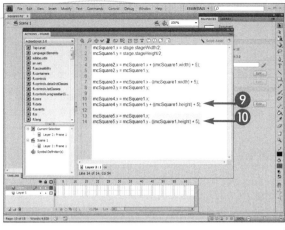

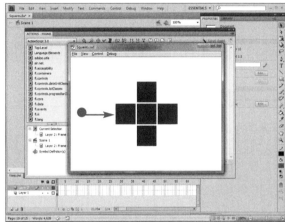

<hr />

## Apply It

The `stage` class has a `frameRate` property, which controls the speed at which the movie plays. This property can
be changed at runtime, allowing you to provide your users with the ability to speed up or slow down your movie:

```
btSpeedUp.addEventListener(MouseEvent.CLICK, speedUp);
btSlowDown.addEventListener(MouseEvent.CLICK, slowDown);
function speedUp(event:MouseEvent):void
{
                stage.frameRate = stage.frameRate + 5;
}
function slowDown(event:MouseEvent):void
{
                stage.frameRate = stage.frameRate -5;
}
```

# Add MovieClips to the Stage through Code

ctionScript classes can be placed into three broad categories. First, there are classes that can be created only visually with the drawing tools, such as `SimpleButton`. Second, there are classes that can be created only through code, such as `Math`, `Date`, and `Array`. Third are the classes that can be created either with the drawing tools or through code. The most common of this last class is `MovieClip`.

`MovieClips` that you plan to add through code can still be created using the drawing tools. The difference is that you will not place an instance of the clip on the Stage but will instead add it through code.

However, you must explicitly tell Flash that you plan to use the symbol in code. By default, instances of symbols that exist in the Flash library that do not have a corresponding instance on the Stage will not be exported to the published SWF. This is done to save file size in the SWF, as many designers will keep a lot of unused symbols in their library because they do not have to worry about those increasing the final sizes of their SWFs. This creates a problem when you are trying to add the clip through code because Flash will not know that it is supposed to include the symbol when it publishes the movie. The solution is to export the clip for ActionScript, which you do via the symbol's Properties dialog box. You can access the Properties dialog box from the Library panel. By default, the box shows only a few properties, but it contains an Advanced mode with other properties, including the setting to allow the symbol to be exported for ActionScript.

## Add MovieClips to the Stage through Code

### CREATE A MOVIECLIP

1 Draw a shape on the Stage using the drawing tools.

2 Click the Selection tool.

3 Double-click the shape to select it.

4 Click Modify.

5 Click Convert to Symbol.

The Convert to Symbol dialog box appears.

6 Type a name for the symbol.

7 Make sure that the type is set to `MovieClip`.

8 Click OK.

The symbol is created and appears in the Library panel. An instance of the symbol is on the Stage.

### REMOVE THE INSTANCE FROM THE STAGE

9 Click the instance of the symbol.

10 Press Delete.

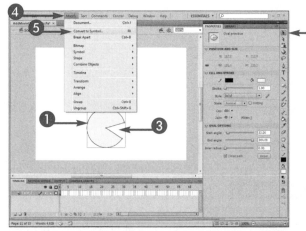

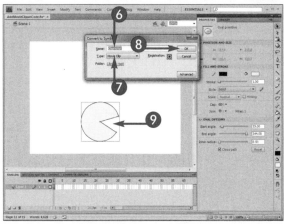

The instance is deleted.

⑪ Right-click the symbol in the Library panel.

⑫ Click Properties.

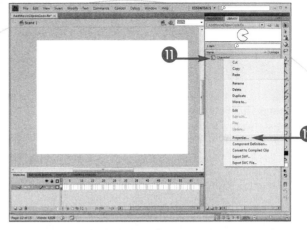

## EXPORT THE MOVIECLIP FOR ACTIONSCRIPT

The Symbol Properties dialog box appears.

⑬ Click Advanced.

The dialog box expands.

⑭ Check Export for ActionScript.

⑮ Click OK.

A dialog box appears, informing you that the classpath for the symbol will be generated.

⑯ Click OK.

The symbol will be exported and available to be used in code.

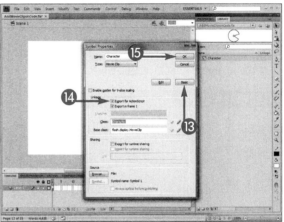

---

### Extra

When you check Export for ActionScript in the Properties dialog box, you will see boxes to specify the class and base class for the symbol. These are used to define the symbol as being an instance of some class other than `MovieClip`. See Chapter 6 for more details.

You will also notice a box labeled Identifier, which will be grayed out and thus inaccessible. This was used in ActionScript versions 1 and 2 to provide a name for the exported symbol. This served the same purpose — exporting the symbol for ActionScript — but was used because those versions of the language did not support the creation of custom classes.

Keep in mind that this extra step is necessary because Flash does not want to export symbols that will not be used and thus needlessly increase the file size of the SWF. Therefore, you should not export any extraneous symbols, either. Only set the Export for ActionScript option on those symbols that you will actually reference in code.

continued →

**A**fter a `MovieClip` has been exported for ActionScript, you can create instances of it in your code. You must first create it as an instance by giving it a name and using the `new` keyword to call its constructor.

Then you can add it to your movie by calling the `addChild()` method of the Stage class, passing as its argument the name of the instance. All objects that appear visually in your movie are part of the display list on the Stage. The display list tells Flash Player what objects should appear on the Stage and in what order. The `addChild()` method adds the instance to this display list as its last item.

The new symbol will be placed at the 0,0 coordinate on the Stage — the top-left corner. You can set the x and y coordinates of the instance to place it elsewhere on the

Stage, just as you would a symbol that you drew on the Stage in Flash. Any other properties of the symbol can also be set as you would normally, and any of the symbol's methods can be called.

You must repeat these steps for each instance that you want to add, so you need to create the instance by naming it and calling its constructor and then call `addChild()` for each.

Creating the `MovieClip` by declaring the variable and using the `new` keyword to call the constructor is fundamentally the same process as dragging an instance of the symbol onto the Stage and then naming it in the Properties panel. Therefore, you should follow the same instance naming conventions for clips created through code as you would for those created visually: Begin with the `mc` prefix and then include the name of the symbol itself and an identifying number.

## Add MovieClips to the Stage through Code *(continued)*

### ADD THE MOVIECLIP THROUGH CODE

**1** Open the Actions panel.

**2** Create the clip as an instance, using the name from step **6** of the first part of this section, such as `var mcCharacter1: Character = new Character();`.

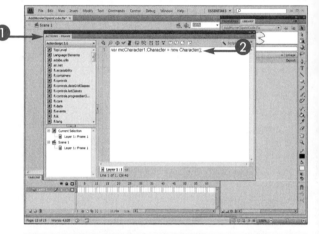

**3** Add the clip to your movie's display list, such as `addChild (mcCharacter1);`.

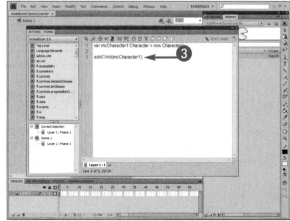

## SET THE MOVIECLIP'S POSITION AND ROTATION

**4** Set the clip's x coordinate, such as `mcCharacter1.x = 100;`.

**5** Set the clip's y coordinate, such as `mcCharacter1.y = 200;`.

**6** Set the clip's rotation, such as `mcCharacter1.rotation = 30;`.

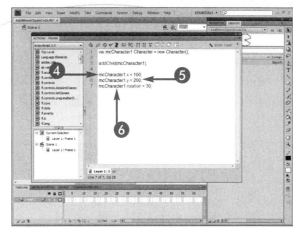

## VIEW THE RESULTS

**7** Press Ctrl + Enter.

The movie plays.

● The instance of the symbol, with the position and rotation properties applied, appears.

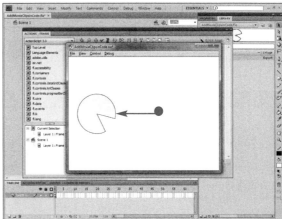

---

### Extra

You can easily create multiple instances of a symbol by placing the line where you declare the instance and the line where you call `addChild()` within a loop. Loops are discussed in Chapter 12.

Overlapping objects appear on the Stage in the order that they are added to the display list, so if you call `addChild()` on two objects and do not specify different x and y coordinates, the second will appear on top of the first. The stacking order can be changed by adding instances using the `addChildAt()` method instead of `addChild()`. This method takes two arguments: the name of the instance to add and a level at which it should be added. The level is given as an integer, and as you would expect, objects placed at higher levels appear on top of those placed at lower levels. Should you accidentally add an object at a level already in use, the object currently using the level and all those above it will be moved up one level to accommodate the new object.

# Remove Elements from the Stage

J ust as `MovieClips` can be added to the Stage with `addChild()`, ActionScript provides a `removeChild()` method to remove objects programmatically. Like its counterpart, the method takes a single argument: the object to be removed. When called, the method removes the specified object from the display list.

However, `removeChild()` does not remove the object from memory, so you can redisplay it by simply calling `addChild()` again. If the object will not be needed anymore, it is a good idea to be sure to remove it from memory as well as the display list, which can be done by setting its value to `null`.

You should also get in the habit of removing any event listeners from the object that you may have added. Even if an object has been removed from memory, its event listeners can remain and continue to consume resources as they try unsuccessfully to respond to events. The code to completely remove a `MovieClip` with a mouse click event might look like this:

```
removeChild(mcStar1);
mcStar1.removeEventListener(MouseEvent.CLICK,
  clickHandler);
mcStar1 = null;
```

If you forget to remove objects from memory as well as the display list, your Flash movie may eventually end up with memory leaks or other potential errors.

## Remove Elements from the Stage

① Export a symbol for ActionScript.

② In the Actions panel, add the code necessary to add the symbol to the Stage.

**Note:** *See the prior task, "Add MovieClips to the Stage through Code" for details on these steps.*

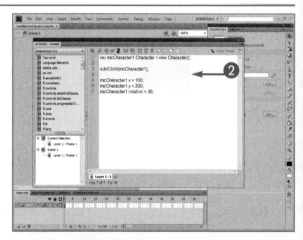

③ Type `removeChild();`.

④ Within the parentheses, type the name of the instance of the symbol to remove.

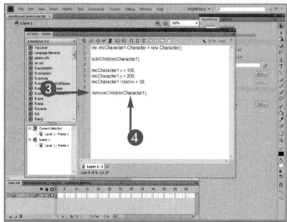

**5** Type the name of the instance.

**6** Type an equals sign.

**7** Type `null` and a semicolon.

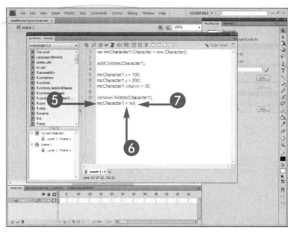

**8** Press Ctrl + Enter.

The movie plays. The symbol that was removed will not appear on the Stage.

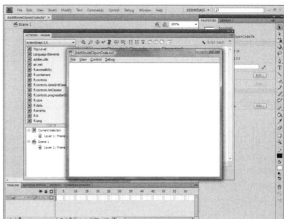

## Apply It

If you need to remove an object where you know the level at which it resides but not its name, you can use the `removeChildAt()` method instead of `removeChild()`. It takes a single argument: an integer representing the level at which the object should be removed. Unlike `removeChild()`, `removeChildAt()` actually removes the object itself by setting its value to null. When you call `removeChildAt()`, all objects on levels above the one removed are moved down one level to fill the vacated space.

Levels are similar conceptually to layers, but they are not the same. Layers define the stacking order of objects that you draw visually on the Stage, whereas levels are used by the display list to order objects that are created in ActionScript. You cannot reference or access the layers in your movie through your code, and you do not have any way to access levels outside of code. In fact, objects added with `addChild()` and `addChildAt()` will not be visible on the Stage, as they are added at runtime.

# Create a Dynamic Text Field Visually

Flash supports three types of text fields: static, dynamic, and input. Static text fields can only be created visually on the Stage using the Text tool, located in the toolbox on the right side of the screen, and contain text that will not change as the movie runs. Headings, labels on navigation buttons, descriptive text, and footer information such as copyright notices are usually placed in static text fields.

Text that will need to change at runtime is placed in dynamic text fields. These fields can be created visually on the Stage using the same Text tool that you use to create a static field, or they can be created through code in ActionScript. Text can be placed in them initially when you draw the field on the Stage, and that text can then be changed as the movie plays via ActionScript.

Alternatively, the field can be left empty initially and populated later through code. You can use dynamic text fields to store player scores in games and quizzes, the name of the user currently viewing the movie, the name of a video or picture that is being displayed, or just about anything else.

When you create a dynamic text field on the Stage, you need to provide an instance name for the field, just as you would for a MovieClip or Button instance. As a convention, text fields are usually named beginning with a txt prefix, followed by a descriptive name for the purpose of the field, so a field used to store a player name could be txtPlayerName.

Dynamic and input text fields are instances of the TextField class. Input text fields are discussed in detail later in this chapter.

## Create a Dynamic Text Field Visually

① Click the Text tool.

② Click and drag on the Stage to draw a field.

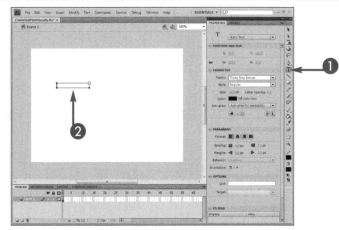

③ Click Static Text.

④ Click Dynamic Text.

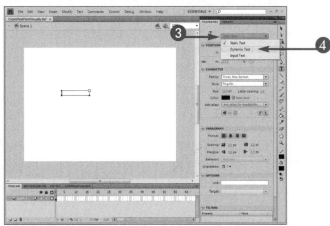

**5** Type an instance name.

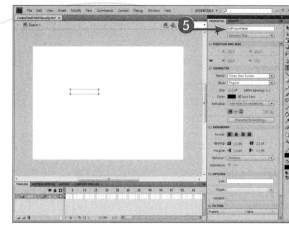

**6** Click File.

**7** Click Save As.

The Save As dialog box appears.

**8** Type a filename.

**9** Click Save.

The file is saved with the dynamic text field on the Stage.

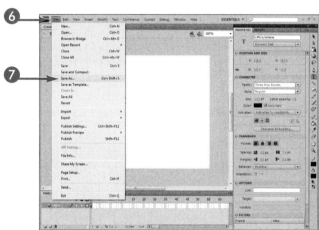

## Extra

When setting the type of field in the Properties panel, be aware that Flash will remember what you used last time. If you create a field and set the type to dynamic text, the next field that you draw will automatically be a dynamic field. To create a different type of field, you can change the setting before you draw it or after; either will work. However, be careful when changing the type before you draw the field to make sure that no existing fields are selected when you make the change. If they are, you will be changing their type rather than setting the type for the next field to be drawn. You can ensure that nothing is selected on the Stage by either clicking a blank area of the Stage with the Selection tool or by clicking Edit ➔ Deselect All. If the menu item is grayed out, nothing is selected.

# Create a Dynamic Text Field in Code

**D**ynamic text fields, like MovieClips, can be created either visually or in code. Likewise, you can create input text fields using either method, but you can only create static text fields visually on the Stage.

Creating a dynamic text field in code involves first creating a variable to reference the field. The variable name should follow the normal conventions for naming a text field, so it should begin with txt and be descriptive of the field's purpose. Set the variable to be of type TextField and use the new keyword to call the TextField class constructor:

```
var txtMyName:TextField = new TextField();
```

You can then add the field to the page by calling the addChild() method of the Stage, passing to it the name of the field that you defined. You can then set properties on the field, such as the width of the field and its x and y position on the Stage.

You can add text to the field through either its text or htmlText property. Simple text can be added by setting the value of the text property to any string. The use of htmlText is discussed in Chapter 10. You can apply formatting to the text in the field through the TextFormat class, which is also discussed in Chapter 10.

## Create a Dynamic Text Field in Code

① Open the Actions panel.

**Note:** *See Chapter 1 for details.*

② Create a txt variable and set its type to TextField, such as var txtPictureName:TextField.

③ Type an equals sign.

④ Type new TextField();.

⑤ Add the field to the page, such as addChild(txtPictureName);.

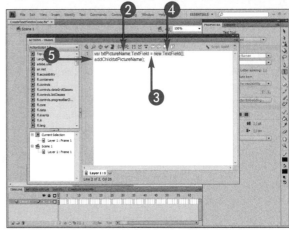

6. Add text to the field, such as `txtPictureName.text = "My first picture";`.

7. Set the field's x position, such as `txtPictureName.x = 50;`.

8. Set the field's y position, such as `txtPictureName.y = 50;`.

9. Set the width of the field, such as `txtPictureName.width = 300;`.

10. Set whether the field has a border, such as `txtPictureName.border = true;`.

11. Press Ctrl + Enter.

   The movie plays, displaying the text field.

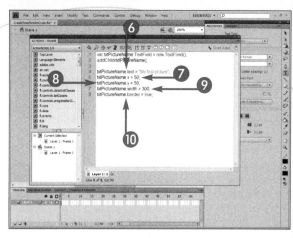

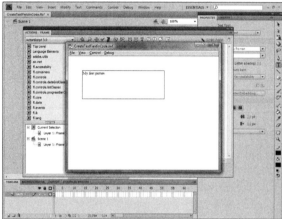

## Apply It

You can set the width of the field to automatically expand to fit whatever text you might place in it by setting the `autoSize` property to one of the three constants defined in the `TextFieldAutoSize` class: `LEFT`, `RIGHT`, or `CENTER`. Which you choose will also define how the text aligns within the field, so if you want to autosize the field and have the text left-aligned, set

```
txtPictureName.autoSize = TextFieldAutoSize .LEFT;
```

If you want the text to wrap within the field, set the `wordWrap` and `multiline` properties to `true`:

```
txtPictureName.multiline = true;
txtPictureName.wordWrap = true;
```

Applying all three values shown here will cause the field to apply any specified width but resize the height to fit the text.

# Create an Input Text Field Visually

In order to allow your user to enter text into your movie, you need to provide input text fields. Input text fields can also be thought of as form fields and behave in much the same way as text fields in HTML forms.

To create an input field visually on the Stage, you use the Text tool, just as you would to create a static or dynamic field. You can set the field type to Input in the Properties panel. As with dynamic fields, you will want to provide an instance name, following the same naming conventions as with other text fields.

You can also use the Properties panel to specify the font face, size, and color of the text that the user will see as he or she types. You can choose to show a border around the field, in which case a thin black line will be drawn around the field. If you leave this setting off, the field will be invisible, so you will need to be sure to provide some other visual clue, such as a rectangle drawn on another layer, to let the user know where the field is. The Properties panel includes a Paragraph formatting section that enables you to designate the field as allowing more than one line of text and an Options section to set the maximum number of allowed characters. You will usually use a static text field to provide a label for the field.

## Create an Input Text Field Visually

① Click the Text tool.

② Click and drag on the Stage to draw a field.

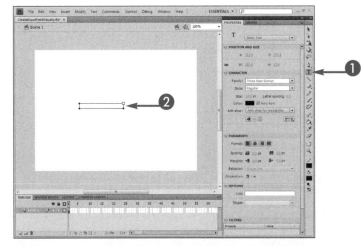

③ In the Properties panel, click the field type.

④ Click Input Text.

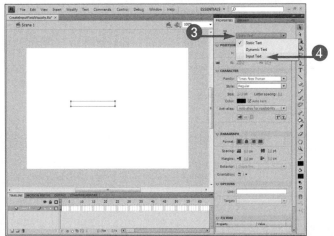

**5** Click here and select a font.

**6** Select a size.

**7** Select a color.

**8** Click the Show Border around Text button to include a border.

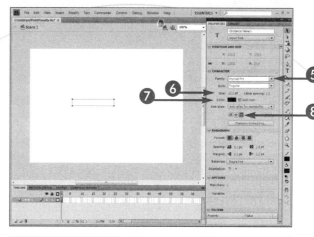

**9** Press Ctrl + Enter.

The movie plays and shows the field.

**10** Click in the text field.

**11** Type text.

The text is entered into the field.

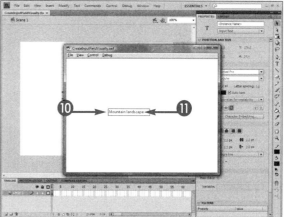

## Extra

Flash automatically embeds fonts used in static text fields but does not automatically embed fonts specified for input fields. Therefore, if you want to use a nonstandard font — anything other than Arial, Times New Roman, Courier, or Verdana — you need to tell Flash to embed the characters for your font. You can do this from the Properties panel by clicking the Character Embedding button and selecting which characters from the font you want to embed. For dynamic fields, you may need to embed all characters from the font, but input fields generally need only those characters that can be directly typed on the keyboard, such as letters, numbers, and punctuation. This will add to the file size of the final SWF. You can avoid this increase by either using a font that you can be relatively sure all users have, such as Arial or Times New Roman, or even better use one of the device fonts: _serif, _sans, or _typewriter, in which case Flash Player will simply use a font of that type from the user's computer.

# Create an Input Text Field in Code

Input text fields, like dynamic fields, are instances of the `TextField` class. Therefore, they are created in code in precisely the same way as dynamic fields. You begin by providing a name and using the `new` keyword to call the class constructor, then use the `addChild()` method to add the field to the display list, and finally, set any other properties, such as position and width:

```
var txtUserName:TextField = new TextField();
addChild(txtUserName);
```

However, if you simply use the preceding code, you will end up with a dynamic field. The difference between a dynamic and input text field in code is the value of the

text field's `type` property, which will be set to one of two constants from the `TextFieldType` class: `DYNAMIC` or `INPUT`:

```
txtUserName.type = TextFieldType.INPUT;
```

As with input fields you draw using the visual tools, input fields created in code will by default not display a border, so you will either need to provide a visual outline for the field elsewhere in your movie or set the `border` property of the field to `true`.

---

### Create an Input Text Field in Code

① Open the Actions panel.

**Note:** *See Chapter 1 for details.*

② Create a `txt` variable and set its type to `TextField`, such as `var txtNewPicName:TextField`.

③ Type an equals sign.

④ Type `new TextField();`.

⑤ Add the field to the page, such as `addChild(txtNewPicName);`.

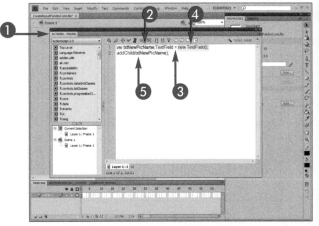

⑥ Set the type as an input field, such as `txtNewPicName.type = TextFieldType.INPUT;`.

⑦ Set the field's x position, such as `txtNewPicName.x = 100;`.

⑧ Set the field's y position, such as `txtNewPicName.y = 50;`.

⑨ Set the width of the field, such as `txtNewPicName.width = 300;`.

⑩ Set whether the field has a border, such as `txtNewPicName.border = true;`.

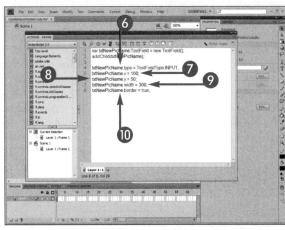

⑪ Press Ctrl + Enter.

The movie plays, displaying the text field.

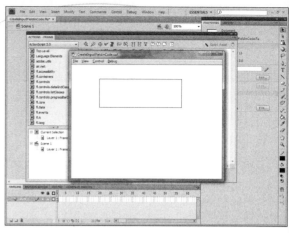

⑫ Click in the text field.

⑬ Type a value.

The value is entered into the field.

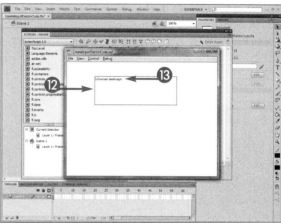

# Work with TextField Events

extFields, like other classes in ActionScript, have events associated with them that allow you to perform actions in response to interactions with the field. In addition to standard events such as `click`, TextFields have four specialized events: `change`, `link`, `scroll`, and `textInput`. Each of these events are represented by related constants of the `TextEvent` class: `CHANGE`, `LINK`, `SCROLL`, and `TEXT_INPUT`.

The `change` event is called whenever the contents of the field are changed in any way. If a user is typing in the field, the event is dispatched after every keystroke. You can use this, for example, to copy the user's input in real time into another field. Note that in other languages such as JavaScript, the `change` event occurs only when the field loses focus, but in ActionScript, it is triggered with each keystroke.

The `link` event is called when a user clicks hyperlinked text within an HTML-formatted text field. HTML-formatted text fields are discussed in Chapter 10.

The `scroll` event occurs when a user scrolls through text. The event is actually dispatched after the user finishes scrolling, so it can be used only for actions that should be triggered after the scroll. For example, you may have a text field that displays a license agreement for a download. You could use the `scroll` event to activate the button to agree to the terms only when the user scrolls to the bottom, thereby forcing the user to at least scroll through the agreement before continuing.

The `textInput` event is dispatched when the user enters text into the field. The text can be entered using a keyboard, speech recognition system, or paste. As with the `change` event, this is triggered after each keystroke if the user is typing.

## Work with TextField Events

① Create an input text field, either through code or by drawing it on the Stage.

**Note:** See the sections "Create an Input Text Field Visually" and "Create an Input Text Field in Code" for details.

② Create a dynamic text field, either through code or by drawing on the Stage.

**Note:** See the first two sections of this chapter for details.

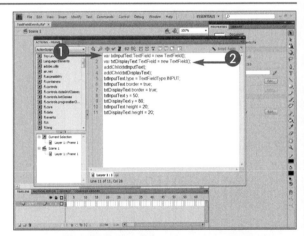

③ Add an event listener, specifying the event that you need, such as
`txtInputText.`
`addEventListener(TextEvent.`
`TEXT_INPUT, textHandler);`.

④ Add an event handler, such as
`function textHandler(event:`
`TextEvent):void.`

⑤ Type a set of curly braces.

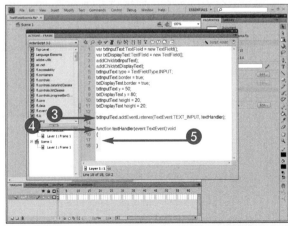

**6** Within the curly braces, add the action that the event will cause, such as

```
txtDisplayText.text
= txtInputText.text.
```

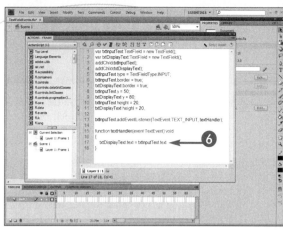

**7** Press Ctrl + Enter.

The movie plays.

**8** Click in the input text field.

**9** Type text.

● In this example, the text is duplicated in the dynamic field.

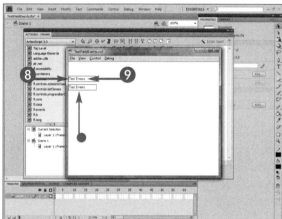

Both the `change` and `textInput` events are dispatched with each character a user types into the field. This can obviously generate a lot of overhead if the user types a lot of text or if something complex happens on the event, particularly if you are using Flash to communicate with a server and are attempting to send data back to the server. You can prevent problems associated with this much added overhead by not using either of these events. Instead, you can wait until the user finishes typing and deal with the text all at once by providing a button and using its `click` event to call your event handler. This will be the preferred method of dealing with user-input text most of the time.

Note that users cannot enter or change text in dynamic text fields, although the text in dynamic fields can be selected and copied, unless you prevent the user from selecting the text in a field by setting its `selectable` property to `false`.

# Find Characters within Strings

**A**ny block of text in ActionScript is an instance of the `String` class. The class contains a set of methods that enable you to work with and manipulate the text.

Some of the most useful of these methods allow you to find particular pieces of text within a string. If you want to return a character from a particular location within the string, you can use `charAt()`. For example, examine this code:

```
var userName:String = "Mal Reynolds";
trace(userName.charAt(4));
```

The `trace` statement would display R. Note that the method begins counting in the string at zero for the first character, not one; hence the *R* is at index 4, not 5.

You can find out where a particular character exists in a string with the `indexOf()` method. Using the same example string as above, `userName.indexOf("a")` would return 1, after finding the first *A* as the second character. Note that like `charAt()`, `indexOf()` counts from zero and as such essentially returns the length of the string up to the found character. The related `lastIndexOf()` method performs the same task but looks at the string from right to left and thus finds the last instance of the character rather than the first.

---

## Find Characters within Strings

**1** Create a text field, such as `var txtPath:TextField = new TextField();`.

**2** Autosize the field and align the text as needed, such as `txtPath.autoSize = TextFieldAutoSize.LEFT;`.

**3** Set the field's x position, such as `txtPath.x = 100;`.

**4** Set the field's y position, such as `txtPath.y = 100;`.

**5** Add the field to the page, such as `addChild(txtPath);`.

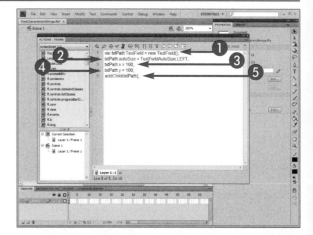

**6** Declare the string variable, such as `var picturePath:String = "mypicture.gif";`.

**7** Find the characters that you need in the string, such as `var dotPosition:Number = picturePath.indexOf(".");`.

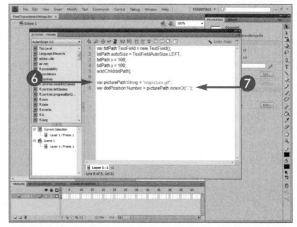

**8** Use the found value as needed, such as `txtPath.text = "The filename is " + dotPosition + " characters long.";`.

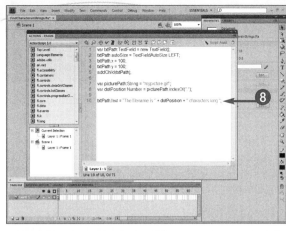

**9** Press Ctrl + Enter.

The movie plays.

● In this example, the length of the filename portion of the string appears in the text field.

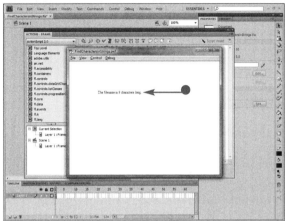

## Apply It

If `indexOf()` does not find the string, it returns -1. This can be useful in determining whether or not a particular character exists in the string, for example —

```
var email:String = "malatserenity.com";
var validateEmail:Number = email.indexOf("@");
if (validateEmail != -1)
{
                trace("Email is valid");
} else {
                trace("Email is invalid");
}
```

`if` statements are covered in more detail in Chapter 11.

# Manipulate Strings

The `String` class contains a single property, `length`, which returns the number of characters in a string. For example, consider this code:

```
var pilot:String = "Hoban Washburne";
var stringLength:Number = pilot.length;
```

The value of the `stringLength` variable would be 15. Note that all characters in the string, including spaces, are counted.

You can convert the string to use specific capitalization using the `toLowerCase()` and `toUpperCase()` methods. Given the `pilot` variable above, `pilot.toLowerCase()` would return hoban washburne, and `pilot.toUpperCase()` would return HOBAN WASHBURNE. The ActionScript documentation notes that there is also a `toLocaleLowerCase()` method that is intended to be locale-specific, but the language actually treats it the same as `toLowerCase()`. This also applies to the `toLocaleUpperCase()` method, which functions just like `toUpperCase()`.

The `String` class also contains a `concat()` method. Normally, concatenation can be performed on strings by simply using the + operator, so `firstName` and `lastName` strings could be combined into a single `fullName` string, including a space, with `var fullName:String = firstName + " " + lastName`. The `concat()` function does essentially the same thing: `var fullName:String = firstName.concat(" ", lastName);`. There is no functional difference between these two approaches.

## Manipulate Strings

1. Create a text field, such as `var txtFile:TextField = new TextField();`.

2. Autosize the field and align the text as needed, such as `txtFile.autoSize = TextFieldAutoSize.LEFT;`.

3. Set the field's x position, such as `txtFile.x = 150;`.

4. Set the field's y position, such as `txtFile.y = 100;`.

5. Add the field to the page, such as `addChild(txtFile);`.

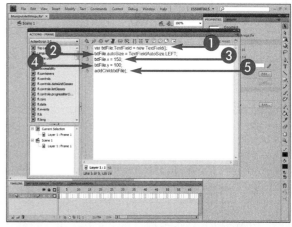

6. Declare the string variable, such as `var filename:String = "MyPicture.GIF";`.

7. Use the `String` property or method that you need, such as `filename = filename.toLowerCase();`.

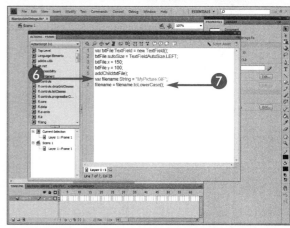

**8** Use the value as needed, such as `txtFile.text = filename;`.

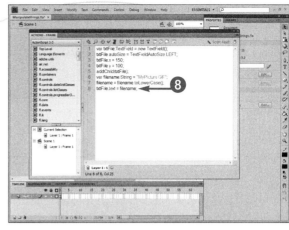

**9** Press Ctrl + Enter.

The movie plays.

● In this example, the filename appears in the text box, with all characters in lowercase.

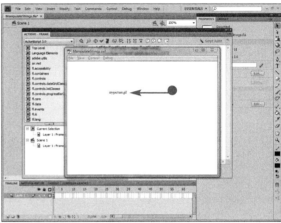

---

**Apply It**

There is some potential confusion when you use `indexOf()`, `lastIndexOf()`, or `charAt()` to find the final character in the string and then compare it to the `length` property. Because the methods begin counting with the first character of the string as zero, `indexOf()` for the final character in the string will be one less than the `length`:

```
var mechanic:String = "Kaylee Frye";
var lastCharacter:Number = mechanic.lastIndexOf("e");
var length:Number = mechanic.length;
trace(lastCharacter) //returns 10;
trace(length) //returns 11;
```

# Get Pieces of Strings

You may find situations in which you need to break strings into smaller component strings. For example, if you have an email address, you may want to separate the username, which precedes the @ sign, from the domain name, which follows the symbol.

ActionScript contains two closely related methods for extracting pieces of strings: substr() and substring(). The first method, substr(), takes two arguments: the starting index from which to extract the string and the number of characters to extract. For example, consider the following:

```
var doctor:String = "Simon Tam";
var stringPart:String = doctor.substr(2, 3);
```

The variable stringPart would then equal mon: the three characters starting with the third character. Note here that the third character has an index of 2, just as if you had used doctor.indexOf("m").

The substring() function also takes two arguments. The first, just as with substr(), indicates the index at which to begin extracting the string. The second argument, however, is also an index — the index of the character after which the extraction should end. Therefore, using the same example string from above, doctor.substring(6,8) would return Tam — the characters beginning at index 6, or the seventh character in the string, and ending just at index 8, or the ninth character.

## Get Pieces of Strings

① Create a text field, such as var txtEmailUser:TextField = new TextField();.

② Autosize the field and align the text as needed, such as txtEmailUser. autoSize = TextFieldAutoSize. LEFT;.

③ Set the field's x position, such as txtEmailUser.x = 150;.

④ Set the field's y position, such as txtEmailUser.y = 150;.

⑤ Add the field to the page, such as addChild(txtEmailUser);.

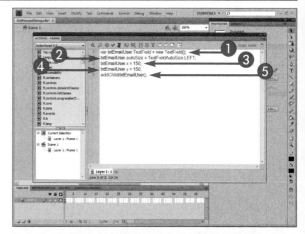

⑥ Create a second text field, such as var txtEmailDomain:TextField = new TextField();.

⑦ Autosize the field and align the text, such as txtEmailDomain.autoSize = TextFieldAutoSize.LEFT;.

⑧ Set the field's x position, such as txtEmailDomain.x = 150;.

⑨ Set the field's y position, such as txtEmailDomain.y = 200;.

⑩ Add the field to the page, such as addChild(txtEmailDomain);.

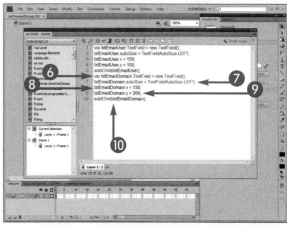

⑪ Declare the string variable, such as `var email:String = "info@ bradystudios.com";`.

⑫ Use the extraction method that you need, such as `var emailUser:String = email. substring(0, email. indexOf("@"));`.

⑬ Extract any other needed characters, such as `var emailDomain:String = email.substring((email. indexOf("@")+1), email. length);`.

⑭ Display one value in the first text field, such as `txtEmailUser.text = emailUser;`.

⑮ Display another value in the second text field, such as `txtEmailDomain. text = emailDomain;`.

⑯ Press Ctrl + Enter.

The movie plays.

● In this example, the first part of the email address is displayed in the first text field, and the second part is displayed in the second text field.

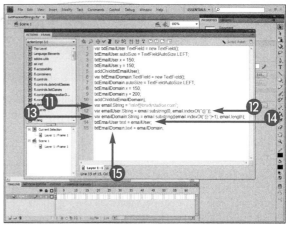

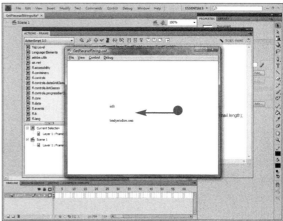

## Apply It

ActionScript also supports the `slice()` method. This method is very similar to `substring()`, and in fact when given positive numbers as its arguments, it is identical. However, the `slice()` method also accepts negative arguments, in which case it searches the string right-to-left, whereas a negative value passed to `substring()` is ignored and causes it to default to 0:

```
var muscle:String = "Jayne Cobb";
trace(muscle.substring(6, muscle.length)); //returns "Cobb"
trace(muscle.slice(6, muscle.length)); //returns "Cobb"
trace(muscle.substring(-3, muscle.length)); // returns "Jayne Cobb"
trace(muscle.slice(-3, muscle.length)); // returns "Cobb"
```

# Convert Data Types

Text fields can display only strings. If you attempt to put any other type of data into a text field, a runtime error will occur. For example, this code will result in an error:

```
txtNumberOfCharacters.text = userName.length;
```

If you run this code, the Compiler Errors panel will appear and display "1067: Implicit coercion of a value of type int to an unrelated type String." This error is the result of trying to put a numeric value — the value of the `length` property — into a text field. You can avoid this error by explicitly converting the offending value to a string. Therefore, modifying the code as follows will succeed:

```
txtNumberOfCharacters.text = String(userName.
  length);
```

The same runtime error will occur if you try to put any other data type into a text field, including Booleans. The solution is the same: Pass the Boolean value to `String()`.

Occasionally, automatic type conversion will occur. For example, if you concatenate a number and a string, the result will be converted to a string, which can be placed directly into a text field. Therefore, `txtResult.text = "The result is " + (5 + 4)` will work without you needing to explicitly convert the mathematical expression to a string.

## Convert Data Types

1. Create a text field, such as `var txtLength:TextField = new TextField();`.

2. Declare a string variable, such as `var userName:String = "theUser";`.

3. Add the text field to the page, such as `addChild(txtLength);`.

4. Try to place the length of the string in the text field, such as `txtLength.text = userName.length;`.

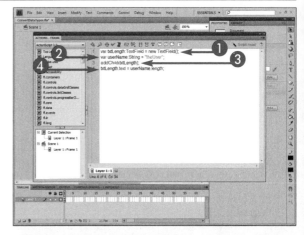

5. Press Ctrl + Enter.

   Flash Player opens.

   • The Compiler Errors panel appears, displaying the "Implicit Coercion" error.

**Note:** If you do not see the Compiler Errors panel, it may be behind Flash Player or the Actions panel.

**6** Close Flash Player.

**7** Retype the line that you wrote in step **4** to convert the length to a string, such as `txtLength.text = String(userName. length);`.

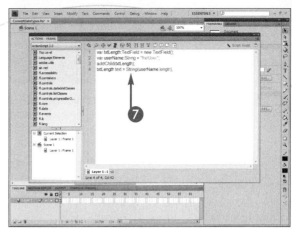

**8** Press Ctrl + Enter.

● The movie plays without error, and the length of the string appears in the text box.

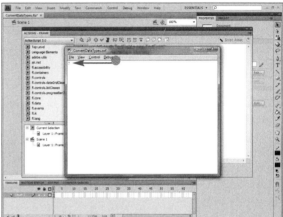

## Extra

Note that complex data types, such as `MovieClips` and `Arrays`, cannot be simply converted to strings. Passing a complex type to `String()` will not return an error, however. The classes that define those complex types contain a special method, `toString()`, which is automatically invoked when you attempt to use them as a string. This method returns a message about the data type, so for example, attempting to put a `MovieClip` directly into a text field will result in [object MovieClip] appearing in the field.

Technically, `String()` is not a method but is rather the constructor for the `String` class. Therefore, the line `String(userName.length)` is actually creating a new string from the variable.

# Understanding the TextFormat Class

**W**hen you create a text field visually using the text tool and dragging on the Stage, you can use the Properties panel to apply formatting. If you create the field in code, however, you must apply formatting via an instance of the `TextFormat` class.

## Class Properties

The `TextFormat` class contains a set of properties for storing formatting information that you plan to apply to a text field. These properties are `align`, `blockIndent`, `bold`, `bullet`, `color`, `font`, `indent`, `italic`, `kerning`, `leading`, `leftMargin`, `letterSpacing`, `rightMargin`, `size`, `tabStops`, `target`, `underline`, and `url`.

### align

The `align` property sets the alignment of text within a field. It takes as its value one of the constants set in the `TextFormatAlign` class, which are `CENTER`, `JUSTIFY`, `LEFT`, and `RIGHT`.

### blockIndent

The `blockIndent` property indents all lines of the field from the left margin by a specified number of pixels. Its value must be set to a valid number.

### bold

The `bold` property renders the text in the indicated field in a bold typeface. Valid values are `true`, `false`, and `null`, which is the same as `false`.

### bullet

You can use the `bullet` property to create a bulleted list. Valid values are `true`, in which case each paragraph within the field will be displayed with a bullet, or `false` and `null`, both of which cause no bullet to appear.

### color

The `color` property sets the text color. You indicate the color by setting the property's value to a valid hexadecimal color value. Hexadecimal is expressed in ActionScript by typing **0x** and then the value, so for example, red is 0xFF0000. The value must always use all six digits of the hexadecimal color; CSS-style three-digit shorthand for the color is not supported, and neither are named values such as `red` or `blue`. A value of `null` is also supported, which causes Flash Player to render the text in black.

### font

Set the font face for the text using the `font` property. You provide the font name as a string, such as `"Arial"` or `"Times New Roman"`.

### indent

The `indent` property indents the first line of text by the specified number of pixels. The value is given as a number; as pixels are the only allowed unit, the unit does not need to be given. Note that `indent` indents only the first line of text, whereas `blockIndent` indents all lines.

### italic

Providing a value of `true` for the `italic` property italicizes the text, and a value of either `false` or `null` does not.

### kerning

In typography, the space between characters in text is known as *kerning,* so the `kerning` property adjusts that spacing. You cannot adjust kerning on individual letter pairs; instead, you simply set this property to `true` to have Flash Player kern text and `false` or `null` to have it not kern. The `kerning` property should be applied only to large text such as that used on headers, and you can apply it only to embedded fonts.

### leading

You can use the `leading` property to adjust the space between lines in text. This property is expressed with a numeric value or as `null`, which sets the leading to zero. Note that a value of `null` or 0 does not remove leading, which would cause lines of text to run on top of one another, but rather simply has the font displayed with a normal amount of leading.

### leftMargin and rightMargin

The `leftMargin` and `rightMargin` properties set the paragraph margins, expressed as a number and set in pixels. The `indent` and `blockIndent` properties indent text from the `leftMargin` if provided.

### letterSpacing

You can increase the space between letters within your text by providing a numeric value for `letterSpacing`. The space is added uniformly between all letters throughout the line; this is in contrast to `kerning`, which adds or removes space only where needed to increase readability. You can provide decimal values for `letterSpacing`.

### size

The `size` property sets the font size. It takes a number. The only valid unit of measurement is pixels, so no unit is given.

### tabStops

The `tabStops` property takes as its value an array of nonnegative numbers. If the text in the field contains tab characters, they will be spaced according to the values in the array. The default tab stop spacing is 4.

### target

The `target` property is used when the text is hyperlinked and the Flash movie is playing in an HTML document in a browser. A value of `_self` causes the linked document to open in the same browser window as the current document, and `_blank` or any custom name causes the linked document to open in a new browser window. Should the wrapper HTML page for the Flash movie be a part of a frameset, `_top`, `_parent`, or a custom name will behave as they would in normal HTML situations.

### underline

The `underline` property causes the text to be displayed as underlined text if the value is set to `true` or to be displayed without underlining if set to `false` or `null`.

### url

The `url` property specifies the target URL as a string for the text in the field. If `url` is set to an empty string or `null`, the text will not appear as a link — which is indicated by underlining. The text field in question must have its `htmlFormat` property set to `true` for `url` to work.

## Default Values

The `font` property defaults to Times New Roman in Windows and Times on Mac OS X and takes a string that is the name of a font. Both `target` and `url` also take strings. For `color`, any hexadecimal value can be used. The default color is black. `size` defaults to 12 (pixels) and takes a numeric value. The default values of `blockIndent`, `indent`, `leading`, `leftMargin`, `letterSpacing`, and `rightMargin` are all 0, and all can be set with new numeric values, whereas `bold`, `bullet`, `italic`, `kerning`, and `underline` all default to `false` but can be set to `true`. The `tabStops` property defaults to an empty array, and both `target` and `url` are set to empty strings. The `align` property defaults to `left`, represented by the constant `TextFormatAlign.LEFT`.

# Apply Formatting to a Text Field

In order to format a text field, you must first create an instance of the `TextFormat` class by creating a variable set as a type of `TextFormat` and then calling the class constructor:

```
var tfInfoText:TextFormat = new TextFormat();
```

You can then add formatting by setting the properties of the class to the values that you want, so for example, you may have something like this:

```
tfInfoText.font = "Verdana";
tfInfoText.color = 0xFF3300;
```

After you have the `TextFormat` instance created and its properties set to the values that you want, you need to apply the format to the text field. Instances of the `TextField` class have a method for this purpose: `setTextFormat`, which takes as its argument the name of an instance of the `TextFormat` class. For example, a text field instance named `txtCopyright` could have `tfInfoText` applied to it with the following line:

```
txtCopyright.setTextFormat(tfInfoText);
```

## Apply Formatting to a Text Field

### CREATE THE TEXTFORMAT INSTANCE

1. Create the instance, such as `var tfNameFormat:TextFormat = new TextFormat();`.

2. Set the font, such as `tfNameFormat.font = "Arial";`.

3. Set the size, such as `tfNameFormat.size = 12;`.

4. Set the color, such as `tfNameFormat.color = 0x009900;`.

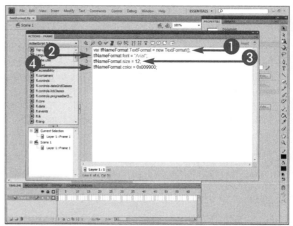

### CREATE THE TEXTFIELD INSTANCE

5. Create a text field, such as `var txtPictureName:TextField = new TextField();`.

6. Place text in the text field, such as `txtPictureName.text = "Sample Picture";`.

7. Set the field's x position, such as `txtPictureName.x = 50;`.

8. Set the field's y position, such as `txtPictureName.y =50;`.

9. Add the field to the page, such as `addChild(txtPictureName);`.

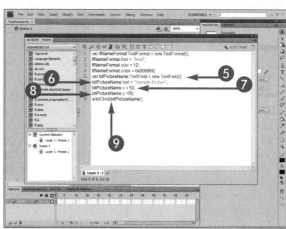

## APPLY THE FORMATTING AND VIEW THE RESULTS

**10** Apply the formatting of the instance from step **1** to the text field from step **5**, such as `txtPictureName.setTextFormat(tfNameFormat);`.

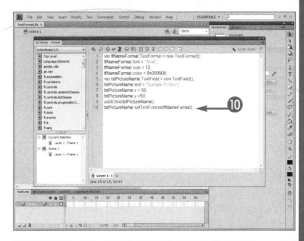

**11** Press Ctrl + Enter.

● The movie plays. The text is displayed in the text box, with the formatting applied.

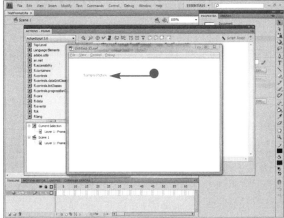

## Extra

Beginning ActionScript developers often wonder why so much work is required to apply formatting and think that it would be a lot easier if the formatting properties were part of the `TextField` class and could thus be applied directly to the field, instead of having to go through the extra steps of creating an additional instance of the `TextFormat` class. It is true that if you are applying formats to a single text field, the approach taken by ActionScript 3.0 is a considerable amount of work.

There is, however, logic behind it. Most of the time, you are going to need to apply the formatting not to a single field but to a group of fields. Imagine an application that was displaying information about products, as in an e-commerce site. Most likely, the product information is going to be made up of a series of fields, displaying the product name, the price, and details about the product. If you wanted the price and details fields to have the same formatting, it would in fact be more work to apply the formatting to them independently. Instead, you can have a single instance of the `TextFormat` class that applies the same formatting to both.

# Using HTML Text

**A**pplying formatting via an instance of the `TextFormat` class allows you to format all the text within a particular text field, but it does not allow you to apply formatting to individual paragraphs, words, or possibly characters within the field. In order to do this kind of formatting, you need to use HTML text.

ActionScript text fields support a small subset of HTML 1.0 tags that you can apply to text within fields. For the most part, the tags supported are those that apply formatting equivalent to that supported by the `TextFormat` class. For example, the class contains a `url` property to set a hyperlink; the HTML `<a>` tag is supported by HTML text to achieve the same results. You can also apply bold through `<b>`, italic via `<i>`, and underline with `<u>`, as well as set the font, color, and size using the `<font>` tag. You can add bulleted text with `<li>`. In addition to the `TextFormat` equivalents, you

can add line breaks by using the `<br>` tag and add inline images with `<img>`. Paragraphs are denoted using the `<p>` tag. You can apply margins, indentation, leading, and tab stops with the `<TextFormat>` tag, which is not technically part of HTML but is supported in ActionScript. A complete list of the supported tags and their values can be found in Appendix C.

For the most part, the standard attributes to these tags are supported just as they are in HTML. For example, to set the font color, you would use `<font color="#006655">`, just as you would in HTML.

In order for any HTML formatting to be applied, you must add the text to the text field via its `htmlText` property, rather than the normal `text` property. Should text be added via both properties, only that added with text will apply.

## Using HTML Text

**1** Create a text field, such as `var txtInfoText:TextField = new TextField();`.

**2** Add the field to the page, such as `addChild(txtInfoText);`.

**3** Set the field's width, such as `txtInfoText.width=200;`.

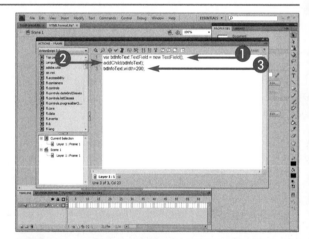

**4** Autosize the field and align the text as needed, such as `txtInfoText.autoSize = TextFieldAutoSize.LEFT;`.

**5** If needed, make the field capable of accepting multiple lines, such as `txtInfoText.multiline = true;`.

**6** If needed, set the text in the field to wrap, such as `txtInfoText.wordWrap = true;`.

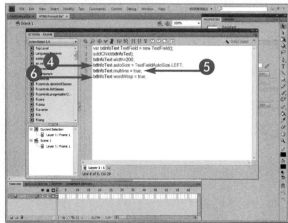

**7** Declare a string variable that includes HTML formatting, such as `var info:String = "<p>A <i>beautiful</i> sunset.</p><p>Photo taken 1/10/09.</p>";`.

**8** Place the string variable's value into the text field, making sure to use the `htmlText` property, such as `txtInfoText.htmlText = info;`.

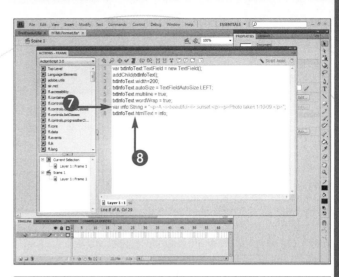

**9** Press Ctrl + Enter.

● The movie plays. The formatted text appears onscreen.

Flash Player also supports the use of character entities, which you must use in HTML text to avoid conflicts over the use of characters that are used as part of the HTML itself. For example, you cannot have an HTML string displaying a mathematical formula such as 5<10, as the HTML text would interpret the less-than symbol as the beginning of a tag. Instead, you would need to use the entity `&lt;`, just as you would in HTML. The entities supported in Flash are `&lt;` for the less than symbol, `&gt;` for greater than, `&amp;` for the ampersand, `&quot;` for the quotation mark, `&apos;` for the apostrophe, and ` ` for a nonbreaking space.

Any HTML tags included within `htmlText` that are not supported by Flash Player will be ignored. For example, if you attempted to add a table through HTML by typing `<table><tr><td>Name</td></tr><tr><td>Mal</td></tr></table>`, all of the unrecognized tags — `<table>`, `<tr>`, `<td>`, and their closing tags — would be stripped, so the resulting text would contain only Name Mal. Empty, unsupported tags are ignored altogether.

# Write an If Statement

In 1979, an extremely popular series of books targeted at young adults hit the shelves. The first such book, written by Edward Packard, was called *The Cave of Time,* and it introduced a novel new concept in which, at the end of each page, readers had to choose between two alternatives. Based on their choice, they jumped to a different page of the book, so no two readings of the book were the same. Eventually, there would be well over 100 of these *Choose Your Own Adventure* titles published.

ActionScript, like other programming languages, provides the ability to have the script make decisions based on what is currently happening in the movie, much like readers of those books could choose their path through the story. The most common decision-making statement is `if`. The `if` clause enables you to provide a test, and if

that test is true, the statements enclosed within the `if`'s curly braces will be executed; if not, processing will continue below the statement.

The test can be almost anything. You can see if the current value of a variable is greater than or less than another variable, or a hard-coded value. You can see if the text property of a text field is empty, or if a variable has been defined, or if an instance of an object has been created.

When comparing two values for equality, you need to be careful to use the equality operator, which is two equals signs (`==`). A single equals sign sets the value of the variable to its left to the value to its right; two equal signs compare the value to the left with the value to the right.

## Write an If Statement

### WRITE A STATEMENT THAT COMPARES TWO VALUES FOR EQUALITY

1. Create a number variable, such as `var firstNum:Number = 42;`.

2. Create a second number variable, such as `var secondNum:Number = 42;`.

3. Create a text field, such as `var txtCompare:TextField = new TextField();`.

4. Add the field to the page, such as `addChild(txtCompare);`.

5. Type `if`.

6. Type a set of parentheses.

7. Within the parentheses, type the name of the first variable, `==`, and the name of the second variable, such as `firstNum == secondNum`.

8. Outside of the parentheses, type a set of curly braces.

9. Within the curly braces, place text in the text field to be displayed if the values match, such as `txtCompare.text = "The values match!";`.

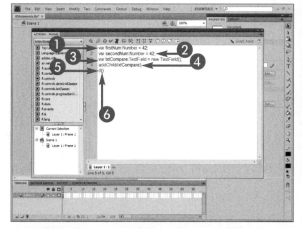

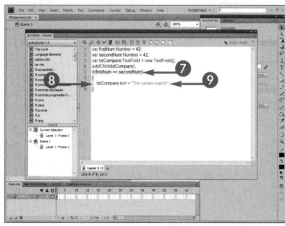

## TEST THE STATEMENT

**10** Press Ctrl + Enter.

The movie plays.

● In this example, the phrase typed in step **9** appears in the text box because the values match.

**11** Click here to close Flash Player.

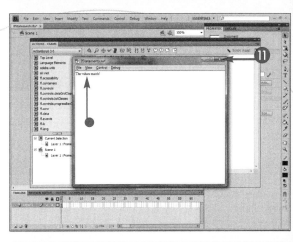

**12** Change the value of the variable that you created in step **2**.

**13** Press Ctrl + Enter.

The movie plays.

● In this example, because the values no longer match, the statement is false, so nothing appears in the text box.

---

### Apply It

In addition to the equality operator (==), you can use other operators to compare values, as shown in the following:

```
if(num1 > num2) //tests to see if num1 is greater than num2.
if(num1 < num2) // tests to see if num1 is less than num2.
if(num1 >= num2) // tests to see if num1 is greater than or equal to num2.
if(num1 <= num2) //tests to see if num1 is less than or equal to num2.
if(num1 != num2) // tests to see that num1 does not equal num2.
if(num1 is String) // tests to see if num1 is of data type String.
if(num1 === num2) // compares values without converting data types. If num1 is 3 (a String)
    and num2 is 3 (a Number), then num1 == num2 is false while num1 === num2 is true.
```

# Using Else and Else If Clauses

A simple `if` statement contains code that will execute if the condition is true; otherwise, processing will continue below the statement. However, ActionScript also includes the ability to provide other options. You can use an `else` clause to say, "if the test is true, do this; otherwise, do something else."

The `else` clause follows the closing curly brace of the `if` statement and contains its own set of braces. The code to be executed by the `else` clause — the code to execute if the `if` condition evaluates to false — is contained within those braces.

For example, say that you have a login script. You will want to have two scenarios: one if the users provide the correct credentials and another if they do not. You could therefore write the `if` statement, testing their input versus the known accepted credentials, and take whatever steps are appropriate if they provide the correct information. However, you do not want to do nothing if they do not, so in an `else` clause, you might provide an informational message stating that their username and password did not match those on file.

You can also test on more than one possible condition using one or more `else if` statements. Like `if`, the `else if` clause contains a test and, within braces, a set of statements to execute if the test is true. But like `else`, the `else if` clause will execute only if the `if` statement — and any `else if` statements above it — have evaluated to false.

You can have as many `else if` clauses as you need, but they must appear after the `if` clause, and before the `else` clause if it is present.

## Using Else and Else If Clauses

① Create a variable, such as `var totalPictures:Number = 15;`.

② Type `if()`.

③ Within the parentheses, check to see if the variable meets a condition, such as `totalPictures < 10`.

④ Outside the parentheses, type a set of curly braces.

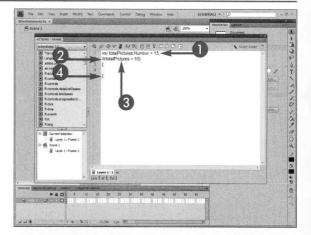

⑤ Within the braces, create the resulting action if the condition is true — for example, displaying certain text, such as `trace("There are less than 10 pictures.");`.

⑥ After the closing curly brace, create an `else if` statement that checks for a different condition, such as `else if(totalPictures == 10)`.

⑦ Type a set of curly braces.

⑧ Within the curly braces, create the resulting action if the second condition is true — for example, displaying different text, such as `trace("There are exactly ten pictures.");`.

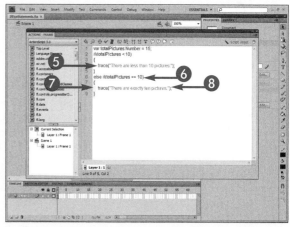

**⑨** After the closing curly brace, type `else`.

**⑩** Type a set of curly braces.

**⑪** Within the curly braces, create the resulting action if the neither the first condition nor the second one is true — for example, displaying some other text, such as `trace("There are more than 10 pictures.");`.

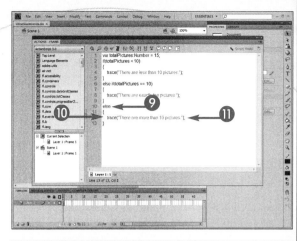

**⑫** Press Ctrl + Enter.

The movie plays.

● Depending on the value set for the variable created in step **1**, one of the three actions occurs — in this example, one of the messages appears in the Output panel.

## Extra

Any expression that evaluates to `true` or `false` can be used in an `if` clause. Boolean values are of course already `true` or `false`, so they can be evaluated as a simple value. For example, if you had `var adminStatus:Boolean = true`, then `if(adminStatus)` would evaluate to `true`. You can test on the opposite result using the `!` character, so `if(!adminStatus)` would be false, as you are in essence saying "if the value of `adminStatus` is not true."

Other data types can also be evaluated directly in the same manner, but you need to be careful that you understand the implications. For example, if you have a variable `num1` set as a `Number`, then `if(num1)` will be true so long as the value of `num1` is not zero or null; otherwise, it will be false. Strings will evaluate to `true` as long as they are not empty or null. The same applies to arrays: They are true as long as they are not null and not empty. Most complex data types will evaluate to `true` as long as they are not null, so `if(mcSquare1)` will be true if a `MovieClip` exists with that instance name and unless you had explicitly written `mcSquare1 = null`.

# Test Multiple Conditions

**W**ithin a single test clause, you can test on multiple conditions using a set of special Boolean operators. These can be helpful when you need to perform one set of actions if two or more conditions are true or if one out of a choice of conditions is true.

The logical AND operator, &&, is used to see if two or more conditions are all true. For example, if you wanted to test to see if a variable shipName contained "Serenity" and a variable captainName contained "Mal", you could write

```
if(shipName == "Serenity" && captainName ==
  "Mal")
```

Note that in this case, *both* conditions must be true. If either is false, then the entire expression is false. If you have a situation in which you need only one of the two values to be true, you could use the logical OR operator, ||:

```
if(shipName == "Millennium Falcon" ||
  captainName == "Lando")
```

In this case, one of the conditions can be false, and the expression will still evaluate to true, as long as the other is true. The expression will evaluate to false only if both conditions are false.

The logical OR operator is two pipe characters. On most keyboards, the pipe character is located directly above the Enter key, on the same key as the backslash. Keyboards tend to label the key as a broken vertical line, but when typed, it will be displayed as an unbroken line.

## Test Multiple Conditions

**1** Create a variable, such as
```
var firstPic:String
= "firstpic.jpg";.
```

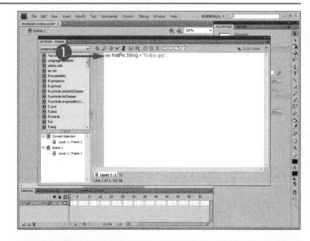

**2** Type if().

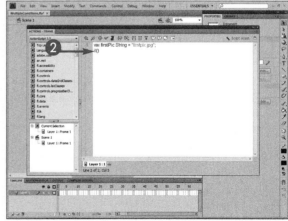

③ Within the parentheses, type the first condition that you want to test for, such as `firstPic.indexOf("jpg") != -1`.

④ Type the comparison operator that you want, such as `||`.

⑤ Type the second condition that you want to test for, such as `firstPic.indexOf("gif") != -1`.

**Note:** See Chapter 9 for details on the `indexOf` method.

⑥ Outside the parentheses, type a set of curly braces.

⑦ Within the curly braces, type the action that you want to occur if the expression evaluates to true, such as `trace("The picture is a JPG or GIF.");`.

⑧ Press Ctrl + Enter.

The movie plays.

● In this example, because the value of the variable in step **1** contains the characters `jpg`, the expression is true, and the phrase from step **7** is displayed in the Output window.

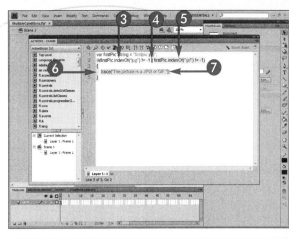

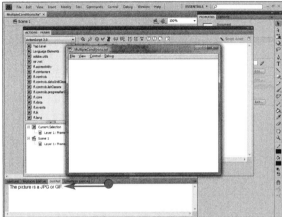

## Apply It

You can test on more than two conditions by combining expressions using the `&&` and `||` operators. For example, this is legal:

```
if(num1 == num2 || num2 >  num3 && num3 < num4)
```

However, you should note that the preceding statement will not execute from left to right. When you combine both logical AND and logical OR statements, the AND statements are evaluated first. Therefore, the preceding condition does not read, "If num1 equals num2 or if num2 is greater than num3 and if num3 is less than num4." Rather, it actually reads, "If num2 is greater than num3 and num3 is less than num4, or if num1 is equal to num2." Often, this distinction will not matter, but it is important to carefully evaluate your expressions in case it does.

If you need to force the logical OR expressions to be read first, you can group them using parentheses:

```
if((num1 == num2 || num2 > num3) && num3 < num4)
```

# Replace If/Else Clauses with a Switch Statement

If you have a long series of conditions that need to be tested, you might be able to save some code by replacing your if/else clauses with a switch statement. The switch statement does the exact same thing as a series of if/else clauses: It evaluates each and, if true, executes the code indicated. However, the switch statement in general uses less code.

To write a switch, you begin with the switch keyword, followed by the variable that you want to test in parentheses:

```
switch(userName)
```

Then, within a set of curly braces, you will include a series of case statements. Each case contains the value against which the variable in the switch should be compared. If they are equal, the statements following the case are executed.

Even if the switch statement finds a case that is equal to the value being compared, it will continue to look at the remainder of the cases. Therefore, you need to include a break clause with each case, which stops the execution of the switch.

The switch statement can end with a default case, which is the equivalent of an else clause in your if statement: It is the code to be executed if none of the other cases matched.

Two significant limitations of switch are that it can test only for equality and only against a single variable: The cases are either equal to or not equal to the variable. If you need to test for inequality or against multiple conditions, you need to use an if statement with if/else clauses.

## Replace If/Else Clauses with a Switch Statement

① Create a variable, such as
   `var timeZone="PST";`.

② Type `switch()`.

③ Within the parentheses, type the name of the variable from step **1**.

④ Type a set of curly braces.

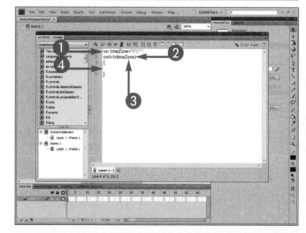

⑤ Within the curly braces, type case, followed by a value that you want to test for and a colon, such as `case "PST":`.

⑥ Create the resulting action if this value matches, such as `trace("Your time is GMT-8");`.

⑦ Type `break;`.

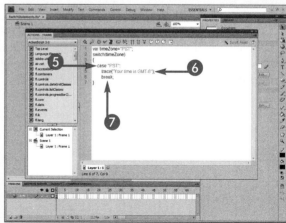

**8** Type `case`, followed by another value that you want to test for and a colon, such as `case "EST":`.

**9** Create the resulting action if this value matches, such as `trace("Your time is GMT-5");`.

**10** Type `break;`.

**11** Type `default:`.

**12** Create the resulting action if none of the other cases match, such as `trace("Cannot determine time zone.");`.

**13** Press Ctrl + Enter.

The movie plays.

● In this example, a message appropriate to the variable created in step **1** is displayed.

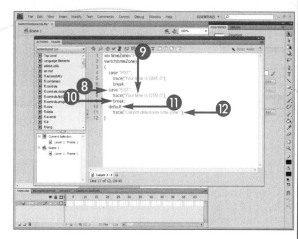

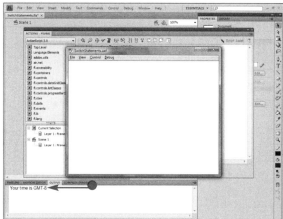

---

**Apply It**

You can test against more than one case at a time by stacking `case` statements. In order to display one message if a user is in either the Pacific or Mountain time zones, for example, you might have the following:

```
case "PST":
case "MST":
              trace("You are in the Pacific or Mountain time zones");
              break;
```

# Write a For Loop

Frequently, you will need to perform repetitive tasks in your scripts. Like other programming languages, ActionScript provides for several different methods of looping over a block of code.

One of the most common types of loops is a `for` loop. To initialize the loop, you need to provide three key elements: the counter variable for the loop, the condition on which the loop will be tested, and a statement to change the value of the counter with each iteration of the loop. Following the initialization line, you will place the code to be executed with each iteration within a set of curly braces. For example, your loop might look like this:

```
for(var i:Number=0; i<10; i++)
{
    trace(i);
}
```

In this example, a variable, i, is created and set to an initial value of 0. After each iteration of the loop, the current value of i will be tested to see if it is less than 10: If it is, the loop will execute again; if not, it will exit. Finally, the value of i is incremented by 1 after each iteration. The code in this example simply outputs the value of i, so if this code were run, the Output panel would display the digits 0 through 9.

## Write a For Loop

① Type `for`.

② Type a set of parentheses.

③ Within the parentheses, create a variable and set its initial value, such as `var i:Number = 0;`.

④ Type the condition for which the loop will be tested, such as `i < 5;`.

⑤ Type a statement to change the value of the counter with each iteration, such as `i++`.

⑥ Outside the parentheses, type a pair of curly braces.

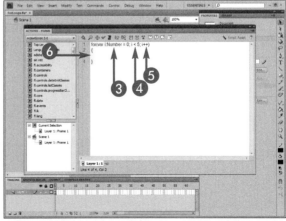

**7** Within the curly braces, type the code to be executed with each iteration — for example, you might display a text field, such as `var txtInput:TextField = new TextField();`.

**8** For a text field, create a border, such as `txtInput.border = true;`.

**9** For a text field, set if you want an input type, such as `txtInput.type = TextFieldType.INPUT;`.

**10** Set the height, such as `txtInput.height = 15;`.

**11** Set the y position, such as `txtInput.y = (txtInput.height + 10) * i;`.

**12** Add the field to the page, such as `addChild(txtInput);`.

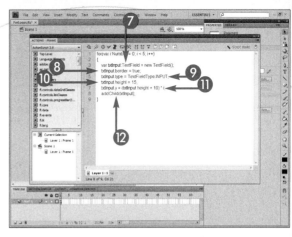

**13** Press Ctrl + Enter.

The movie plays.

● In this example, five input text fields are created and displayed, each placed proportionally lower than the previous one.

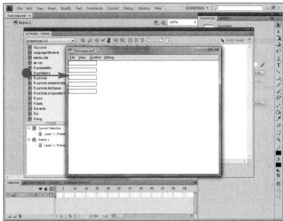

## Apply It

You will likely encounter situations in which you need to programmatically stop a loop from processing. A common example is a loop that contains a conditional statement. For example, if you were looping over an array and attempting to find a particular value, you would want to stop the loop from continuing to process the rest of the array as soon as the value that you want is found. To do otherwise is at best a waste of resources and at worse might cause unexpected results if the value was discovered more than once in the array.

You can terminate a loop programmatically with the `break` statement. ActionScript will stop the loop immediately when the statement is encountered and pass the processing to whatever statement immediately follows the loop's closing curly brace.

Most often, the `break` statement will be contained within an `if` statement or some other conditional clause so that the script will encounter it only if a certain condition is met, such as a particular value being found.

# Write a While Loop

You will use a `for` loop any time that you need to execute the same block of code a certain number of times. In the example presented in the section "Write a For Loop," exactly five text fields were created, so a `for` loop made sense. However, there will be times when, instead of looping a predetermined number of times, you will instead want to perform a set of instructions while a condition is true.

ActionScript provides a second looping construct for this scenario — the `while` loop. Whereas a `for` loop contains the creation of the variable, the test, and the increment within the initialization statement, a `while` loop contains only the test. The variable against which you will be testing will be created elsewhere in the code — somewhere above the `while` loop — and the incrementing of the variable will occur within the code to be executed by the loop.

In many situations, a `for` loop and a `while` loop can be written to achieve the same results, and for the most part, it will not matter which you use. A general rule is that if you have to loop over a variable that already exists in your code, you should use a `while` loop; if you are looping over a variable that will exist only for the purpose of the loop, then a `for` loop will usually be more appropriate.

In the example shown here, a `while` loop is used to step over a string containing a comma-separated list of names and counts the number of commas. After the loop, the number of names, which is known to be one more than the number of commas, is output. The loop relies on an `if` statement, which is discussed in detail in Chapter 11.

## Write a While Loop

### COUNT THE NUMBER OF NAMES IN A LIST

① Create a string with a comma-separated list of names, such as `var pictures: String ="First Picture, Second Picture, Third Picture";`.

② Create a `count` variable and set its initial value to 0, such as `var count:Number = 0;`.

③ Create a test varlable and set its initial value to 0, such as `var i: Number = 0;`.

④ Type `while()`.

⑤ Within the parentheses, type the variable name from step **3**, `<`, the variable name from step **1**, a period, and `length`, such as `i < pictures.length`.

⑥ Type a set of curly braces.

⑦ Within the curly braces, type `if(StringVariable. charAt(TestVariable) == ",")`, replacing *StringVariable* with the name of the variable in step **1** and *TestVariable* with the name of the variable in step **3**.

⑧ Type a set of curly braces.

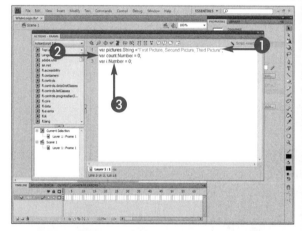

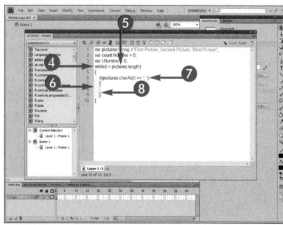

**9** Within the nested set of braces, type `count++;`.

**10** Outside of the nested braces but inside the braces for the `while` loop, type the variable name from step **3** and `++;`.

**11** Outside both sets of curly braces, create a variable to contain the number of names, such as `var totalNames:Number = count +1;`.

**12** Display the variable's value, such as `trace(totalNames);`.

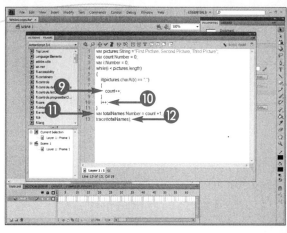

## TEST THE MOVIE

**13** Press Ctrl + Enter.

The movie plays.

- In this example, the Output panel displays the value of the `totalNames` variable — 3.

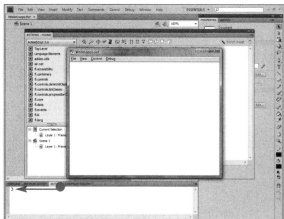

---

### Apply It

A third type of loop structure exists: the `do while` loop, which is similar conceptually to a `while` loop, but it has one major difference: The condition is at the bottom of the code, so the loop will execute before the condition is evaluated. This means that the loop's code is guaranteed to execute at least once, even if the condition is initially false — for example:

```
var x:Number = 5;
while(x < 5)
{
                trace(x);
}
```

Executing this code would result in nothing being displayed in the Output panel, as the value of x is not less than 5. However, if you write this as a `do while` loop, using the same variable:

```
do
{
                trace(x);
} while (x<5)
```

This code would cause 5 to appear, as the code within the loop — the `trace` statement — executes once before the conditional is tested.

# Loop over an Array

**A**n array is a special type of variable that enables you to store multiple values in one variable name. For example, if you have multiple characters in a story, you can create an array to store them together:

```
var characters:Array = ["Mal", "Zoe", "Wash",
  "Jayne", "Kaylee", "Inara", "Simon", "River",
  "Book"];
```

Individual elements of the array can be returned by referencing the array name and, in square brackets, the element that you want to view. Keep in mind that the first element of the array is 0. Therefore, in the preceding array, `characters[5]` would return `Inara`.

To access all elements of the array, you can use a loop. You could use a `for` loop, setting the test to one less than the length of the array, which can be determined with `array.length`. Or, if you were removing the elements as you accessed them, you could use a `while` loop, continuing until there were no elements left. Although both of these alternatives work, ActionScript actually provides a loop structure specifically designed for arrays, known as a `for each..in` loop.

The basic initialization of the loop is simple: `for each (CounterVariable in Array)`. `CounterVariable` is some arbitrary variable that will represent each returned element, and `Array` is the name of the array over which you are looping. As with other loops, you will follow the initialization statement with a set of curly braces, and within the braces, you will have the code that you want to execute, which will usually involve using a counter to view or manipulate the elements.

## Loop over an Array

### PLACE THE VALUES OF AN ARRAY IN TEXT FIELDS

1 Create an array, such as `var caption Array:Array = ["First Picture", "Second Picture", "Third Picture"];`.

2 Create a variable for the original `x` position of a field, such as `var xPos:Number = 60;`.

3 Create a variable for the original `y` position of a field, such as `var yPos:Number = 100;`.

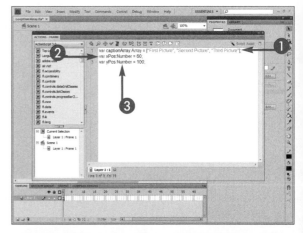

4 Initialize the loop, such as `for each(var i in captionArray)`.

5 Type a set of curly braces.

6 Within the curly braces, create a text field, such as `var txtCaption:TextField = new TextField();`.

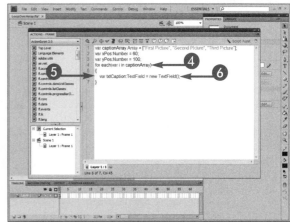

**7** Set the field's text to the counter variable, such as `txtCaption.text = i;`.

**8** Set the field's height, such as `txtCaption.height = 25;`.

**9** Set the field's x position to the variable from step **2**, such as `txtCaption.x = xPos;`.

**10** Set the field's y position to the variable from step **3**, such as `txtCaption.y = yPos;`.

**11** Add the field to the page, such as `addChild(txtCaption);`.

**12** Move the x position for subsequent fields, such as `xPos += txtCaption.width+ 10;`.

## TEST THE MOVIE

**13** Press Ctrl + Enter.

The movie plays.

● In this example, three text fields are created, each populated with an individual value from the array.

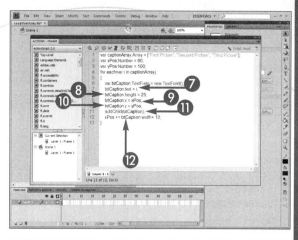

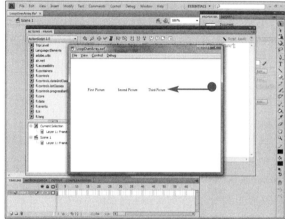

## Extra

You can also use the `for each..in` loop to loop over the elements in an XML file. Using XML and looping over its values are covered in Chapter 17. The examples shown in this section are using the shorthand method of creating an array. For more information on arrays and alternative syntaxes for creating them, see Chapter 2.

Note that in a `for each..in` loop, the counter variable automatically contains the value from each element of the array, so if you are looping over array characters with a counter `i`, you simply reference each element directly using `i`. This is in contrast to using a `for` loop with the array, in which you would need to reference `characters[i]` as the counter in the loop will not be a reference to the actual element but will instead simply be a digit.

In the initialization statement for the `for each..in` loop, do not declare the counter variable as being of a particular data type. Because the values in an array can be of any type, you cannot predict what type the value being returned will be with each iteration.

# Using the EnterFrame Event

**A**lthough today's Flash platform does many things, at its heart Flash is always, and hopefully always will be, an animation tool. Traditionally, animation was created by applying tweens to objects on the Stage and controlling them through the Timeline. Although this approach still works, and has in fact been vastly improved in Flash CS4 Professional, you also have the ability to animate objects entirely through code.

A common misconception about animating in ActionScript is that it relies on loops. To an extent, there is some logic there: It makes sense that if you wanted to move an object across the Stage, you might create a `while` loop that increments the x property of the object repeatedly until it reaches the opposite edge of the Stage. The

problem, however, is that loops force the screen to redraw, so that kind of loop would simply cause the object to appear at the far edge of the screen.

This problem can be avoided by instead recalling that ActionScript is event-driven, and like all other actions, animation relies on an event to occur. The most common event to use is `EnterFrame`, which is called at the movie's frame rate. In other words, if you are using the default 20 frames-per-second rate, the event will occur 20 times per second. You use the event just as you would any other — by creating an event handler to specify what you want to happen with the event and a listener to attach it to an object. See Chapter 7 for more specifics on events.

## Using the EnterFrame Event

### MOVE AN OBJECT ACROSS THE STAGE HORIZONTALLY

1. Create a `MovieClip` and place a named instance of it near the left edge of the Stage.

**Note:** See Chapter 3 for details on creating clips and naming instances.

2. Click the New Layer button to create a new layer and name it "actions."

3. Click in the first frame of the new layer.

4. Press F9 to open the Actions panel.

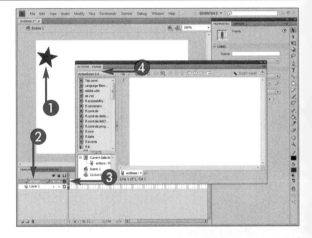

5. Type the name of the instance created in step **1** and a period.

6. Type `addEventListener();`.

7. Within the parentheses, type `Event.ENTER_FRAME`, a comma and a space, and the name of the event handler that you will add, such as `animateClip`.

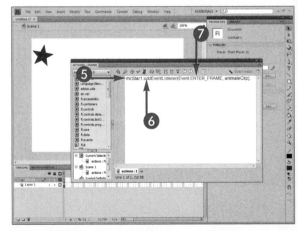

**8** Add the event handler, such as
`function animateClip
(event:Event):void`.

**9** Type a pair of curly braces.

**10** Within the braces, type `event.
target.x += 10;`.

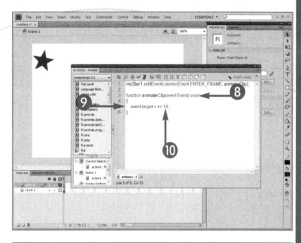

## TEST THE MOVIE

**11** Press Ctrl + Enter.

The movie plays.

● The clip animates, moving
horizontally across the Stage.

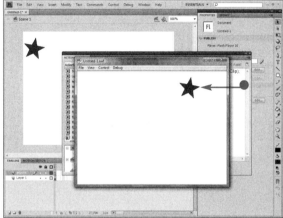

---

### Apply It

Any properties of the `MovieClip` can be altered in the event. If you want the clip to move diagonally from the top-left corner to the bottom-right corner while rotating, you can simply add the code to alter those properties as well:

```
mcSquare1.x += 10;
mcSquare1.y += 10;
mcSquare1.rotation += 30;
```

As mentioned earlier, the `+=` operator is used as a shortcut for adding a new value to an existing value, so the line `mcSquare1.x += 10` is the same as `mcSquare1.x = mcSquare1.x + 10`.

You can also use the `random` method of the `Math` class to move clips at random speeds:

```
mcSquare1.x += Math.round(Math.random() *10) + 1;
```

# Animate MovieClips That Scale and Fade

**M**ost animation involves moving objects from one location to another. However, you can apply any change to an object such as a `MovieClip` over time and have that change animate.

You can change the size of a clip over time by adjusting its `width` and `height` properties. The properties take as their values an integer. There is no direct property in the language that allows you to scale the width and height in proportion to each other or to the initial values, but you can maintain proportions by using mathematical expressions to calculate the new values and being careful to use the same expression on both.

You can also scale clips by adjusting the `scaleX` and `scaleY` properties. Both take a number that represents a

multiplier of the original value. The end result of using these properties, versus multiplying the width or height, is the same. For example, if you want to double the size of a clip, you could either use `mcClip1.width *= 2` or `mcClip2.scaleX = 2`. To scale a clip down, provide a decimal value for these properties.

You can also fade clips using the `alpha` property. `alpha` is expressed as a number between 0 and 1, where 1 is completely opaque and 0 completely transparent. Levels of semitransparency are then expressed as a decimal number, so 50% transparent would be an alpha of .5. Be aware that alpha animations can be very processor-intensive at runtime in Flash Player, so they should be used sparingly.

## Animate MovieClips That Scale and Fade

### HAVE A CENTRAL OBJECT GROW AND FADE IN

1. Create a `MovieClip` and place a named instance on the Stage.

**Note:** See Chapter 3 for details on creating clips and naming instances.

2. Click the New Layer button.

3. Name the new layer "actions."

4. Click in the first frame of the new layer.

5. Press F9 to open the Actions panel.

**Note:** The following steps assume that the instance name given in step **1** is `mcStar1`. If you named your instance something else, adjust the code accordingly.

6. Type `mcStar1.x = stage.stageWidth/2;`.

7. Type `mcStar1.y = stage.stageHeight/2;`.

**Note:** See Chapter 8 for details on working with the Stage.

8. Type `mcStar1.scaleX = .25;`.

9. Type `mcStar1.scaleY = .25;`.

10. Type `mcStar1.alpha = 0;`.

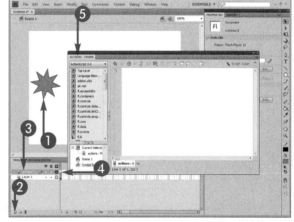

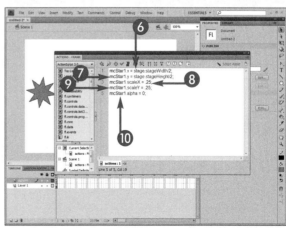

**Note:** *The following steps assume that you use the name* `scaleAndFade` *for the event handler.*

**⑪** Type `mcStar1.addEventListener(Event.ENTER_FRAME, scaleAndFade);`.

**⑫** Type `function scaleAndFade (event:Event):void`.

**⑬** Type a pair of curly braces.

**⑭** Within the curly braces, type `event.target.scaleX += 0.1;`.

**⑮** Type `event.target.scaleY += 0.1;`.

**⑯** Type `event.target.alpha += 0.01;`.

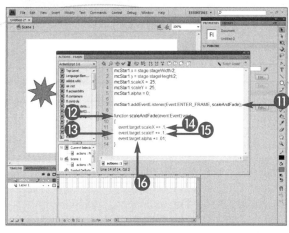

## TEST THE MOVIE

**⑰** Press Ctrl + Enter.

The movie plays.

● The clip is centered on the Stage, shrunk and faded out, but as it animates, it grows and fades in.

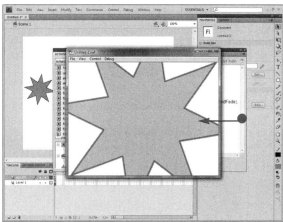

---

## Extra

Unfortunately, Flash is inconsistent in its use of the `alpha` property. If you want to adjust the alpha visually on the Stage with the Properties panel, its values are expressed as percentages, with 0% being transparent and 100% opaque. Prior versions of ActionScript treated the property the same, but ActionScript 3.0 changed it to use a decimal between 0 and 1. A common error in code-based fade animations is to forget this and attempt to set the `alpha` property using a number that represents a percent. This can be a difficult error to diagnose, as the code will run without generating an error, but any value greater than 1 is simply treated as opaque, so no fading will occur.

Of course, scaling and fading animations can be combined with movement. You can easily alter the `x`, `y`, `width`, `height`, `alpha`, and any other properties that you want at the same time to achieve whatever animation effect you need.

# Change the Speed
# of Animation

**O**bjects in motion in the real world rarely travel at a consistent rate of speed. Rather, they accelerate or decelerate over time. Although we cannot necessarily see this, we know instinctively that a ball falling toward the ground speeds up as it falls and that a ball being thrown up in the air slows down as it rises.

You can add realism to your animations by having objects follow these same principles. When animating using tweens, you can apply *easing* to your tweens to have them speed up or slow down over the course of the animation. In ActionScript, you can achieve the same effect by using a combination of variables and basic math to alter the rate at which an object moves.

Simple animation in code involves modifying the x and y coordinates of an object over time by manipulating their values within an `EnterFrame` event handler. The rate at which the variables change affects the speed at which they move: An object whose x coordinate is changing by 1 pixel in each event will move slower than one that is changing by 10 pixels. Rather than hard-coding this change into your handler, however, you can instead set the initial speed of the object — this rate at which the object will change — as a variable, which can in turn be modified within the event handler. This way, the speed at which the object moves will vary from one call to the handler to the next, causing the rate at which the object moves to speed up or slow down.

## Change the Speed of Animation

### MOVE AN OBJECT ACROSS THE STAGE HORIZONTALLY AND HAVE IT SPEED UP

1 Create a `MovieClip` and place a named instance of it near the left edge of the Stage.

**Note:** *See Chapter 3 for details on creating clips and naming instances.*

2 Click the New Layer button.

3 Name the new layer "actions."

4 Click in the first frame of the new layer.

5 Press F9 to open the Actions panel.

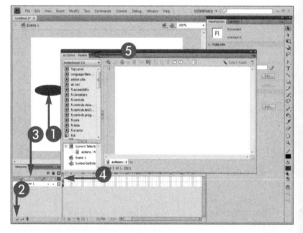

6 Create a number variable and set its initial value to 5, such as `var velocity: Number = 5;`.

7 Type the name of the instance created in step **1** and a period.

8 Type `addEventListener();`.

9 Within the parentheses, type `Event.ENTER_ FRAME`, a comma and a space, and the name of the event handler that you will add, such as `animateClip`.

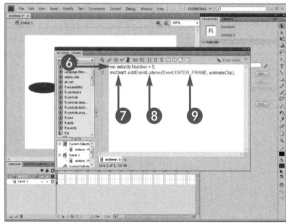

**10** Add the event handler, such as `function animateClip (event:Event):void`.

**11** Type a pair of curly braces.

**12** Within the braces, type `event. target.x += NumberVariable;`, replacing `NumberVariable` with the variable created in step **6**.

**13** Type the name of the variable created in step **6**, followed by `+= 5;`.

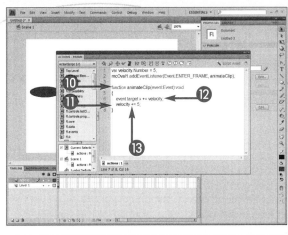

## TEST THE MOVIE

**14** Press Ctrl + Enter.

The movie plays.

● The clip animates, moving horizontally across the Stage. As it moves, it will gradually speed up.

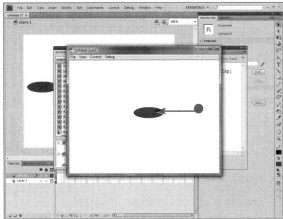

It is possible to easily simulate the effect of gravity on an object by getting a bit creative with your velocity variable, as in the following:

```
var mcBall1:MovieClip = new Ball();
addChild(mcBall1);
var xVelocity:Number = 2;
var yVelocity:Number = -10;
mcBall1.addEventListener(Event.ENTER_FRAME, bouncingBall);
function bouncingBall(event:Event):void
{
            mcBall1.x += xVelocity;
            mcBall1.y += yVelocity;
            yVelocity ++;
}
```

In this code, the ball will move horizontally at a consistent rate. However, it will begin moving up and slow down because the y coordinates are being altered by a negative value. After ten iterations of the event, however, the `yVelocity` variable will be 0 — stopping the object. After that, `yVelocity` begins to be set to a positive value, causing the ball to begin moving back down and speeding up.

# Using the Timer Class

If you are familiar with Timeline-based animation in Flash, then using the `EnterFrame` event will make sense to you. However, it does have a couple of important limitations. First, the frequency with which it occurs is based on the movie's frame rate; therefore, the frequency with which your animation occurs will change if the frame rate changes. Second, there are limits to how fast Flash Player can reliably play back a movie. In theory, the frame rate can be set as high as 120 frames per second, but in practice the actual rate at which your movie can be played smoothly is much less. This performance issue has been steadily improving with each new version of Flash Player, but even with Flash Player 10, you cannot rely on animations that run at much faster than 25 or 30 frames per second. Unfortunately, this has as much to do with your user's computers, so it is extremely difficult to accurately test.

The alternative to the `EnterFrame` event is to animate via an instance of the `Timer` class. These time-based animations will be measured in milliseconds, so they are reliable and consistent across movies and varying frame rates.

To use timer-based animation, you need to first create an instance of the `Timer` class, using the standard notation with the `new` keyword and a call to its constructor. The constructor takes a required argument that represents the delay, in milliseconds, before the timer fires. You can then add an event listener, using the `TIMER` constant of the `TimerEvent` class, and perform any actions that you want.

When you instantiate the class, the timer does not start automatically. Instead, you need to call its `start()` method.

## Using the Timer Class

### MOVE AN OBJECT ACROSS THE STAGE HORIZONTALLY AND HAVE IT SPEED UP

1. Create a `MovieClip` and place a named instance of it near the left edge of the Stage.

**Note:** *See Chapter 3 for details on creating clips and naming instances.*

2. Click the New Layer button.

3. Name the new layer "actions."

4. Click in the first frame of the new layer.

5. Press F9 to open the Actions panel.

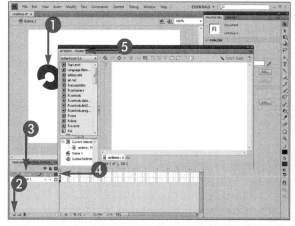

6. Create a number variable and set its initial value, such as `var velocity:Number = 5;`.

7. Create an instance of the `Timer` class and set the delay, such as `var myTimer:Timer = new Timer(100);`.

8. Call the timer's `start()` method, such as `myTimer.start();`.

9. Add an event listener for the timer, such as `myTimer.addEventListener();`.

10. Within the parentheses, type `TimerEvent.TIMER`, a comma and a space, and the name of the event handler that you will add, such as `animateClip`.

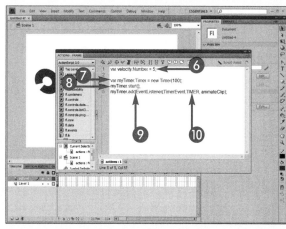

**11** Add the event handler, such as
```
function animateClip
(event:TimerEvent):void.
```

**12** Type a pair of curly braces.

**13** Within the braces, type the name of the instance from step **1** and a period.

**14** Type `x += NumberVariable;`, replacing `NumberVariable` with the variable created in step **6**.

**15** Type the name of the variable created in step **6**, followed by `++;`.

## TEST THE MOVIE

**16** Press Ctrl + Enter.

The movie plays.

● The clip animates, moving horizontally across the Stage. In this example, the movement is updated every 1/10 of a second. As it moves, it will gradually speed up.

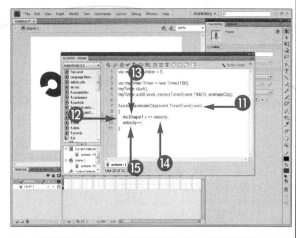

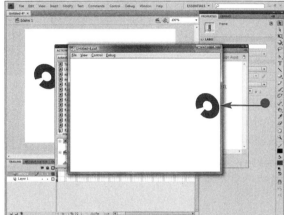

## Extra

The constructor for the `Timer` class can take as a second, optional argument the number of times that the timer will repeat. Omitting this parameter will cause the timer to fire infinitely; providing a numeric value will cause it to fire only that number of times. Each of these repeats occurs after the delay specified in the first argument.

You must be certain to always call the `start` method of the class. The timer will not work otherwise. The class also has a `stop` method, which can be used to programmatically end the timer even if it still has repetitions to perform, and a `reset` method, which both stops the timer and resets the repeat count to 0. You could use these in a stopwatch application, which has the user click one button to start the timer — the button's event handler would therefore call the start method — another button to stop it, and a third to reset it back to 0.

# Create Tweens in Script

Simple animations can be created visually on the Stage through the process of tweening. In this process, you as the designer define the object as a symbol and define its starting and ending locations and the number of frames over which the animation should occur. Flash then calculates the necessary position for the symbol in each of the frames between the start and end and handles the animation for you.

Tweens can be created in code as well. You do not have as much control over the animation when coding a tween as you do when you simply alter the properties of the object directly, but it can be a way to quickly get an object from one point to another without worrying about details such as precise locations.

To use a tween, you must first import the Tween class and the classes in the easing package. You will then create an instance of the Tween class by using the new keyword and calling its constructor. The constructor takes a series of arguments. The first is an instance of the object that you want to move. The second is the property that you want to alter with the tween. The third is a reference to a predefined function for easing, which is covered in more detail in the next section, "Ease Tweened Animation." Next, you provide the beginning and ending values for the property you will be altering and the duration of the tween. Finally, you need to provide a Boolean value, where true states that you will use seconds to evaluate the duration and false that you will use frames.

## Create Tweens in Script

### MOVE AN OBJECT ACROSS THE STAGE HORIZONTALLY

1. Create a MovieClip and place a named instance of it near the left edge of the Stage.

   **Note:** See Chapter 3 for details on creating clips and naming instances.

2. Click the New Layer button.

3. Name the new layer "actions."

4. Click in the first frame of the new layer.

5. Press F9 to open the Actions panel.

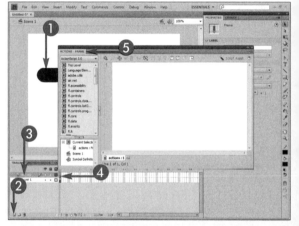

6. Import the Tween class, such as
   ```
   import fl.transitions.
   Tween;
   ```

7. Import the classes in the easing package, such as
   ```
   import
   fl.transitions.easing.*;
   ```

   **Note:** See the following section, "Ease Tweened Animation," for more details on this line.

8. Type the name of the instance created in step **1** and a period.

9. Set the object's initial x position, such as `x = 100;`.

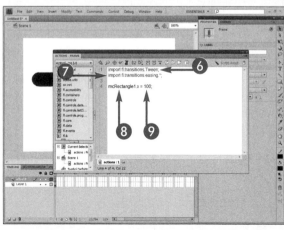

**10** Create an instance of the `Tween` class, such as `var myTween:Tween = new Tween();`.

**11** Within the parentheses, type the name of the instance from step **1** and a comma.

**12** Type `"x"`, `None.easeOut`, *InitialX*, *FinalX*, *Seconds*, `true`, replacing *InitialX* with the number that you set in step **9**, *FinalX* with the final x position that you want, and *Seconds* with the span that you want, such as 2.

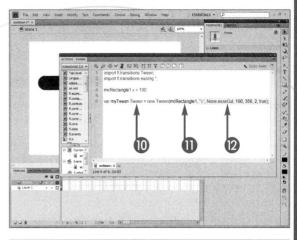

## TEST THE MOVIE

**13** Press Ctrl + Enter.

The movie plays.

● In this example, the clips starts at an x of 100 and moves to the right to an x of 350 over the span of 2 seconds.

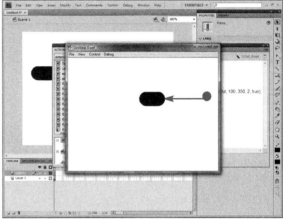

---

### Apply It

You need to create a separate instance of the `Tween` class for each property that you want to animate. Although this might seem tedious, it has a big advantage: Each property can be timed individually. In the following example, a `MovieClip` named `mcSquare1` has its `x` and `y` properties tweened over the course of 3 seconds, while its `alpha` property tweens to fade the clip from transparent to opaque over the course of 5 seconds. Therefore, the clip will stop moving before it finishes fading in.

```
import fl.transitions.Tween;
import fl.transitions.easing.*;
mcSquare1.x = 100;
mcSquare1.y = 100;
mcSquare1.alpha = 0;
var myTweenX:Tween = new Tween(mcSquare1, "x", None.easeOut, 100, stage.width, 3, true);
var myTweenY:Tween = new Tween(mcSquare1, "y", None.easeOut, 100, stage.height, 3, true);
var myTweenAlpha:Tween = new Tween(mcSquare1, "alpha", None.easeOut, 0, 1, 3, true);
```

# Ease Tweened Animation

You can use easing to change the speed at which an animation occurs to be nonlinear. When creating animation in code by manually adjusting property values, you can simulate easing by altering the value by which the property changes over time; see the section "Change the Speed of Animation" earlier in this chapter for details. When using tweens, you can use one of the classes in the easing package to apply a similar effect.

The easing package contains a set of classes that apply easing to tweens: Back, Bounce, Elastic, None, Regular, and Strong. Each class supports *easing in* through its easeIn method and *easing out* through the easeOut method. The Back class backs up the object and then moves it toward the target when easing in and overshoots the target and then backs to it when easing out. Bounce does what its name implies: It bounces the object.

Bounce.easeIn increases the speed of the bounce, and easeOut slows it down. Elastic causes the object to bounce in an exponentially decaying sine wave, accelerating with easeIn and decelerating with easeOut. None applies no easing. Regular simply speeds the object up gradually when easing in and slows it down when easing out. Strong functions much like Regular but is more pronounced.

You must import the class or classes that you want to use when applying an ease. You can be most efficient in your code by importing only the specific ease class you want to use, so if you plan to use Bounce, you could write import fl.transitions.easing.Bounce. However, you will need to write a separate import statement for each ease you will use; therefore, the generally accepted practice is to simply import all the classes by using the asterisk wildcard: import fl.transitions.easing.*.

## Ease Tweened Animation

### BOUNCE AN OBJECT USING THE ELASTIC CLASS

1. Create a MovieClip and place a named instance of it near the left edge of the Stage.

**Note:** See Chapter 3 for details on creating clips and naming instances.

2. Click the New Layer button.

3. Name the new layer "actions."

4. Click in the first frame of the new layer.

5. Press F9 to open the Actions panel.

**Note:** Easing can only be used in conjunction with code-based tweening. See the preceding section, "Create Tweens in Script," for details.

6. Type import fl.transitions.Tween;.

7. Type import fl.transitions. easing.*;

8. Type the name of the instance created in step **1** and a period.

9. Set the x position, such as x = 100;.

10. Repeat steps **8** and **9** to set the y coordinate to a number such as 100.

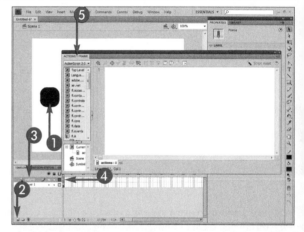

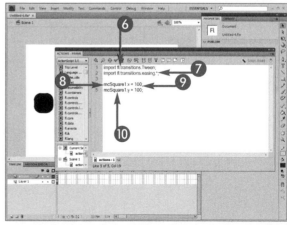

**⑪** Create an instance of the `Tween` class, such as `var myTweenX:Tween = new Tween();`.

**⑫** Within the parentheses, type the name of the instance from step **1** and a comma.

**⑬** Type `"x", Elastic.easeIn, InitialX, FinalX, Seconds, true,` replacing *InitialX* with the number that you set in step **9**, *FinalX* with the final x position that you want, and *Seconds* with the span that you want, such as 2.

**⑭** Repeat steps **11** to **13** to create another tween instance that animates the `y` property.

**TEST THE MOVIE**

**⑮** Press Ctrl + Enter.

The movie plays.

● The clips bounces on the Stage.

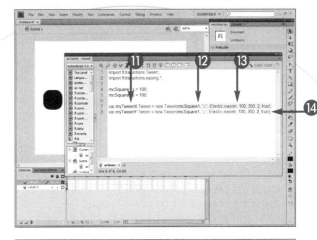

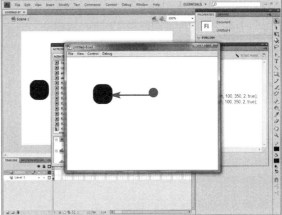

---

**Extra**

The `easing` classes, except `None`, support a third method, `easeInOut`, that enables you to apply both the in and out effect on the same ease. You must always provide a reference to one of the `easing` classes as part of the constructor for the `Tween` class. The `None` easing class is provided to allow you to reference easing without actually applying it. The class actually contains four methods: `easeIn`, `easeOut`, `easeNone`, and `easeInOut`, although all four do the exact same thing: They do not apply easing. Therefore, it makes no difference at all which of the four methods you choose to call. `easeNone` is provided as it makes the most logical sense; the other three exist to provide consistency with the other ease classes.

You cannot apply more than one ease to any given tween; however, each instance of a tween could in theory use a difference ease. Take care when applying different tweens to related properties. For example, applying a `Bounce` ease to the x property and an `Elastic` ease to the y property of the same object is possible but will likely produce an extremely strange result.

# Allow Users to Drag and Drop Objects

Y ou can add an additional level of interactivity to your movies by adding drag-and-drop capabilities. This way, your users will be able to "pick up" objects on the Stage and move them to other locations.

The Sprite class contains two methods to enable dragging and dropping. The appropriately named startDrag() method enables you to specify an object that the user can drag. You can then allow them to "let go" of the object — drop it — with the equally appropriate stopDrag() method.

Almost always, you will use the MOUSE_DOWN and MOUSE_UP events to trigger drag and drop. Although you can in theory use any event to trigger the action, these are the ones your user will most likely expect you to use. They are also the easiest to use because they represent opposing actions.

When dragging objects, you can test to determine whether it is touching another object by calling the hitTestObject() method. The method takes a single required argument: a reference to the object that you want to test to see if the object being dragged is hitting. For example, if you wanted to see if a MovieClip named mcStar1 was touching another clip, mcTarget1, when it was dropped, you would write mcStar1. hitTestObject(mcTarget1). The method returns a Boolean value and is thus almost always used as the condition in an if statement. A related hitTestPoint() method can be used to determine if an object has been dragged over a given x and y coordinate point. It therefore takes two required arguments: the x and y coordinates against which you want to test.

## Allow Users to Drag and Drop Objects

### CREATE TWO DRAGGABLE OBJECTS

1. Create two MovieClips on the Stage and name each instance.

2. Press F9 to open the ActionScript panel.

3. Type the name of one of the MovieClips and a period.

4. Add an event listener for the drag event handler that you will create, such as addEventListener (MouseEvent.MOUSE_DOWN, drag);.

5. Repeat step 3, referencing the same clip.

6. Add an event listener for the drop event handler that you will create, such as addEventListener (MouseEvent.MOUSE_UP, drop);.

7. Create the drag event handler, such as function drag(event:MouseEvent):void.

8. Type a pair of curly braces.

9. Within the braces, type event.target. startDrag();.

10. Below the closing brace, create the drop event handler, such as function drop(event: MouseEvent):void.

11. Type a pair of curly braces.

12. Within the braces, type event.target. stopDrag();.

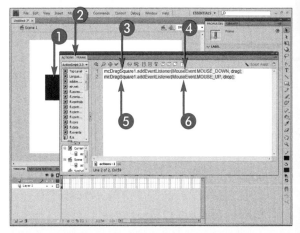

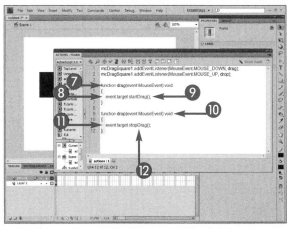

## MAKE ONE MOVE TO A SPECIFIED LOCATION IF DRAGGED OVER THE OTHER

⑬ Type `if(event.target.hitTestObject())`.

⑭ Within the inner parentheses, type the name of the second clip on the Stage.

⑮ Type a pair of curly braces.

⑯ Within the braces, type `event.target.x =`, a space, the x position that you want the object to move to (such as 100), and a semicolon.

## TEST THE MOVIE

⑰ Press Ctrl + Enter.

The movie plays.

⑱ Press and hold your mouse over the first clip and drag it.

The clip moves with the mouse cursor.

⑲ Release your mouse over the second clip.

The first clip jumps to the location specified in step **16**.

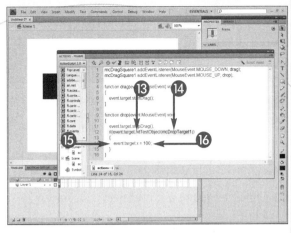

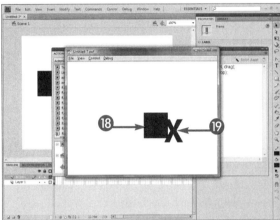

## Extra

The `startDrag()` method accepts an optional argument, `lockCenter`. You can provide a Boolean value to the argument; when `true`, the clip's center point will lock onto, or *snap to,* the mouse position. If you provide a value of `false`, the object will be dragged from whichever point the user actually clicked on it. The default value for the argument is `false`.

Likewise, the `hitTestPoint()` method also accepts an additional, optional argument, `shapeFlag`. This argument, also a Boolean, determines whether Flash Player should determine whether the shape is over the target pixel based on its actual pixels if true or its bounding box if false. Obviously, if the shape is rectangular, these are the same, and the argument is meaningless; however, if the shape is an ellipse, polygon, star, or other shape, then its bounding box will be larger than its actual pixels. If the argument is set to true and the shape is dragged over the target such that its bounding box, but not its pixels, are over the point, the method will return `false`. The default value of the argument is `false`.

# Animate in 3D

One of the most exciting additions to Flash Player 10 and Flash CS4 Professional is the ability to animate objects in three dimensions. 3D animation can be done on the Stage using the new 3D tools, which enable you to rotate objects not just along x and y axes, but also on the z axis. You can also move objects along the same z axis, the effect of which is to move the object toward or away from an imaginary vanishing point.

These properties also exist in ActionScript. Therefore, in addition to rotating objects in 2D by altering the rotationX and rotationY properties, you can use the rotationZ property to spin an object along that axis, providing a "flip" effect. You can also move an object toward or away from the vanishing point by changing the z property.

Increasing the z property causes the object to appear to move closer to the "camera," whereas decreasing it moves the object away. In effect, Flash will scale the shape up or down as it applies the effect, but the scaling will maintain perspective. If you want to use the rotationZ property, you must also use either rotationX or rotationY or both, as you will be unable to see the effect of the z rotation by itself.

Support for the z and rotationZ properties is unique to Flash Player 10. This version of the player was released in October 2008 alongside Flash CS4 Professional. Past experience suggests that it should take no more than one year for this version of Flash Player to reach 90% or better adoption. You can view version-specific adoption statistics for Flash Player at www.adobe.com/products/player_census/flashplayer/version_penetration.html.

## Animate in 3D

### ROTATE AN OBJECT

① Create a MovieClip and place a named instance of it near the left edge of the Stage.

**Note:** *See Chapter 3 for details on creating clips and naming instances.*

② Click the New Layer button.

③ Name the new layer "actions."

④ Click in the first frame of the new layer.

⑤ Press F9 to open the Actions panel.

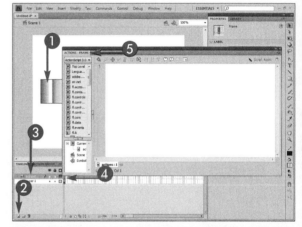

⑥ Create a number variable and set its initial value, such as var velocity:Number = 5;.

⑦ Type the name of the instance created in step **1** and a period.

⑧ Type addEventListener();.

⑨ Within the parentheses, type Event. ENTER_FRAME, a comma and a space, and the name of the event handler that you will add, such as animateClip.

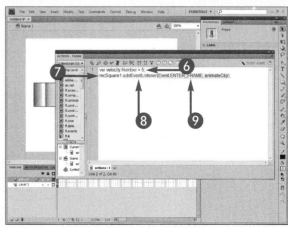

**10** Add the event handler, such as `function animateClip(event:Event):void`.

**11** Type a pair of curly braces.

**12** Within the braces, type `event.target.rotationX += NumberVariable;`, replacing `NumberVariable` with the variable created in step **6**.

**13** Repeat step **12**, replacing `rotationX` with `rotationY`.

**14** Repeat step **12** again, replacing `rotationX` with `rotationZ` this time.

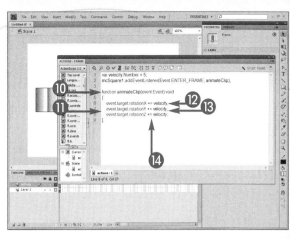

## TEST THE MOVIE

**15** Press Ctrl + Enter.

The movie plays.

● The clip animates, appearing to rotate in 3D space.

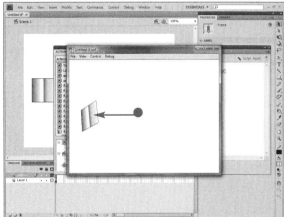

---

## Extra

Flash Player does not provide for "true" 3D effects. When you draw a shape on the Stage, it is a flat, 2D object. You can move or spin this object in all three dimensions, but it will remain a flat shape. Because of this, some developers have referred to the Flash 3D model as "postcards in space." True 3D animation — taking a shape that is actually drawn in all three dimensions and so actually has multiple sides and planes — requires a specific 3D tool such as Maya 3D or Bryce 3D.

You will most often apply these 3D effects to `MovieClips`. As `MovieClips` can contain almost any other object, the possibilities for 3D animation are almost endless. For example, you could use the clip to display images that could then be rotated in 3D. You can even insert video into the clip that will continue to play even as it is rotated.

# React to a Key Press

W hen developing interactive environments, it can be easy to become focused on dealing with the mouse and forget about the other important input device attached to every computer — the keyboard. However, keyboard input can be just as important — if not more important — than mouse input.

There are many advantages to responding to keyboard input. First, not everyone can use a mouse. For example, people with motor skill disabilities and the blind or visually impaired cannot use a mouse. Second, any given computer can have only a single mouse in use, but there are at least 85 keys on most standard keyboards, and ones with numeric keypads can have at least 102 keys. Because your script can be written to respond to each key press independently, you have many more options for interaction with the keyboard than with the mouse.

You can capture the keyboard input and respond to it by adding an event listener. The listener will use one of two constants of the `KeyboardEvent` class — `KEY_UP` or `KEY_DOWN`.

Every key has a key code associated with it. For example, the code for the up arrow key is 38, and the down arrow key is 40. This code is available to the event handler via the event's `keyCode` property. Using a simple `if` statement, you can test to see if the key you wanted to use has been pressed and then respond accordingly.

Only objects that have focus can respond to the keyboard. Users could in theory give a `MovieClip` or similar object on the Stage focus by clicking it, but if your goal in responding to the keyboard is to not require mouse interaction, you will generally need to attach the `Keyboard` event to the Stage.

## HAVE A KEY PRESS MOVE AN OBJECT

1. Create a `MovieClip` and place a named instance of it on the Stage.

*Note:* See Chapter 3 for details.

2. Click the New Layer button.

3. Name the new layer "actions."

4. Press F9 to open the Actions panel.

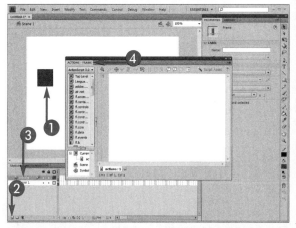

5. Add an event listener using `KEY_DOWN` for a handler that you will add, such as `stage.addEventListener (KeyboardEvent.KEY_DOWN, moveClip);`.

6. Add the event handler using `KeyboardEvent`, such as `function moveClip(event: KeyboardEvent):void`.

7. Type a pair of curly braces.

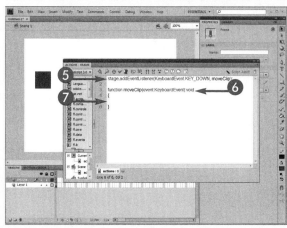

**8** Within the curly braces, type `if(event. keyCode == `*Number*`)`, replacing *Number* with the number of the key to which you want to react.

**9** Type a pair of curly braces.

**10** Within the inner braces, type the name of the clip that you created in step **1** and a period.

**11** Type the position change that you want for the reaction, such as `y += 10;`.

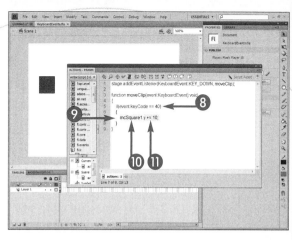

**TEST THE MOVIE**

**12** Press Ctrl + Enter.

The movie plays.

**13** Press the key that you specified in step **8** — the down arrow key in the sample code.

● In this example, the clip moves down 10 pixels.

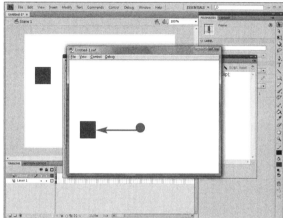

## Extra

You can determine which key has been pressed by placing a `trace` statement within the event handler and tracing the value of the `keyCode` property: `trace(event.keyCode);`. A complete list of the codes associated with each key can also be found at http://livedocs.adobe.com/flash/9.0/main/wwhelp/wwhimpl/common/html/wwhelp. htm?context=LiveDocs_Parts&file=00000311.html.

Flash CS4 Professional has a series of keyboard shortcuts used for selecting tools in the toolbox. For example, pressing the letter *V* on your keyboard activates the Selection tool, and pressing *T* gives you the Text tool. In normal usage, these shortcuts will speed up your design time. However, they pose a problem when attempting to test movies that respond to key presses. When you press Ctrl + Enter to test a movie, Flash Player launches, but Flash Professional is still running as well, so pressing the letter *V* will still select the Selection tool, even if your ActionScript code is written to do something else when pressing *V*. In order to get around this, you need to click Commands ➔ Disable Keyboard Shortcuts in the test movie window. Alternatively, you can click File ➔ Publish Preview ➔ Flash.

# Using Keyboard Constants

As mentioned in the preceding section, "React to a Key Press," you can determine which key was pressed by your user via the `keyCode` property of the `KeyboardEvent`. By comparing this to the proper code, you can make your movie react in specific ways depending on the pressed key.

However, using the actual codes for the keys is cumbersome. You could use a `trace` statement and while running your movie compare the output to the keys you press and determine the codes for each, but even still your movie is going to be difficult to maintain, as you are unlikely to easily remember that 38 is the code for the up arrow key. To work around this issue, ActionScript contains a `Keyboard` class, which contains a set of

constants that represent those keys commonly used in applications. Therefore, instead of this:

```
if(event.keyCode == 38)
```

You can write this:

```
if(event.keyCode == Keyboard.UP)
```

The `Keyboard` class is a static class, which simply means that you do not need to create an instance of it in order to use its constants. Static classes represent those things of which there can logically exist only a single instance, such as the keyboard and mouse. A complete list of the constants within the class can be viewed in the code hints in Flash when you type **Keyboard** and a period.

## Using Keyboard Constants

### HAVE A KEY PRESS MOVE AN OBJECT

1 Create a `MovieClip` and place a named instance of it on the Stage.

**Note:** See Chapter 3 for details.

2 Click the New Layer button.

3 Name the new layer "actions."

4 Press F9 to open the Actions panel.

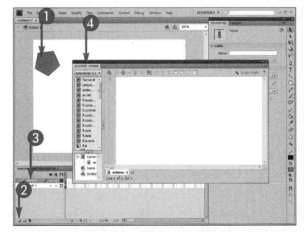

5 Add an event listener using `KEY_DOWN` for a handler that you will add, such as `stage.addEventListener(KeyboardEvent.KEY_DOWN, moveClip);`.

6 Add the event handler using `KeyboardEvent`, such as `function moveClip(event: KeyboardEvent):void`.

7 Type a pair of curly braces.

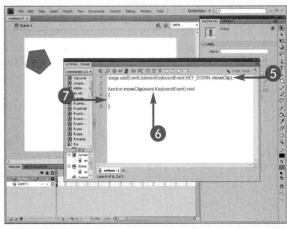

**8** Within the curly braces, type `if(event.keyCode == Keyboard.KEY)`, replacing *KEY* with the name of the key to which you want to react, such as `LEFT` for the left arrow key.

**9** Type a pair of curly braces.

**10** Within the inner braces, type the name of the clip that you created in step **1** and a period.

**11** Type the position change that you want for the reaction, such as `x += 10;`.

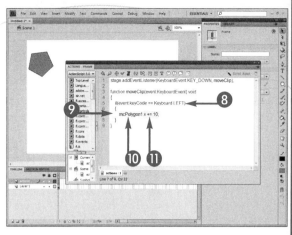

## TEST THE MOVIE

**12** Press Ctrl + Enter.

The movie plays.

**13** Press the key that you specified in step **8** — the left arrow key in the sample code.

● In this example, the clip moves 10 pixels to the left.

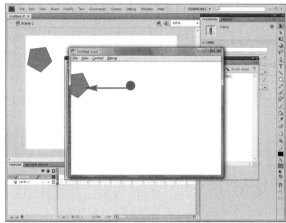

## Apply It

When testing against many keys, you may find it clearer to use a `switch` statement:

```
switch(event.keyCode)
{
                case Keyboard.UP:
                    mcStar.y -= 10;
                    break;
                case Keyboard.DOWN:
                    mcStar.y += 10;
                    break;
                case Keyboard.LEFT:
                    mcStar.x -= 10;
                    break;
                case Keyboard.RIGHT:
                    mcStar.x += 10;
                    break;
}
```

# Understanding Sound in Flash

**F**ew things can enliven your movie like sound. Whether it is a short sound effect clip or background music, voice narrations, or musical scores, a judicious use of sound can often make the difference in a project.

## Understanding Digital Sounds

Although not visible to the naked eye, sounds are made of waves that vary in frequency and amplitude. Digital sounds are visually represented as *waveforms*. Waveforms appear as vertically stacked lines of varying heights, resembling the output from a seismic chart of an earthquake. The more intense the sound, the taller and denser the waveform line measurement.

For computer usage, sounds are transformed into mathematical equations, called *digital sampling*. Digital quality is measured by how many samples exist in a single second of the sound, called the *sampling rate*. Sampling rates are expressed in *kilohertz* (kHz). Higher sampling rates result in larger files and clearer sounds. Typically, sampling size is measured in 8, 16, or 24 bits. The *bit rate* is the amount of data that is streamed or encoded for each second that plays in a sound file. Higher bit rates result in higher-quality sound waves.

Like graphics, sounds can consume large amounts of disk space and RAM, and stereo sounds use twice as much data as mono sounds. You can set compression options for reducing event sounds and streaming sounds when publishing and exporting your Flash files. Compression simply reduces the overall file size of an audio clip. Keep in mind that the more you compress a sound and lower the sampling rate, the smaller the sound file and the lower the sound quality. It may take some experimentation to find the right balance between file size and sound quality in your own Flash movies.

## Sounds on the Timeline

All sounds that you add in Flash, whether music, narration, or sound effects, fall into two categories: event driven and streamed. An action in your movie triggers event-driven sounds, and these types of sounds must be downloaded completely before playing in your movie. Using the Timeline, you can assign an event sound to start playing on a specific keyframe, and it will continue to play independently of the Timeline for your movie. If the event sound is longer than your movie, it continues to play even when your movie stops. You can use event sounds when you do not want to synchronize a sound clip with frames in your movie.

Streamed sounds are downloaded as they are needed and start playing even if the entire clip has not yet finished downloading. Flash synchronizes streamed sounds with the frames of your movie and attempts to keep any animation in sync with the streamed sounds.

When assigning event or streamed sounds, you can use the options in the Property Inspector to specify the sound type. Flash offers four sync options — event, stream, start, and stop — based on what you want the sound to do.

## Sound File Formats

Flash recognizes a large variety of sound file formats. You can import WAV, AIFF, MP3, System 7 Sounds (Mac), Sun AU, Sound Designer II (Mac), and QuickTime file formats into your movies. You need to install QuickTime 4 or later to support some of the sound file formats. When importing sounds, Flash works best with 16-bit sounds.

You can export the audio you use in your Flash movies in MP3 format, or you can compress it as ADPCM, MP3, or RAW. You can find compression options in the Publish Settings dialog box. You can check the file format for any sound clip using the Sound Properties dialog box. The dialog box offers detailed information about the sound clip, including file size and compression assigned to the clip.

If you create Flash content for mobile devices, you can publish your Flash movie with device sounds, which are encoded in the device's native file format. Device sound formats include MIDI, MFi, and SMAF.

## Adding Sounds in Flash

You can import sounds from other sources to use in your Flash movies. Flash stores imported sounds in the library. You add sound clips in the same way that you add other frame content. Although you can add only one sound per frame in Flash, you can use multiple layers for different sounds. For example, you can add new sounds to the same frame but assign them to different layers. To help keep your movie organized, it is a good practice to add sounds to their own layers in a movie.

## Controlling Sounds

You can use the Property Inspector to control sounds in a movie, such as changing the sound type and creating sounds that repeat, or *loop.* You can also apply sound effects to fade sound in or out or appear to emanate from the left speaker channel or right speaker channel. You can also find a few rudimentary features for editing sounds in Flash using the Edit Envelope dialog box. This dialog box enables you to set beginning and end points for a sound and control the volume of a sound while it plays in a movie.

However, you should keep in mind that Flash is not designed to be an audio editing tool. If your movie sounds require more detailed editing, use a sound editing program, such as Adobe Soundbooth CS4 or Apple Logic Pro 7, to modify the sound clip before importing it for use in Flash.

You can also use ActionScript to control how a sound plays in a movie. ActionScript can be used to set up buttons that can start or stop sounds or control the volume, as well as for importing the sound and setting what kinds of events can be used as triggers for the sound.

## Using Sound Judiciously

Although sound can add a degree of professionalism to a project if done right, it can as easily detract from the project if done incorrectly. There are several factors to consider when adding sound files. First, you must think about whether the sound is actually enhancing your project or if you are adding it simply because you can. Second, consider that many users may be unable to hear the sound, either due to a physical disability or, more often, due simply to the fact that they either do not have speakers or they are turned off. You must think about how these users will be able to obtain information from your site if that information is presented only through sound. Third, keep in mind that sound files will increase the file size of your movie, possibly dramatically.

# Add a Sound to the Library and Play It

Two options exist for playing sounds in a Flash movie. First, you can import a sound directly into the project's library, export it for ActionScript, and then create an instance of it to play. Second, you can load an external sound file.

Both methods have their pros and cons. The biggest advantage of playing sounds from the library is that you do not need to deal with remembering to upload additional files to the server. Loading an external sound is covered in the next section, "Load and Play an External Sound."

Playing a sound from the library involves a process almost identical to that used when creating instances of `MovieClip`s in code. You begin by adding the sound to the library. See the preceding section, "Understanding Sound in Flash," for information on what formats are

supported by Flash. Once imported, you can right-click the sound file in the library to access its properties. Just as you would do for a `MovieClip`, when you export the file for ActionScript, you provide a unique class name for the sound.

After you have the sound marked for export, you can add it to your code and create an instance. For example, if you exported a sound as `SoundTrack`, you might type something like this: `var mySound:Sound = new SoundTrack();`.

Finally, you can call the `play()` method of the `Sound` class to have your sound file play. You can call this method directly in your code, in which case the sound will begin playing as soon as your movie loads and will play in its entirety, or you can call it within an event handler.

## Add a Sound to the Library and Play It

① Click File → Import → Import to Library.

The Import to Library dialog box opens.

② Navigate to the folder that contains your sound file.

③ Click the sound file.

④ Click Open.

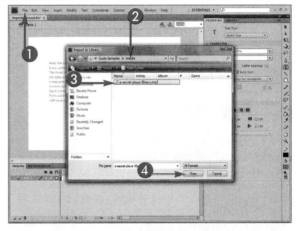

The sound is imported to the library.

⑤ Click Library.

⑥ Right-click the sound.

⑦ Click Properties.

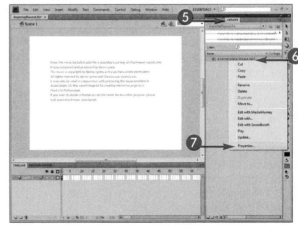

The Sound Properties dialog box appears.

⑧ Check Export for ActionScript.

⑨ Type a class name for the sound.

⑩ Click OK.

A dialog box appears stating that the classpath will be automatically generated.

⑪ Click OK.

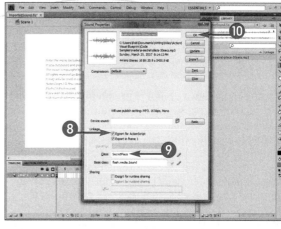

The sound is exported for script.

⑫ Press F9 to open the Actions panel.

⑬ Type var *variableName*: Sound = new, replacing *variableName* with the name that you want for your sound variable.

⑭ Type the class name you used in step **9** and a pair of parentheses.

⑮ Type the sound variable name from step **13**, a period, and then play();.

⑯ Press Ctrl + Enter.

Flash Player runs. In this example, the movie is blank visually, but the sound plays.

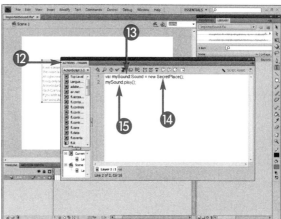

## Extra

When you export the sound for ActionScript, Flash will provide a default class name for your sound file, which will simply be the same as the file itself. Unfortunately, this default class name will not work, as it will contain the file extension. Although the extension by itself is not a problem, the dot separating the filename from the extension will cause your ActionScript code to fail because class names cannot contain dots. For example, if you import a sound file weddingmusic.mp3 and accept the default class name of weddingmusic.wav, when you try to create an instance of that class, you would need to type

```
var theMusic:Sound = wedddingmusic.mp3();
```

You can see that this appears to be an attempt to call an mp3 method of class weddingmusic. Therefore, you should change the class name. At the very least, you should remove the dot and file extension, but to maintain coding standards, you should also convert the filename to the standard casing scheme used for classes. Therefore, the preceding example should be given a class name of WeddingMusic.

# Load and Play an External Sound

Rather than play a sound from the library, you can load an external sound file at runtime. This offers advantages over playing sounds from the library. First, by loading sounds into the library, you are increasing the file size of your movie. If you load external sounds, your movie's file size will remain smaller, so it can load and play faster. This is particularly beneficial if you do not believe that all your users will encounter the section of the movie that contains the sound. Second, by keeping the sounds apart from your Flash movie, you can change them at will by simply placing new sounds on the Web server. If you have sounds playing from the library, you would need to open Flash CS4 Professional, import the sound, export for ActionScript, and then republish your movie every time you wanted to change the sound.

In order to load external sounds, you must first create an instance of the Sound class. Then you can call its load() method. This method takes as an argument an instance of the URLRequest class, which is used any time that you want to call files from a Web server. The URLRequest class simplifies the process by which Flash can call external resources and is discussed in more detail in Chapter 17.

Once loaded, the sound can be started by calling its play() method. Other methods of the Sound class also exist to further control the sound; they are discussed in detail later in this chapter.

## Load and Play an External Sound

① Open the Actions panel.

② Type the beginning of a string variable, such as var filePath:String, and an equals sign.

③ Within quotation marks, type the name of the sound file to be loaded and a semicolon.

**Note:** If necessary, you may need to include the directory in which the sound resides.

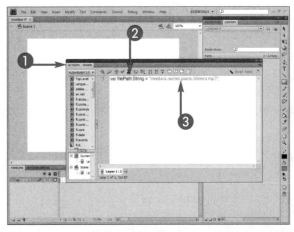

④ Create an instance of the URLRequest class and pass it the variable from step **2**, such as var request: URLRequest = new URLRequest(filePath);.

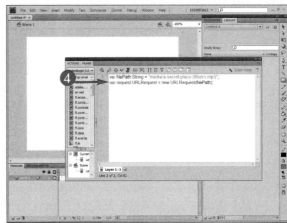

⑤ Create an instance of the Sound class, such as `var mySound:Sound = new Sound();`.

⑥ Call its `load()` method and pass it the variable from step **4**, such as `mySound.load(request);`.

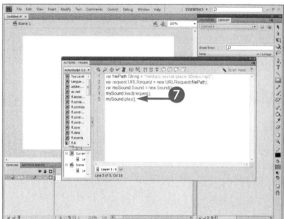

⑦ Type the variable name from step **5**, a period, and then `play();`.

⑧ Press Ctrl + Enter.

Flash Player runs. In this example, the movie is blank visually, but the sound plays.

**Note:** *You may need to save the file before you can test it.*

## Extra

It is worth noting that although loading an external sound file will reduce the size of the SWF when compared to those with sounds imported in the library, the actual download time for the user will, in the end, be the same. For example, there is no real logical difference between downloading a 1MB SWF that includes embedded sounds and downloading a 200KB SWF and then downloading an 800KB MP3: You end up downloading 1MB either way. The file size advantage to loading sounds at runtime is that the SWF will download *initially* much faster, so the user can begin interacting with it immediately.

In the example shown here, only the filename is given for the sound, which means that the sound file must be in the same directory on the Web server as the SWF. If you want to store your sounds in another directory, you can provide a relative path to the file instead. For example, instead of setting a `filePath` variable above to `"music.mp3"`, you could use `"sounds/music.mp3"`, or even a more complex path such as `"../sounds/soundtrack/music.mp3"`.

# Avoid Errors Due to Loading Delays

**W**hen your users access your movie over the Internet, there will likely be a delay before an externally loaded sound file can play due to download time. Any attempt to play the sound before loading will cause an error.

You can avoid this error by adding an event listener to your sound instance and listening for the Complete event. This event is broadcast any time you load an external file, and not surprisingly, it is broadcast when the file has completed downloading. By placing your sound's play command within the event handler, you can ensure that Flash Player will not attempt to play the sound until it is downloaded and ready.

Any time you begin relying on external sources for your content, you increase the possibility of errors. The sound

file may not actually be on the server, or its path may have been specified incorrectly. The server may be down, or the user may have lost his or her Internet connection.

You can prevent potential runtime errors from occurring by testing to be sure that the sound loads successfully. The easiest method for doing this is to add an event listener to the sound that listens for the I/O error event. I/O stands for *input/output,* and the event will occur only if something — anything — happens to prevent the sound from loading successfully. Therefore, if you have a sound instance called theTheme, you could write theTheme.addEventListener(IOErrorEvent.IO_ERROR, loadError). The loadError method could then simply contain some sort of friendly output to your users explaining that an error occurred in loading the sound and that they should try again later.

## Avoid Errors Due to Loading Delays

### WAIT FOR THE SOUND TO LOAD

**1** Create an instance of the URLRequest class, passing to it a file path to a sound file.

**2** Create an instance of the Sound class and then call its load method, passing the URLRequest instance.

**Note:** *See the preceding section, "Load and Play an External Sound," for details on these steps.*

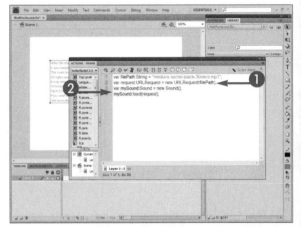

**3** Type the name of the sound instance created in step **2** and a period.

**4** Type addEventListener(Event. COMPLETE, a comma and a space, and the name of the event handler that you will add, such as completionHandler, followed by );.

**5** Add the event handler, such as function completionHandler (event:Event):void, and a pair of curly braces.

**6** Within the braces, type event. target.play();.

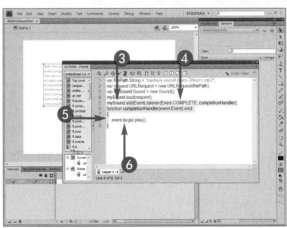

## HANDLE LOADING ERRORS

**7** Create a text field to display an error message, such as `var txtError Display:TextField = new TextField();`.

**8** Add the field to the page, such as `addChild(txtErrorDisplay);`.

**9** Type the name of the sound instance created in step **2** and a period.

**10** Type `addEventListener (IOErrorEvent.IO_ERROR, loadError);`.

**11** Type `function loadError(event: IOErrorEvent):void`.

**12** Type a pair of curly braces.

**13** Within the curly braces, place the error message in the field, such as `txtErrorDisplay.text = "An error occurred in loading the file.";`.

**14** Press Ctrl + Enter.

The movie plays. The sound plays. If an error occurs, it will be displayed in the text box.

**Note:** *You can force an error to test the error handler by intentionally entering an incorrect file path in step **1**.*

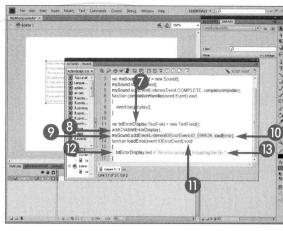

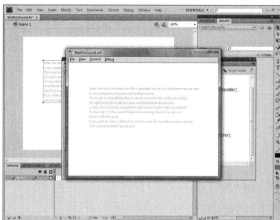

---

### Apply It

You can create a progress indication to let the user know that a large file is downloading. You can use the `Progress` event to test the number of bytes that have loaded, and by dividing this by the total number of bytes in the file, you can determine how much of the file has loaded. You can then either use this number to manipulate a drawn object, as shown in the following, or display the number in a text field.

```
var request:URLRequest = new URLRequest("music.mp3");
var mySound:Sound = new Sound();
mySound.load(request);
mySound.addEventListener(ProgressEvent.PROGRESS, showProgress);
function showProgress(event:ProgressEvent):void
{
            progressBar.width = 100 * (event.bytesLoaded/event.bytesTotal);
}
```

# Pause and Resume Sounds

**A**lthough sounds can be played directly using the `play()` method of the `Sound` class, you can establish more control over your sound by isolating it in a channel. Audio professionals have long worked with multitrack recordings, which allow individual recordings so that they can be edited later. The ActionScript `SoundChannel` class mimics this functionality, although it has applications beyond mere recording of audio. You should note that the channels created by the class are not left and right channels but rather represent individual tracks of sound. Either stereo or mono sounds can be placed in a channel.

One particular advantage of using channels is that they allow you to further control the sound by stopping, pausing, and resuming it. You can stop a sound by

calling the `stop()` method; note, however, that this is a method of the channel, not the sound, whereas `play()` is a method of the sound itself.

You also pause a sound by calling the channel's `stop()` method. Generally, the difference between pausing and stopping is that with a pause, you will want the sound to resume playing at the point at which it was paused. Fortunately, the channel contains a `position` property that stores the point at which the sound is currently playing. By storing this value in a variable before you pause, you can pass it back to the `play` method and resume where you left off.

All of these actions can of course be placed into event handlers for buttons or other user interface objects, allowing your user to start, stop, and pause the playback of the sound in your movie.

## Pause and Resume Sounds

### CREATE BUTTONS TO PAUSE AND RESUME THE SOUNDS

1. Create a pause and resume button, giving each an appropriate instance name.

2. Create a new layer named "actions."

3. Click in the first frame of the new layer.

4. Press F9 to open the ActionScript panel.

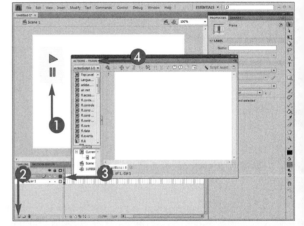

5. Create an instance of the `URLRequest` class, passing to it a file path to a sound file.

6. Create an instance of the `Sound` class called `mySound` and call its `load` method, passing the `URLRequest` instance.

7. Create an instance of the `SoundChannel` class called `myChannel`, such as `var myChannel:SoundChannel = new SoundChannel();`.

8. Type `myChannel = mySound.play();`.

9. Type the name of the pause button and a period.

10. Type `addEventListener(MouseEvent. CLICK, pauseHandlerName);`, using the name of the event handler that you will add.

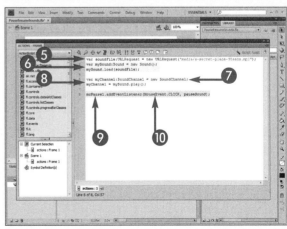

⑪ Add the event handler, such as `function pauseSound (event:MouseEvent):void`, and a pair of curly braces.

⑫ Type `var position = myChannel.position;`.

⑬ Type `myChannel.stop();`.

⑭ Type the name of the resume button, a period, and `addEventListener(MouseEvent.CLICK, resume HandlerName);` using the name of the resume event handler that you will add.

⑮ Add the event handler, such as `function resume Sound(event:MouseEvent):void`, and a pair of curly braces.

⑯ Type `myChannel = mySound.play(myChannel. position);`.

**TEST THE MOVIE**

⑰ Press Ctrl + Enter.

The movie loads in Flash Player. The sound starts playing.

⑱ Click the pause button.

The sound stops.

⑲ Click the resume button.

The sound resumes.

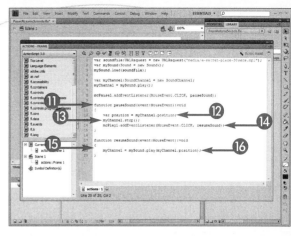

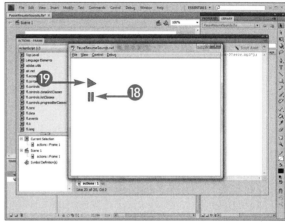

---

**Apply It**

In the example shown here, two buttons are used. It is possible to do this with a single button instead. To do this, you would need to create a `MovieClip` with two keyframes. In one frame, draw the symbol to represent pause and in the other, the symbol representing resume or play. Label each frame.

Then you could write the pause event handler as the following:

```
function pauseSound(event:MouseEvent):void
{
                myButton.removeEventListener(MouseEvent.CLICK, pauseSound);
                myButton.gotoAndStop("resume");
                var position:Number = channel.position;
                channel.stop();
                myButton.addEventListener(MouseEvent.CLICK, resumeSound);
}
```

Your resume function would look very similar:

```
function resumeSound(event:MouseEvent):void
{
                myButton.removeEventListener(MouseEvent.CLICK, resumeSound);
                myButton.gotoAndStop("pause");
                channel.play(position);
                myButton.addEventListener(MouseEvent.CLICK, pauseSound);
}
```

# Control Sound Volume

ActionScript provides a `SoundTransform` class that enables you to manipulate the volume of sound during playback. You set the volume by manipulating the `volume` property of an instance of the `transform` object. The value is expressed as a number ranging from 0 to 1, with 0 representing no volume or mute and 1 representing full volume.

The `SoundChannel` class contains a `soundTransform` property that represents an instance of the `transform` class. By setting the volume in an instance of the `transform` class and then applying that instance to the channel, you can adjust the volume.

The user interface to manipulate volume can be handled in any way that you choose. At the simplest level, you could simply have a button that, when clicked, mutes the sound, and that when clicked again, restores the volume. Alternatively, you could have a series of buttons representing various volume levels or even a more complex `MovieClip` that allows the user to drag a slider up to increase the volume or down to decrease it. See Chapter 13 for details on using drag and drop in your movies. You could even, in theory, control volume simply through mouse movement by detecting the `mouseX` coordinates relative to the Stage and then increasing the volume as the user moves the mouse right and decreasing it on a left move. You could also use the `mouseY` coordinates to achieve the same effect with up and down movement, although you should keep in mind that in Flash, downward movement increases the `y` value, so you would actually need to calculate the opposite of the `mouseY` coordinate. To keep the code in the example here simple, only a mute/unmute button will be shown.

## Control Sound Volume

### CREATE A MUTE/UNMUTE BUTTON

1. Create a `MovieClip` with two keyframes in its Timeline. In one frame, labeled "mute," draw a shape representing mute; in the other, labeled "unmute," draw an opposite symbol.

2. Place an instance of the symbol on the Stage and give it an instance name of `mcVolume`.

3. Return to the main Timeline.

4. Create a new layer named "actions" and click in its first frame.

5. Press F9 to open the Actions panel.

6. Create an instance of `SoundChannel`, such as `var channel:SoundChannel = new SoundChannel();`.

7. Create an instance of `SoundTransform`, such as `var muteControl:SoundTransform = new SoundTransform();`.

8. Create an instance of `URLRequest`, passing to it a file path to a sound file.

9. Create an instance of `Sound` and call its `load` method, passing the `URLRequest` instance.

10. Call the play method for the channel, such as `channel = mySound.play();`.

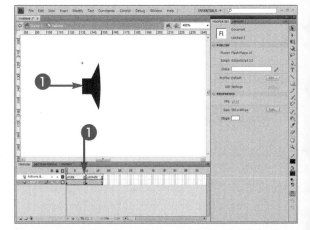

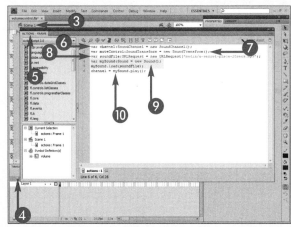

⑪ Type the mute event listener, such as `mcVolume.addEventListener(MouseEvent.CLICK, muteSound);`.

⑫ Type the mute event handler, such as `function muteSound(event:MouseEvent):void`, and a pair of curly braces.

⑬ Remove the listener, such as `event.target.removeEventListener(MouseEvent.CLICK, muteSound);`.

⑭ Type `event.target.gotoAndStop("mute");`.

⑮ Mute the control, such as `muteControl.volume = 0;`.

⑯ Set the channel to the mute variable, such as `channel.soundTransform = muteControl;`.

⑰ Add the unmute listener, such as `event.target.addEventListener(MouseEvent.CLICK, unMuteSound);`.

⑱ Repeat steps **12** to **17** to create the unmute handler.

**TEST THE MOVIE**

⑲ Press Ctrl + Enter.

The movie loads, and the sound plays.

⑳ Click the button.

The sound is muted, and the button changes to show the unmute state.

㉑ Click the button again.

The sound's volume is restored.

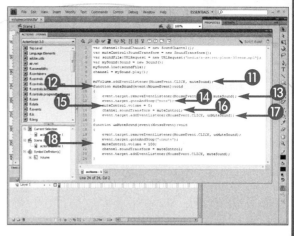

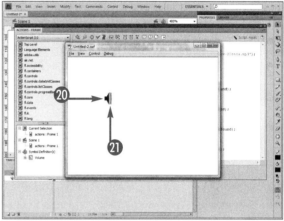

---

**Extra**

If you have more than one sound playing, you can stop all sounds by calling the `stopAllSounds()` method of the `SoundMixer` class. The class is static; you do not need to create an instance of it to use it. You can also apply effects created with a `SoundTransform` instance, such as volume control, by applying the `SoundTransform` instance to the `SoundMixer`'s `soundTransform` property.

If you are using stereo sound, you can manipulate the `SoundTransform`'s pan property to pan the sound between the two speakers. Values for the property range from –1 to 1. A value of –1 puts all the sound in the left speaker, whereas a value of 1 uses only the right speaker. A value of 0, the default, evenly divides the sound. Although it can be fun to play with panning, keep in mind that very few computer users have speakers properly positioned to hear true stereo sound, so the effect will be limited or potentially lost altogether for them.

# Display Information about Sound Files

When recording sound, most MP3 encoders have the ability to inject metadata into the file. *Metadata* is data about data — generally, text that describes the data. Metadata is generally used for search purposes, as it provides text on which to search otherwise unsearchable binary files. Modern MP3 encoders almost universally follow a standard developed in the late 1990s: Called *ID3,* it provides a standard set of "tags" to describe music files.

ActionScript contains an `ID3Info` class that can be used to read ID3 tags in your music. You can use this to display the title of the song, the artist, the album, the length of the music, or any other piece of information that was encoded into the file. A total of seven ID3 tags are represented by properties of the `id3` property of the

Sound class: `comment`, `album`, `genre`, `songName`, `artist`, `track`, and `year`. If, for example, you have a sound clip named `mySound`, you could read the track's title into a text field named `txtSongTitle` like so:

```
txtSongTitle.text = mySound.id3.songName;
```

The remaining ID3 tags are represented by four-letter constants. The composer, for example, would be read using `mySound.id3.TCOM`. You can view a complete list of the tags and their associated constants online at http://livedocs.adobe.com/flash/9.0/ActionScriptLangRefV3/flash/media/Sound.html#id3.

When reading a tag directly, ActionScript will always return `undefined` for tags that are not encoded within a particular sound.

## Display Information about Sound Files

### DISPLAY THE SONG TITLE AND LENGTH

① Create an instance of the `URLRequest` class, passing to it a file path to a sound file.

② Create an instance of the `Sound` class and call its `load` method, passing the `URLRequest` instance.

③ Add the event listener, such as `mySound.addEvent Listener(Event.COMPLETE,displayInfo);`.

④ Add the event handler, such as `function displayInfo(event:Event):void`

⑤ Type a pair of curly braces.

⑥ Within the braces, call the `play` method, such as `mySound.play();`.

⑦ Create a text field to display the song title, such as `var txtSongTitle:TextField = new TextField();`.

⑧ Create a text field to display the song length, such as `txtSongLength:TextField = new TextField();`.

⑨ Set the y position for the first field, such as `txtSongTitle.y = 10;`.

⑩ Set the y position for the second field in relation to the first, such as `txtSongLength.y = txtSong Title.y + txtSongTitle.height + 10;`.

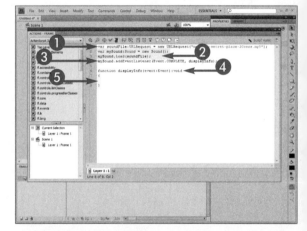

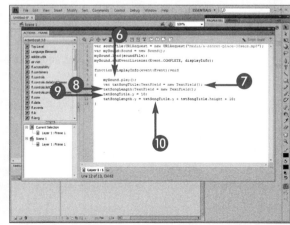

⑪ Set the text of the first field to the song title ID3 information, such as `txtSongTitle.text = mySound.id3.songName;`.

⑫ Set the text of the second field to the song length ID3 information, such as `txtSongLength.text = mySound.id3.TLEN;`.

⑬ Add the song title field to the page, such as `addChild(txtSongTitle);`.

⑭ Add the song length field to the page, such as `addChild(txtSongLength);`.

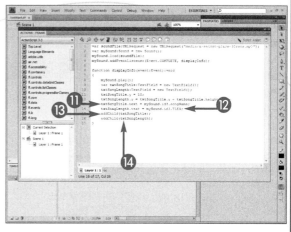

**TEST THE MOVIE**

⑮ Press Ctrl + Enter.

The movie runs, and the song plays.

● The title and length of the track are displayed in the text fields.

**Note:** *If an error occurs, then the ID3 tag for that particular property has not been encoded into your MP3. This can be avoided by wrapping the statement that applies the tag to the text field in an `if` statement.*

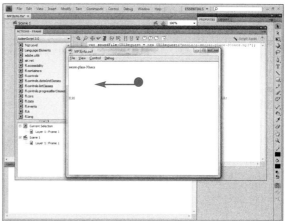

**Apply It**

ActionScript also supports an `ID3` event, which is called whenever Flash Player encounters an ID3 tag. Using this event and a `for` loop, you could theoretically return a list of all of a particular song's ID3 data:

```
mySound.addEventListener(Event.ID3, displayAllTags);
function displayAllTags(event:Event):void
{
            var id3Properties:ID3Info = event.target.id3;
            for(var propertyName:String in id3Properties)
            {
                trace("ID3 Tag: " & propertyName & "=" & id3Properties[propertyName]);
            }
}
```

# Convert Video to Flash Video

Although you can import a variety of formats of images and sound files into your Flash projects, only one format is supported for video: Flash Video. In order to work in video in Flash, you need to convert it from whichever format it was created in to the Flash Video format. Flash Video files provide a small file size while maintaining quality. Flash Video is commonly referred to as *FLV*, after the file extension used with converted movies.

When you install Flash CS4 Professional, the Adobe Media Encoder is automatically installed as well. You need to use the Adobe Media Encoder in order to convert video from its original source format to FLV. You can access it either from the first screen of the Import Video dialog box or directly from the operating system through the Start menu or the Dock.

The Media Encoder allows you to select a source video file. Almost every widely supported video format, including AVI, MOV, and MPEG, are supported by the encoder. You can either choose to encode it as FLV, to use in Flash movies; the new F4V format, which offers higher-quality conversion than FLV; or the H.264 format for use on the Apple iPhone. You can select from a list of presets for the size and quality of the movie and select a path to which the resulting file is saved. The Media Encoder also supports batch converting, so if you have multiple videos to convert, you can add them all to the encoder and then leave it to run by itself. Encoding can be a very slow process.

## Convert Video to Flash Video

1 Click File.

2 Click Import.

3 Click Import Video.

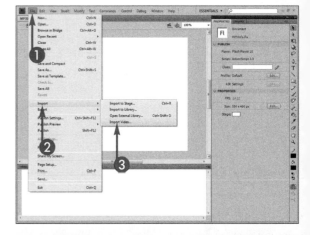

The Import Video dialog box appears.

4 Click Launch Adobe Media Encoder.

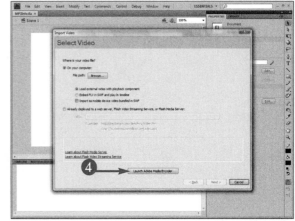

The Adobe Media Encoder
launches.

**⑤** Click Add.

The Open dialog box appears.

**⑥** Navigate to the folder containing
the video that you want to convert.

**⑦** Click the video file.

**⑧** Click Open.

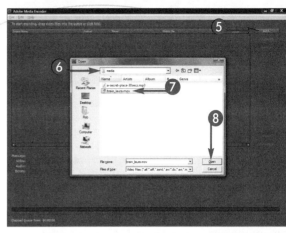

**⑨** Click here and select a format.

**⑩** Select a preset.

**⑪** Click Start Queue.

The video is converted to FLV
format.

---

**Extra**

You can also convert videos to the Flash Video format directly from within Adobe's video suite of products. These include Adobe Premiere Pro CS4, a professional-level video editing application and Adobe After Effects CS4, a powerful animation tool used by most professional producers to create title sequences, work with blue- and green-screen effects, and much more. These two products, along with Adobe Encore CS4 for burning DVD and Blu-ray discs, Adobe Soundbooth CS4 for audio editing, and Adobe OnLocation CS4 for recording live video, can be purchased as part of the Adobe Creative Suite 4 Production Premium suite. The suite also includes Flash, Photoshop CS4, and Illustrator CS4.

The Flash Video format is a noneditable format, much like SWF. All the editing that you need to do with your video must be done in a video editing tool such as Adobe Premiere Pro or Final Cut Pro. The techniques involved in effectively shooting and editing video are beyond the scope of this book.

# Using the FLVPlayback Component Visually

The simplest method of inserting Flash Video into a Flash movie is to use the `FLVPlayback` component. Components are special `MovieClips` that are included with Flash and contain prebuilt functionality. The FLV component greatly simplifies the process of inserting Flash Video into a movie. It relies on ActionScript, but all the coding and implementation are hidden from view.

You need to convert your video to the FLV format before you can use the component. See the previous section, "Convert Video to Flash Video," for details on how to convert to FLV.

Flash includes a wizard that steps you through the process of loading the FLV into the component. The wizard provides a simple, three-step process for conversion. You can select a video on your hard drive and configure the look and feel of the control buttons. After you complete the wizard, Flash places an instance of the playback component on the Stage. The `FLVPlayback` component includes all the visual elements and code necessary to control the video. You can then simply save the file, upload both it and the FLV file to your Web server, and enjoy the video.

You can select the instance of the component on the Stage and use the Component Inspector panel to alter its settings if you want to. A few of the available settings include the *skin,* or playback controls, and whether the video plays automatically. You can open the Component Inspector from the Window menu.

## Using the FLVPlayback Component Visually

**Note:** If the Import Video dialog box is already open, skip to step **2**.

1. Click File → Import → Import Video.

   The Import Video Wizard appears.

2. Click Browse.

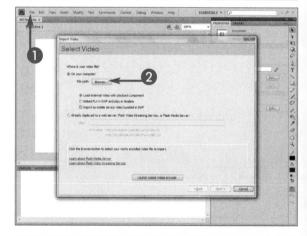

The Open dialog box appears.

3. Navigate to the folder containing the video that you want to use.

4. Click the video file.

**Note:** Be sure to select an FLV video.

5. Click Open.

   You are returned to the Import Video Wizard.

6. Click Next.

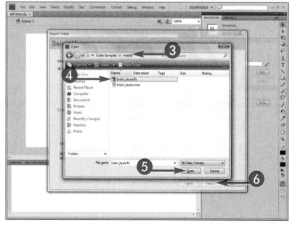

**7** Click here and select a skin.

**8** If needed, click here and select a color for the skin.

**9** Click Next.

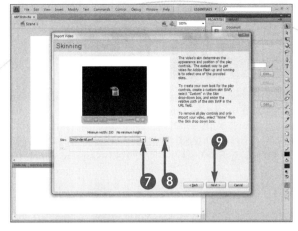

The Finish Video Import screen appears.

**10** Click Finish.

The wizard closes, and an instance of the component is placed on the Stage.

## Extra

You can also add video to your movie without using the Import Video Wizard, as long as the video has already been converted to FLV. You can click Window → Components to open the Components panel. Click the plus sign next to Video to expand that category and then drag the FLVPlayback component to the Stage. You can then open the Component Inspector panel by using the Window menu or the keyboard shortcut Shift + F7. Within the Component Inspector panel, you will see a Source setting. Clicking in the Value box for this setting produces a magnifying glass icon; clicking the icon will allow you to browse your hard drive for the FLV. You can also select a skin and change its colors and configure any other settings that you want.

There is no particular advantage or disadvantage to inserting the video via the wizard or doing it yourself by dragging the component to the Stage and configuring it manually. The end result is the same either way.

# Using the FLVPlayback Component in Code

Instead of creating the `FLVPlayback` component visually on the Stage and using the Import Video Wizard and Component Inspector panels to configure its settings, you can instantiate it through code. This provides additional flexibility not offered when using the component visually.

Before you can use the component in code, you still must place an instance of it in your library. You can do this by dragging the `FLVPlayback` component either to the Stage or directly to the library. If you drag it to the Stage, you will want to remove the instance before proceeding.

In your code, you will need to import the classes from the `fl.video` package, using the `*` wildcard. Then you can create an instance of the `FLVPlayback` class, set its

source property to the path to the FLV file, and finally, use the `addChild()` method to add it to the Stage.

If you do not add a skin to your component, it will play but only once, not providing your users with any method by which they can rewind the video or play it again. You can add a skin to your video by setting the `FLVPlayback` instance's `skin` property to the name of one of the prebuilt skins that come with Flash. You can browse through the available skins using the Component Inspector. You can also modify the `skinBackgroundColor` and `skinBackgroundAlpha` properties to change the appearance of the skin to better match your Web site. The `skinBackgroundColor` property takes any valid hexadecimal color, and the `skinBackgroundAlpha` property takes a number between 0 for transparent and 1 for opaque.

## Using the FLVPlayback Component in Code

### ADD THE FLVPLAYBACK COMPONENT TO YOUR LIBRARY

1. Click Window → Components.

2. Click the plus sign next to Video.

3. Drag the `FLVPlayback` component to the Stage.

4. Click the component instance and press the Delete key.

- The component is added to the library.

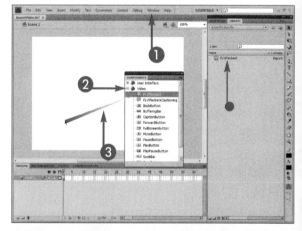

### USE THE COMPONENT IN CODE

5. Press F9 to open the Actions panel.

6. Type `import fl.video.*;`.

7. Create an instance of the `FLVPlayback` class, such as
`var myVideo:FLVPlayback = new FLVPlayback();`.

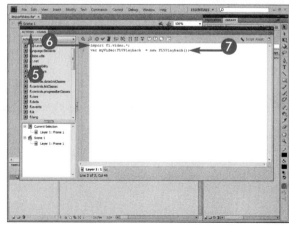

**8** Type the variable name from step **7**, a period, `source`, an equals sign, and the path to the FLV file.

**9** Add the video to the page, such as `addChild(myVideo);`.

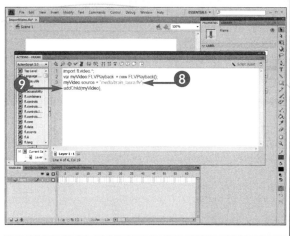

**10** Press Ctrl + Enter.

The movie loads in Flash Player, and the video plays. If set, the skin shows under the video.

**Note:** *If you do not see the video, check to be sure that the path specified in step **8** is correct.*

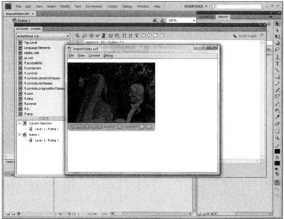

## Extra

You need to be aware that your FLV file remains independent of your SWF at all times. This allows you to have even long videos in your Flash movies without the corresponding dramatic file size increase. However, you also will need to be aware that as a separate file, you need to be sure that you place the FLV in a folder that can be referenced from the SWF; generally, it is a good idea to either place the FLV directly in the same folder as the SWF or in a subfolder under the SWF's. In addition, you need to be sure that you remember to upload the FLV to your Web server.

Your Web server may need to be configured in order to play back FLVs. If you use a third-party, commercial Web host, you will need to check to be sure that its servers support Flash Video.

# Go Full Screen

Just as you could in Flash Player 9, in Flash Player 10, you can add controls to your video to allow your user to expand and play the video full screen. Flash Player 9 and later supports true full screen; that is, the video will expand to completely fill the screen and not be limited by the browser window or other elements onscreen.

You should keep in mind that all video are *rasters;* that is, they are pixel-based and resolution dependent. Although you can in theory expand any video to full screen, smaller videos will be pixilated, possibly to the point of being unwatchable. You also want to make sure that when you encode the video in the Adobe Media Encoder that you select the option to deinterlace. This

allows the two fields used to create digital video to be properly converted into the Flash Video frames. Turning this option on will greatly reduce the jagged lines that can appear around the edges of objects in your video.

In order to provide for full-screen viewing, you need to use one of the skins that contains either "Full Screen" or "All" as part of its name. These skins provide the user with a button to expand Flash Player to full-screen mode. Finally, you need to add the `allowFullScreen` parameter to the HTML tags that are responsible for inserting the video into the page. The simplest way to do this if you are unfamiliar with HTML is to select the Flash Only – Allow Full Screen template in the Publish Settings dialog box.

## Go Full Screen

① Create an instance of the `FLVPlayback` component.

**Note:** *See either the section "Using the FLVPlayback Component Visually" or "Using the FLVPlayback Component in Code" for details.*

**Note:** *Be sure to select or set a skin that contains either "Full Screen" or "All" as part of its name.*

② Click File.

③ Click Publish Settings.

The Publish Settings dialog box appears.

④ Click the HTML tab.

⑤ Click Flash Only.

⑥ Click Flash Only – Allow Full Screen.

⑦ Click OK.

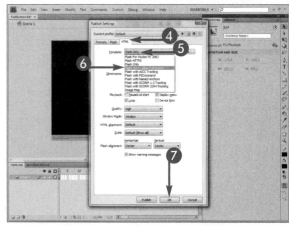

**8** Click File.

**9** Click Publish Preview.

**10** Click Default - (HTML).

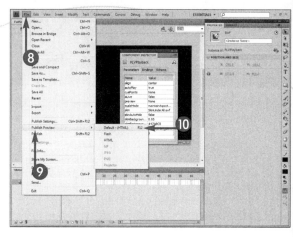

The default Web browser opens and displays the page.

**11** Click the Full Screen button.

The video expands and plays full screen.

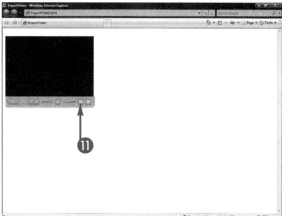

If you want to use your own HTML page, you need to slightly modify the HTML `<object>` tag's parameters to allow for full-screen display. The `<object>` tag contains a set of parameters that control the playback of the SWF. To allow full screen, you need to add an additional `<param>` tag somewhere within the `<object>` tag:

```
<param name="allowFullScreen" value="true" />
```

If you use Adobe Dreamweaver CS4 to create your Web pages, you can simply insert the SWF from the Insert panel, then switch to Code view, and add the necessary `<param>` tag. You can follow a similar process if you use another editor for creating your pages.

# Add Closed Captioning

You must always take into account the reality that many of your users will be unable to hear the audio track of your video. Although the most obvious cause of this is a user with a hearing impairment, the disabled are not the only ones who may not be able to hear your video's audio. Many users whose hearing is perfectly fine may be in an environment where they either do not have speakers attached to their computers or their speakers are turned off. You can provide an alternative means for all of these users — disabled or not — to still benefit from the information in your video by adding closed captioning.

Before you can add captions to your video, you need to create the captions themselves. Flash Video supports an XML standard created by the World Wide Web Consortium

known as the timed text (TT) format or, more formally, the distribution format exchange profile, or DFXP.

The TT document is simply an XML file. XML is a format similar to HTML that allows you to define data. The TT document actually looks very much like an HTML page. It has both a head and a body, and the body, where the captions are actually defined, is made up of `div` and `p` tags. However, the `p` tags, each of which represents a specific caption, will contain a `begin` attribute with a time code to note when the caption appears and usually either a `dur` attribute for the caption's duration or an `end` attribute for the time code for the caption to disappear. Both the `dur` and `end` attributes are optional; if omitted, the caption will vanish as soon as the next caption needs to appear.

## Add Closed Captioning

### CREATE YOUR CLOSED CAPTIONING DOCUMENT

1 Open a text editor.

**Note:** *This example shows using Notepad, but any simple text editor will work. HTML editors such as Dreamweaver or dedicated XML editors will work as well.*

2 Type `<?xml version="1.0" encoding="utf-8" ?>`.

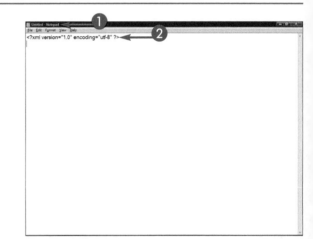

3 Type `<tt xmlns="http://www.w3.org/2006/04/ttaf1">`.

4 Type `<head>`.

5 Type `</head>`.

6 Type `<body>`.

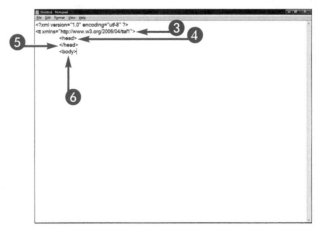

7. Type `<div>`.

8. Create the first caption, setting the time code for the caption to begin and a duration, such as `<p begin="00:00:05.00" dur="00:00:02.00">Welcome to Brady Studios.</p>`.

You can add as many captions as you need using the same format as in step **8**.

9. Type `</div>`.

10. Type `</body>`.

11. Type `</tt>`.

12. Save the file.

**Note:** *Be sure to give it an .xml extension.*

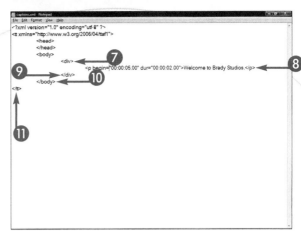

## Extra

The first line of the code in this section simply declares the document as being XML. The second is the opening tag of the document, similar to the `<html>` tag. The `xmlns` attribute defines the namespace for the tags; in essence, it provides a reference to the document, in this case one on the servers for the W3C, that defines the TT format. More details on XML can be found in Chapter 17 and in *XML: Your visual blueprint for building expert Web sites with XML, CSS, XHTML, and XSLT*, published by Wiley.

The time codes are given in *full clock format,* which is `"HH:MM:SS.m"`, where m is milliseconds. You can also use *partial clock format,* `"MM:SS.m"`, or *offset time,* where `"1s"` is one second. Full clock format will be used throughout this text for clarity.

Video editing tools such as Adobe Premiere Pro and many audio editing tools such as Adobe Soundbooth will allow you to "scrub" through video to find the precise times at which text is being spoken to help synchronize your captions.

continued →

**A**fter you have created your TT document, you need to add the captions to your Flash Video file. The FLVPlayback component contains a built-in text field for captions, but it cannot interface with the TT document directly. Rather, you need an instance of the FLVPlaybackCaptioning component. This is a nonvisual component and is responsible for reading the TT document and passing the text into the FLVPlayback's text field at the appropriate time.

Like the FLVPlayback component, the FLVPlaybackCaptioning component can be added to the Stage either visually, by dragging an instance of it from the Components panel, or through code, although as before the component must exist in the movie's library before it can be added in code. Also note that even

though the component will not be visible, you must still call the addChild() method to add it to the movie if using the code-based approach.

Once added, you can simply set the captioning component's source to the path to the TT document. As long as you have only a single instance of the FLVPlayback component on the Stage, the captioning component will automatically associate itself with the playback component.

The playback component has a showCaption property that allows you to turn the captions on or off when the movie first loads; the default is for captions to be off. Unless you set this to on, you need to be sure that the playback component is using a skin that either contains "Caption" or "All." Otherwise, the user will be unable to turn captions on and view them.

## Add Closed Captioning (continued)

### ADD THE CAPTIONS TO YOUR FLASH VIDEO

**1** Return to Flash CS4 Professional.

**2** Click Window → Components.

The Components panel opens.

**3** Click the plus sign next to Video.

**4** Drag the FLVPlaybackCaptioning component and the FLVPlayback component to the Stage.

**5** Click each instance and press Delete to remove them from the Stage.

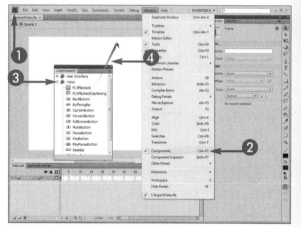

**6** Press F9 to open the Actions panel.

**7** Type import fl.video.*;.

**8** Create an instance of the FLVPlayback class, such as var myVideo:FLV Playback = new FLVPlayback();.

**9** Type the variable name from step **8**, a period, source =, the name of the video file, and a semicolon.

**10** Add a skin to your video that enables the use of captions, such as myVideo.skin = "SkinUnderAll.swf";.

**11** Add the instance to the page, such as addChild(myVideo);.

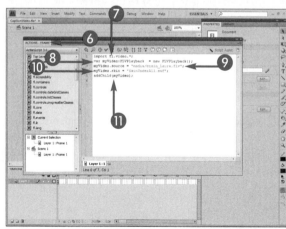

**12** Create an instance of the `FLVPlayback Captioning` class, such as `var myCaption:FLVPlaybackCaptioning = new FLVPlaybackCaptioning();`.

**13** Type the variable name from step **12**, a period, `source =`, the name of the XML captions file, and a semicolon.

**14** Add the instance to the page, such as `addChild(myCaption);`.

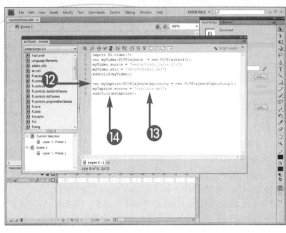

**15** Press Ctrl + Enter.

The movie plays. The video begins.

**16** Click the Closed Caption button on the skin.

The captions appear.

**Note:** *If you do not see the captions or you get an error, double-check the filename and path to the captions document in step **13**.*

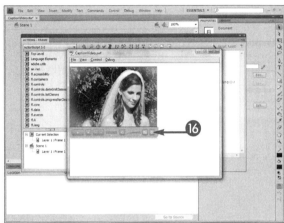

## Extra

In the United States, Section 508 of the Rehabilitation Act of 1973 provides that any agency of the U.S. government must make content provided on Web sites accessible to people with disabilities. Many state and local governments in the United States have similar policies, and many other governments around the world have adopted statutes requiring accessible content. In addition, several lawsuits against private corporations have been filed and in some cases won to force them to provide for accessibility. Captioning is the primary method by which video content can be made accessible, so it is a good idea to always provide it.

Adobe Soundbooth CS4, which is included with Flash in both the Production Premium and Web Premium suites, has an audio transcription feature that will "listen" to audio files and provide a text transcription. Unfortunately, this transcription is not automatically formatted using the TT standard, but it can at least save you from having to type in the text manually, as you can copy and paste it from Soundbooth.

# Style Closed Captions

The default appearance of captions is similar to what you see on TV: a black bar along the bottom of the screen with white text. Although this might work in certain situations, at other times you may like to have control over the appearance of the captions.

You can change many properties of the captions by using a slightly modified version of cascading style sheets within the TT document that contains your captions. Within the head of the document, you can add a pair of `styling` tags. Inside the tag, you can add one or more `style` tags. Each `style` tag must contain a unique ID. You can then set the appearance of the captions using a series of additional attributes. All attributes will begin with a `tts` prefix, followed by a colon and the name of the style. The style names have adopted standard CSS names, with the exception that multiword names in CSS use hyphens, and the `tts` standard combines the words

into a single word using camel case. Therefore, the CSS `color` property can be set with `tts:color`, and the CSS `background-color` becomes `tts:backgroundColor`.

You can apply the styles to selected captions by referencing the style's unique ID in the `style` attribute of the caption's `p` tag. You can also add a `<span>` around selected words and apply the style there.

You will need to add an additional attribute to the opening `tt` tag in your caption document to establish the `tts` namespace. This attribute will always read `xmlns:tts="http://www.w3.org/2006/04/ttaf1#styling"`.

Flash supports only a subset of the `tts` standard. You can view a list of the attributes that are and are not supported online at http://help.adobe.com/en_US/ActionScript/3.0_UsingComponentsAS3/WS5b3ccc516d4fbf351e63e3d118a9c65b32-7ee5.html.

## Style Closed Captions

① In a text editor, open a TT document.

② After the opening `<head>` tag, type `<styling>`.

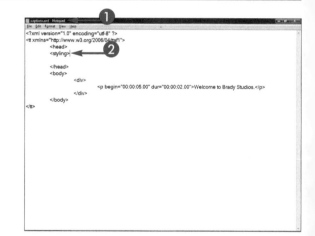

③ Type `<style id=`, followed by the name of the caption style that you will define, such as `"mainCaption"`.

④ Type `tts:fontFamily=`, followed by the font that you want, such as `"Arial"`.

⑤ Type `tts:fontSize=`, followed by the font size that you want, such as `"18"`.

⑥ Close the `style` tag with `/>`.

You can add as many `style` tags and attributes as needed using the same format as in steps **3** to **6**.

⑦ Type `</styling>`.

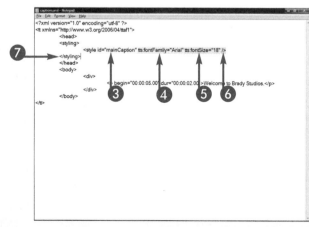

8 Within the `<p>` tag of the captions, type `style=`, followed by the name of the caption style that you defined in steps **3** to **6**, such as `"mainCaption"`.

9 Within the opening `tt` tag, add `xmlns:tts="http://www.w3.org/2006/04/ttaf1#styling"`.

10 Save the document.

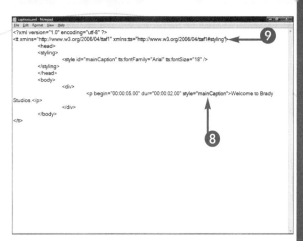

11 Return to Flash CS4 Professional.

12 If necessary, open a movie that contains a video and captioning associated with the document from the prior steps.

13 Press Ctrl + Enter.

The movie plays. The video begins.

14 Click the Closed Caption button.

Closed captions appear, showing the styles.

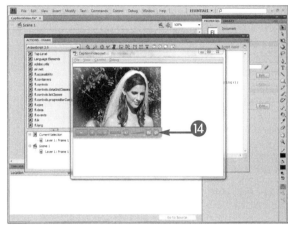

---

## Apply It

You can apply multiple styles to the same text by grouping them. For example, if you wanted captions to be a consistent color and size but use different alignment, you could create a style for the first two attributes:

```
<style id="colorAndSize" tts:color="#FF9900" tts:fontSize="18" />
```

Then create separate styles for the alignment:

```
<style id="alignLeft" tts:textAlign="left" />
<style id="alignCenter" tts:textAlign="center" />
```

Finally, create two styles for the combinations that you want:

```
<style id="leftCaption" style="colorAndSize alignLeft" />
<style id="centerCaption" style="colorAndSize alignCenter" />
```

You could then apply `"leftCaption"` to one set of captions and `"centerCaption"` to the other. All captions would be 18 pixels and orange, but one group would be left-aligned and the other centered.

# Understanding XML and E4X

Your Flash movie will be running entirely on the client; that is, everything that happens in Flash happens on your user's computer. In a simple Flash movie, all the information required by the movie needs to be imported into the FLA and thus included in the SWF. Although this is certainly the simplest approach, it has some limitations, the most important of which is that any time the data needs to change, you have to republish and re-upload your SWF. Fortunately, Flash movies have the capability, thanks to ActionScript, to communicate back to the Web server at runtime and access additional information, provided that the information being returned to the SWF is in the correct format. Although several formats actually exist that work well with Flash movies, perhaps the easiest to understand and work with is XML.

## The Background of XML

XML, or the Extensible Markup Language, was developed in the mid-to-late 1990s by the World Wide Web Consortium, or W3C. The W3C is a standards organization that is responsible for developing languages such as HTML, XHTML, and CSS. Today, XML is widely used as a universal data exchange format. Because anyone can develop XML documents without licensing restrictions and without the need to purchase expensive development tools, it is very popular in business, government, and private sectors.

## Writing XML

If you are familiar with HTML or XHTML, you know that they provide a defined set of elements with specific purposes. XML, on the other hand, does not. When you write XML documents, you invent the set of elements that you need for that document's purposes. You can also create your own attributes and entities. Although many XML documents can share the same structure, others will not — and that is part of the design of the language. It is, in fact, what is meant by "extensible" in XML's name.

## XML and HTML Similarities

Although XML does not rely on a fixed set of tags, it is still tag-based. XML documents look similar to HTML documents. Both are simple text documents that can be created in almost any editor.

Also, neither XML nor HTML can actually "do" anything as they are not programming languages. Both require some other application to parse and interpret them and respond accordingly. In the case of HTML, the helper application is most often a Web browser. XML can be parsed and interpreted by browsers, but there are many other applications available today capable of using XML.

## XML Syntax

XML follows a very strict syntax. Although this can sometimes present problems for developers coming from a language such as HTML with its loose syntax rules, programmers using languages such as ActionScript should already be comfortable with issues such as paying attention to case.

### Document Structure

As mentioned earlier, like HTML, XML is a tag-based language. XML documents must follow a strict structure. They must always contain a single root element. The root element will be the parent of all the other elements on the page. Every tag on the page must be properly nested within its respective parent tag. For example, if you have a `<picture>` element with a `<picture-name>` child element, you must close the `<picture-name>` element before you can close the `<picture>` element.

### Case Sensitivity

XML is case-sensitive. There are no specific rules stating that tags and attributes must be a particular case, but you must be consistent in the casing structure that you follow. Developers coming from an HTML background will often use all lowercase for everything in their document, as this is the standard in that language. Developers with an object-oriented programming background will likely use camel casing for tag and attribute names as they will likely be comfortable and familiar with that standard.

### Whitespace

XML parsers ignore whitespace outside of tags, but most pay attention to it within tags. You should space out your document to maximize readability and code editing.

### Comments

XML documents can contain comments just like ActionScript. The syntax for comments is the same as it is in HTML: The comment begins with `<!--` and ends with `-->`. Comments can span multiple lines.

### Reserved Characters and CDATA

The data within your document cannot contain the less-than symbol (<), greater-than symbol (>), ampersand (&), apostrophe ('), or quotation mark ("). Each of these characters should be represented in your data with a character entity. An *entity* is a code that the parser uses to interpret these characters. All entities begin with an ampersand and end with a semicolon. The entity for the less-than symbol is `&lt;`. The greater-than symbol is represented with `&gt;`. The ampersand uses `&amp;`, the apostrophe is `&apos;`, and the quotation mark is `&quot;`.

If you have a long block of text that may need multiple instances of these characters, such as a block of HTML stored within your XML file, you can create a CDATA section. This is a block of data within your XML that will be entirely ignored by the parser and treated as literal text. The

CDATA block will begin with `<![CDATA[`, and end with `]]>`. In addition to HTML, you will want to wrap any ActionScript code that may be part of your XML in a CDATA block as well. An example of ActionScript embedded within XML might look like this:

```
<code>
<![CDATA[
function parseHTML(sample:String):String
{
    var codeBlock = "<p>Sample text:<i>" &
  sample & "</i></p>";
    return codeBlock;
}
]]>
</code>
```

### Parsing Instructions

XML documents can contain parsing instructions. These code blocks do not represent data within the document; instead, they contain instructions for the XML parser that will process the document. Parsing instructions are most often found at the top of a XML document. They begin with `<?` and the instruction name and end with `?>`. An example of a parsing instruction found on every XML document is the XML declaration:

```
<?xml version="1.0" encoding="UTF-8" ?>
```

## E4X

ECMA for XML, or E4X, is another standard developed by the W3C. E4X is a standard for writing and reading XML documents. Basically, E4X allows you to treat XML data as an object and deal with it through familiar dot notation. ActionScript treats E4X as a native data type.

# Embed XML in ActionScript

**M**ost often, the XML that you use for data in your Flash applications will be stored in separate XML files that are loaded at runtime. The process for doing this is covered later in this chapter in the section "Load XML at Runtime." However, there are times when it may be helpful to embed XML directly into your ActionScript code.

You can use XML embedded within your ActionScript to store complex data that requires relationships between pieces of data. Lists of data points can be stored in an array, but you cannot provide an association between the data points with arrays. An array is useful if you simply need a single variable that, for example, stores the names of a series of photos that you will load into your application.

However, it would not be particularly useful to store that same data in an array if, in addition to the filename of the photo, you also needed to store a caption, the name of the photographer, and the date and location the picture was taken. In this case, you need to provide not just the data but also a way to label each data point, and XML provides a useful means for describing this data.

When embedding XML, you simply need to create a variable as an instance of the XML class. You can then populate this variable with your XML. In many languages, XML is treated as a string, but in ActionScript, you do need to worry about quotes or line breaks because XML is understood as an actual data type. After your XML is embedded as a variable, you can read the data from it using simple dot notation.

## Embed XML in ActionScript

### STORE RELATED DATA

**1** In the Actions panel, type the beginning of an XML variable, such as `var myPictures:XML`, and a equals sign.

**2** Press Enter.

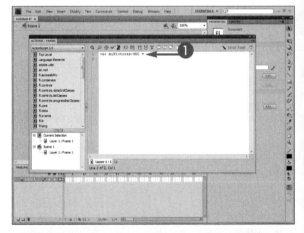

**3** Type an opening parent tag to contain the related data, such as `<pictures>`.

**4** Type a child node for the first piece of data, such as `<pictureName>Half Dome at Dusk</pictureName>`.

**5** Type a child node for the second piece of data, such as `<photographer>Ann Sel Adams</photographer>`.

**6** Type a child node for the third piece of data, such as `<pictureDate> 07-23-2008</pictureDate>`.

**7** Type a child node for the fourth piece of data, such as `<pictureLocation> Yosemite NP</pictureLocation>`.

You can include as much data as necessary.

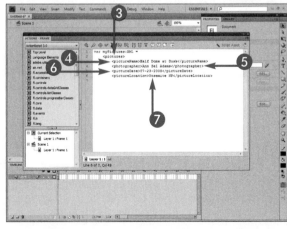

**8** Type the closing tag corresponding to step **3**'s tag, such as `</pictures>;`.

**Note:** *Do not forget the semicolon at the end of this line.*

**9** Display the data that you want, such as `trace(myPictures. pictureName);`.

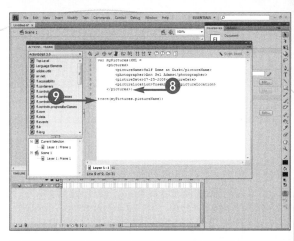

## TEST THE MOVIE

**10** Press Ctrl + Enter.

The movie plays.

● In this example, the value of the `pictureName` node is displayed in the Output panel.

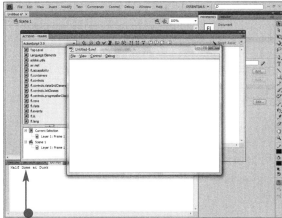

---

### Extra

The XML that you embed in your ActionScript must follow the syntax rules for the language, with a few additional caveats. First, although dashes are valid as part of a name of an element in XML, you cannot use them in element names in XML that you want to use in ActionScript. This is due to the fact that the element names are treated as properties of the XML object; therefore, they must adhere to the standard rules for property or variable names in ActionScript. Second, you omit the XML declaration. Although the declaration is technically optional in regular XML documents, its purpose is to declare to the parser that the document is XML. Because you are placing this data into an instance of the XML class, no such declaration is necessary.

Note that the entire block of XML is treated as a single statement in ActionScript. Only the last line should have a semicolon.

When outputting your XML, you treat the child nodes as properties of the XML instance. The root node is ignored, but nonetheless required. In the example in this section, the `<pictureName>` node is a child of `<pictures>`, but the proper syntax for tracing the name is `myPictures.pictureName`, not `myPictures.pictures. pictureName`.

# Read XML

E4X makes it very simple to read XML into your ActionScript code. Because XML data is treated as a native object, you do not need to do anything complicated to parse the XML.

However, even though E4X and the XML class in ActionScript simplify using the data, you should still understand a few things that are going on behind the scenes. A better understanding of what is happening with the class will prevent errors and frustration when the simplicity causes unexpected results.

For example, if you had nodes containing numeric data, you might think that you would have to explicitly cast them as strings before putting them in text boxes, as the text property cannot contain a number. You may be surprised, then, when it actually works to simply read the XML directly into the text property because all data returned from XML is text. It is therefore a good idea to specifically cast any data being returned from XML if you do *not* want to treat it as a string.

If you have a node that contains multiple, repeating child nodes and then attempt to read the parent node, an instance of the XMLList class is automatically created for you. The XMLList class will take the repeating node and generate what amounts to an array. For example, say you had a <pictures> parent node that contained three <picture> nodes, which in turn each contained a <pictureName> node, and then placed all of this XML into a variable named myPictures. You could output the first <pictureName> with myPictures.picture[0].pictureName. You could as easily loop over the picture node to return all three names.

## Read XML

1. In the Actions panel, type the beginning of an XML variable, such as var myPictures:XML, and a equals sign.

2. Type an opening parent node to contain all the related data, such as <pictures>.

3. Type an opening child node that will in turn contain one set of the related data, such as <picture>.

4. Type a child node for the first piece of data, such as <pictureName>Half Dome at Dusk</pictureName>.

5. Type as many child nodes as needed for each piece of data in the set.

6. Type the closing tag corresponding to step **3**'s tag, such as </picture>.

7. Repeat step **3**.

8. Again, type as many child nodes as needed for each piece of data in the set.

9. Repeat step **6**.

   You can include as many sets of data as necessary.

10. Close step **2**'s tag, such as </pictures>;.

**Note:** Be sure to include the semicolon after this line.

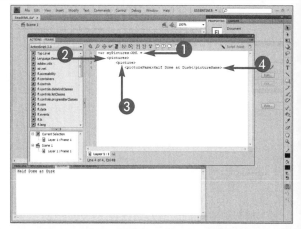

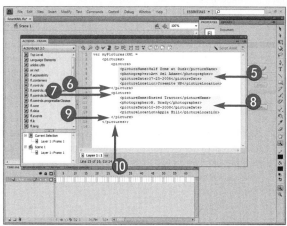

⑪ Display all the individual sets of data, such as `trace ("All pictures:" + myPictures.picture);`.

⑫ Use an index number to display a particular piece of data that you want, such as `trace("Second picture name:" + myPictures. picture[1]. pictureName);`.

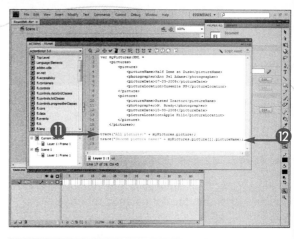

⑬ Press Ctrl + Enter.

The movie plays.

● In this example, the XML from both `<picture>` nodes is displayed in the Output window, along with the name of the second picture.

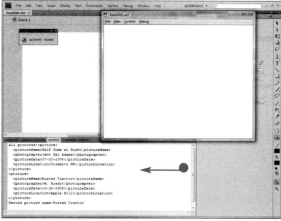

When writing XML, you can use variables as data for the nodes by placing the variable names in curly braces:

```
var shipName:String = "Serenity";
var captainName:String = "Malcolm Reynolds";
var shipData:XML =
<ships>
                <ship>
                    <name>{shipName}</name>
                    <captain>{captainName}</name>
                </ship>
</ships>;
trace(shipData.captain); //returns Malcolm Reynolds
```

# Filter XML

When addressing nodes in E4X, you can use conditionals to filter the results. This can be particularly useful when you need to return only a subset of your data. Rather than looping over all the data and then using the `if` statement in the loop, which not only takes a lot of time to write but is also processor-intensive, you can instead simply provide the condition directly within the dot notation that references the XML.

Take, for example, an embedded XML structure in a variable called `myPictures` with a root node of `<pictures>` and a set of repeating `<picture>` nodes. Within these `<picture>` nodes, you have a `<pictureName>` and `<photographer>` node, along with a `<pictureWidth>` and `<pictureHeight>` node. You need to return all the pictures whose width is less than 1024 pixels. This can be accomplished using a conditional within the reference to the node:

```
trace(myPictures.picture.(pictureWidth <
    1024));
```

As with other conditional statements, you need to be sure to use two equal signs when comparing a literal value. Using this same sample structure, you could return all the photos with a height of exactly 800 pixels using the following:

```
trace(myPictures.picture.(pictureHeight ==
    800));
```

Filter XML

## DISPLAY FILTERED DATA IN A TEXT FIELD

1. Create an XML variable that contains a structure with a repeating child node.

**Note:** *See the preceding section, "Read XML," for an example.*

2. Create a variable that filters for a particular piece of data, such as `var smallPictures:XMLList = myPictures.picture. (pictureWidth <= 400);`.

3. Begin a text field variable, such as `var picName:TextField;`.

4. Create a variable for the y position, such as `var yPos = 10;`.

5. Type a `for` loop that uses the variable in step **2**, such as `for (var i in small Pictures)`, and a pair of curly braces.

6. Within the braces, create the text field, such as `picName = new TextField();`.

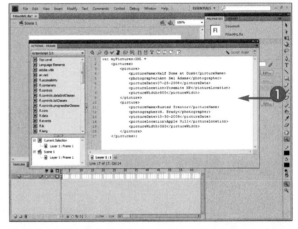

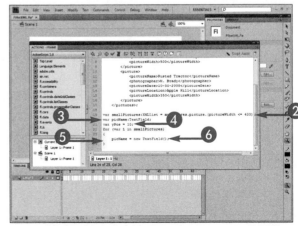

**7** Set the text of the field to an identifying piece of data, such as `picName.text = small Pictures[i].pictureName;`.

**8** Set the field's y position to the variable in step **4**, such as `picName.y = yPos;`.

**9** Change the y position as needed for subsequent fields, such as `yPos += 50;`.

**10** Add the text field to the page, such as `addChild(picName);`.

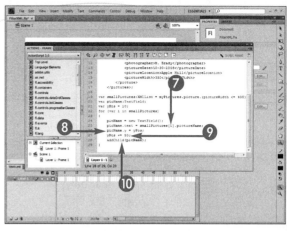

## TEST THE MOVIE

**11** Press Ctrl + Enter.

The movie plays.

● The names of the selected nodes are displayed in the text fields. In this example, the name shown is that of the pictures with a width of no more than 400 pixels.

### Apply It

Occasionally, you may have a child node that is common to several parent nodes but appears in a different location within each parent. Take the following example:

```
var coolShips:XML =
<ships>
                <ship>
                    <shipName>Serenity</shipName>
                    <movieTitle>Serenity</movieTitle>
                </ship>
                <ship>
                    <shipName>Millennium Falcon</shipName>
                    <movies>
                        <movieTitle>Star Wars Episode IV</movieTitle>
                        <movieTitle>Star Wars Episode V</movieTitle>
                        <movieTitle>Star Wars Episode VI</movieTitle>
                    </movies>
                </ship>
    </ships>
```

The `movieTitle` node is the direct child of the `ship` node in the first case but not in the second. To access this node regardless of its position, use two dots instead of one, the E4X standard for finding a node at any level:

```
trace(coolShips..movieTitle);
```

# Write XML

In addition to reading XML, ActionScript can also write XML for output. You may have decided to store the project's data in an XML structure and need to add more data to it based on user input. Or you might be planning to take data submitted by the user and eventually pass it to the server for more processing, and you decided that XML made sense for that purpose.

Regardless of how you use it, writing XML via ActionScript is essentially the same process as reading it. You first create a variable as an instance of XML and then assign nodes to it. After that, you can either assign additional nodes or data.

Any valid XML file must contain a root node, so you should always begin by explicitly creating one, as in `var playerData:XML = <players />;`. All XML tags must always be closed. Normally, you expressly close a tag:

`</players>`. Although it would be possible in this example to write `<players></players>`, in this case you are creating an empty tag — one that, at least temporarily, contains nothing else, so you can use the shortcut of merely placing the slash before the closing bracket.

You can create additional nodes in a similar manner: `playerData.player = <player />;`. Data could be assigned to nodes using dot syntax and assigning a string. For example, if you added another node to the examples shown previously, called `playerName`, and then wanted to assign data to it, you would write `userPictures.player.playerName = "Inara Serra";`. Alternatively, of course, the value being assigned could be a variable or value from another source, such as a text field: `userPictures.player.playerName = txtPlayerName.text;`.

## Write XML

① In the Actions panel, create the root node, such as `var pictureData:XML = <pictures />;`.

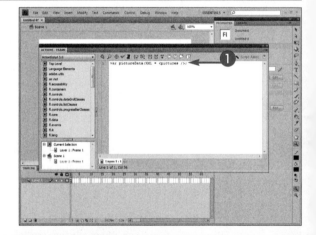

② Type a child node that will contain one set of the related data, such as `pictureData.picture = <picture />;`.

③ Type a child node for the first piece of data, such as `pictureData.picture.pictureName = <pictureName />;`.

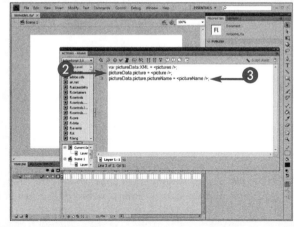

④ Assign data to the first node, such as `pictureData.picture.pictureName = "First Photo";`.

⑤ Continue adding child nodes to the element and appropriate data.

You can include as many sets of data as necessary.

⑥ Display the XML, such as `trace(pictureData);`.

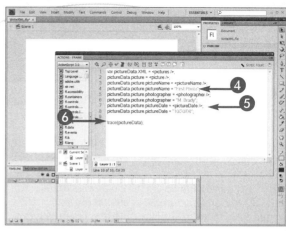

⑦ Press Ctrl + Enter.

The movie plays.

● The XML is displayed in the Output window.

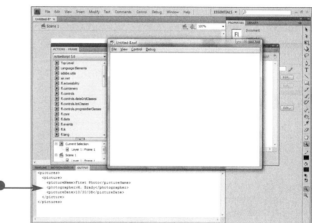

## Apply It

In addition to nodes and text, you can also read and write attributes in your XML, again relying on a standard notation from E4X. If your node contains an attribute, such as the following:

```
<photographer staff="true">Ann Sel Adams</photographer>
```

You can read the attribute by appending the @ symbol to it. Assuming that the preceding code snippet is a node contained in an XML variable `pictureData` and has a parent node, you could trace the value of the attribute with this:

```
trace(pictureData.picture.photographer.@staff);
```

When writing XML, you can add attributes to nodes in much the same way:

```
var pictureData:XML = <pictures />;
pictureData.picture = <picture />;
pictureData.picture.photographer = <photographer />;
pictureData.picture.photographer.@staff = true;
```

# Load XML at Runtime

Although you may find it convenient to use XML as a data type to store information within your movies, you will most likely more often want to use it to store data that is kept apart from the movie itself.

Using external XML files for your data provides many benefits. XML embedded directly in your ActionScript can be changed only by opening the movie in Flash CS4 Professional, editing it, and then republishing and re-uploading it. External files are called by Flash Player at runtime, so they can be freely changed at any time without needing to touch the SWF. Any time you need large amounts of data, and you know or suspect that that data may need to change, you should consider placing it in an external file that will be called at runtime.

Calling an external file is done with the URLLoader class. After creating an instance of the class, you can call its load method, into which you pass an instance of the URLRequest class. The URLRequest takes as its argument the path to the file that you want to have loaded.

Because the potential exists for delay in loading the file, you should always add an event listener to the loader instance for the Complete event. The event handler can then perform whatever processing you need to parse the XML. The information from the file will be automatically passed to the handler as a data property of the target, so if your handler argument is called event, you can read it with event.target.data.

Once received, you can read the XML data just as you would XML embedded in your document. See the prior tasks in this chapter for information on reading XML.

## Load XML at Runtime

1. In a text editor, write an XML file such as the one shown here.

**Note:** *Any plain text editor, such as Notepad on Windows, will work. HTML editors or a dedicated XML editor will work as well. See the earlier sections of this chapter for details on writing the XML.*

2. Save the file with an .xml extension.

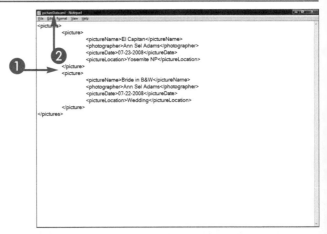

3. Return to Flash CS4 Professional.

4. In the Actions panel, type an XML variable, such as var pictureData:XML;.

5. Create an instance of the URLLoader class, such as var loader:URLLoader = new URLLoader();.

6. Call its load method and pass it an instance of the URLRequest class, using your XML file, such as loader.load(new URL Request("pictureData.xml"));.

**Note:** *Be sure to use the filename of the file that you saved in step 2.*

7. Add an event listener, such as loader. addEventListener(Event.COMPLETE, readXML);.

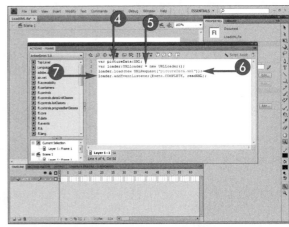

**8** Add the event handler, such as `function readXML(event:Event):void`, and a pair of curly braces.

**9** Within the braces, type `trace(event. target.data);`.

**10** Save the file.

***Note:*** *Be sure to save the file in the same directory as the XML file.*

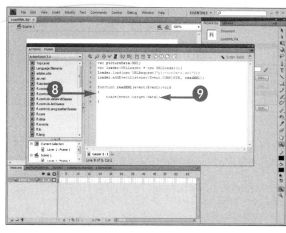

**11** Press Ctrl + Enter.

The movie plays.

● The XML data is displayed in the Output panel.

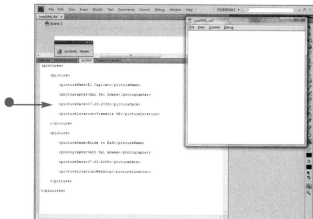

---

## Extra

Remember that Flash Player runs locally on your user's computer. Therefore, it cannot write XML — or any other type of information — to your server. It can send data to the server, as discussed in Chapter 18, but you will need some kind of server-side script to write the data. For security reasons, Flash Player cannot write files to your user's hard drive, either.

Also for security reasons, Flash Player runs in what is known as a "security sandbox" that prevents it from making requests for data from any server other than the one from which the SWF was called. So although it is legal to pass a complete URL as the argument for the `URLRequest` object, if the URL does not match the one from which Flash Player detects the current movie came, the request will fail. Two workarounds exist for this problem, although both require working on Web servers. You can read more about this issue and the solutions on Adobe's Web site at www.adobe.com/devnet/flashplayer/articles/flash_player10_security_wp.html.

# Download the Apache Web Server

Your Flash applications have the capability to make requests back to a script running on a Web server. These requests can send user-generated data that can be processed by the script, which in turn can send responses specific to the data. For example, you can have a user enter his or her personal information into a form in your Flash application, have the server-side script insert that data into a database, and then return a response that can be displayed in Flash Player.

In order to test that your applications are working properly, you should set up a testing server on your personal computer. To do this, you will need to install a Web server and a server-side application server. If you use Windows, you can choose between the free Apache Web server or Microsoft's own Internet Information Services (IIS). For the purposes of these examples,

Apache will be used. If you run a Mac with at least OS X, Apache is already on your computer. See the Extra at the end of this section for details on enabling it.

To use Apache, you first need to download it from the Apache Web site. As an open source project, the Web server is free to download and use for any purpose. In fact, you can even download the raw source code for the server, but you probably will not need to because Apache provides a precompiled installer similar to what you are used to from other programs.

When you visit the Web site to download the server, you see links to the latest "stable" release, as well as past versions and new, still-in-development versions. You want to get whatever version is being offered as the latest "stable" release.

## Download the Apache Web Server

① Browse to www.apache.org.

The main Apache Web site opens.

② Click HTTP Server.

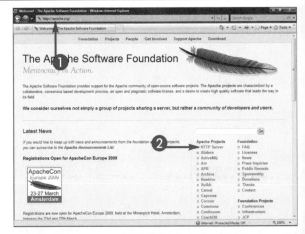

The Apache HTTP Server Project page appears.

③ Click Download.

**Note:** The text of the heading and link may be slightly different if a newer version is available.

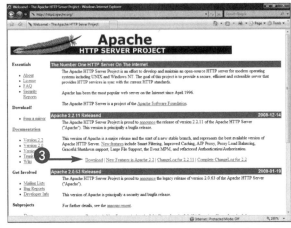

The download page appears.

④ Click the version for your operating system.

The File Download dialog box appears.

⑤ Click Save.

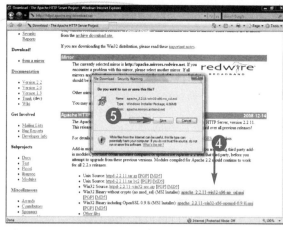

The Save As dialog box appears.

⑥ Click Save.

The software downloads.

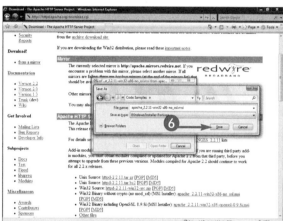

## Extra

If you use a Macintosh running at least OS X, you will have Apache preinstalled, but not configured, for your computer. To enable it, you need to go into the Sharing panel in System Preferences and check the Web Sharing box.

You can also open a Terminal window and type

```
sudo apachect1 start
```

You will be prompted to enter the computer's root password. If you need to restart the server at some later point, for example after making changes to its configuration settings, you can return to a Terminal window and type

```
sudo apachect1 restart
```

# Install the Apache Server

A lthough the actual process of installing Apache in Windows is very straightforward — it uses an installer wizard that guides you through the steps — there are several important configuration issues that you should address. You need to provide administrative information such as the domain name of the Web site and a contact email address, both of which are displayed in default error messages. If you are creating a testing computer for your own use, you can enter anything you want into either of these fields. The same applies to the email address: For testing purposes, it is not necessary to be accurate.

You can also choose to install Apache completely or perform a custom installation to choose which

components you want to have available. In most cases, the default installation will be fine for testing purposes.

You can also decide whether you want to run Apache as a service and control how it starts. If you run it as a service, it is configured to run "silently" in the background, which simply means that you do not have a visual indicator that it is running while working. You can have the server start automatically when you start Windows, or you can set it so that you have to manually start the server when you want to use it. Most of the time, it makes the most sense to have it run as a service and start automatically, although you can choose either of the other options if you prefer more control.

## Install the Apache Server

① Double-click the installer.

The Installation Wizard launches, and the Welcome screen appears.

② Click Next.

The License Agreement screen appears.

③ Click I Accept the Terms in the License Agreement.

④ Click Next.

The Read This First screen appears.

⑤ Click Next.

The Server Information screen appears.

6 Type a name for your network.

7 Type a name for your server.

8 Type an administrative email address.

9 Click Next.

The Setup Type screen appears.

10 Click Typical.

11 Click Next.

The Destination Folder screen appears.

12 Click Next to use the folder that the wizard suggests.

The Ready to Install the Program screen appears.

13 Click Install.

The installation begins.

When the installation is completed, the Installation Wizard Completed screen appears.

14 Click Finish.

Apache is installed.

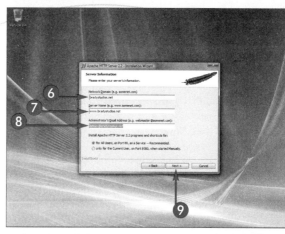

## Extra

Before you begin attempting to test Flash applications against a server, you need to be sure that it is running. The easiest way to tell if the server is running is to open your Web browser and go to http://localhost. If a page appears with information about Apache, the server is running. If you get a Page Not Found error, you need to be sure that the server installed correctly and that it has been started.

With the default installation, the server should start automatically when you launch Windows. If you want to control it manually, you can start and stop the server by clicking Start → All Programs → Apache. Within this folder, you will find a set of applets that start or stop the server. You can also click Start → Control Panel → Administrative Tools → Services and start or stop the server there.

# Download Adobe ColdFusion

In addition to a Web server, you need an application server to actually process the data. Flash Player cannot communicate with services such as databases directly; instead, it simply makes a request to the server, which in turn must pass the request to an application server for processing. Several solutions exist for this purpose. A few of the most popular are Adobe ColdFusion, Microsoft ASP.NET, and open source PHP. The one you choose depends mostly on personal preference; Flash applications can work with any of them.

Adobe ColdFusion is a commercial product, with a Standard Edition that retails for about $1,300 and an Enterprise Edition for around $7,500. However, you can develop and test applications in ColdFusion using the Developer Edition, which can be downloaded for free from the Adobe Web site.

The Developer Edition of ColdFusion includes all the features of the Enterprise Edition but is limited to access from only two other computers. It is designed so that developers can create ColdFusion applications without needing to purchase a license. You need to deploy your application to a server that is running one of the two commercial editions of ColdFusion, but you can find third-party hosting companies that offer ColdFusion hosting. With some comparison shopping, you can find ColdFusion hosting plans for the same cost as, and in some cases less than, that for other technologies such as PHP.

ColdFusion runs with almost any operating system, as it is available for Windows, Macintosh, and several varieties of UNIX. The installation package is a very large file, so it may take some time to download over slower Internet connections.

## Download Adobe ColdFusion

① Browse to www.adobe.com/products/coldfusion.

② Click Download the Free Developer Edition.

A login page appears.

③ If you have an Adobe account, log in.

If you do not have an account, you can click Create an Adobe Account on this page, which takes you to a form to create a free Adobe membership.

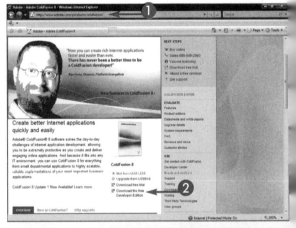

④ Click the version for your operating system.

⑤ Click Download.

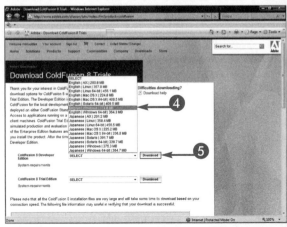

The File Download
dialog box appears.

**6** Click Save.

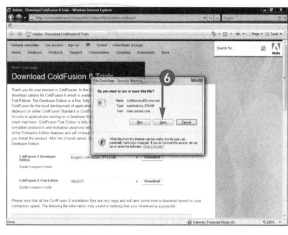

The Save As dialog box
appears.

**7** Click Save.

The download begins. A
message appears when
the download is
complete.

# Install ColdFusion

Once downloaded, ColdFusion can be installed by using the install wizard. It takes you through a series of steps to install the program and get it set up. Once completed, you can begin using ColdFusion immediately.

ColdFusion can be run with a Web server such as Apache or IIS, but the Developer Edition can also be run with its own standalone server. If you are going to use Apache or IIS, you need to be sure that the server is installed and running before you install ColdFusion. You can also install the database connectors, search services, and documentation for ColdFusion.

Your ColdFusion server is configured through an administrator, which requires a password that you set during installation. You will be prompted for this password when you need to access the administrator. ColdFusion will also ask if you want to enable Remote Development Services, or RDS. RDS is used by programs such as Dreamweaver to communicate with ColdFusion. You can choose to install it if you use Dreamweaver, but it is not necessary for testing with Flash.

Once complete, ColdFusion launches your Web browser and completes a few additional configuration steps. This does not require your input and generally takes only a few minutes. When the installation succeeds, you are taken to the login page for the administrator. You can log in to explore the configuration and administrative settings for the server, but these are beyond the scope of this book, as the standard settings will all work well. You can return to the administrator at any point by clicking Start → All Programs → Adobe → Adobe ColdFusion → Administrator in Windows.

## Install ColdFusion

① Double-click the file that you downloaded from the Adobe Web site.

② In the Open File dialog box, click Run.

③ Complete the initial screens, clicking Next to move to each screen.

The License Agreement screen appears.

④ Click I Accept the Terms of the License Agreement.

⑤ Click Next.

The Install Type screen appears.

⑥ Click Developer Edition.

⑦ Click Next.

The Installer Configuration screen appears.

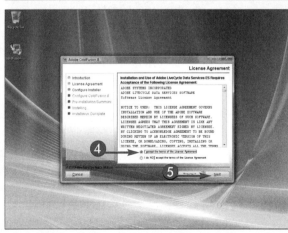

⑧ Click Server Configuration.

⑨ Click Next.

⑩ On the next screen, select the components that you want.

⑪ Click Next on this and the following screens.

⑫ Complete the screens regarding installation of LiveCycle Data Services ES.

⑬ On the next screen, click All IIS Websites.

**Note:** *If you do not want to use IIS or Apache, click Built-in Web Server.*

⑭ Click Next on this and the following screens.

The Administrator Password screen appears.

⑮ Type an administrator password twice.

⑯ Click Next.

⑰ On the next screen, choose if you want to enable RDS.

**Note:** *If you do not want to use RDS, skip to step* **19**.

⑱ Type an RDS password twice.

⑲ Click Next.

The Pre-Installation Summary screen appears.

⑳ Click Install.

The application installs. Once complete, a message is displayed.

㉑ Click Done.

## Extra

Along the way when installing ColdFusion, you will be asked to install and configure LiveCycle Data Services ES. This is a free, somewhat limited version of Adobe's LiveCycle Data Services, or LCDS. Although LCDS is not used in normal Flash development, it plays an important role in the overall Flash platform, as it is the primary means by which Flex applications communicate with server resources. Flex is a companion development environment to Flash. It offers a more developer-centric and code-oriented workflow, in which you can build applications using a combination of ActionScript and an XML-based markup language known as *MXML*. You can learn more about Flex in *Flex 3 Bible,* by David Gassner, published by Wiley.

Sometime in late 2009 or early 2010, Adobe is planning to release the next version of Flex, along with a new application in the Flash platform, known as *Flash Catalyst,* which will provide a more designer-based workflow for building Flex applications.

# Download PHP

PHP, like the Apache server, is open source and can be downloaded and used without charge. When you visit the download site at www.php.net/downloads, you will see several options for downloading the same version of PHP. You can download the raw source code for PHP, but this should only be attempted by experienced developers. Instead, you should download either a Windows installer that provides a simple wizard-based installation or a ZIP archive that contains all the files you need but requires that you manually copy them to specific locations on your computer and then manually configure your Web server to work with PHP. Although some developers like the fine-tuned control offered by the ZIP method, it is fastest and easiest to use the Windows installer.

You should download the latest stable release of PHP. At the time of this writing, that is version 5.2.9; however, a later version, possibly even PHP 6, may be available when you visit the site. For the purposes of the examples presented in this book, any version of PHP will work.

If you are using a Macintosh running OS X or later, PHP should already be installed on your system. Therefore, you do not need to do anything to get started developing sites in PHP on the Mac, other than configuring the Apache server. See the section "Download the Apache Web Server" earlier in this chapter for details on configuring the server on the Mac. However, if you have had your Mac for a while, you may want to see if a more up-to-date version of PHP is available if you want to become a more advanced developer.

## Download PHP

① Browse to www.php.net/downloads.php.

② Click PHP 5.2.6 Installer.

**Note:** *The version number may be different.*

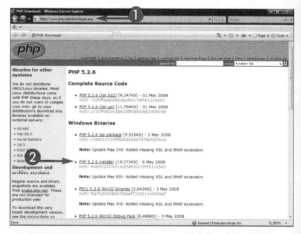

The Get Download page appears.

③ Click a mirror site close to you.

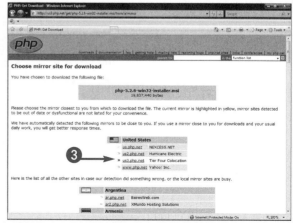

The File Download
dialog box appears.

④ Click Save.

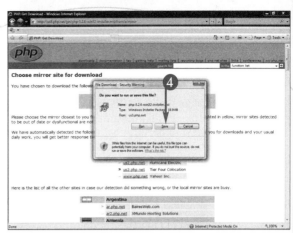

The Save As dialog
box appears.

⑤ Click Save.

The file downloads.

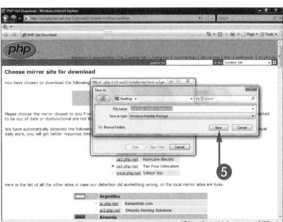

## Extra

When you download PHP, you will have the option to download it from one of many mirror sites. These are merely Web servers that host the download files, as a way of spreading the bandwidth costs. Which mirror site you choose only matters to a point. Mirror sites that are closer to you may download the file faster than those far away, particularly if they are on a different continent, but there are many other factors that may affect your download speed, including your connection speed and the number of other users currently attempting to download from the same server. Most likely, you will not see any noticeable difference between downloading from one mirror or another.

The various subreleases of PHP 5 do not have significant differences, so although the text discusses PHP 5.2.6, everything will work the same if you have a slightly later or earlier release. PHP 6, on the other hand, will likely offer many very big differences from past versions, but it is supposed to be backwards-compatible, so the examples in the text should work even if you end up downloading that version.

# Install PHP

**A**fter you have downloaded PHP, you can install it by following the steps outlined in the installation wizard. You need to be sure that either Apache or IIS is installed and running on your computer before you begin the installation.

As with other software installers, PHP begins by asking you to read and agree to an end-user license agreement. It then asks you to confirm the directory into which you want to have it installed and the Web server you are using.

A default installation of PHP installs only the minimum files needed to run it. In order to communicate with a database, you must install the appropriate database modules. You can do this in the installer on the Choose Items to Install page by expanding Extensions and then

selecting the appropriate modules. Although almost any database can be used with PHP, the overwhelming majority of PHP developers use MySQL. The examples later in this chapter that discuss communicating with databases use MySQL as well, so you will want to choose the MySQL extensions. After you have completed these steps, the actual installation should be fairly quick.

As mentioned previously, Macintosh computers come with PHP preinstalled. If, however, you find that you want to upgrade your preinstalled version of PHP to a newer one, the easiest method is to use MAMP, which contains Apache, MySQL, and PHP in a single package, specifically designed for Macs. You can download the latest version of MAMP and read details on installing and configuring it at www.mamp.info/en/index.html.

## Install PHP

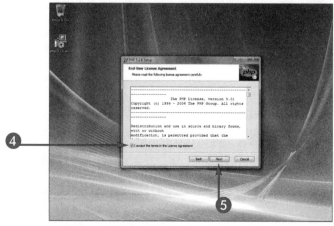

① Double-click the file that you downloaded from the PHP Web site.

The Windows security warning appears.

② Click Run.

The installer Welcome screen appears.

③ Click Next.

The End-User License Agreement screen appears.

④ Click I Accept the Terms in the License Agreement.

⑤ Click Next.

The Destination Folder screen appears.

⑥ Click Next.

The Web Server Setup screen appears.

⑦ Click the proper version of your Web server.

**Note:** *If you are using a recent version of Apache, click Apache 2.2.x Module; if you use IIS, you want the IIS ISAPI Module.*

⑧ Click Next on this and the following screens.

The Choose Items to Install screen appears.

**9** Click the Add button.

**10** Click MySQL.

**11** Click Will Be Installed on Local Hard Drive.

**12** Click Next.

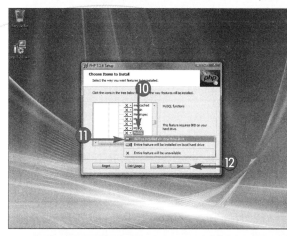

The Ready to Install PHP screen appears.

**13** Click Install.

PHP installs. When complete, a message appears.

**14** Click Finish.

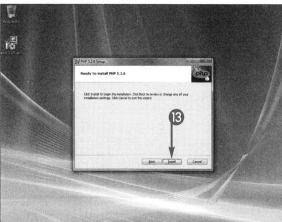

## Extra

If you forget to install the MySQL extensions or you decide later that you want to modify other aspects of your installation, you can run the installer again. If PHP detects that the same version is already installed, it will run in Repair mode. You can tell it that you want to change your installation and then select the modules that you want to install.

You can also manually install modules by downloading the files from http://pecl.php.net/packages.php or http://pear.php.net, following the instructions provided in the PHP documentation online to install the module, and configuring PHP to use it. Note that many of the modules are packaged as TAR files, so you need a special application such as gzip or WinRAR to extract them if you are running Windows, as the WinZip utility installed on most Windows machines does not support the TAR format. You can use a search engine such as Google to find those applications.

# Send Data to the Server

A fter you have your testing environment set up by installing a Web server and an application server, you can configure your Flash application to connect to the server to send and retrieve data. This is most often handled with the URLRequest class.

Flash Player ultimately connects to Web servers in exactly the same way as a regular HTML page. Both send a request via HTTP to a server and then await a response. Two methods exist for sending this data: get and post. A request via get appends the data being sent from the client, whether Flash or HTML-based, to the URL in name=value pairs. For example, if you are sending a get request to a server at www.bradystudios.net and have a variable userName with a value Mal, the get request would look like www.bradystudios. com?userName=Mal. You can have multiple data points,

but servers do limit the total length of the URL string, usually to about 1,024 characters, so large blocks of data cannot be sent. post, on the other hand, allows you to send large blocks of data, as the information is sent in the background of the request. post requests are hidden from direct view from users.

The address to which you are making the request is provided directly to the constructor for the class. Additional data points can be added by placing them within a single variable and then assigning this variable to the data property of the class.

The default method when sending data with URLRequest is get, but this can be changed by setting the method property of the class to a constant, either URLRequestMethod.GET or URLRequestMethod.POST.

## Send Data to the Server

### SEND DATA VIA A TEXT FIELD AND A SUBMIT BUTTON

1 On the Stage, create an input text field with an instance name of something like txtUserName.

**Note:** See Chapter 9 for details on creating text fields.

2 Create a MovieClip named something like mcSubmitButton.

**Note:** See Chapter 3 for details on creating and naming MovieClips.

3 Create a new layer named "actions."

4 Click frame 1 of the actions layer.

5 Press F9 to open the Actions panel.

6 Add the event listener for the handler that will have the button submit the data to the server, such as mcSubmitButton.
addEventListener(MouseEvent.CLICK, submitData);.

7 Add the event handler, such as function submitData(event:MouseEvent):void, and a pair of curly braces.

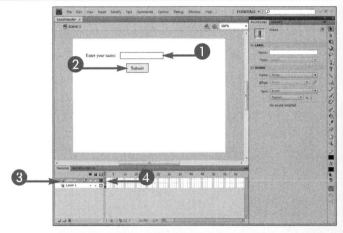

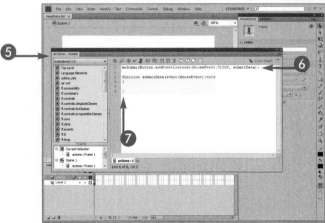

**8** Within the braces, create a variable that sets the data typed into the text field as the data to send to the server, such as `var dataToSend:String = "userName=" + txtUserName.text;`.

**9** Create an instance of the `URLRequest` class, such as `var theRequest:URLRequest = new URLRequest("http://localhost");`.

**10** Set the variable from step **9**'s data to the variable in step **8**, such as `theRequest.data = dataToSend;`.

**11** Save the file to your Web server's root directory.

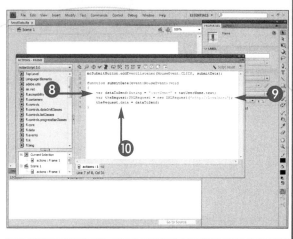

## TEST THE MOVIE

**12** Press Ctrl + Enter.

The movie runs.

**13** Type the requested data in the text field.

**14** Click the button.

Your Web browser launches, displaying the default page for the Web server. In this example, the data from the Flash application will appear in the Address bar as something like `http://localhost?userName=Rob`.

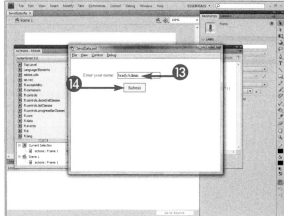

---

### Extra

In order to respond to requests for documents, Web servers have a root directory configured. All documents that you want to be accessible from the server need to be saved either in this directory or a subdirectory of it.

On Windows, the default root directory for the Apache server, assuming a default installation, is c:/Program Files/Apache Software Foundation/Apache2.2/htdocs. The default directory for a normal installation of Internet Information Services is c:/intepub/wwwroot. The configuration settings for either server allow you to change this root.

On the Macintosh, the default root directory for Apache can be found at /Library/WebServer/Documents/.

You need to be sure to save any files that you want to use for communication with the server in this root directory. Otherwise, you will get an error.

You can make a request to the server located on your machine using the special reserved URL `localhost`. This will send a request to the local server, which will attempt to find the document in the root directory.

# Create XML with ColdFusion

In order to respond to a request from the client, rather than from Flash Player or an HTML document, you need to write a script in the language supported by the application server you are using. For ColdFusion, this involves writing in CFML, of ColdFusion Markup Language. CFML closely resembles HTML in that it uses a tag-based architecture.

You can write CFML in any text editor. However, Adobe Dreamweaver provides several important features that make coding CFML easier. If you purchased Flash in one of the CS4 suites, you likely already have Dreamweaver as they are included together in the suites.

You can create a variable in CFML using the `<cfset>` tag. Variables in ColdFusion follow the same naming rules as ActionScript variables: They must begin with a letter and then can only contain letters, numbers, and underscores. However, unlike ActionScript, CFML is not case-sensitive.

The easiest format to use when sending data back to Flash is XML. CFML has many tags that it can use to both read and write XML. The simplest of these is simply `<cfxml>`. You provide a name for the variable for reference later via the `variable` attribute of the tag. Between the opening and closing tags, you can provide a valid XML document, which may either be hard-coded or constructed with variables or other ColdFusion tags.

You can view the value of ColdFusion variables with the `<cfoutput>` tag. Literal text can be output directly with the tag, whereas ColdFusion values must be placed within pound, or *hash,* symbols. You can determine the current date and time from the server with the `now()` function and format it by using the `dateformat()` function.

## Create XML with ColdFusion

### DISPLAY A NAME AND THE CURRENT DATE

① Create a new ColdFusion document in your text editor.

*Note: If your editor adds any code to the page by default, delete it.*

② Create a variable for the name, such as `<cfset companyName="BradyStudios">`.

③ Create a variable for the current date and format it, such as `<cfset today=dateformat(now(), "mm/dd/yy")>`.

④ Open a `<cfxml>` tag to read and write the data, giving it a variable name, such as `<cfxml variable="xmlData">`.

⑤ Create a parent node for the data, such as `<myData>`.

⑥ Create a child node to output the name, such as `<company><cfoutput>#companyName# </cfoutput></company>`.

⑦ Create a child node to output the current date, such as `<dateCreated><cfoutput>#today# </cfoutput></dateCreated>`.

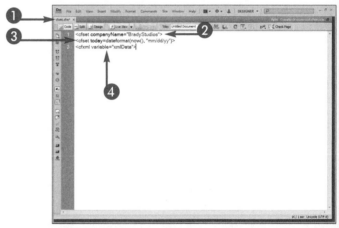

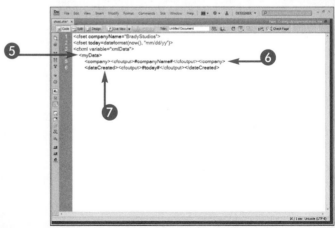

**8** Close the parent node, such as
`</myData>`.

**9** Type `</cfxml>`.

**10** Output all the data, such as
`<cfoutput>#xmlData#`
`</cfoutput>`.

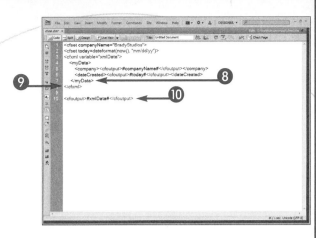

**11** Save the document to the root directory of your Web server.

## TEST THE COLDFUSION

**12** Open a Web browser.

**13** Type `http://localhost/` and the name of the file.

● The page is displayed in your browser. The XML created by ColdFusion is displayed as the source of the page.

## Extra

A detailed explanation of ColdFusion is well beyond the scope of this book. Additional details on the language can be found online. You can visit http://livedocs.adobe.com/coldfusion/8/htmldocs/help.html to browse Adobe's official ColdFusion documentation. Many ColdFusion tutorials are available at the Adobe Developer Center at http://developer.adobe.com, and Adobe has a series of video tutorials on the topic at http://tv.adobe.com. In addition, ColdFusion enjoys a large and vibrant developer community. You may have a ColdFusion user group in your area that you can join to learn more about the language and network with other local developers; go to http://groups.adobe.com to see if one is available.

ColdFusion is not case-sensitive, but you should keep in mind that XML is, so although you can use any case that you want for the ColdFusion tags and variable names, you need to be sure that the resulting XML will use a consistent case.

# Create XML with PHP

ou can create PHP documents in any plain text editor. Most HTML editors, including visual editors such as Adobe Dreamweaver, also support PHP development. Your documents will contain a mixture of PHP and regular HTML. All PHP will be placed within PHP delimiters, which begin with `<?php` and end with `?>`. Like ActionScript, PHP variable names are case-sensitive; function names, however, are not.

PHP, via its DOM XML extension, provides the ability to read and write XML. The extension includes a series of objects, properties, and methods to manipulate XML.

You can begin writing an XML document in PHP by creating a new instance of `DomDocument`, passing the version of XML that you want to use to its constructor. Creating new instances of objects in PHP uses the exact

same syntax as ActionScript, except that PHP variables must begin with a dollar sign.

You can then create elements within your XML document via the `createElement` method. Once created, you can insert an element into your document via the `appendChild` method. In both cases, you associate the method with the object using the `->` characters.

You can add text data to the XML with the `createTextNode` method. The syntax is basically the same as creating an element, so you need to also call `appendChild` to add the text node to the document.

After the XML has been created, you can output the entire result by setting a variable to a call to the DOM XML instance's `saveXML()` method. In PHP, you can output strings to the browser by calling the `echo` method.

## Create XML with PHP

### DISPLAY A NAME

**1** Open a new PHP document in your text editor.

**Note:** *If your editor adds anything to the document by default, delete it.*

**2** Type `<?php`.

**3** Create a variable for the name, such as
`$companyName = "Brady Studios";`.

**4** Create an instance of `DomDocument`, such as
`$myXML = new DomDocument('1.0');`.

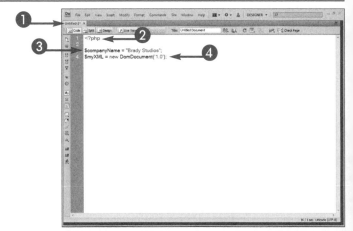

**5** Create an element that will be the parent node for the data, such as `$rootElement = $myXML -> createElement('myData');`.

**6** Add the element to the document, such as
`$rootElement = $myXML -> appendChild($rootElement);`.

**7** Create an element that will be the child node for the name, such as `$company = $myXML -> createElement('company');`.

**8** Add the element to the document, such as
`$company = $myXML -> appendChild($company);`.

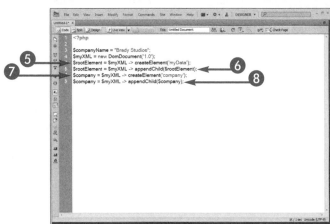

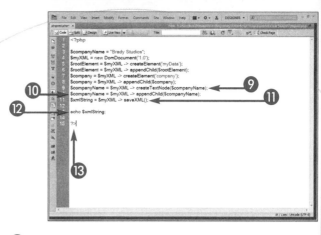

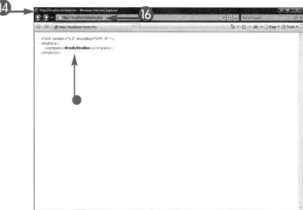

**9** Add the text data for the name, such as
`$companyName = $myXML -> createTextNode($companyName);`.

**10** Add the text node to the document, such as
`$companyName = $myXML -> appendChild($companyName);`.

**11** Output the result, such as `$xmlString = $myXML -> saveXML();`.

**12** Output the string to the browser, such as
`echo $xmlString;`.

**13** Type `?>`.

**14** Save the file to the root of your Web server.

**TEST THE PHP**

**15** Open a Web browser.

**16** Type `http://localhost/` and the filename.

● The page loads, displaying the XML data.

---

## Extra

A detailed examination of PHP is beyond the scope of this book. Additional information about the language can be found online. The official Web site of PHP at www.php.net contains a detailed reference guide to the language. In addition, many detailed tutorials exist online; you can use a search engine such as Google to search for tutorials on any specific topic. You can also learn the language through books such as *PHP 5: Your visual blueprint for creating open source, server-side content,* by Toby Boudreaux, and *Flash and PHP Bible,* by Matthew Keefe, both published by Wiley.

The DOM XML was introduced into the language in version 4 but was subsequently removed with version 5. Therefore, if you are using PHP 5 or later, you will need to download and install it as a separate extension. You can visit the PECL library of PHP extensions at http://pecl.php.net. From there, simply search for "DOM XML" and follow the instructions provided on the site to download and install the extension.

# Read Data from the Server

The process of receiving data from the server is essentially the same as that for sending the data. When a client makes a request to a server-side script, the Web server will automatically send any data created by the script back to the client. This is true regardless of the technologies used, so whether the client uses HTML or a Flash-based solution and whether the server script is written in ColdFusion, PHP, or some other language, the process is the same.

To use data from a server in your Flash application, you must therefore begin by having the application send a request to the server. Often, this will involve creating a form with input text fields for your users to input the data that they want to send. This data will be appended to the `URLRequest` object's `data` property. It can be structured as a simple string, or for larger, more complex data, it may be easier to work with it as XML.

You will also need to have your Flash movie set up to handle the data that is returned. This can be accomplished by simply adding dynamic text fields that will display the information from the server.

In the example shown here, a simple form will request that the user enter his or her name and email address. This data will be sent to the server; in the second half of this section, a ColdFusion script will process the data and send it back to the Flash movie for display. In this example, the data will be structured as a string for simplicity.

## Read Data from the Server

### CREATE A FORM THAT REQUESTS AND RETURNS A NAME AND EMAIL ADDRESS

① On the Stage, create an input text field for the username.

② Create another input text field for the email address.

③ Create a `MovieClip` to act as a submit button.

④ Create two dynamic text fields to receive the name and email address back from the server.

⑤ Create a new layer named "actions."

⑥ Click frame 1 of the actions layer.

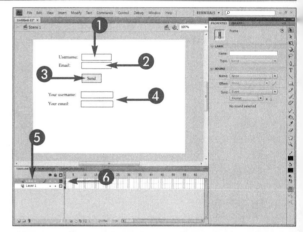

⑦ In the Actions panel, add an event listener for the handler that will submit the data to the server, such as `mcSubmitButton.addEventListener(MouseEvent.CLICK, submitData);`.

⑧ Create an instance of the `URLRequest` class, such as `var theRequest:URLRequest;`.

⑨ Create an instance of the `URLLoader` class, such as `var theLoader:URLLoader = new URLLoader();`.

⑩ Add the event handler, such as `function submitData(event:MouseEvent):void`.

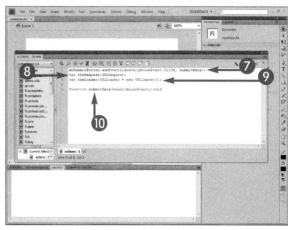

(11) Type a pair of curly braces.

(12) Within the braces, create a variable to display the name, such as `var dataToSend:String = "userName=" + txtSendUserName.text;`.

(13) Add the email address to that data, such as `dataToSend += "&email=" + txtSendEmailAddress.text;`.

(14) Pass the `URLRequest` variable the path to the file, such as `theRequest= new URLRequest("http://localhost/readdata.cfm");`.

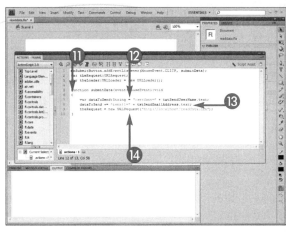

(15) Set its data to the variable from step **12**, such as `theRequest.data = dataToSend;`.

(16) Call its `load` method, such as `theLoader.load(theRequest);`.

(17) Add an event listener for the handler to process the data, such as `theLoader.addEventListener(Event.COMPLETE, processData);`.

(18) Save the file with an .fla extension to the root of your Web server.

The Flash form is created.

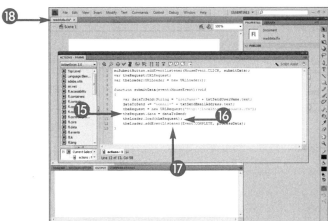

## Extra

This example focuses on a simple send-response mechanism, which is the standard method by which browsers and servers communicate. If you have experience building HTML-based Web applications, this method should be familiar to you.

However, ActionScript does support the use of sockets. Send-response systems are equivalent to email communication: Each side sends its data and then closes its connection to the server. By comparison, a socket-based system allows the client to open a connection to the server and then hold it open, allowing the client and server to communicate back and forth as much as necessary. Server-side push, whereby the server sends data to the client without the client requesting it, is only possible with sockets.

Unfortunately, socket communication requires that additional software be installed on the server. Many Java-based socket servers exist, including red5, Unity, and Electro Server. Adobe's BlazeDS, an open source implementation of its commercial LiveCycleDS, can also be used.

continued ➡

You will need a script on the server to process the data being sent by Flash. This script may compare the data sent from Flash with existing database information, as is the case in application login scripts, or it may insert that data into the database. ColdFusion and PHP, along with other languages such as ASP.NET and JSP, are practically limitless as to what they can do with the data, including sending and receiving email and reading and writing files on the server. The details of using any of these languages are beyond the scope of this book; you should explore the possibilities of your language of choice to get a better idea of what can be done.

Regardless of what the script does, in the end it needs to send its data back to your Flash application. Although there are many possibilities as to how this data can be

structured, XML is generally the easiest format in which to work, as XML is recognized as a native data format in ActionScript. See the sections earlier in this chapter for examples of how to use ColdFusion or PHP to construct the XML data.

Once received, the data can simply be handled as would any other XML data. As with any interaction with the server, you should wrap the code needed to receive the data into an event handler and the Complete event of the request. This will ensure that the data has been received before ActionScript attempts to use it; otherwise, runtime errors may occur if the data is delayed from the server.

## Read Data from the Server (continued)

### CREATE THE COLDFUSION SCRIPT TO RETURN THE NAME AND EMAIL ADDRESS

1 Open a new ColdFusion file in your text editor.

2 Open a `<cfxml>` tag to read and write the data, giving it a variable name, such as `<cfxml variable="sendData">`.

3 Create a parent node with two child nodes to output the name and email address.

4 Type `</cfxml>`.

5 Output all the data, such as `<cfoutput>#sendData#</cfoutput>`.

6 Save the file to the root of your Web server.

**Note:** Be sure that the filename matches the one referenced by the URLRequest object. See step **14** in the first half of this section.

### FINISH THE FLASH FILE

1 Return to Flash CS4 Professional.

2 In the ActionScript panel, type the event handler to process the data, such as `function processData(event:Event):void`, and a pair of curly braces.

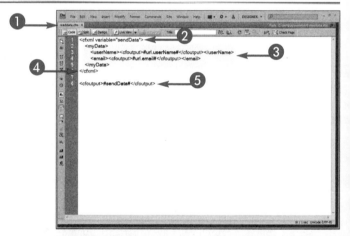

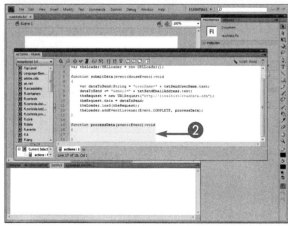

③ Within the braces, create a variable to read the data, such as `var dataRec:XML = new XML(event.target.data);`.

④ Set the text of the first dynamic field to the name, such as `txtRecUserName.text = dataRec.userName;`.

⑤ Set the text of the second dynamic field to the email address, such as `txtRecEmailAddress.text = dataRec.email;`.

⑥ Remove the event listener to the handler to process the data, such as `theLoader. removeEventListener(Event. COMPLETE, processData);`.

⑦ Save the file.

⑧ Click File ➔ Publish.

## TEST THE SCRIPT

⑨ Open a Web browser.

⑩ Type `http://localhost/` and the name of the file.

⑪ Type a username and an email address.

⑫ Click the button.

● The Flash movie sends the data to the script, which then returns it.

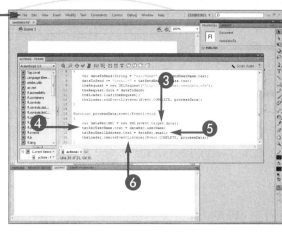

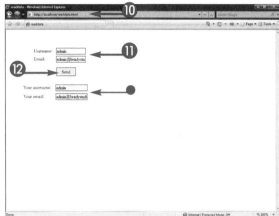

---

### Apply It

Ideally, the ActionScript should include a mechanism to inform the user in case the server script fails or is unavailable. This can be accomplished by adding code to handle the `IOError` event, which is automatically fired whenever an error occurs when receiving data:

```
myRequest.addEventListener(IOErrorEvent.IO_ERROR, handleError);
function handleError(event:IOErrorEvent):void
{
    txtErrorField.text = "An error occurred: " + event.text;
}
```

# Draw Lines in Code

**A**ctionScript provides a full programming interface that allows you to draw objects onscreen through code, freeing you from having to rely on the Flash Professional drawing tools. This interface is particularly helpful in that you can have objects drawn at runtime based on user-provided variables.

Drawing in ActionScript relies on the `Graphics` class, which defines line and fill styles and lets you draw lines, curves, and shapes. All the methods of the class can be called via the `graphics` property of the display object onto which you are drawing. It can be helpful, although not required, to create a specific object, often using the `Sprite` class, to hold your drawings rather than place them directly onto the Stage, as this provides a central reference that allows you to later move or resize the drawn shapes as a group if needed.

To draw lines, you need to first call the `lineStyle` method. The first argument for the method is the width or thickness of the line, in pixels. The second argument is the color, given as a hexadecimal value.

Next, you need to draw the actual line. You begin by calling the `moveTo` method, which takes x and y coordinates to define the starting point of the line and then calling the `lineTo` method, passing the line's endpoint as x and y arguments. You can continue drawing connected lines by repeatedly calling `lineTo`, or you can start a new line with a new call to the `moveTo` method. You can change the appearance of the line at any point by recalling the `lineStyle` method.

## Draw Lines in Code

① Create an instance of the `Sprite` class, such as `var canvas:Sprite = new Sprite();`.

② Create a `Graphics` variable and set it to the object's `graphics` property, such as `var drawing:Graphics = canvas.graphics;`.

③ Add step **1**'s object to the page, such as `addChild(canvas);`.

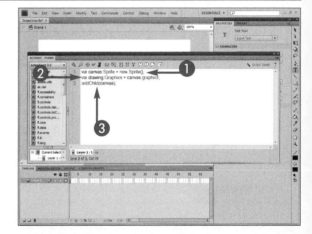

④ Call the `lineStyle` method and set the line's thickness and color, such as `drawing.lineStyle(1, 0xFF9900);`.

⑤ Define the starting point of the line, such as `drawing. moveTo(100,100);`.

⑥ Specify the line's endpoint, such as `drawing.lineTo(200,200);`.

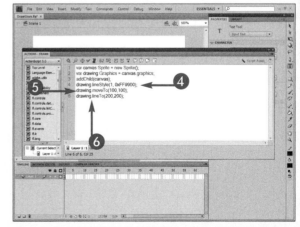

⑦ To draw a connected line, specify a new endpoint, such as `drawing.lineTo(200,300);`.

⑧ To start a new line, repeat step **4** with new arguments, such as `drawing.lineStyle(2,0x000066);`.

⑨ Define the starting point of the new line, such as `drawing.moveTo(300,350);`.

⑩ Specify the new line's endpoint, such as `drawing.lineTo(400,300);`.

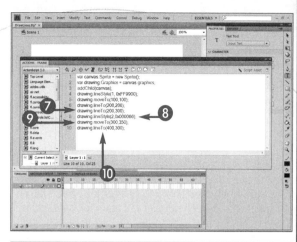

⑪ Press Ctrl + Enter.

The movie plays.

● In this example, two lines are shown.

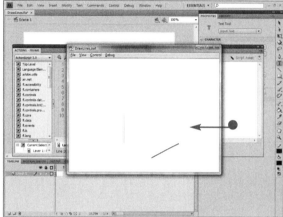

# Draw Curves in Code

You can draw curves in code by defining a `lineStyle` method and determining a starting point with the `moveTo` method. See the previous section, "Draw Lines in Code," for details on these two methods.

After setting the style and initial point, you can call the `curveTo` method to draw a curve. Like other vector-based drawing tools, Flash draws Bezier curves. However, other programs such as Adobe Illustrator and Adobe Fireworks use what is known as a *cubic curve model,* in which the curve is defined using separate control points or handles for each endpoint on the curve. Flash, on the other hand, uses a quadratic Bezier model, whereby the curve is defined by a single control point for the curve. Although this can cause confusion when drawing on the Stage in

Flash, if you are experienced with other vector tools, it greatly simplifies the code needed to draw the curve. Thus, the `curveTo` method takes four arguments: two numbers to specify the x and y coordinates of the control point and two numbers for the x and y coordinates of the end of the line. The control point is the imaginary point where the control handles would meet. Determining the exact location of the control point in your code requires a bit of practice and a lot of trial and error.

Once done, you should get in the habit of resetting the drawing point to an arbitrary place on the Stage to prevent future lines from connecting to your existing shape. You simply need to call the `moveTo` method to accomplish this.

## Draw Curves in Code

① Create an instance of the `Sprite` class, such as `var curve:Sprite = new Sprite();`.

② Create a `Graphics` variable and set it to the object's `graphics` property, such as `var drawing:Graphics = curve.graphics;`.

③ Add step **1**'s object to the page, such as `addChild(curve);`.

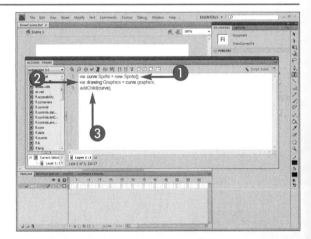

④ Call the `lineStyle` method and set the line's thickness and color, such as `drawing.lineStyle(2, 0x333333);`.

⑤ Define the starting point of the curve, such as `drawing.moveTo(150,150);`.

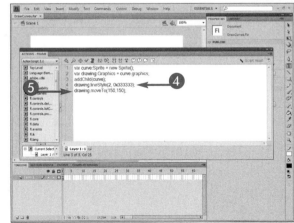

**6** Specify the curve's control point and endpoint, such as `drawing.curveTo(200, 0, 250,150);`.

**7** Reset the drawing point to somewhere else on the Stage, such as `drawing. moveTo(0,0);`.

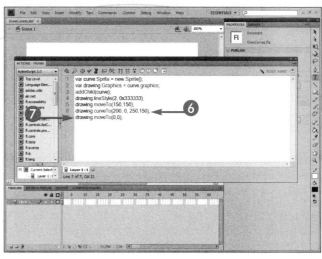

**8** Press Ctrl + Enter.

The movie plays.

● A curve is drawn on the screen.

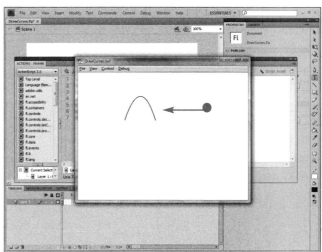

---

**Apply It**

It is possible to draw a circle by repeatedly calling the `curveTo` method, but ActionScript includes a `drawCircle` method that greatly simplifies this process. The method is discussed in the following section, "Draw Shapes in Code."

You can clear an existing line style by calling the `lineStyle` method but providing no arguments.

You can freely switch between drawing curves and lines based on the order in which you call successive `lineTo` and `curveTo` methods. Therefore, a straight line, followed by a curve, followed by a straight line could be created like this:

```
drawing.moveTo(100,100);
drawing.lineTo(150, 100);
drawing.curveTo(200,0,200,100);
drawing.lineTo(250,100);
```

# Draw Shapes in Code

**A**lthough you can draw complete shapes by creating a series of connected lines or curves, ActionScript provides a far easier path via its `drawCircle`, `drawEllipse`, `drawRect`, and `drawRoundRect` methods. Each offers an easy way to draw closed shapes.

The `drawCircle` method takes as its arguments three numbers: The first and second represent the x and y coordinates of the center of the circle, and the third is the radius, in pixels. The related `drawEllipse` method takes four arguments: The first two are the same as for the circle — the x and y of the shape's center, and the final two arguments are the width and height of the ellipse, both in pixels.

You can draw a rectangle with square corners by using the `drawRect` method. Like the ellipse, it takes as its first two arguments x and y coordinates, although they represent the top-left corner of the rectangle rather than its center, and as its last two arguments the width and height of the shape. Finally, the `drawRoundRect` draws a rectangle with rounded corners. Its first four arguments are the same as that of the rectangle, but it includes a fifth argument, in which you specify the corner radius, in pixels as usual.

Any of these methods should be preceded by a call to the `lineStyle` method, discussed in the previous sections of this chapter, to set the appearance of their lines. You need not call the `moveTo` method because the shapes reference the point at which they are drawn directly. You can fill the shapes with solid or gradient colors, which is covered in the following section, "Create Fills."

## Draw Shapes in Code

① Create an instance of the `Sprite` class, such as `var shapes:Sprite = new Sprite();`.

② Create a `Graphics` variable and set it to the object's `graphics` property, such as `var drawing:Graphics = shapes.graphics;`.

③ Call the `lineStyle` method and set the line's thickness and color, such as `graphics.lineStyle(1, 0x000000);`.

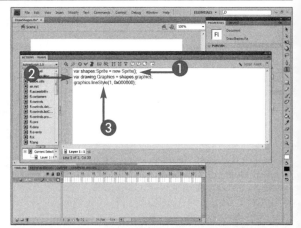

④ To draw a circle, define its center and radius, such as `graphics.drawCircle(50,50,100);`.

⑤ To change the line's appearance for the next shape, repeat step **3** with different arguments, such as `graphics.lineStyle(0,0x99ccff);`.

⑥ To draw an ellipse, define its center, width, and height, such as `graphics.drawEllipse(150,150,20,100);`.

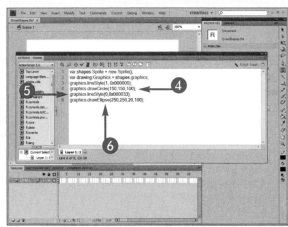

**7** To change the line's appearance for the next shape, repeat step **3** again with different arguments, such as `graphics.lineStyle(3,0x66ffcc);`.

**8** To draw a rectangle, define its top-left corner, width, and height, such as `graphics.drawRect(300, 100, 50, 100);`.

**9** To change the line's appearance for the next shape, repeat step **3** yet again with different arguments, such as `graphics.lineStyle(1, 0xcc6633);`.

**10** To draw a rounded rectangle, define its top-left corner, width, height, and corner radius, such as `graphics.drawRoundRect(400,100,75, 150, 5);`.

**11** Press Ctrl + Enter.

The movie plays.

● In this example, four shapes are displayed on the screen.

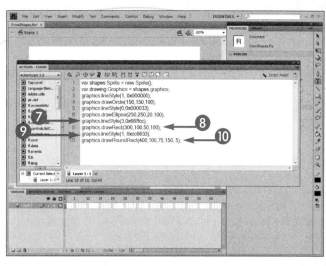

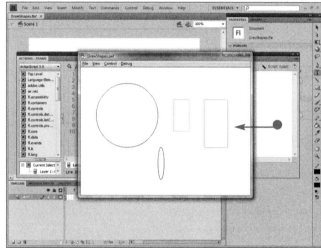

## Extra

When calling the `lineStyle` method, you can set its width to 0, which sets it to a hairline thickness. The maximum thickness of the line is 255 pixels; if you pass in a value greater than that, it will be ignored and the thickness set to 255. The parameter must be an integer, so you cannot set a thickness to, say, 1.5. The caps, joints, and miter settings of the method are not always obvious when simply drawing lines but will be clear if you apply them to rectangles.

ActionScript does not provide methods to draw stars and polygons, even though tools exist for those shapes in Flash Professional. You need to draw them manually with the `moveTo` and `lineTo` methods to draw a series of lines. Closed shapes can be drawn by simply having a final `lineTo` method return to the original point specified by the initial `moveTo` call.

# Create Fills

While drawing shapes, you can also add fills. When creating a filled shape using the drawing tools in Flash Professional, you can set the fill color and its alpha, or transparency. You can do the same when adding fills in code.

Before you begin drawing the lines or curves, you need to call the `beginFill` method. It takes two arguments: the color of the fill and its alpha. The color is a hexadecimal value, and the alpha is a number between 0 and 1, where 0 is completely transparent and 1 completely opaque. The alpha value is optional and defaults to 1.

After setting the fill, you can draw the line using the `moveTo`, `lineTo`, and `curveTo` methods. See the prior sections in this chapter for details on these methods. You

need to call the `endFill` method, which takes no arguments, after any `lineTo` or `curveTo` calls to complete the shape.

Using the drawing tools, you can use gradients to fill shapes, and you can also use them when drawing in code. Rather than call the `beginFill` method, you use the `beginGradientFill` method. This method takes four arguments. The first defines the type of gradient, using either the `RADIAL` or `LINEAR` constants of the `GradientType` class. Second, you provide an array of colors that will be used to fill the gradient. Third is an array of alpha for each color, and the final argument is an array of ratios that determine how the gradient is applied. Just as with the `beginFill` method, you complete your shape by calling the `endFill` method.

## CREATE A FILL

1️⃣ Create an instance of the `Sprite` class, such as `var filledShapes:Sprite = new Sprite();`.

2️⃣ Set a `Graphics` variable to the object's `graphics` property, such as `var drawing:Graphics = filledShapes.graphics;`.

3️⃣ Add step **1**'s object to the page, such as `addChild(filledShapes);`.

4️⃣ Set the line's thickness and color, such as `drawing.lineStyle(1, 0x000000);`.

5️⃣ Call the `beginFill` method and set the fill's color (and optionally, its `alpha`), such as `drawing.beginFill(0xff0000);`.

6️⃣ Define the shape that you want, such as `drawing.drawCircle(150,150,50);`.

7️⃣ Complete the shape, such as `drawing.endFill();`.

## CREATE A GRADIENT

8️⃣ Define the gradient type, such as `var gradientType:String = GradientType.LINEAR;`.

9️⃣ Specify the colors in an array, such as `var colors:Array = [0x000000, 0xFFFFFF];`.

🔟 Specify the alphas in an array, such as `var alphas:Array = [1, 1];`.

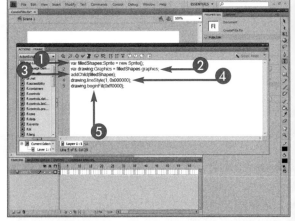

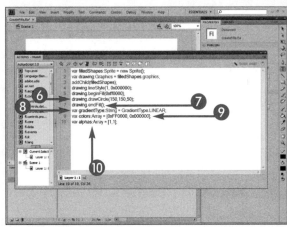

⑪ Set ratios in an array to determine how the gradient is applied, such as `var ratios:Array = [0, 255];`.

⑫ Set the line's thickness and color, such as `drawing.lineStyle(1, 0x000000);`.

⑬ Call the `beginGradientFill` method and set the preceding variables as its arguments, such as `drawing.beginGradientFill(gradientType, colors, alphas, ratios);`.

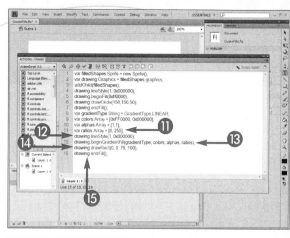

⑭ Define the shape that you want, such as `drawing.drawRect(200, 200, 50, 100);`.

⑮ Complete the shape, such as `drawing.endFill();`.

⑯ Press Ctrl + Enter.

The movie plays.

● In this example, two shapes, a circle with a solid fill and a rectangle with a gradient, are displayed.

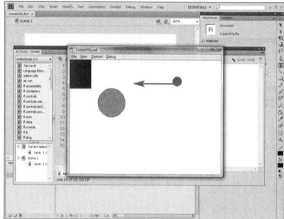

## Extra

The `beginGradientFill` method takes arrays as its arguments instead of simple values because gradients can take more than one color, alpha, or ratio value. You can, for example, specify as many colors as you want for a gradient.

The ratios argument defines how the gradient is applied through the shape. In the example shown here where the values are set to 0 and 255, the gradient is applied evenly through the shape. A ratio of 0, 127 would cause the gradient to be applied only over the first third or so of the shape, so the second color would be solid through most of it. A ratio of 127, 255 would have the opposite effect: The first color would be solid through the first two-thirds of the shape, with the gradient being applied only in the last third. These settings mimic the ability to drag the color stops to the left and right in the Color Mixer panel in Flash CS4 Professional to adjust the ratios of the gradients.

You can have a gradient move from transparent to opaque by adding an array of alphas going from 0 to 1. You still need to provide at least two colors. Even though the first color will be transparent when it starts, it will be somewhat visible as the alpha shifts over the course of the gradient.

# Transform Visual Objects

You can change the color of an object on the Stage at runtime through an instance of the `ColorTransform` class. This class allows you to adjust the red, green, and blue channels that make up the object, as well as its alpha, or transparency, channel.

When using the `ColorTransform` class, you can change the channels with either a multiplier or an offset. Using the multipliers, you can, for example, double the amount of red in the object by setting the `redMultiplier` property to 2, or you can cut the amount of blue in half by setting the `blueMultiplier` to .5. If you would prefer, you can use the offsets instead, setting the channels to a value between -255 and 255. The new value will be added or subtracted to the current value to achieve a new color or alpha setting.

Once created, the instance of the `ColorTransform` class can be applied to one or more clips on the Stage by setting the instance to the `colorTransform` property of the display object's `transform` object. Therefore, if you created an instance of `ColorTransform` called `ct`, you could apply it to a `MovieClip` called `mcBox1` with the following:

```
mcBox1.transform.colorTransform = ct;
```

In the example shown here, the `Math` object's `random` method will be used to calculate random offsets for a `Sprite`'s color. The `Math` object and the `random` method are discussed in Chapter 4.

## Transform Visual Objects

### CHANGE A FILLED OBJECT'S COLOR AT RANDOM

1. Create an instance of the `Sprite` class, such as `var newRect:Sprite = new Sprite();`.

2. Add it to the page, such as `addChild(newRect);`.

3. Set a `Graphics` variable to the object's `graphics` property, such as `var drawing:Graphics = newRect.graphics;`.

4. Set the line's thickness and color, such as `drawing.lineStyle(1, 0x000000);`.

5. Call the `beginFill` method and set the fill's color (and optionally, its alpha), such as `drawing.beginFill(0xff0000);`.

6. Define the shape that you want, such as `drawing.drawRect(200, 200, 50, 100);`.

7. Complete the shape, such as `drawing.endFill();`.

8. Create an instance of the `ColorTransform` class, such as `var ct:ColorTransform = new ColorTransform();`.

9. Calculate a random red offset, such as `ct.redOffset = Math.round((Math.random() * 510)-255);`.

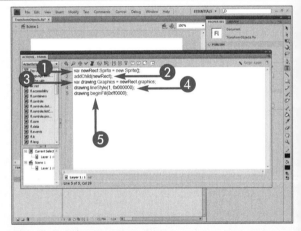

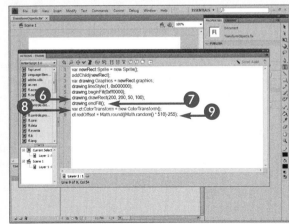

**10** Calculate a random green offset, such as `ct.greenOffset = Math. round((Math.random() * 510)- 255);`.

**11** Calculate a random blue offset, such as `ct.blueOffset = Math.round((Math. random() * 510)-255);`.

**12** Set the instance from step **8** to the `colorTransform` property of its `transform` object, such as `newRect. transform.colorTransform = ct;`.

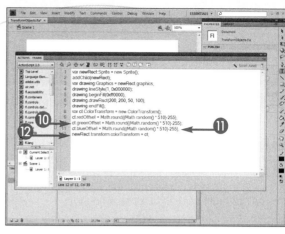

## TEST THE MOVIE

**13** Press Ctrl + Enter.

The movie plays.

● The shape is displayed with a random color.

**14** Press Ctrl + Enter again.

The movie is regenerated.

● The shape is displayed with another random color.

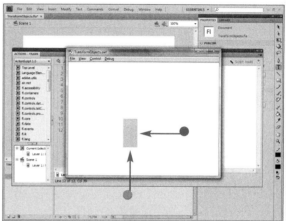

---

## Apply It

Any time you need to apply a series of properties to a single object, you can reduce the amount of typing needed by using the `with` operator. The code to set the properties of the `ColorTransform` object shown in this section is written as follows:

```
ct:ColorTransform = new ColorTransform();
ct.redOffset = Math.round((Math.random() * 510)-255);
ct.greenOffset = Math.round((Math.random() * 510)-255);
ct.blueOffset = Math.round((Math.random() * 510)-255);
```

Instead, it could be written using `with`:

```
ct:ColorTransform = new ColorTransform();
with(ct)
{
            redOffset = Math.round((Math.random() * 510)-255);
            greenOffset = Math.round((Math.random() * 510)-255);
            blueOffset = Math.round((Math.random() * 510)-255);
}
```

Unfortunately, the ActionScript panel in Flash Professional will not provide code hinting when using `with`, so you need to weigh the advantages of code hinting against not needing to type the object name when deciding whether or not you use it.

# Add Filters through Code

ilters, first introduced in Flash 8, allow you to apply visual effects to objects on the Stage such as drop shadows, blur, and bevel. Although the Properties panel allows you to set up and apply these filters, you can also do so through code. Fortunately, the code required almost exactly mirrors the settings in the Properties panel, so if you are familiar with the panel, you will not find this code difficult to remember.

Each of the filters has a corresponding class in ActionScript: `DropShadowFilter`, `BlurFilter`, `GlowFilter`, `BevelFilter`, `GradientGlowFilter`, and `GradientBevelFilter`. In order to use the filter, you need to first create an instance of the appropriate class and set its properties. For example, if you want to create a dark gray drop shadow that will be 5 pixels from the object, have x and y blurs of 15 pixels, and a 75% alpha, you might create a `DropShadowFilter` instance called `ds` and then add `ds.color=0x888888`, `ds.distance=5`, `ds.blurX=15`, `ds.blurY=15`, and `ds.alpha=.75`.

Once created, filters can be applied to an object by calling the object's `filters` property. The property takes as its value an array of filters, which allows you to apply multiple filters to the same object at once.

If the object to which you are applying filters is animated, the filter will animate with it. You could alter the properties of the filter over time as you animate the object if you want to have it animate on its own; for example, you may want a shadow to become lighter and blurrier as the shape moves away from the Stage. However, you should be aware that animating filters is extremely processor-intensive, so it should be used with caution.

## Add Filters through Code

### APPLY THE DROP SHADOW FILTER TO A FILLED OBJECT

1. Perform steps **1** to **5** in the preceding section, "Transform Visual Objects."

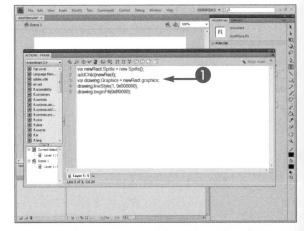

2. Perform steps **6** and **7** in the preceding section, "Transform Visual Objects."

3. Create an instance of the `DropShadowFilter` class, such as `var ds:DropShadowFilter = new DropShadowFilter();`.

4. Set the color, such as `ds.color=0x999999;`.

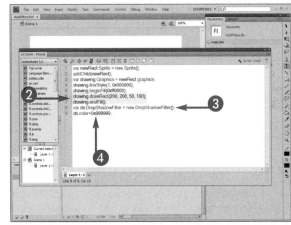

5 Set the alpha, such as `ds.alpha = .8;`.

6 Set the x blur, such as `ds.blurX = 5;`.

7 Set the y blur, such as `ds.blurY = 5;`.

8 Set the angle, such as `ds.angle = 45;`.

9 Apply the filter to the object created in step **1**, such as `newRect.filters = [ds];`.

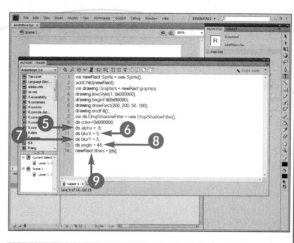

**TEST THE MOVIE**

10 Press Ctrl + Enter.

The movie plays.

● The shape is displayed with a drop shadow.

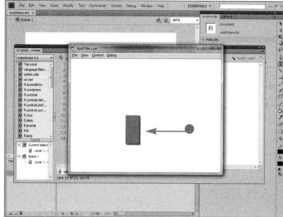

---

**Extra**

Although the example in this section demonstrates the ability to apply a filter to a `Sprite` drawn in code, filters can in fact be applied to objects that you place or draw directly on the Stage as well. Therefore, instead of using the initial lines in the example to draw a `Sprite`, you could manually draw a shape on the Stage, convert it to a `MovieClip`, and then apply the filter to the clip. Alternatively, you could import a bitmap image of some kind, convert it to a `MovieClip`, and then apply the filter. Of course, there would be no functional difference at that point between applying the filter in code versus applying it through the Properties panel, so most often you will see code-generation filters applied only to those objects that are created, or at least instantiated, through code themselves.

The easiest way to determine the available properties of a filter is to look at the Properties panel for that filter. You can also reference the filter's class on the online ActionScript reference at http://livedocs.adobe.com/flash/9.0/ActionScriptLangRefV3/.

# Cache Vectors As Bitmaps

**C**omputer graphics can be drawn as either vectors or bitmaps. Vectors use mathematical calculations to draw lines or curves between defined points, whereas bitmaps fill individual pixels with colors. Flash is primarily a vector drawing program; all the drawing you do with the tools from the Tools panel and all the drawing done thus far in this chapter have relied on vectors.

However, you can work with bitmaps in Flash. Bitmaps, most often photographs, can be imported from other applications such as Adobe Photoshop, directly from a digital camera or scanner, or downloaded from a stock photo service online such as iStockphoto (www. istockphoto.com).

Rather than import graphics, you can temporarily convert vectors to bitmaps in Flash. When animating, vectors require considerable processing overhead, as they must

be constantly recalculated. Bitmaps, on the other hand, require no processing as they are based on filled pixels rather than calculated lines and curves.

You can cache a vector as a bitmap by simply setting its `cacheAsBitmap` property to `true`. When you do this, Flash creates a *surface,* or bitmap representation of the vector. The appearance will not be affected; if the vector needs to be scaled or changed, Flash will discard the bitmap, modify the vector, and then create a new bitmap. Therefore, your user will not be able to tell visually when this process occurs. However, they may be able to notice that you are caching bitmaps because if the image is not changing as it animates, storing it as a bitmap will save processor cycles and may result in your movie playing faster or giving you smoother playback.

## Cache Vectors As Bitmaps

### CACHE A FILLED OBJECT AS A BITMAP

1. Perform steps **1** to **5** in the section "Transform Visual Objects."

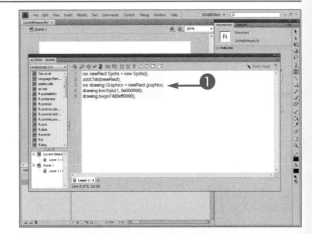

2. Perform steps **6** and **7** in the section "Transform Visual Objects."

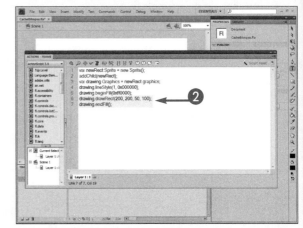

**3** Set the object's `cacheAsBitmap` property to `true`, such as `newRect.cacheAsBitmap = true;`.

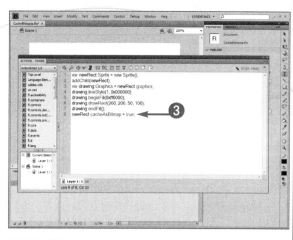

## TEST THE MOVIE

**4** Press Ctrl + Enter.

The movie plays.

● The shape is displayed, after being converted to a bitmap.

**Note:** *With only a single element on the Stage, you will not be able to see any appreciable performance gain, but in large, complex projects, the result may be noticeable.*

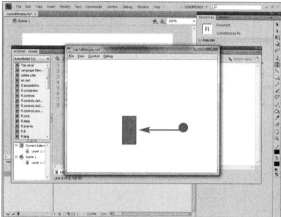

---

### Extra

When you create a nonrectangular shape in Flash, either through the drawing tools or ActionScript, the shape is given a transparent background. You can achieve even greater performance gains by applying solid backgrounds to shapes so that the transparency can be ignored as well. ActionScript provides an `opaqueBackground` property, which takes a hexadecimal color value, that allows you to set this background color.

The performance gains achieved by caching a vector as a bitmap will be noticeable only on relatively static objects, such as backgrounds in your animations. If the object is moving or being scaled repeatedly, any performance savings gained by the caching will be lost by the need to constantly delete and regenerate the new bitmaps. In general, it should only be used sparingly and only when you notice that you have performance lags that you believe may be helped by the technique.

# Draw a Bitmap

You can create shapes through code that are stored internally as bitmaps rather than vectors. You can fill the bitmap with either a solid fill or a picture from the library. This section demonstrates using a solid fill, and the next section, "Add an Image to the Library and Create a Bitmap from It," shows how to insert an image from the library.

In order to draw a bitmap, you must first create an instance of the BitmapData class. This class defines the visual aspects of the bitmap but does not create the image itself. An example of creating the bitmap might look like this:

```
var bitData:BitmapData = new BitmapData(150,
  150, false, 0xFF0000FF);
```

As you can see, the class constructor takes four arguments. The first two are the width and height of the image, in pixels. The third, a Boolean, defines whether the object can support transparency. The final argument defines the color to be used to fill the bitmap. As usual with colors, it is given in hexadecimal format, but note here that it takes four pairs of values, rather than the normal three. The additional pair, given first, is the alpha, or transparency value.

As noted earlier, the BitmapData class merely defines the pixels to be used; it does not draw the shape. The drawing is handled by an instance of the Bitmap class, whose constructor takes an instance of the BitmapData class. Once created, you can simply call the addChild method to add the Bitmap instance to the Stage.

## Draw a Bitmap

① Type the beginning of an instance of the BitmapData class, such as var myBitmapData:BitmapData, and an equals sign.

② Call the class constructor and set the width and height, whether it supports transparency, and the color, such as new BitmapData(150, 150, false, 0xFF993366);.

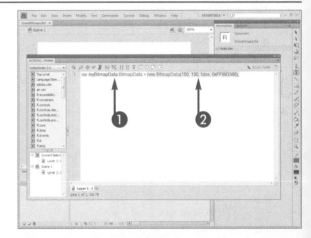

③ Type the beginning of an instance of the Bitmap class, such as var myBitmap:Bitmap, and an equals sign.

④ Call the class constructor and set it to step 1's variable, such as new Bitmap(myBitmapData);.

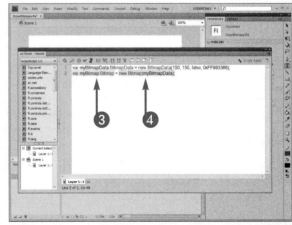

**⑤** Add the bitmap to the page, such as
`addChild(myBitmap);`.

**⑥** Press Ctrl + Enter.

The movie plays.

● A colored square is drawn on the Stage.

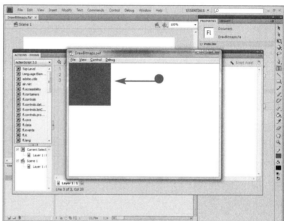

---

## Extra

Creating semitransparent bitmaps can be a bit challenging due to the need to use hexadecimal to specify the alpha value rather than an integer. You need to understand that hexadecimal is a method of counting from 0 to 255 in two digits rather than three. This is done by using a base-16 counting system, in which the letters A to F represent the additional six digits.

You can convert from decimal to hexadecimal by taking the decimal number and dividing by 16. The whole portion of the result becomes the first digit, and the remainder is the second. For example, take a decimal value of 127. 127/16 is 7, with a remainder of 15. 15 is the equivalent of F in hexadecimal, so 127 is the same as 7F. As 127 is approximately half of 255, a value of 7F would roughly equal an alpha transparency of 50%. Remember that in order to use transparency, you must also set the third argument of the `BitmapData`'s constructor to `true`. For example, if you wanted a blue square with 50% transparency, you could write `var mySquare:BitmapData = new BitmapData(100, 100, true, 0x7FFF0000);`.

# Add an Image to the Library and Create a Bitmap from It

Rather than draw a solid fill in a bitmap shape, you can use an image that you have imported into Flash and stored in the library. This allows you to create bitmap images from any image that you may have on your computer.

Before you can use a library image, you must first export it for ActionScript and give it a class name. It can be anything, but to maintain consistency, it should be a single word that uses Pascal case, so it should begin with a capital letter.

In your code, you can then create an instance of the `BitmapData` class, as discussed in the preceding section, "Draw a Bitmap." However, rather than create the

instance by calling the `BitmapData`'s constructor, you should call the constructor of the new image class that you created when you exported the image. You must pass to the constructor a width and height, but oddly, these will be ignored and the actual width and height of the image used. For ease of use, it can be helpful to set both values at 0 — for example,

```
var myImage:BitmapData = new
  WeddingPhoto(0,0);
```

Finally, you can create an instance of the `Bitmap` class, passing the `BitmapData` variable to it. Call `addChild` to actually draw the bitmap on the screen, and your image will appear.

---

### Add an Image to the Library and Create a Bitmap from It

## ADD THE IMAGE TO THE LIBRARY

**1** Click File → Import → Import to Library.

The Import to Library dialog box appears.

**2** Navigate to the folder that contains the image.

**3** Click the image file.

**4** Click Open.

The image is imported to the library.

## EXPORT THE IMAGE FOR ACTIONSCRIPT

**5** If necessary, open the library.

**6** Right-click (⌘ + click) the image.

**7** Click Properties.

The Bitmap Properties dialog box appears.

**8** Click Advanced.

**9** Click Export for ActionScript.

**10** Type a class name.

**11** Click OK.

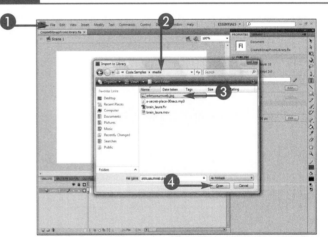

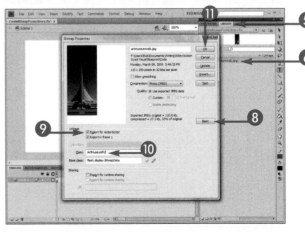

## CREATE THE BITMAP

⓬ Press F9 to open the Actions panel.

⓭ Create an instance of the `BitmapData` class, calling the constructor of the new image class, such as `var myPictureData:BitmapData = new ArtMuseumPic(0,0);`.

**Note:** *Be sure to use the class name you created in step* **10**.

⓮ Draw the shape, such as `var myPicture:Bitmap = new Bitmap(myPictureData);`.

⓯ Add the bitmap to the page, such as `addChild(myPicture);`.

## TEST THE MOVIE

⓰ Press Ctrl + Enter.

The movie plays.

● The image is displayed onscreen.

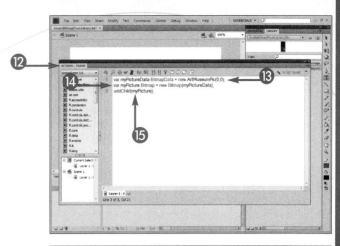

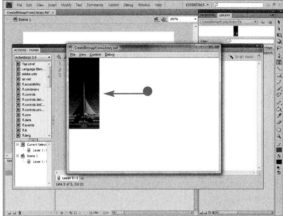

---

### Apply It

You can retrieve the width and height of the `BitmapData` object by calling those properties. If, for example, you have a `BitmapData` object named `myPicData`, you could display its width and height in the Output window using this:

```
trace("The width is " + myPicData.width);
trace("The height is " + myPicData.height);
```

If you animate a `Bitmap` off the Stage, it is a good idea to remove it from memory to free up those resources. This can be accomplished via the `dispose()` method. Once called, the method sets the width and height each to 0 and causes any other calls to the object to fail:

```
myPicData.dispose();
myPicData.hitTest(); //fails and throws exception
```

# Understanding AIR

The Adobe Integrated Runtime, or AIR, allows you to take the skills that you have already developed in building rich Internet applications and apply them to desktop applications. Your applications need not be bound to a Web browser; with AIR, you can create true desktop applications that work across multiple platforms.

## The Adobe Integrated Runtime

The foundation of these cross-platform applications is the Adobe Integrated Runtime. Similar conceptually to the Java Runtime, Adobe's runtime allows you to develop an application once and be assured that it will run in Windows, Macintosh, or Linux environments. The runtime takes your code and translates it into platform-specific code so that you do not need to worry about any differences that may exist.

Your users must have AIR installed on their machines in order to run your application. However, the installation is seamless: When a user attempts to install your application, the installer will check to see if AIR exists on the user's computer and will automatically download and install it if needed. AIR is free to both you and your users.

## AIR Development Environments

As of this writing, Adobe offers three primary tools for developing AIR applications: Dreamweaver CS4, the Flex platform, and Flash CS4 Professional. If you are familiar with developing applications using XHTML, CSS, and possibly Ajax, then you can apply those skills directly to AIR development using Dreamweaver CS4. Flex developers can create AIR applications through the open-source Flex SDK, or they can use Flex Builder, Adobe's commercial tool for Flex development.

Flash CS4 Professional introduced AIR development to the Flash community. The remainder of this chapter covers the basics of creating a simple AIR application using Flash.

## AIR Components

The runtime for AIR includes an integrated Web browser based on the open-source WebKit rendering engine, the same engine used by Apple for its Safari browser and by Adobe for Dreamweaver CS4's Live View feature. Thus, any XHTML, CSS, and Ajax that are supported by WebKit can be used with AIR. AIR also includes the Adobe Reader software, enabling it to view PDF files. The runtime includes a copy of the SQLLite database for data storage, and most importantly for this discussion, it includes a full copy of Flash Player 10.

## AIR Capabilities

AIR applications can do anything that your Web application could do. Your application can display images, PDF files, and Flash movies. It can play sound and video. It can access server-based resources.

For security reasons, Web-based applications, whether written in Flash or HTML or any other technology, do not have local file system access. Web applications can write cookies to the user's hard drive and then later read those cookies, but that is the extent of the browser's access to your user's hard drive. A browser-based system cannot, for example, open a Microsoft Word document on the user's hard drive.

AIR applications do not suffer from this limitation. Because an AIR application is installed on your user's computer, it can fully access the user's hard drive, allowing for not only reading and writing existing files, but even for creating and deleting files. AIR applications also have access to other hardware on the user's machine, such as the printer, and they can access and consume network resources. It is these additional capabilities that will set your AIR application apart from traditional Web applications.

## ActionScript and AIR

Because AIR includes Flash Player 10, any ActionScript that you would write in a traditional, Web-based Flash movie can be written for an AIR application. Adobe has also created a set of classes for ActionScript that are specific to AIR to enable the additional functionality available in those applications. For example, ActionScript includes a set of SQL classes to allow you to interact with AIR's built-in SQLLite database. The complete ActionScript Language and Components Reference, available at http://livedocs.adobe.com/flash/9.0/ActionScriptLangRefV3/, designates these AIR-only classes by placing a small AIR logo next to each.

## AIR and Web Applications

You can have an AIR application and a Web application that perform the same tasks. In certain situations, it may be helpful to have some users access the application via a traditional Web- and browser-based interface and have others download and install an AIR application. Although the AIR application and the Web-based application will need to be two separate files, they can be created from the same source: You could create your Web application, save a copy, and then convert that copy to AIR. Unfortunately, it will then be necessary to maintain both independently; changes to one would not be reflected automatically in the other. You may also end up adding additional, AIR-specific functionality to that application that would not apply to the Web version.

## Connected and Disconnected Applications

Obviously, Web applications are built with the assumption that the user will be online when he or she interacts with the application. Desktop applications, however, are not always built with this assumption. You can use Microsoft Word or Adobe Photoshop in the same way whether you are connected to the Internet or not.

AIR applications can be built so that they require an Internet connection. For example, you might be populating the application with information that must be requested at runtime from a server. However, because the applications

are desktop applications, they can also be built to run without a connection. AIR includes the SQLLite database for exactly this reason: Your application can keep its own set of data internally, without the need to connect back to a server.

Your application can also be written so that it can run in either scenario. You might, for example, have the application make a call back to a server if available to get data, but if the server is unavailable, it could simply use data stored internally.

## Custom Logos

Once installed, your AIR application will work exactly like any other application on your users' computers. If they use Windows, they can access it from the Start menu; on Macintosh, it will be available in the Dock. Either way, your application will be represented in the operating system by an icon. You can use the default icon for AIR applications, which looks like a rocket blasting off; this is a reference to "Apollo," AIR's development codename. You can also create your own custom icon, using any modern graphics application such as Adobe Fireworks, Photoshop, Illustrator, or even Flash itself. The icon must be in PNG format, and you can create up to four icons, at sizes of 128 pixels x 128 pixels, 48 x 48, 32 x 32, and 16 x 16.

## Testing AIR Applications

While working in Flash CS4 Professional, you can test AIR applications just as you would a regular Flash application, by pressing Ctrl + Enter on Windows or ⌘ + Enter on Macintosh or by clicking Control → Test Movie. Before deploying the application, you should publish the file and go through the installation process.

# Create a New AIR Application

You need to designate to Flash that you are creating an AIR application so that when it is published, Flash creates an AIR file, rather than the traditional SWF. You can do this in the Publish Settings dialog box on the Flash tab by selecting AIR 1.1 under the player version. You can also have Flash do this for you by simply selecting Flash File (Adobe AIR) from the Start screen, as shown here, or from the New Document dialog box.

Regardless of the method used to set the application to AIR, you need to configure some settings for the application through the Publish Settings dialog box. In the AIR settings, you can designate a name and version for your application, provide a description that will be visible when your user installs the application, insert copyright data, and configure the installer.

After you have configured these settings, you can proceed with the development of your project. When you begin planning an AIR application, you should keep in mind that everything you would normally do in a Flash application can be done in AIR. Therefore, most of the design and development process will be identical in both cases. You can therefore add text fields to capture user input, insert images, add symbols, and include animation. The ActionScript needed to handle all of these is identical to that needed for a regular Flash movie.

Remember that your AIR application will be running independent of the browser. Although many Flash developers tend to keep their Flash movies small to allow for room for the browser's menus and toolbars and for any HTML that might be on the page, you can make your AIR application any size that you want.

## Create a New AIR Application

① From the Start screen, Click Flash File (Adobe AIR).

**Note:** *If you do not see the Start screen, click File → New and then select Flash File (Adobe AIR).*

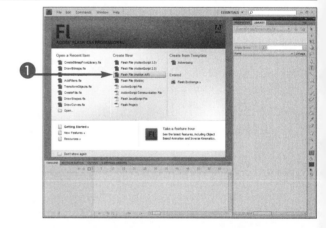

The file is created.

② Click File.

③ Click Publish Settings.

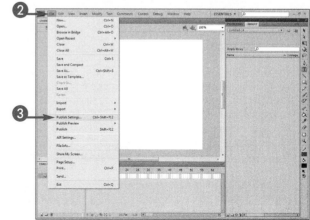

The Publish Settings dialog box appears.

④ Click the Flash tab.

⑤ Click Settings.

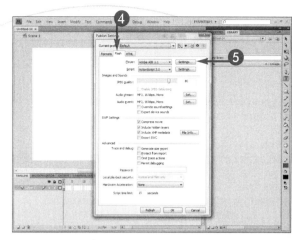

The Settings dialog box appears.

⑥ Type information into the dialog box to describe your application.

⑦ Click OK.

You are returned to the Publish Settings dialog box.

⑧ Click OK.

The new file is created and configured to run on AIR.

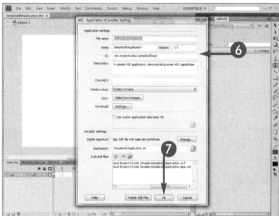

## Extra

Most of the settings for AIR are beyond the scope of this chapter, the purpose of which is merely to provide an introduction to AIR development, not a comprehensive look at it. Much more information on developing AIR applications can be found online at www.adobe.com/products/air/ or in *Adobe AIR Bible,* by Benjamin Gorton, Ryan Taylor, and Jeff Yamada, published by Wiley.

You may also want to download and install the Tour de Flex application, available from www.flex.org/tour. Itself an AIR application, Tour de Flex was created by the Adobe Flex team as a resource for its developers. Although obviously focused on Flex, the application does include a comprehensive ActionScript resource, valuable to anyone using either Flex or Flash, and it includes all the AIR-specific classes, along with examples.

# Digitally Sign Your Application

As you are no doubt aware, many malicious programs exist on the Internet. When you download a program such as the latest version of Flash Player, you can be confident that you are getting the actual application created by Adobe, and not a piece of malware that happens to have the same filename as the Flash Player installer, because the software will identify itself as having been created by Adobe. This identification is done via a digital signature.

You should digitally sign your AIR applications so that your users know that the program is coming from you, a presumably trusted source. In fact, AIR applications *require* a digital signature; you can create an intermediate, unsigned file for testing but cannot distribute an unsigned file.

You can create your own digital signature, which simply identifies you as the program's developer, in the AIR Settings dialog box. You can create a new signature file if you do not already have one, in which you will identify yourself, create a password, and determine the level of encryption to be used by the signature file.

Once created, you can specify the location on your computer of the signature file and a password to prevent others from signing their programs as you whenever you create another AIR application.

This signature information will be displayed on the first screen of the installation process for the application. Your users can review this and, if they recognize that you are a developer who they trust, they can install the application.

## Digitally Sign Your Application

① Open an existing AIR application or create a new one.

② Click File → Publish Settings.

③ Click the Flash tab.

④ Click the Settings button to the right of Player.

  The Settings dialog box appears.

⑤ Click Set.

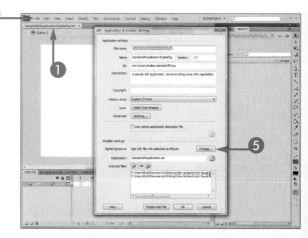

  The Digital Signature dialog box appears.

⑥ Click Create.

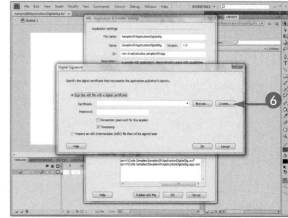

The Create Self-Signed Digital Certificate dialog box appears.

**7** Fill in your name, organization unit, organization name, and country.

**8** Type a password twice.

**9** Set the encryption type.

**10** Enter a location to save the file.

**11** Click OK.

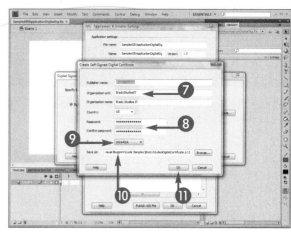

You are returned to the Digital Signature dialog box.

**12** Enter your password.

**13** Click OK.

You are returned to the Settings dialog box.

**14** Click OK.

**15** Click OK in the Publish Settings dialog box.

The digital signature is created and saved with the file.

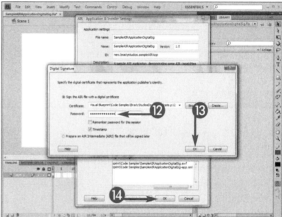

When your users install an AIR application that uses a self-signed certificate, they will receive a security warning stating that the publisher is unknown. This is because self-signed certificates cannot be trusted. There is nothing to prevent you from claiming to be anyone when you set up the certificate. In other words, in the steps shown here, you could easily enter a publisher name of "Adobe Systems, Inc."

The solution to this issue is to use a certificate issued by a trusted third party. When you install an AIR application that is actually created by Adobe, AIR will not generate the security warning because the certificate is not one created by Adobe, but instead Verisign. Verisign is the industry leader in certificates; almost all the certificates used to identify Web sites in e-commerce transactions, where the same issues exist, come from Verisign. If you want to distribute your application and have it be trusted, you need to go to Verisign's Website at www.verisign.com and purchase a certificate.

# Detect User Inactivity

AIR applications have the capability to detect whether users are interacting with their computers and can respond based on this interaction. This is similar to the concept used by your computer's screensaver: After you have failed to interact with your computer for a number of minutes, it turns the screensaver on. An AIR application can be set up to simply display a status message informing the users that they have been inactive, or it can perform other actions such as logging inactive users out of an application or automatically saving data.

Your AIR application is represented in ActionScript as the `nativeApplication` instance of the `Native Application` class. This class provides a set of methods and properties that allows you to interact with the

application as a whole. One of these properties is `idleThreshold`, which can be set to an integer representing a number of seconds. Any time your users stop interacting with the application by not using either their keyboard or their mouse, AIR will begin an internal countdown; when this countdown reaches the value of `idleThreshold`, a `userIdle` event will be dispatched. Note that unlike many other timer functions in ActionScript, `idleThreshold` is set to a number of seconds, not milliseconds.

You can create an event handler to listen for this event and deal with it accordingly. In the example shown here, a message will be displayed, informing the users that they have timed out, using the `trace` method. For the purposes of the example, a very low threshold is being set; obviously, for real applications, you would want this number set much higher.

## Detect User Inactivity

1. Open an existing AIR application or create a new one.

2. Press F9 to open the Actions panel.

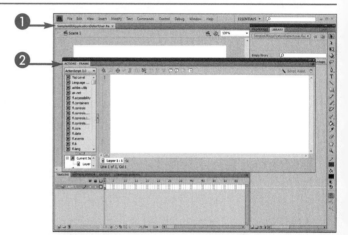

3. Create a number variable to hold the timer value, such as `var timeOut: Number = 5;`.

4. Type `NativeApplication.native Application.idleThreshold = numberVariable;`, replacing `numberVariable` with the variable from step **3**.

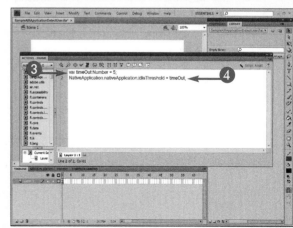

**5** Add an event listener for the handler that will react to the period of inactivity, such as `NativeApplication.native Application.addEventListener (Event.USER_IDLE, alertTimeOut);`.

**6** Add the event handler, such as `function alertTimeOut(event:Event):void`, and a pair of curly braces.

**7** Within the curly braces, create the action that you want to occur when the inactivity period reaches the specified number of seconds, such as `trace("You have timed out of the application");`.

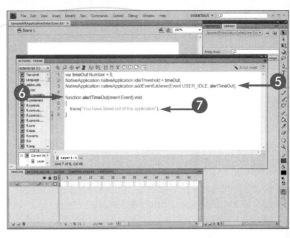

**8** Press Ctrl + Enter.

The AIR application launches.

**9** Do nothing on your computer for the specified number of seconds.

● In this example, the Output panel in Flash displays the message informing you that you have timed out.

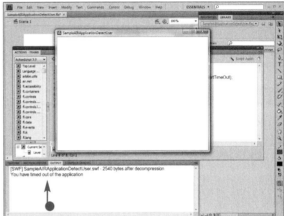

## Extra

When you use `idleThreshold`, you are not just detecting that the user is inactive. AIR applications can also be used to detect the opposite: When the next keyboard or mouse action occurs, a `userPresent` event is triggered. This could be used to display a "Welcome Back" message or something similar to the user.

Should you need to determine precisely how many seconds have elapsed since the last user input, you can read the `lastUserInput` property of `nativeApplication`. For example, you may have an application that users must log in to and plan to use `idleThreshold` to automatically log them out after a period of time. You can then use the `lastUserInput` property to display a warning to users shortly before they are logged out to tell them that they need to do something to prevent being logged out.

# Allow Users to Save Data

O ne of the nicest features of AIR is its local file system access. Because it is an application that has been installed locally on a machine, it has full access to the user's hard drive, meaning that AIR applications can not only read, but also write data to the local file system.

One practical application of this is a simple word processor. You can use a text field for input, setting it to allow multiple lines and wrap text. Unfortunately, Flash does not include a rich text editor that would allow for formatting, although third-party components for this do exist. Keep in mind, however, that Flash text fields do support a subset of HTML, so basic formatting is possible.

After the users have entered their text, they could click a Save button. In a word processor, they would expect a

dialog box to open to prompt them to name the file and provide a location for it. In your AIR application, you can have this same functionality, thanks to the `File` and `FileStream` classes. The `File` class includes a `browseForSave` method that generates a Save As dialog box. It can take as an argument a string, representing the title of the dialog box.

The `browseForSave` method generates a `SELECT` event when the user clicks the Save button in the Save As dialog box. Using this event, you can invoke an instance of the `FileStream` class. You can use the `open` method of this class to open the new file, the `writeUTFBytes` method to write the data to it, and the `close` method to close it, all of which have the effect of creating a new file on the user's computer.

## Allow Users to Save Data

### USE A BUTTON TO SAVE DATA FROM A TEXT FIELD

1. Create a multiline input text box with a border, rendered as HTML.

2. Create a button.

3. Create a new actions layer and click in its first frame.

4. In the Actions panel, type the name of the button, a period, and `addEventListener (MouseEvent.CLICK, handlerName);` replacing *handlerName* with the name of the handler.

5. Type the handler, such as `function saveAs(event:MouseEvent):void`, and a pair of curly braces.

6. Within the braces, create an instance of the `File` class, such as `var fileInstance: File = new File();`.

7. Generate a Save As dialog box, such as `fileInstance.browseForSave ("Save As");`.

8. Add an event listener for the handler to save the file, such as `fileInstance. addEventListener(Event.SELECT, saveFile);`.

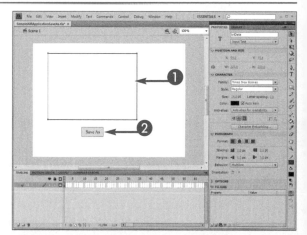

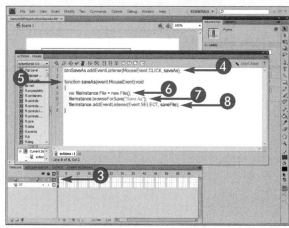

9 Outside of the braces, type the handler, such as `function saveFile(event:Event): void`, and a pair of curly braces.

10 Within the braces, create an instance of the `FileStream` class, such as `var stream: FileStream = new FileStream();`.

11 Open a new file for the saved text, such as `stream.open(event.target as File, FileMode.WRITE);`.

12 Write the text to the file, such as `stream.writeUTFBytes(txtData.htmlText);`.

13 Close the new file, such as `stream.close();`.

## TEST THE MOVIE

14 Press Ctrl + Enter.

15 Type text into the text field.

16 Click the button.

A Save As dialog box appears.

17 Navigate to the folder in which you want to save the text.

18 Type a filename and .txt extension.

19 Click Save.

The file is saved.

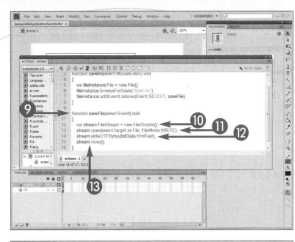

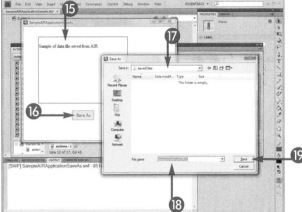

---

## Apply It

You can control the directory that initially appears in the Save As dialog box by setting the `File` instance to either `File.desktopDirectory` or `File.documentsDirectory`. The former will open the dialog box at the desktop; the latter will open it in the user's documents folder:

```
var fileInstance:File = File.desktopDirectory();
var fileInstance:File = File.documentsDirectory();.
```

The `File` class contains many more properties and a host of useful methods; you can explore these at http://livedocs.adobe.com/flash/9.0/ActionScriptLangRefV3/flash/filesystem/File.html.

The example shown in this section writes the data using the `FileStream`'s `writeUTFBytes` method, which takes a string of text encoded as UTF-8 and writes it to the file. Other write methods of the class include `writeBoolean`, `writeByte`, `writeBytes`, `writeDouble`, `writeFloat`, `writeInt`, `writeMultiByte`, `writeObject`, `writeShort`, `writeUnsignedInt`, and `writeUTF`. You can explore the rest of the methods and properties of the class at http://livedocs.adobe.com/flash/9.0/ActionScriptLangRefV3/flash/filesystem/FileStream.html.

# ActionScript Class Reference

The following is a list of all the ActionScript 3.0 classes supported by Flash CS4 Professional, Flash Player, and AIR. Note that this list excludes those classes that are unique to the Flex platform. A complete ActionScript reference, including Flex classes, is available as a free PDF at www.adobe.com/devnet/actionscript/articles/atp_ria_guide/atp_ria_guide.pdf.

The classes are listed alphabetically. Each class listing denotes the class name, its package, what if any class it extends, and its properties, methods, and constants.

## Accessibility

**Package: flash.accessibility**

**Extends Object**

**PROPERTY:**

active:Boolean

**METHOD:**

updateProperties():void

## AccessibilityProperties

**Package: flash.accessibility**

**Extends Object**

**PROPERTIES:**

description:String

forceSimple:Boolean

name:String

noAutoLabeling:Boolean

shortcut:String

silent:Boolean

**METHOD:**

AccessibilityProperties()

## ActionScriptVersion

**Package: flash.display**

**Extends Object**

**CONSTANTS:**

ACTIONSCRIPT2:uint

ACTIONSCRIPT3:uint

## AntiAliasType

**Package: flash.text**

**Extends Object**

**CONSTANTS:**

ADVANCED:String

NORMAL:String

## ApplicationDomain

**Package: flash.system**

**PROPERTIES:**

currentDomain:ApplicationDomain

domainMemory:ByteArray

parentDomain:ApplicationDomain

**CONSTANTS:**

MIN_DOMAIN_MEMORY_LENGTH: uint

**METHODS:**

ApplicationDomain()

getDefinition():Object

hasDefinition():Boolean

## ArgumentError

**Package: Top Level**

**Extends Error**

**METHOD:**

ArgumentError()

## Arguments

**Package: Top Level**

**PROPERTIES:**

callee:Function

length:Number

## Array

**Package: Top Level**

**Extends Object**

**PROPERTY:**

length:uint

**CONSTANTS:**

CASEINSENSITIVE:uint

DESCENDING:uint

NUMERIC:uint

RETURNINDEXEDARRAY:uint

UNIQUESORT:uint

**METHODS:**

Array()

concat():Array

every():Boolean

filter():Array

forEach():void

indexOf():int

join():String

lastIndexOf():int

map():Array

pop():*

push():uint

reverse():Array

shift():*

slice():Array

some():Boolean

sort():Array

sortOn():Array

splice():Array

toLocaleString():String

toString():String

unshift():uint

continued ➡

## AsyncErrorEvent

Package: flash.events

Extends ErrorEvent

**PROPERTY:**
error:Error

**CONSTANT:**
ASYNC_ERROR:String

**METHODS:**
AsyncErrorEvent()

clone():Event

toString():String

## AuthenticationMethod

(AIR only)

Package: flash.net.drm

Extends Object

**CONSTANTS:**
ANONYMOUS:String

USERNAME_AND_PASSWORD:String

## AVM1Movie

Package: flash.display

Extends Display Object

## BevelFilter

Package: flash.filters

Extends BitmapFilter

**PROPERTIES:**
angle:Number

blurX:Number

blurY:Number

distance:Number

highlightAlpha:Number

highlightColor:uint

knockout:Boolean

quality:int

shadowAlpha:Number

shadowColor:uint

strength:Number

type:String

**METHODS:**
BevelFilter()

clone():BitmapFilter

## Bitmap

**Package: flash.display**

**Extends DisplayObject**

PROPERTIES:

bitmapData:BitmapData

pixelSnapping:String

smoothing:Boolean

METHOD:

Bitmap()

## BitmapDataChannel

**Package: flash.display**

**Extends Object**

CONSTANTS:

ALPHA:uint

BLUE:uint

GREEN:uint

RED:uint

## BitmapData

**Package: flash.display**

**Extends Object|BitmapDrawable**

PROPERTIES:

height:int

rect:Rectangle

transparent:Boolean

width:int

Methods:

applyFilter():void

BitmapData()

clone():BitmapData

colorTransform():void

compare():Object

copyChannel():void

copyPixels():void

dispose():void

draw():void

fillRect():void

floodFill():void

generateFilterRect():Rectangle

getColorBoundsRect():Rectangle

getPixel():uint

getPixel32():uint

getPixels():ByteArray

hitTest():Boolean

lock():void

merge():void

noise():void

paletteMap():void

perlinNoise():void

pixelDissolve():int

scroll():void

setPixel():void

setPixel32():void

setPixels():void

setVector():void

threshold():uint

unlock():void

continued ➡

## BitmapFilter

**Package: flash.filters**

**Extends Object**

**METHOD:**

clone():BitmapFilter

## BitmapFilterQuality

**Package: flash.filters**

**Extends Object**

**CONSTANTS:**

HIGH:int

LOW:int

MEDIUM:int

## BitmapFilterType

**Package: flash.filters**

**Extends Object**

**CONSTANTS:**

FULL:String

INNER:String

OUTER:String

## BlendMode

**Package: flash.display**

**Extends Object**

**CONSTANTS:**

ADD:String

ALPHA:String

DARKEN:String

DIFFERENCE:String

ERASE:String

HARDLIGHT:String

INVERT:String

LAYER:String

LIGHTEN:String

MULTIPLY:String

NORMAL:String

OVERLAY:String

SCREEN:String

SHADER:String

SUBTRACT:String

## BlurFilter

**Package: flash.filters**

**Extends BitmapFilter**

**PROPERTIES:**

blurX:Number

blurY:Number

quality:int

**METHODS:**

BlurFilter()

clone():BitmapFilter

## Boolean

**Package: Top Level**

**Extends Object**

METHODS:
Boolean()
toString():String
valueOf():Boolean

## BreakOpportunity

**Package: flash.text.engine**

**Extends Object**

CONSTANTS:
ALL:String
ANY:String
AUTO:String
NONE:String

## BrowserInvokeEvent

**Package: flash.events**

**Extends Event**

PROPERTIES:
arguments:Array
isHTTPS:Boolean
isUserEvent:Boolean

sandboxType:String
securityDomain:String

CONSTANT:
BROWSER_INVOKE:String

METHODS:
BrowserInvokeEvent()
clone():Event

continued ➡

# ActionScript
# Class Reference (continued)

## ByteArray

**Package: flash.utils**

**Extends Object**

**IMPLEMENTS:**

IDataInput

IDataOutput

**PROPERTIES:**

bytesAvailable:uint

defaultObjectEncoding:uint

endian:String

length:uint

objectEncoding:uint

position:uint

**METHODS:**

ByteArray()

compress():void

readBoolean():Boolean

readByte():int

readBytes():void

readDouble():Number

readFloat():Number

readInt():int

readMultiByte():String

readObject():*

readShort():int

readUnsignedByte():uint

readUnsignedInt():uint

readUnsignedShort():uint

readUTF():String

readUTFBytes():String

toString():String

uncompress():void

writeBoolean():void

writeByte():void

writeBytes():void

writeDouble():void

writeFloat():void

writeInt():void

writeMultiByte():void

writeObject():void

writeShort():void

writeUnsignedInt():void

writeUTF():void

writeUTFBytes():void

## Camera

Package: flash.media

Extends EventDispatcher

PROPERTIES:

activityLevel:Number

bandwidth:int

currentFPS:Number

fps:Number

height:int

index:int

keyFrameInterval:int

loopback:Boolean

motionLevel:int

motionTimeout:int

muted:Boolean

name:String

names:Array

quality:int

width:int

METHODS:

getCamera():Camera

setKeyFrameInterval():void

setLoopback():void

setMode():void

setMotionLevel():void

setQuality():void

## Capabilities

Package: flash.system

Extends Object

PROPERTIES:

avHardwareDisable:Boolean

hasAccessibility:Boolean

hasAudio:Boolean

hasAudioEncoder:Boolean

hasEmbeddedVideo:Boolean

hasIME:Boolean

hasMP3:Boolean

hasPrinting:Boolean

hasScreenBroadcast:Boolean

hasScreenPlayback:Boolean

hasStreamingAudio:Boolean

hasStreamingVideo:Boolean

hasTLS:Boolean

hasVideoEncoder:Boolean

isDebugger:Boolean

language:String

localFileReadDisable:Boolean

manufacturer:String

os:String

pixelAspectRatio:Number

playerType:String

screenColor:String

screenDPI:Number

screenResolutionX:Number

screenResolutionY:Number

serverString:String

version:String

continued ➡

## CapsStyle

**Package: flash.display**

**Extends Object**

CONSTANTS:

NONE:String

ROUND:String

SQUARE:String

## CFFHinting

**Package: flash.text.engine**

**Extends Object**

CONSTANTS:

HORIZONTAL_STEM:String

NONE:String

## Class

**Package: Top Level**

**Extends Object**

## Clipboard

(AIR only)

**Package: flash.desktop**

**Extends Object**

PROPERTIES:

formats:Array

generalClipboard:Clipboard

METHODS:

clear():void

clearData():void

Clipboard()

getData():Object

hasFormat():Boolean

setData():Boolean

setDataHandler():Boolean

## ClipboardFormats

(AIR only)

**Package: flash.desktop**

**Extends Object**

CONSTANTS:

BITMAP_FORMAT:String

FILE_LIST_FORMAT:String

HTML_FORMAT:String

RICH_TEXT_FORMAT:String

TEXT_FORMAT:String

URL_FORMAT:String

## ClipboardTransferMode

**(AIR Only)**

**Package: flash.desktop**

**Extends Object**

CONSTANTS:
CLONE_ONLY:String
CLONE_PREFERRED:String
ORIGINAL_ONLY:String
ORIGINAL_PREFERRED:String

## ColorCorrection

**Package: flash.display**

**Extends Object**

CONSTANTS:
DEFAULT:String
OFF:String
ON:String

## ColorCorrectionSupport

**Package: flash.display**

**Extends Object**

CONSTANTS:
DEFAULT_OFF:String
DEFAULT_ON:String
UNSUPPORTED:String

## ColorMatrixFilter

**Package: flash.filters**

**Extends BitmapFilter**

PROPERTY:
matrix:Array

METHODS:
clone():BitmapFilter
ColorMatrixFilter()

## ColorTransform

**Package: flash.geom**

**Extends Object**

PROPERTIES:
alphaMultiplier:Number
alphaOffset:Number
blueMultiplier:Number
blueOffset:Number
color:uint
greenMultiplier:Number
greenOffset:Number
redMultiplier:Number
redOffset:Number

METHODS:
ColorTransform()
concat():void
toString():String

continued ➡

## CompressionAlgorithm

**(AIR only)**

**Package: flash.utils**

**Extends Object**

CONSTANTS:
DEFLATE:String
ZLIB:String

## ContentElement

**Package: flash.text.engine**

**Extends Object**

PROPERTIES:
elementFormat:ElementFormat
eventMirror:EventDispatcher
groupElement:GroupElement
rawText:String
text:String
textBlock:TextBlock
textBlockBeginIndex:int
textRotation:String
userData:*

CONSTANT:
GRAPHIC_ELEMENT:uint

METHOD:
ContentElement()

## ContextMenu

**Package: flash.ui**

**Extends NativeMenu**

PROPERTIES:
builtInItems:ContextMenuBuiltInItems
customItems:Array

METHODS:
ContextMenu()
display():void
hideBuiltInItems():void

## ContextMenuBuiltInItems

**Package: flash.ui**

**Extends Object**

PROPERTIES:
forwardAndBack:Boolean
loop:Boolean
play:Boolean
print:Boolean
quality:Boolean
rewind:Boolean
save:Boolean
zoom:Boolean

METHOD:
ContextMenuBuiltInItems()

## ContextMenuClipboardItems

**Package: flash.ui**

**Extends Object**

PROPERTIES:
clear:Boolean
copy:Boolean
cut:Boolean
paste:Boolean
selectAll:Boolean

## ContextMenuEvent

**Package: flash.events**

**Extends Event**

PROPERTIES:
contextMenuOwner:InteractiveObject
MENU_ITEM_SELECT:String
mouseTarget:InteractiveObject

CONSTANT:
MENU_SELECT:String

METHODS:
clone():Event
ContextMenuEvent()
toString():String

## ContextMenuItem

**Package: flash.ui**

**Extends NativeMenuItem**

PROPERTIES:
caption:String
separatorBefore:Boolean
visible:Boolean

METHODS:
ContextMenuItem()
systemClearMenuItem():ContextMenuItem
systemCopyLinkMenuItem():ContextMenuItem
systemCopyMenuItem():ContextMenuItem
systemCutMenuItem():ContextMenuItem
systemOpenLinkMenuItem():ContextMenuItem
systemPasteMenuItem():ContextMenuItem
systemSelectAllMenuItem():ContextMenuItem

## CSMSettings

**Package: flash.text**

**Extends Object**

PROPERTIES:
fontSize:Number
insideCutoff:Number
outsideCutoff:Number

METHOD:
CSMSettings()

continued

## DataEvent

**Package: flash.events**

**Extends TextEvent**

**PROPERTY:**

data:String

**CONSTANTS:**

DATA:String

UPLOAD_COMPLETE_DATA:String

**METHODS:**

clone():Event

DataEvent()

toString():String

## Date

**Package: Top Level**

**Extends Object**

**PROPERTIES:**

date:Number

dateUTC:Number

day:Number

dayUTC:Number

fullYear:Number

fullYearUTC:Number

hours:Number

hoursUTC:Number

milliseconds:Number

millisecondsUTC:Number

minutes:Number

minutesUTC:Number

month:Number

monthUTC:Number

seconds:Number

secondsUTC:Number

time:Number

timezoneOffset:Number

**METHODS:**

Date()

getDate():Number

getDay():Number

getFullYear():Number

getHours():Number

getMilliseconds():Number

getMinutes():Number

getMonth():Number

getSeconds():Number

getTime():Number

getTimezoneOffset():Number

getUTCDate():Number

getUTCDay():Number

getUTCFullYear():Number

getUTCHours():Number

getUTCMilliseconds():Number

**Date** *(continued)*

| | |
|---|---|
| getUTCMinutes():Number | setUTCHours():Number |
| getUTCMonth():Number | setUTCMilliseconds():Number |
| getUTCSeconds():Number | setUTCMinutes():Number |
| parse():Number | setUTCMonth():Number |
| setDate():Number | setUTCSeconds():Number |
| setFullYear():Number | toDateString():String |
| setHours():Number | toLocaleDateString():String |
| setMilliseconds():Number | toLocaleString():String |
| setMinutes():Number | toLocaleTimeString():String |
| setMonth():Number | toString():String |
| setSeconds():Number | toTimeString():String |
| setTime():Number | toUTCString():String |
| setUTCDate():Number | UTC():Number |
| setUTCFullYear():Number | valueOf():Number |

## DefinitionError

**Package: Top Level**

**Extends Error**

**METHOD:**
DefinitionError()

## DeleteObjectSample

**Package: flash.sampler**

**Extends Sample**

**PROPERTIES:**
id:Number
size:Number

## Dictionary

**Package: flash.utils**

**Extends Object**

## DigitCase

**Package: flash.text.engine**

**Extends Object**

**PROPERTY:**
delta:Number

**CONSTANTS:**
DEFAULT:String
LINING:String
OLD_STYLE:String

## DigitWidth

**Package: flash.text.engine**

**Extends Object**

**CONSTANTS:**
DEFAULT:String
PROPORTIONAL:String
TABULAR:String

continued →

## DisplacementMapFilter

**Package: flash.filters**

**Extends BitmapFilter**

**PROPERTIES:**

alpha:Number

color:uint

componentX:uint

componentY:uint

mapBitmap:BitmapData

mapPoint:Point

mode:String

scaleX:Number

scaleY:Number

**METHODS:**

clone():BitmapFilter

DisplacementMapFilter()

## DisplacementMapFilterMode

**Package: flash.filters**

**Extends Object**

**CONSTANTS:**

CLAMP:String

COLOR:String

IGNORE:String

WRAP:String

## DisplayObject

**Package: flash.system**

**Extends EventDispatcher**

**Implements IBitmapDrawable**

**PROPERTIES:**

accessibilityProperties:AccessibilityProperties

alpha:Number

blendMode:String

blendShader:void

cacheAsBitmap:Boolean

filters:Array

height:Number

loaderInfo:LoaderInfo

mask:DisplayObject

mouseX:Number

mouseY:Number

name:String

opaqueBackground:Object

parent:DisplayObjectContainer

root:DisplayObject

rotation:Number

rotationX:Number

rotationY:Number

rotationZ:Number

## DisplayObject (continued)

scale9Grid:Rectangle

scaleX:Number

scaleY:Number

scaleZ:Number

scrollRect:Rectangle

stage:Stage

transform:Transform

visible:Boolean

width:Number

x:Number

y:Number

z:Number

**METHODS:**

getBounds():Rectangle

getRect():Rectangle

globalToLocal():Point

globalToLocal3D():Vector3D

hitTestObject():Boolean

hitTestPoint():Boolean

local3DToGlobal():Point

localToGlobal():Point

## DisplayObjectContainer

**Package: flash.display**

**Extends InteractiveObject**

**PROPERTIES:**

mouseChildren:Boolean

numChildren:int

tabChildren:Boolean

textSnapshot:TextSnapshot

**METHODS:**

addChild():DisplayObject

addChildAt():DisplayObject

areInaccessibleObjectsUnderPoint():Boolean

contains():Boolean

DisplayObjectContainer()

getChildAt():DisplayObject

getChildByName():DisplayObject

getChildIndex():int

getObjectsUnderPoint():Array

removeChild():DisplayObject

removeChildAt():DisplayObject

setChildIndex():void

swapChildren():void

swapChildrenAt():void

## DockIcon

**(AIR only)**

**Package: flash.desktop**

**Extends InteractiveIcon**

**PROPERTIES:**

bitmaps:Array

height:int

menu:NativeMenu

width:int

**METHOD:**

bounce()

continued ➡

# ActionScript
# Class Reference (continued)

## DRMAuthenticateEvent

**(AIR only)**

**Package: flash.events**

**Extends Event**

**PROPERTIES:**
authenticationType:String
header:String
originater:Object
passwordPrompt:String
urlPrompt:String
usernamePrompt:String

**CONSTANTS:**
AUTHENTICATION_TYPE_DRM:String
AUTHENTICATION_TYPE_PROXY:String
DRM_AUTHENTICATE:String

**METHODS:**
clone():Event
DRMAuthenticateEvent()
toString():String

## DRMAuthenticationCompleteEvent

**(AIR only)**

**Package: flash.events**

**Extends Event**

**PROPERTIES:**
domain:String
serverURL:String
token:flash.utils:ByteArray

**CONSTANT:**
AUTHENTICATION_COMPLETE:String

## DRMAuthenticationErrorEvent

**(AIR Only)**

**Package: flash.events**

**Extends ErrorEvent**

**PROPERTIES:**
domain:String
serverURL:String
subErrorID:int

**CONSTANT:**
AUTHENTICATION_ERROR:String

## DRMContentData

(AIR only)

Package: flash.net.drm

Extends Object

**PROPERTIES:**
authenticationMethod:String
domain:String
licenseID:String
serverURL:String

## DRMManager

(AIR only)

Package: flash.net.drm

Extends EventDispatcher

**METHODS:**
authenticate():void
getDRMManager():DRMManager
loadVoucher():void
resetDRMVouchers():void
setAuthenticationToken():void

## DRMErrorEvent

(AIR only)

Package: flash.events

Extends ErrorEvent

**PROPERTIES:**
contentData:DRMContentData
subErrorCode:int

**CONSTANT:**
DRM_ERROR:String

**METHODS:**
clone():Event
DRMErrorEvent()
toString():String

## DRMManagerError

(AIR only)

Package: flash.errors

Extends Error

**PROPERTY:**
subErrorID:int

## DRMPlaybackTimeWindow

(AIR only)

Package: flash.net.drm

Extends Object

**PROPERTIES:**
endDate:Date
period:uint
startDate:Date

continued →

## DRMStatusEvent

**(AIR only)**

**Package: flash.events**

**Extends Event**

**PROPERTIES:**

contentData:DRMContentData

detail:String

isAnonymous:Boolean

isAvailableOffline:Boolean

isLocal:Boolean

offlineLeasePeriod:uint

voucher:DRMVoucher

voucherEndDate:Date

**CONSTANT:**

DRM_STATUS:String

**METHODS:**

clone():Event

DRMStatusEvent()

preloadEmbeddedData():void

toString():String

## DRMVoucher

**(AIR only)**

**Package: flash.net.drm**

**Extends Object**

**PROPERTIES:**

offlineLeaseEndDate:Date

offlineLeaseStartDate:Date

playbackTimeWindow:DRMPlaybackTimeWindow

policies:Object

voucherEndDate:Date

voucherStartDate:Date

## EastAsianJustifier

**Package: flash.text.engine**

**Extends TextJustifier**

**PROPERTY:**

justificationStyle:String

**METHODS:**

clone():TextJustifier

EastAsianJustifier()

## ElementFormat

**Package: flash.text.engine**

**Extends Object**

**PROPERTIES:**

alignmentBaseline:String

alpha:Number

baselineShift:Number

breakOpportunity:String

color:uint

digitCase:String

digitWidth:String

dominantBaseline:String

fontDescription:FontDescription

fontSize:Number

kerning:String

ligatureLevel:String

locale:String

locked:Boolean

textRotation:String

trackingLeft:Number

trackingRight:Number

typographicCase:String

**METHODS:**

clone():ElementFormat

ElementFormat()

getFontMetrics():FontMetrics

## Endian

**Package: flash.utils**

**Extends Object**

**CONSTANTS:**

BIG_ENDIAN:String

LITTLE_ENDIAN:String

## EOFError

**Package: flash.errors**

**Extends Error**

**METHOD:**

EOFError()

## Error

**Package: Top Level**

**Extends Object**

**PROPERTIES:**

length:int = 1

message:String

name:String

**METHODS:**

Error()

getStackTrace():String

toString():String

continued ➡

## ErrorEvent

**Package: flash.events**

**Extends TextEvent**

**PROPERTY:**

errorID:int

**CONSTANT:**

ERROR:String

**METHODS:**

clone():Event

ErrorEvent()

toString():String

## EvalError

**Package: Top Level**

**Extends Error**

**METHOD:**

EvalError()

## Event

**Package: flash.events**

**Extends Object**

**PROPERTIES:**

bubbles:Boolean

cancelable:Boolean

currentTarget:Object

eventPhase:uint

target:Object

type:String

**CONSTANTS:**

ACTIVATE:String

ADDED:String

ADDED_TO_STAGE:String

CANCEL:String

CHANGE:String

CLEAR:String

CLOSE:String

CLOSING:String

COMPLETE:String

CONNECT:String

COPY:String

CUT:String

DEACTIVATE:String

DISPLAYING:String

ENTER_FRAME:String

EXITING:String

FULLSCREEN:String

HTML_BOUNDS_CHANGE:String

HTML_DOM_INITIALIZE:String

HTML_RENDER:String

ID3:String

## Event (continued)

INIT:String

LOCATION_CHANGE:String

MOUSE_LEAVE:String

NETWORK_CHANGE:String

OPEN:String

PASTE:String

REMOVED:String

REMOVED_FROM_STAGE:String

RENDER:String

RESIZE:String

SCROLL:String

SELECT:String

SELECT_ALL:String

SOUND_COMPLETE:String

TAB_CHILDREN_CHANGE:String

TAB_ENABLED_CHANGE:String

TAB_INDEX_CHANGE:String

UNLOAD:String

USER_IDLE:String

USER_PRESENT:String

**METHODS:**

clone():Event

Event()

formatToString():String

isDefaultPrevented():Boolean

preventDefault():void

stopImmediatePropagation():void

stopPropagation():void

toString():String

## EventDispatcher

**Package: flash.events**

**Extends Object**

**Implements IEventDispatcher**

**METHODS:**

addEventListener():void

dispatchEvent():Boolean

EventDispatcher():void

hasEventListener():Boolean

removeEventListener():void

willTrigger():Boolean

## EventPhase

**Package: flash.events**

**Extends Object**

**CONSTANTS:**

AT_TARGET:uint

BUBBLING_PHASE:uint

CAPTURING_PHASE:uint

continued ➡

## File

| | |
|---|---|
| **(AIR only)** | browseForOpenMultiple():void |
| | browseForSave():void |
| **Package: flash.filesystem** | cancel():void |
| | canonicalize():void |
| **Extends FileReference** | clone():File |
| | copyTo():void |
| **PROPERTIES:** | copyToAsync():void |
| applicationDirectory:File | createDirectory():void |
| applicationStorageDirectory:File | createTempDirectory():File |
| desktopDirectory:File | createTempFile():File |
| documentsDirectory:File | deleteDirectory():void |
| exists:Boolean | deleteDirectoryAsync():void |
| icon:Icon | deleteFile():void |
| isDirectory:Boolean | deleteFileAsync():void |
| isHidden:Boolean | File() |
| isPackage:Boolean | getDirectoryListing():Array |
| isSymbolicLink:Boolean | getDirectoryListingAsync():void |
| lineEnding:String | getRelativePath():String |
| nativePath:String | getRootDirectories():Array |
| parent:File | moveTo():void |
| separator:String | moveToAsync():void |
| systemCharset:String | moveToTrash():void |
| url:String | moveToTrashAsync():void |
| userDirectory:File | resolvePath():File |
| | |
| **METHODS:** | |
| browseForDirectory():void | |
| browseForOpen():void | |

## FileFilter

Package: flash.net

Extends Object

**PROPERTIES:**
description:String
extension:String
macType:String

**METHOD:**
FileFilter():void

## FileListEvent

(AIR only)

Package: flash.events

Extends Event

**PROPERTY:**
files:Array

**CONSTANTS:**
DIRECTORY_LISTING:String
SELECT_MULTIPLE:String

**METHOD:**
FileListEvent()

## FileMode

(AIR only)

Package: flash.filesystem

Extends Object

**CONSTANTS:**
APPEND:String
READ:String
UPDATE:String
WRITE:String

## FileReference

Package: flash.net

Extends EventDispatcher

**PROPERTIES:**
creationDate:Date
creator:String
extension:String
modificationDate:Date
name:String
size:Number
type:String

**METHODS:**
browse():Boolean
cancel():void
download():void
FileReference()
upload():void
uploadUnencoded():void

## FileReferenceList

Package: flash.net

Extends EventDispatcher

**PROPERTY:**
fileList:Array

**METHODS:**
browse():Boolean
FileReferenceList()

continued

## FileStream

**(AIR only)**

**Package: flash.filesystem**

**Extends EventDispatcher**

**Implements IDataInput, IDataOutput**

**PROPERTIES:**

bytesAvailable:uint

endian:String

objectEncoding:uint

position:Number

readAhead:Number

**METHODS:**

close():void

FileStream()

open():void

openAsync():void

readBoolean():Boolean

readByte():int

readBytes():void

readDouble():Number

readFloat():Number

readInt():int

readMultiByte():String

readObject():*

readShort():int

readUnsignedByte():uint

readUnsignedInt():uint

readUnsignedShort():uint

readUTF():String

readUTFBytes():String

truncate():void

writeBoolean():void

writeByte():void

writeBytes():void

writeDouble():void

writeFloat():void

writeInt():void

writeMultiByte():void

writeObject():void

writeShort():void

writeUnsignedInt():void

writeUTF():void

writeUTFBytes():void

## FocusDirection

(AIR only)

Package: flash.display

Extends Object

**CONSTANTS:**

BOTTOM:String

NONE:String

TOP:String

## FocusEvent

Package: flash.events

Extends Event

**PROPERTIES:**

direction:String

keyCode:uint

relatedObject:InteractiveObject

shiftKey:Boolean

**CONSTANTS:**

FOCUS_IN:String

FOCUS_OUT:String

KEY_FOCUS_CHANGE:String

MOUSE_FOCUS_CHANGE:String

**METHODS:**

clone():Event

FocusEvent()

toString():String

## Font

Package: flash.text

Extends Object

**PROPERTIES:**

fontName:String

fontStyle:String

fontType:String

**METHODS:**

enumerateFonts():Array

hasGlyphs():Boolean

registerFont():void

## FontDescription

Package: flash.text.engine

Extends Object

**PROPERTIES:**

cffHinting:String

fontLookup:String

fontName:String

fontPosture:String

fontWeight:String

locked:Boolean

renderingMode:String

**METHODS:**

FontDescription()

clone():FontDescription

isFontCompatible():Boolean

continued ➡

## FontLookup

Package: flash.text.engine

Extends Object

CONSTANTS:
DEVICE:String
EMBEDDED_FF:String

## FontMetrics

Package: flash.text.engine

Extends Object

PROPERTIES:
emBox:Rectangle
strikethroughOffset:Number
strikethroughThickness:Number
underlineOffset:Number
underlineThickness:Number
subscriptOffset:Number
subscriptScale:Number
superscriptOffset:Number
superscriptScale:Number

METHOD:
FontMetrics()

## FontPosture

Package: flash.text.engine

Extends Object

CONSTANTS:
ITALIC:String
NORMAL:String

## FontStyle

Package: flash.text

Extends Object

CONSTANTS:
BOLD:String
BOLD_ITALIC:String
ITALIC:String
REGULAR:String

## FontType

Package: flash.text

Extends Object

CONSTANTS:
DEVICE:String
EMBEDDED:String
EMBEDDED_CFF:String

## FontWeight

**Package: flash.text.engine**

**Extends Object**

**CONSTANTS:**

BOLD:String

NORMAL:String

## FrameLabel

**Package: flash.display**

**Extends Object**

**PROPERTY:**

frame:intname:String

## FullScreenEvent

**Package: flash.events**

**Extends ActivityEvent**

**PROPERTY:**

fullScreen:Boolean

**CONSTANT:**

FULL_SCREEN:String

**METHODS:**

clone():Event

FullScreenEvent()

toString():String

## Function

**Package: Top Level**

**Extends Object**

**METHODS:**

apply():*

call():*

## GlowFilter

**Package: flash.filters**

**Extends BitmapFilter**

**PROPERTIES:**

alpha:Number

blurX:Number

blurY:Number

color:uint

inner:Boolean

knockout:Boolean

quality:int

strength:Number

**METHODS:**

clone():BitmapFilter

GlowFilter()

continued →

## GradientBevelFilter

**Package: flash.filters**

**Extends BitmapFilter**

**PROPERTIES:**

alphas:Array

angle:Number

blurX:Number

blurY:Number

colors:Array

distance:Number

knockout:Boolean

quality:int

ratios:Array

strength:Number

type:String

**METHODS:**

clone():BitmapFilter

GradientBevelFilter()

## GradientGlowFilter

**Package: flash.filters**

**Extends BitmapFilter**

**PROPERTIES:**

alphas:Array

angle:Number

blurX:Number

blurY:Number

colors:Array

distance:Number

knockout:Boolean

quality:int

ratios:Array

strength:Number

type:String

**METHODS:**

clone():BitmapFilter

GradientGlowFilter()

## GradientType

**Package: flash.display**

**Extends Object**

**CONSTANTS:**

LINEAR:String = "linear"

RADIAL:String = "radial"

## GraphicElement

**Package: flash.text.engine**

**Extends ContentElement**

**PROPERTIES:**

elementHeight:Number

elementWidth:Number

graphic:DisplayObject

**METHOD:**

GraphicElement()

## Graphics

**Package: flash.display**

**Extends Object**

**METHODS:**

beginBitmapFill():void

beginFill():void

beginGradientFill():void

clear():void

curveTo():void

drawCircle():void

drawEllipse():void

drawRect():void

drawRoundRect():void

endFill():void

lineGradientStyle():void

lineStyle():void

lineTo():void

moveTo():void

## GraphicsBitmapFill

**Package: flash.display**

**Extends Object**

**Implements IGraphicsData, IGraphicsFill**

**PROPERTIES:**

bitmapData:BitmapData

matrix:Matrix

repeat:Boolean

smooth:Boolean

**METHOD:**

GraphicsBitmapFill()

## GraphicsGradientFill

**Package: flash.display**

**Extends ObjectIGraphicsData**

**Implements IGraphicsFill**

**PROPERITES:**

alphas:Array

colors:Array

focalPointRatio:Number

interpolationMethod:String

matrix:Matrix

ratios:Array

spreadMethod:String

type:String

## GraphicsEndFill

**Package: flash.display**

**Extends Object**

**Implements IGraphicsData, IGraphicsFill**

**METHOD:**

GraphicsEndFill()

continued ➡

## GraphicsPath

**Package:** flash.display

**Extends Object**

**Implements IGraphicsData, IGraphicsPath**

**PROPERTIES:**
commands:Vector.<int>
data:Vector.<Number>
winding:String

**METHODS:**
curveTo():void
lineTo():void
moveTo():void
wideLineTo():void
wideMoveTo():void

## GraphicsPathCommand

**Package:** flash.display

**Extends Object**

**CONSTANTS:**
CURVE_TO:int
LINE_TO:int
MOVE_TO:int
NO_OP:int
WIDE_LINE_TO:int
WIDE_MOVE_TO:int

## GraphicsPathWinding

**Package:** flash.display

**Extends Object**

**CONSTANTS:**
EVEN_ODD:String
NON_ZERO:String

## GraphicsShaderFill

**Package:** flash.display

**Extends Object**

**Implements IGraphicsData, IGraphicsFill**

**PROPERTIES:**
matrix:Matrix
shader:Shader

## GraphicsSolidFill

**Package:** flash.display

**Extends Object**

**Implements IGraphicsData, IGraphicsFill**

**PROPERTIES:**
alpha:Number
color:uint

## GraphicsStroke

Package: flash.display

Extends Object

Implements IGraphicsData, IGraphicsStroke

PROPERTIES:
caps:String
fill:IGraphicsFill
joints:String
miterLimit:Number
pixelHinting:Boolean
scaleMode:String
thickness:Number

## GraphicsTrianglePath

Package: flash.display

Extends Object

Implements IGraphicsData, IGraphicsPath

PROPERTIES:
culling:String
indices:Vector.<int>
uvtData:Vector.<Number>
vertices:Vector.<Number>

## GridFitType

Package: flash.text

Extends Object

CONSTANTS:
NONE:String
PIXEL:String
SUBPIXEL:String

## GroupElement

Package: flash.text.engine

Extends ContentElement

PROPERTY:
elementCount:int

METHODS:
getElementAt():ContentElement
getElementAtCharIndex():ContentElement
getElementIndex():int
groupElements():GroupElement
mergeTextElements():TextElement
replaceElements():Vector.<ContentElement>
setElements():void
splitTextElement():TextElement
ungroupElements():void

## HTMLHistoryItem

(AIR only)

Package: flash.html

Extends Object

PROPERTIES:
isPost:Boolean
originalUrl:String
title:String
url:String

METHOD:
HTMLHistoryItem():void

continued ➡

## HTMLHost

**(AIR only)**

**Package: flash.html**

**Extends Object**

**PROPERTIES:**

htmlLoader:HTMLLoader

windowRect:Rectangle

**METHODS:**

createWindow():HTMLLoader

HTMLHost()

updateLocation():void

updateStatus():void

updateTitle():void

windowBlur():void

windowClose():void

windowFocus():void

## HTMLLoader

**(AIR Only)**

**Package: flash.html**

**Extends Sprite**

**PROPERTIES:**

authenticate:Boolean

cacheResponse:Boolean

contentHeight:Number

contentWidth:Number

hasFocusableContent:Boolean

height:Number

historyLength:uint

historyPosition:uint

htmlHost:HTMLHost

loaded:Boolean

location:String

manageCookies:Boolean

paintsDefaultBackground:Boolean

pdfCapability:int

placeLoadStringContentInApplicationSandbox:Boolean

runtimeApplicationDomain:ApplicationDomain

scrollH:Number

scrollV:Number

textEncodingFallback:String

textEncodingOverride:String

useCache:Boolean

userAgent:String

width:Number

window:Object

## HTMLLoader *(continued)*

**METHODS:**

cancelLoad():void

createRootWindow():HTMLLoader

getHistoryAt():HTMLHistoryItem

historyBack():void

historyForward():void

historyGo():void

HTMLLoader()

load():void

loadString():void

reload():void

## HTMLPDFCapability

(AIR only)

Package: flash.html

Extends Object

**CONSTANTS:**

ERROR_CANNOT_LOAD_READER:int

ERROR_INSTALLED_READER_NOT_FOUND:int

ERROR_INSTALLED_READER_TOO_OLD:int

ERROR_PREFERRED_READER_TOO_OLD:int

STATUS_OK:int

## HTMLUncaughtScriptExceptionEvent

(AIR only)

Package: flash.events

Extends Event

**PROPERTIES:**

exceptionValue:*

stackTrace:Array

**CONSTANT:**

UNCAUGHT_SCRIPT_EXCEPTION:*

**METHODS:**

clone():Event

HTMLUncaughtScriptExceptionEvent():void

## HTMLWindowCreateOptions

(AIR only)

Package: flash.html

Extends Event

**PROPERTIES:**

fullscreen:Boolean

height:Number

locationBarVisible:Boolean

menuBarVisible:Boolean

resizable:Boolean

scrollBarsVisible:Boolean

statusBarVisible:Boolean

toolBarVisible:Boolean

width:Number

x:Number

y:Number

continued ➡

# ActionScript
# Class Reference (continued)

## HTTPStatusEvent

**Package: flash.events**

**Extends Event**

**PROPERTIES:**
responseHeaders:Array
responseURL:String
status:int

**CONSTANTS:**
HTTP_RESPONSE_STATUS:String
HTTP_STATUS:String

**METHODS:**
clone():Event
HTTPStatusEvent()
toString():String

## IBitmapDrawable

**Package: flash.display**

## Icon

**(AIR only)**

**Package: flash.desktop**

**Extends EventDispatcher**

**PROPERTY:**
bitmaps:Array

## ID3Info

**Package: flash.media**

**Extends Object**

**PROPERTIES:**
album:String
artist:String
comment:String
genre:String
songName:String
track:String
year:String

## IDataInput

**Package: flash.utils**

**PROPERTIES:**

bytesAvailable:uint

endian:String

objectEncoding:uint

**METHODS:**

readBoolean():Boolean

readByte():int

readBytes():void

readDouble():Number

readFloat():Number

readInt():int

readMultiByte():String

readObject():*

readShort():int

readUnsignedByte():uint

readUnsignedInt():uint

readUnsignedShort():uint

readUTF():String

readUTFBytes():String

## IDataOutput

**Package: flash.utils**

**PROPERTIES:**

endian:String

objectEncoding:uint

**METHODS:**

writeBoolean():void

writeByte():void

writeBytes():void

writeDouble():void

writeFloat():void

writeInt():void

writeMultiByte():void

writeObject():void

writeShort():void

writeUnsignedInt():void

writeUTF():void

writeUTFBytes():void

## IDynamicPropertyOutput

**Package: flash.net**

**METHOD:**

writeDynamicProperty():void

## IDynamicPropertyWriter

**Package: flash.net**

**METHOD:**

writeDynamicProperties():void

continued ➡

## IEventDispatcher

**Package: flash.events**

**METHODS:**

addEventListener():void

dispatchEvent():Boolean

hasEventListener():Boolean

removeEventListener():void

willTrigger():Boolean

## IExternalizable

**Package: flash.utils**

**METHODS:**

readExternal():void

writeExternal():void

## IGraphicsData

**Package: flash.display**

**Extends Object**

## IGraphicsFill

**Package: flash.display**

**Extends Object**

## IGraphicsPath

**Package: flash.display**

**Extends Object**

## IGraphicsStroke

**Package: flash.display**

**Extends Object**

## IllegalOperationError

**Package: flash.errors**

**Extends Error**

**METHOD:**

IllegalOperationError()

## IME

**Package: flash.system**

**Extends EventDispatcher**

**PROPERTIES:**

conversionMode:String

enabled:Boolean

**METHODS:**

compositionAbandoned():void

compositionSelectionChanged():void

doConversion():void

setCompositionString():void

## IMEConversionMode

**Package:** flash.system

**Extends Object**

**CONSTANTS:**

ALPHANUMERIC_FULL:String

ALPHANUMERIC_HALF:String

CHINESE:String

JAPANESE_HIRAGANA:String

JAPANESE_KATAKANA_FULL:String

JAPANESE_KATAKANA_HALF:String

KOREAN:String

UNKNOWN:String

## Int

**Package:** Top Level

**Extends Object**

**CONSTANTS:**

MAX_VALUE:int

MIN_VALUE:int

**METHODS:**

int()

toExponential():String

toFixed():String

toPrecision():String

toString():String

valueOf():int

## IMEEvent

**Package:** flash.events

**Extends TextEvent**

**CONSTANT:**

IME_COMPOSITION:String

**METHODS:**

clone():Event

IMEEvent()

toString():String

## InteractiveIcon

**(AIR only)**

**Package:** flash.desktop

**Extends Icon**

**PROPERTIES:**

bitmaps:Array

height:int

width:int

continued ➡

## InteractiveObject

**Package: flash.display**

**Extends Display Object**

**PROPERTIES:**

contextMenu:NativeMenu

doubleClickEnabled:Boolean

focusRect:Object

mouseEnabled:Boolean

tabEnabled:Boolean

tabIndex:int

**METHOD:**

InteractiveObject():void

## InterpolationMethod

**Package: flash.display**

**Extends Object**

**CONSTANTS:**

LINEAR_RGB:String

RGB:String

## InvalidSWFError

**Package: flash.errors**

**Extends Error**

**METHOD:**

InvalidSWFError()

## InvokeEvent

**(AIR only)**

**Package: flash.events**

**Extends Event**

**PROPERTIES:**

arguments:Array

currentDirectory:File

**CONSTANT:**

INVOKE:String

**METHODS:**

clone():Event

InvokeEvent()

## IOError

**Package: flash.errors**

**Extends Error**

**METHOD:**

IOError()

## IOErrorEvent

**Package: flash.events**

**Extends ErrorEvent**

**CONSTANT:**

IO_ERROR:String

**METHODS:**

clone():Event

IOErrorEvent()

toString():String

## IURIDereferencer

(AIR only)

**Package: flash.security**

**METHOD:**
dereference():IDataInput

## JointStyle

**Package: flash.display**

**Extends Object**

**CONSTANTS:**
BEVEL:String
MITER:String
ROUND:String

## JPEGLoaderContext

**Package: flash.system**

**Extends LoaderContext**

**PROPERTY:**
deblockingFilter:Number

## Keyboard

**Package: flash.ui**

**Extends Object**

**PROPERTIES:**
capsLock:Boolean
CharCodeStrings:Array
numLock:Boolean

**CONSTANTS:**
A:uint
ALTERNATE:uint
B:uint
BACKQUOTE:uint
BACKSLASH:uint
BACKSPACE:uint

## JustificationStyle

**Package: flash.text.engine**

**Extends Object**

**CONSTANTS:**
PRIORITIZE_LEAST_ADJUSTMENT:String
PUSH_IN_KINSOKU:String
PUSH_OUT_ONLY:String

## Kerning

**Package: flash.text.engine**

**Extends Object**

**CONSTANTS:**
AUTO:String
OFF:String
ON:String

continued

# ActionScript
## Class Reference (continued)

| | |
|---|---|
| C:uint | H:uint |
| CAPS_LOCK:uint | HOME:uint |
| COMMA:uint | I:uint |
| COMMAND:uint | INSERT:uint |
| CONTROL:uint | J:uint |
| D:uint | K:uint |
| DELETE:uint | KEYNAME_BEGIN:String |
| DOWN:uint | KEYNAME_BREAK:String |
| E:uint | KEYNAME_CLEARDISPLAY:String |
| END:uint | KEYNAME_CLEARLINE:String |
| ENTER:uint | KEYNAME_DELETE:String |
| EQUAL:uint | KEYNAME_DELETECHAR:String |
| ESCAPE:uint | KEYNAME_DELETELINE:String |
| F:uint | KEYNAME_DOWNARROW:String |
| F1:uint | KEYNAME_END:String |
| F2:uint | KEYNAME_EXECUTE:String |
| F3:uint | KEYNAME_F1:String |
| F4:uint | KEYNAME_F2:String |
| F5:uint | KEYNAME_F3:String |
| F6:uint | KEYNAME_F4:String |
| F7:uint | KEYNAME_F5:String |
| F8:uint | KEYNAME_F6:String |
| F9:uint | KEYNAME_F7:String |
| F10:uint | KEYNAME_F8:String |
| F11:uint | KEYNAME_F9:String |
| F12:uint | KEYNAME_F10:String |
| F13:uint | KEYNAME_F11:String |
| F14:uint | KEYNAME_F12:String |
| F15:uint | KEYNAME_F13:String |
| G:uint | KEYNAME_F14:String |

| | |
|---|---|
| KEYNAME_F15:String | KEYNAME_PREV:String |
| KEYNAME_F16:String | KEYNAME_PRINT:String |
| KEYNAME_F17:String | KEYNAME_PRINTSCREEN:String |
| KEYNAME_F18:String | KEYNAME_REDO:String |
| KEYNAME_F19:String | KEYNAME_RESET:String |
| KEYNAME_F20:String | KEYNAME_RIGHTARROW:String |
| KEYNAME_F21:String | KEYNAME_SCROLLLOCK:String |
| KEYNAME_F22:String | KEYNAME_SELECT:String |
| KEYNAME_F23:String | KEYNAME_STOP:String |
| KEYNAME_F24:String | KEYNAME_SYSREQ:String |
| KEYNAME_F25:String | KEYNAME_SYSTEM:String |
| KEYNAME_F26:String | KEYNAME_UNDO:String |
| KEYNAME_F27:String | KEYNAME_UPARROW:String |
| KEYNAME_F28:String | KEYNAME_USER:String |
| KEYNAME_F29:String | L:uint |
| KEYNAME_F30:String | LEFT:uint |
| KEYNAME_F31:String | LEFTBRACKET:uint |
| KEYNAME_F32:String | M:uint |
| KEYNAME_F33:String | MINUS:uint |
| KEYNAME_F34:String | N:uint |
| KEYNAME_F35:String | NUMBER_0:uint |
| KEYNAME_FIND:String | NUMBER_1:uint |
| KEYNAME_HELP:String | NUMBER_2:uint |
| KEYNAME_HOME:String | NUMBER_3:uint |
| KEYNAME_INSERT:String | NUMBER_4:uint |
| KEYNAME_INSERTCHAR:String | NUMBER_5:uint |
| KEYNAME_INSERTLINE:String | NUMBER_6:uint |
| KEYNAME_LEFTARROW:String | NUMBER_7:uint |
| KEYNAME_MENU:String | NUMBER_8:uint |
| KEYNAME_MODESWITCH:String | NUMBER_9:uint |
| KEYNAME_NEXT:String | NUMPAD:uint |
| KEYNAME_PAGEDOWN:String | NUMPAD_0:uint |
| KEYNAME_PAGEUP:String | NUMPAD_1:uint |
| KEYNAME_PAUSE:String | NUMPAD_2:uint |

continued ➡

**Keyboard** *(continued)*

| | |
|---|---|
| NUMPAD_3:uint | STRING_BEGIN:String |
| NUMPAD_4:uint | STRING_BREAK:String |
| NUMPAD_5:uint | STRING_CLEARDISPLAY:String |
| NUMPAD_6:uint | STRING_CLEARLINE:String |
| NUMPAD_7:uint | STRING_DELETE:String |
| NUMPAD_8:uint | STRING_DELETECHAR:String |
| NUMPAD_9:uint | STRING_DELETELINE:String |
| NUMPAD_ADD:uint | STRING_DOWNARROW:String |
| NUMPAD_DECIMAL:uint | STRING_END:String |
| NUMPAD_DIVIDE:uint | STRING_EXECUTE:String |
| NUMPAD_ENTER:uint | STRING_F1:String |
| NUMPAD_MULTIPLY:uint | STRING_F2:String |
| NUMPAD_SUBTRACT:uint | STRING_F3:String |
| O:uint | STRING_F4:String |
| P:uint | STRING_F5:String |
| PAGE_DOWN:uint | STRING_F6:String |
| PAGE_UP:uint | STRING_F7:String |
| PERIOD:uint | STRING_F8:String |
| Q:uint | STRING_F9:String |
| QUOTE:uint | STRING_F10:String |
| R:uint | STRING_F11:String |
| RIGHT:uint | STRING_F12:String |
| RIGHTBRACKET:uint | STRING_F13:String |
| S:uint | STRING_F14:String |
| SEMICOLON:uint | STRING_F15:String |
| SHIFT:uint | STRING_F16:String |
| SLASH:uint | STRING_F17:String |
| SPACE:uint | STRING_F18:String |

**Keyboard** *(continued)*

| | |
|---|---|
| STRING_F19:String | STRING_PAGEUP:String |
| STRING_F20:String | STRING_PAUSE:String |
| STRING_F21:String | STRING_PREV:String |
| STRING_F22:String | STRING_PRINT:String |
| STRING_F23:String | STRING_PRINTSCREEN:String |
| STRING_F24:String | STRING_REDO:String |
| STRING_F25:String | STRING_RESET:String |
| STRING_F26:String | STRING_RIGHTARROW:String |
| STRING_F27:String | STRING_SCROLLLOCK:String |
| STRING_F28:String | STRING_SELECT:String |
| STRING_F29:String | STRING_STOP:String |
| STRING_F30:String | STRING_SYSREQ:String |
| STRING_F31:String | STRING_SYSTEM:String |
| STRING_F32:String | STRING_UNDO:String |
| STRING_F33:String | STRING_UPARROW:String |
| STRING_F34:String | STRING_USER:String |
| STRING_F35:String | T:uint |
| STRING_FIND:String | TAB:uint |
| STRING_HELP:String | U:uint |
| STRING_HOME:String | UP:uint |
| STRING_INSERT:String | V:uint |
| STRING_INSERTCHAR:String | W:uint |
| STRING_INSERTLINE:String | X:uint |
| STRING_LEFTARROW:String | Y:uint |
| STRING_MENU:String | Z:uint |
| STRING_MODESWITCH:String | **METHOD:** |
| STRING_NEXT:String | isAccessible():Boolean |
| STRING_PAGEDOWN:String | |

continued ➡

## KeyboardEvent

**Package: flash.events**

**Extends Event**

**PROPERTIES:**

altKey:Boolean

charCode:uint

commandKey:Boolean

controlKey:Boolean

ctrlKey:Boolean

keyCode:uint

keyLocation:uint

shiftKey:Boolean

**CONSTANTS:**

KEY_DOWN:String

KEY_UP:String

**METHODS:**

clone():Event

KeyboardEvent()

toString():String

updateAfterEvent():void

## KeyLocation

**Package: flash.ui**

**Extends Object**

**CONSTANTS:**

LEFT:uint

NUM_PAD:uint

RIGHT:uint

STANDARD:uint

## LigatureLevel

**Package: flash.text.engine**

**Extends Object**

**CONSTANTS:**

COMMON:String

EXOTIC:String

MINIMUM:String

NONE:String

UNCOMMON:String

## LineJustification

Package: flash.text.engine

Extends Object

CONSTANTS:
ALL_BUT_LAST:String
ALL_INCLUDING_LAST:String
UNJUSTIFIED:String

## LineScaleMode

Package: flash.display

Extends Object

CONSTANTS:
HORIZONTAL:String
NONE:String
NORMAL:String
VERTICAL:String

## Loader

Package: flash.display

Extends DisplayObjectContainer

PROPERTIES:
content:DisplayObject
contentLoaderInfo:LoaderInfo

METHODS:
close():void
load():void
loadBytes():void
Loader()
unload():void

## LoaderContext

Package: flash.system

Extends Object

PROPERTIES:
applicationDomain:ApplicationDomain
checkPolicyFile:Boolean
securityDomain:SecurityDomain

METHOD:
LoaderContext()

continued ➡

# ActionScript
# Class Reference (continued)

## LoaderInfo

**Package: flash.display**

**Extends EventDispatcher**

**PROPERTIES:**

actionScriptVersion:uint

applicationDomain:ApplicationDomain

bytes:ByteArray

bytesLoaded:uint

bytesTotal:uint

childAllowsParent:Boolean

childSandboxBridge:Object

content:DisplayObject

contentType:String

frameRate:Number

height:int

loader:Loader

loaderURL:String

parameters:Object

parentAllowsChild:Boolean

parentSandboxBridge:Object

sameDomain:Boolean

sharedEvents:EventDispatcher

swfVersion:uint

url:String

width:int

**METHOD:**

getLoaderInfoByDefinition():LoaderInfo

## LoadVoucherSetting

**(AIR only)**

**Package: flash.net.drm**

**Extends Object**

**CONSTANTS:**

ALLOW_SERVER:String

FORCE_REFRESH:String

LOCAL_ONLY:String

## LocalConnection

**Package: flash.net**

**Extends EventDispatcher**

**PROPERTIES:**

client:Object

domain:String

**METHODS:**

allowDomain():void

allowInsecureDomain():void

close():void

connect():void

LocalConnection()

send():void

## Math

| | |
|---|---|
| **Package: Top Level** | atan():Number |
| | atan2():Number |
| **Extends Object** | ceil():Number |
| | cos():Number |
| **CONSTANTS:** | exp():Number |
| E:Number | floor():Number |
| LN2:Number | log():Number |
| LN10:Number | max():Number |
| LOG2E:Number | min():Number |
| LOG10E:Number | pow():Number |
| PI:Number | random():Number |
| SQRT1_2:Number | round():Number |
| SQRT2:Number | sin():Number |
| | sqrt():Number |
| **METHODS:** | tan():Number |
| abs():Number | |
| acos():Number | |
| asin():Number | |

## Matrix

| | |
|---|---|
| **Package: flash.geom** | createBox():void |
| | createGradientBox():void |
| **Extends Object** | deltaTransformPoint():Point |
| | identity():void |
| **PROPERTIES:** | invert():void |
| a:Number | Matrix() |
| b:Number | rotate():void |
| c:Number | scale():void |
| d:Number | toString():String |
| tx:Number | transformPoint():Point |
| ty:Number | translate():void |
| | |
| **METHODS:** | |
| clone():Matrix | |
| concat():void | |

continued ➡

# ActionScript Class Reference (continued)

## Matrix3D

**Package: flash.geom**

**Extends Object**

**PROPERTIES:**

determinant:Number

position:Vector3D

rawData:Vector.<Number>

**METHODS:**

append():void

appendRotation():void

appendScale():void

appendTranslation():void

clone():Matrix3D

decompose():Vector.<Vector3D>

deltaTransformVector():Vector3D

identity():void

interpolate():Matrix3D

interpolateTo():void

invert():Boolean

pointAt():void

prepend():void

prependRotation():void

prependScale():void

prependTranslation():void

recompose():Boolean

transformVector():Vector3D

transformVectors():void

transpose():void

## MemoryError

**Package: flash.errors**

**Extends Error**

**METHOD:**

MemoryError():void

## Microphone

**Package: flash.media**

**Extends EventDispatcher**

**PROPERTIES:**

activityLevel:Number

codec:String

encodeQuality:int

framesPerPacket:int

gain:Number

index:int

muted:Boolean

name:String

names:Array

rate:int

silenceLevel:Number

silenceTimeout:int

soundTransform:SoundTransform

useEchoSuppression:Boolean

**METHODS:**

getMicrophone():Microphone

setLoopBack():void

setSilenceLevel():void

setUseEchoSuppression():void

## MorphShape

**Package: flash.display**

**Extends Display Object**

## Mouse

**Package: flash.ui**

**Extends Object**

**PROPERTY:**

cursor:String

**METHODS:**

hide():void

show():void

## MouseCursor

**Package: flash.ui**

**Extends Object**

**CONSTANTS:**

ARROW:String

AUTO:String

BUTTON:String

HAND:String

IBEAM:String

continued ➡

# ActionScript
## Class Reference (continued)

**MouseEvent**

| | |
|---|---|
| **Package: flash.events** | DOUBLE_CLICK:String |
| | MIDDLE_CLICK:String |
| **Extends Event** | MIDDLE_MOUSE_DOWN:String |
| | MIDDLE_MOUSE_UP:String |
| **PROPERTIES:** | MOUSE_DOWN:String |
| altKey:Boolean | MOUSE_MOVE:String |
| buttonDown:Boolean | MOUSE_OUT:String |
| clickCount:int | MOUSE_OVER:String |
| commandKey:Boolean | MOUSE_UP:String |
| controlKey:Boolean | MOUSE_WHEEL:String |
| ctrlKey:Boolean | RIGHT_CLICK:String |
| delta:int | RIGHT_MOUSE_DOWN:String |
| localX:Number | RIGHT_MOUSE_UP:String |
| localY:Number | ROLL_OUT:String |
| relatedObject:InteractiveObject | ROLL_OVER:String |
| shiftKey:Boolean | |
| stageX:Number | **METHODS:** |
| stageY:Number | clone():Event |
| | MouseEvent() |
| **CONSTANTS:** | toString():String |
| CLICK:String | updateAfterEvent():void |
| CONTEXT_MENU:String | |

## MovieClip

**Package: flash.display**

**Extends Sprite**

**PROPERTIES:**

currentFrame:int

currentFrameLabel:String

currentLabel:String

currentLabels:Array

currentScene:Scene

enabled:Boolean

framesLoaded:int

scenes:Array

totalFrames:int

trackAsMenu:Boolean

**METHODS:**

gotoAndPlay():void

gotoAndStop():void

MovieClip()

nextFrame():void

nextScene():void

play():void

prevFrame():void

prevScene():void

stop():void

## Namespace

**Package: Top Level**

**Extends Object**

**PROPERTIES:**

prefix:String

uri:String

**METHODS:**

Namespace():void

toString():String

valueOf():String

continued

## NativeApplication

| | |
|---|---|
| **(AIR only)** | supportsSystemTrayIcon:Boolean |
| | timeSinceLastUserInput:int |
| **Package: flash.desktop** | |
| | **METHODS:** |
| **Extends EventDispatcher** | activate():void |
| | addEventListener():void |
| **PROPERTIES:** | clear():Boolean |
| activeWindow:NativeWindow | copy():Boolean |
| applicationDescriptor:XML | cut():Boolean |
| applicationID:String | dispatchEvent():Boolean |
| autoExit:Boolean | exit():void |
| icon:InteractiveIcon | getDefaultApplication():String |
| idleThreshold:int | isSetAsDefaultApplication():Boolean |
| menu:NativeMenu | paste():Boolean |
| nativeApplication:NativeApplication | redo():Boolean |
| openedWindows:Array | removeAsDefaultApplication():void |
| publisherID:String | removeEventListener():void |
| runtimePatchLevel:uint | selectAll():Boolean |
| runtimeVersion:String | setAsDefaultApplication():void |
| startAtLogin:Boolean | undo():Boolean |
| supportsDockIcon:Boolean | |
| supportsMenu:Boolean | |

## NativeDragActions

(AIR Only)

Package: flash.desktop

Extends Object

**CONSTANTS:**

COPY:String

LINK:String

MOVE:String

NONE:String

## NativeDragEvent

(AIR Only)

Package: flash.events

Extends MouseEvent

**PROPERTIES:**

allowedActions:NativeDragOptions

clipboard:Clipboard

dropAction:String

**CONSTANTS:**

NATIVE_DRAG_COMPLETE:String

NATIVE_DRAG_DROP:String

NATIVE_DRAG_ENTER:String

NATIVE_DRAG_EXIT:String

NATIVE_DRAG_OVER:String

NATIVE_DRAG_START:String

NATIVE_DRAG_UPDATE:String

**METHODS:**

clone():Event

NativeDragEvent()

toString():String

## NativeDragManager

(AIR Only)

Package: flash.desktop

Extends Object

**PROPERTIES:**

dragInitiator:InteractiveObject

dropAction:String

isDragging:Boolean

**METHODS:**

acceptDragDrop():void

doDrag():void

## NativeDragOptions

(AIR Only)

Package: flash.desktop

Extends Object

**PROPERTIES:**

allowCopy:Boolean

allowLink:Boolean

allowMove:Boolean

**METHOD:**

toString():String

continued ➡

313

## NativeMenu

| | |
|---|---|
| **(AIR Only)** | addSubmenu():NativeMenuItem |
| | addSubmenuAt():NativeMenuItem |
| **Package: flash.display** | clone():NativeMenu |
| | containsItem():Boolean |
| **Extends EventDispatcher** | display():void |
| **PROPERTIES:** | getItemAt():NativeMenuItem |
| items:Array | getItemByName():NativeMenuItem |
| numItems:int | getItemIndex():int |
| parent:NativeMenu | removeItem():NativeMenuItem |
| | removeItemAt():NativeMenuItem |
| **METHODS:** | setItemIndex():void |
| addItem():NativeMenuItem | |
| addItemAt():NativeMenuItem | |

## NativeMenuItem

| | |
|---|---|
| **(AIR Only)** | label:String |
| | menu:NativeMenu |
| **Package: flash.display** | mnemonicIndex:int |
| | name:String |
| **Extends EventDispatcher** | submenu:NativeMenu |
| **PROPERTIES:** | **METHODS:** |
| checked:Boolean | clone():NativeMenuItem |
| data:Object | NativeMenuItem() |
| enabled:Boolean | toString():String |
| isSeparator:Boolean | |
| keyEquivalent:String | |
| keyEquivalentModifiers:Array | |

## NativeWindow

| | |
|---|---|
| **(AIR Only)** | title:String |
| | transparent:Boolean |
| **Package: flash.display** | type:String |
| | visible:Boolean |
| **Extends EventDispatcher** | width:Number |
| | x:Number |
| **PROPERTIES:** | y:Number |
| active:Boolean | |
| alwaysInFront:Boolean | **METHODS:** |
| bounds:Rectangle | activate():void |
| closed:Boolean | close():void |
| displayState:String | globalToScreen():Point |
| height:Number | maximize():void |
| maximizable:Boolean | minimize():void |
| maxSize:Point | NativeWindow() |
| menu:NativeMenu | notifyUser():void |
| minimizable:Boolean | orderInBackOf():Boolean |
| minSize:Point | orderInFrontOf():Boolean |
| resizable:Boolean | orderToBack():Boolean |
| stage:Stage | orderToFront():Boolean |
| supportsMenu:Boolean | restore():void |
| supportsNotification:Boolean | startMove():Boolean |
| systemChrome:String | startResize():Boolean |
| systemMaxSize:Point | |
| systemMinSize:Point | |

continued ➡

## NativeWindowBoundsEvent

**(AIR Only)**

**Package: flash.events**

**Extends Events**

**PROPERTIES:**

afterBounds:Rectangle

beforeBounds:Rectangle

**CONSTANTS:**

MOVE:String

MOVING:String

RESIZE:String

RESIZING:String

**METHODS:**

clone():Event

NativeWindowBoundsEvent()

toString():String

## NativeWindowDisplayState

**(AIR Only)**

**Package: flash.display**

**Extends Object**

**CONSTANTS:**

MAXIMIZED:String

MINIMIZED:String

NORMAL:String

## NativeWindowDisplayStateEvent

**(AIR Only)**

**Package: flash.events**

**Extends Event**

**PROPERTIES:**

afterDisplayState:String

beforeDisplayState:String

**CONSTANTS:**

DISPLAY_STATE_CHANGE:String

DISPLAY_STATE_CHANGING:String

**METHODS:**

clone():Event

NativeWindowDisplayStateEvent()

toString():String

## NativeWindowInitOptions

(AIR Only)

Package: flash.display

Extends Object

**PROPERTIES:**

hasMenu:Boolean

maximizable:Boolean

minimizable:Boolean

resizable:Boolean

systemChrome:String

transparent:Boolean

type:String

**METHOD:**

NativeWindowInitOptions()

## NativeWindowSystemChrome

(AIR Only)

Package: flash.display

Extends Object

**CONSTANTS:**

NONE:String

STANDARD:String

UTILITY:String

## NativeWindowResize

(AIR Only)

Package: flash.display

Extends Object

**CONSTANTS:**

BOTTOM:String

BOTTOM_LEFT:String

BOTTOM_RIGHT:String

LEFT:String

NONE:String

RIGHT:String

TOP:String

TOP_LEFT:String

TOP_RIGHT:String

## NativeWindowType

(AIR Only)

Package: flash.dlsplay

Extends Object

**CONSTANTS:**

LIGHTWEIGHT:String

NORMAL:String

UTILITY:String

continued ➡

## NetConnection

**Package: flash.net**

**Extends EventDispatcher**

**PROPERTIES:**

client:Object

connected:Boolean

connectedProxyType:String

defaultObjectEncoding:uint

farID:String

farNonce:String

maxPeerConnections:uint

nearID:String

nearNonce:String

objectEncoding:uint

protocol:String

proxyType:String

unconnectedPeerStreams:Array

uri:String

usingTLS:Boolean

**METHODS:**

addHeader():void

call():void

close():void

connect():void

NetConnection()

## NetStatusEvent

**Package: flash.events**

**Extends Event**

**PROPERTY:**

info:Object

**CONSTANT:**

NET_STATUS:String

**METHODS:**

clone():Event

NetStatusEvent()

toString():String

| | |
|---|---|
| **Package: flash.net** | **METHODS:** |
| | attachAudio():void |
| **Extends EventDispatcher** | attachCamera():void |
| | close():void |
| **PROPERTIES:** | NetStream() |
| bufferLength:Number | onPeerConnect():Boolean |
| bufferTime:Number | pause():void |
| bytesLoaded:uint | play():void |
| bytesTotal:uint | play2():void |
| checkPolicyFile:Boolean | preloadEmbeddedData():void |
| client:Object | publish():void |
| currentFPS:Number | receiveAudio():void |
| farID:String | receiveVideo():void |
| farNonce:String | receiveVideoFPS():void |
| info:NetStreamInfo | resetDRMVouchers():void |
| liveDelay:Number | resume():void |
| nearNonce:String | seek():void |
| objectEncoding:uint | send():void |
| peerStreams:Array | setDRMAuthenticationCredentials():void |
| soundTransform:SoundTransform | togglePause():void |
| time:Number | |
| | |
| **CONSTANTS:** | |
| CONNECT_TO_FMS:String | |
| DIRECT_CONNECTIONS:String | |

continued ➡

**Package: flash.net**

**Extends Object**

PROPERTIES:

audioBufferByteLength:Number

audioBufferLength:Number

audioByteCount:Number

audioBytesPerSecond:Number

audioLossRate:Number

byteCount:Number

currentBytesPerSecond:Number

dataBufferByteLength:Number

dataBufferLength:Number

dataByteCount:Number

dataBytesPerSecond:Number

droppedFrames:Number

maxBytesPerSecond:Number

playbackBytesPerSecond:Number

SRTT:Number

videoBufferByteLength:Number

videoBufferLength:Number

videoByteCount:Number

videoBytesPerSecond:Number

CONSTANT:

EMBEDDED_CFF:String

METHOD:

toString():String

## NetStreamPlayOptions

**Package: flash.net**

**Extends EventDispatcher**

PROPERTIES:

len:Number

oldStreamName:String

start:Number

streamName:String

transition:String

## NetStreamPlayTransitions

**Package: flash.net**

**Extends Object**

CONSTANTS:

APPEND:*

RESET:*

STOP:*

SWAP:*

SWITCH:*

## NewObjectSample

**Package: flash.sampler**

**Extends Sample**

PROPERTIES:
id:Number
object:*
type:Class

## NotificationType

**(AIR only)**

**Package: flash.desktop**

**Extends Object**

CONSTANTS:
CRITICAL:String
INFORMATIONAL:String

## Number

**Package: Top Level**

**Extends Object**

CONSTANTS:
MAX_VALUE:Number
MIN_VALUE:Number
NaN:Number
NEGATIVE_INFINITY:Number
POSITIVE_INFINITY:Number

METHODS:
Number()
toExponential():String
toFixed():String
toPrecision():String
toString():String
valueOf():Number

## Object

**Package: Top Level**

PROPERTIES:
constructor:Object
prototype:Object

METHODS:
hasOwnProperty():Boolean
isPrototypeOf():Boolean
Object()
propertyIsEnumerable():Boolean
setPropertyIsEnumerable():void
toString():String
valueOf():Object

## ObjectEncoding

**Package: flash.net**

**Extends Object**

PROPERTY:
dynamicPropertyWriter:IDynamicPropertyWriter

CONSTANTS:
AMF0:uint
AMF3:uint
DEFAULT:uint

## Orientation3D

**Package: flash.geom**

**Extends Object**

CONSTANTS:
AXIS_ANGLE:String
EULER_ANGLES:String
QUATERNION:String

continued →

# ActionScript
# Class Reference (continued)

## OutputProgressEvent

**Package: flash.events**

**Extends Event**

**PROPERTIES:**

bytesPending:Number

bytesTotal:Number

**CONSTANT:**

OUTPUT_PROGRESS:String

**METHODS:**

clone():Event

OutputProgressEvent():void

toString():String

## PerspectiveProjection

**Package: flash.geom**

**Extends Object**

**PROPERTIES:**

fieldOfView:Number

focalLength:Number

projectionCenter:Point

**METHOD:**

toMatrix3D():Matrix3D

## PixelSnapping

**Package: flash.display**

**Extends Object**

**CONSTANTS:**

ALWAYS:String

AUTO:String

NEVER:String

## Point

**Package: flash.geom**

**Extends Object**

**PROPERTIES:**

length:Number

x:Number

y:Number

**METHODS:**

add():Point

clone():Point

distance():Number

equals():Boolean

interpolate():Point

normalize():void

offset():void

Point()

polar():Point

subtract():Point

toString():String

## PrintJob

**Package: flash.printing**

**Extends EventDispatcher**

**PROPERTIES:**

orientation:String

pageHeight:int

pageWidth:int

paperHeight:int

paperWidth:int

**METHODS:**

addPage():void

PrintJob()

send():void

start():Boolean

## PrintJobOptions

**Package: flash.printing**

**Extends Object**

**PROPERTY:**

printAsBitmap:Boolean

**METHOD:**

PrintJobOptions()

## PrintJobOrientation

**Package: flash.printing**

**Extends Object**

**CONSTANTS:**

LANDSCAPE:String

PORTRAIT:String

## ProgressEvent

**Package: flash.events**

**Extends Event**

**PROPERTIES:**

bytesLoaded:Number

bytesTotal:Number

**CONSTANTS:**

PROGRESS:String

SOCKET_DATA:String

**METHODS:**

clone():Event

ProgressEvent()

toString():String

## Proxy

**Package: flash.utils**

**Extends Object**

**METHODS:**

callProperty():*

deleteProperty():Boolean

getDescendants():*

getProperty():*

hasProperty():Boolean

isAttribute():Boolean

nextName():String

nextNameIndex():int

nextValue():*

setProperty():void

continued ➡

## QName

**Package: Top Level**

**Extends Object**

**PROPERTIES:**

localName:String

uri:String

**METHODS:**

QName()

toString():String

valueOf():QName

## RangeError

**Package: Top Level**

**Extends Error**

**METHOD:**

RangeError()

## Rectangle

**Package: flash.geom**

**Extends Object**

**PROPERTIES:**

bottom:Number

bottomRight:Point

height:Number

left:Number

right:Number

size:Point

top:Number

topLeft:Point

width:Number

x:Number

y:Number

**METHODS:**

clone():Rectangle

contains():Boolean

containsPoint():Boolean

containsRect():Boolean

equals():Boolean

inflate():void

inflatePoint():void

intersection():Rectangle

intersects():Boolean

isEmpty():Boolean

offset():void

offsetPoint():void

Rectangle()

setEmpty():void

toString():String

union():Rectangle

## ReferenceError

**Package: Top Level**

**Extends Error**

**METHOD:**
ReferenceError()

## Responder

**Package: flash.net**

**Extends Object**

## RegExp

**Package: Top Level**

**Extends Object**

**PROPERTIES:**
dotall:Boolean
extended:Boolean
global:Boolean
ignoreCase:Boolean
lastIndex:Number
multiline:Boolean
source:String

**METHODS:**
exec():Object
RegExp()
test():Boolean

## RevocationCheckSettings

**(AIR only)**

**Package: flash.security**

**Extends Object**

**CONSTANTS:**
ALWAYS_REQUIRED:*
BEST_EFFORT:*
NEVER:*
REQUIRED_IF_AVAILABLE:*

## RenderingMode

**Package: flash.text.engine**

**Extends Object**

**CONSTANTS:**
NORMAL:String
CFF:String

## Sample

**Package: flash.sampler**

**Extends Object**

**PROPERTIES:**
stack:Array
time:Number

continued ➡

## SampleDataEvent

**Package: flash.events**

**Extends Event**

**PROPERTIES:**

data:ByteArray

position:Number

**CONSTANT:**

SAMPLE_DATA:String

**METHODS:**

clone():Event

toString():String

## Screen

**(AIR Only)**

**Package: flash.display**

**Extends EventDispatcher**

**PROPERTIES:**

bounds:Rectangle

colorDepth:int

mainScreen:Screen

screens:Array

visibleBounds:Rectangle

**METHOD:**

getScreensForRectangle():Array

## Scene

**Package: flash.display**

**Extends Object**

**PROPERTIES:**

labels:Array

name:String

numFrames:int

## ScreenMouseEvent

**(AIR only)**

**Package: flash.events**

**Extends MouseEvent**

**PROPERTIES:**

screenX:Number

screenY:Number

**METHODS:**

clone():Event

ScreenMouseEvent()

toString():String

## ScriptTimeoutError

**Package: flash.errors**

**Extends Error**

PROPERTY:

ScriptTimeoutError()

## SecurityError

**Package: Top Level**

**Extends Error**

METHOD:

SecurityError():void

## Security

**Package: flash.system**

**Extends Object**

PROPERTIES:

exactSettings:Boolean

sandboxType:String

CONSTANTS:

APPLICATION:String

LOCAL_TRUSTED:String

LOCAL_WITH_FILE:String

LOCAL_WITH_NETWORK:String

REMOTE:String

METHODS:

allowDomain():void

allowInsecureDomain():void

loadPolicyFile():void

showSettings():void

## SecurityErrorEvent

**Package: flash.events**

**Extends ErrorEvent**

CONSTANT:

SECURITY_ERROR:String

METHODS:

clone():Event

SecurityErrorEvent()

toString():String

## SecurityPanel

**Package: flash.system**

**Extends Object**

CONSTANTS:

CAMERA:String

DEFAULT:String

DISPLAY:String

LOCAL_STORAGE:String

MICROPHONE:String

PRIVACY:String

SETTINGS_MANAGER:String

## SecurityDomain

**Package: flash.system**

**Extends Object**

PROPERTY:

currentDomain:SecurityDomain

continued ➡

# ActionScript
# Class Reference (continued)

## ServiceMonitor

**(AIR only)**

**Package: air.net**

**Extends EventDispatcher**

**PROPERTIES:**

available:Boolean

lastUpdated:Date

pollInterval:Number

running:Boolean

**METHODS:**

augmentPrototype():void

checkStatus():void

ServiceMonitor()

start():void

stop():void

toString():String

## Shader

**Package: flash.display**

**Extends Object**

**PROPERTIES:**

byteCode:ByteArray

data:ShaderData

precisionHint:String

## ShaderData

**Package: flash.display**

**Extends Object**

**METHOD:**

ShaderData()

## ShaderEvent

**Package: flash.events**

**Extends Event**

**PROPERTIES:**

bitmapData:BitmapData

byteArray:ByteArray

vector:Vector.<Number>

**CONSTANT:**

COMPLETE:String

**METHODS:**

clone():Event

toString():String

## ShaderFilter

**Package: flash.filters**

**Extends BitmapFilter**

**PROPERTIES:**

bottomExtension:int

leftExtension:int

rightExtension:int

shader:Shader

topExtension:int

## ShaderParameter

**Package: flash.display**

**Extends Object**

**PROPERTIES:**

index:int

type:String

value:Array

## ShaderInput

**Package: flash.display**

**Extends Object**

**PROPERTIES:**

channels:int

height:int

index:int

input:Object

width:int

## ShaderParameterType

**Package: flash.display**

**Extends Object**

**CONSTANTS:**

BOOL:String

BOOL2:String

BOOL3:String

BOOL4:String

FLOAT:String

FLOAT2:String

FLOAT3:String

FLOAT4:String

INT:String

INT2:String

INT3:String

INT4:String

MATRIX2X2:String

MATRIX3X3:String

MATRIX4X4:String

## ShaderJob

**Package: flash.display**

**Extends EventDispatcher**

**PROPERTIES:**

height:int

progress:Number

shader:Shader

target:Object

width:int

**METHODS:**

cancel():void

start():void

continued →

## ShaderPrecision

**Package: flash.display**

**Extends Object**

CONSTANTS:

FAST:String

FULL:String

## Shape

**Package: flash.display**

**Extends Display Object**

PROPERTY:

graphics:Graphics

METHOD:

Shape()

## SharedObject

**Package: flash.net**

**Extends EventDispatcher**

PROPERTIES:

client:Object

data:Object

defaultObjectEncoding:uint

fps:Number

objectEncoding:uint

size:uint

METHODS:

clear():void

close():void

connect():void

flush():String

getLocal():SharedObject

getRemote():SharedObject

send():void

setDirty():void

setProperty():void

## SharedObjectFlushStatus

**Package: flash.net**

**Extends Object**

CONSTANTS:

FLUSHED:String

PENDING:String

## SignatureStatus

(AIR only)

Package: flash.security

Extends Object

CONSTANTS:
INVALID:String
UNKNOWN:String
VALID:String

## SignerTrustSettings

(AIR only)

Package: flash.security

Extends Object

CONSTANTS:
CODE_SIGNING:String
PLAYLIST_SIGNING:String
SIGNING:String

## SimpleButton

Package: flash.display

Extends InteractiveObject

PROPERTIES:
downState:DisplayObject
enabled:Boolean
hitTestState:DisplayObject
overState:DisplayObject

soundTransform:SoundTransform
trackAsMenu:Boolean
upState:DisplayObject
useHandCursor:Boolean

METHOD:
SimpleButton()

continued ➡

## Socket

**Package: flash.net**

**Extends EventDispatcher**

**Implements IDataInput, IDataOutput**

**PROPERTIES:**

bytesAvailable:uint

connected:Boolean

endian:String

objectEncoding:uint

**METHODS:**

close():void

connect():void

flush():void

readBoolean():Boolean

readByte():int

readBytes():void

readDouble():Number

readFloat():Number

readInt():int

readMultiByte():String

readObject():*

readShort():int

readUnsignedByte():uint

readUnsignedInt():uint

readUnsignedShort():uint

readUTF():String

readUTFBytes():String

Socket()

writeBoolean():void

writeByte():void

writeBytes():void

writeDouble():void

writeFloat():void

writeInt():void

writeMultiByte():void

writeObject():void

writeShort():void

writeUnsignedInt():void

writeUTF():void

writeUTFBytes():void

## SocketMonitor

**(AIR only)**

**Package: air.net**

**Extends ServiceMonitor**

**PROPERTIES:**

host:String

port:int

**METHODS:**

checkStatus():void

SocketMonitor()

toString():String

## Sound

Package: flash.media

Extends EventDispatcher

PROPERTIES:

bytesLoaded:uint

bytesTotal:int

id3:ID3Info

isBuffering:Boolean

length:Number

url:String

METHODS:

close():void

extract():Number

load():void

play():SoundChannel

Sound()

## SoundChannel

Package: flash.media

Extends EventDispatcher

PROPERTIES:

leftPeak:Number

position:Number

rightPeak:Number

soundTransform:SoundTransform

METHOD:

stop():void

## SoundCodec

Package: flash.media

Extends Object

CONSTANTS:

NELLYMOSER:String

SPEEX:String

## SoundLoaderContext

Package: flash.media

Extends Object

PROPERTIES:

bufferTime:Number

checkPolicyFile:Boolean

METHOD:

SoundLoaderContext()

## SoundMixer

Package: flash.media

Extends Object

PROPERTIES:

bufferTime:int

soundTransform:SoundTransform

METHODS:

areSoundsInaccessible():Boolean

computeSpectrum():void

stopAll():void

continued ➡

## SoundTransform

**Package: flash.media**

**Extends Object**

PROPERTIES:

leftToLeft:Number

leftToRight:Number

pan:Number

rightToLeft:Number

rightToRight:Number

volume:Number

METHOD:

SoundTransform()

## SpaceJustifier

**Package: flash.text.engine**

**Extends TextJustifier**

PROPERTY:

letterSpacing:Boolean

METHOD:

clone():TextJustifier

## SpreadMethod

**Package: flash.display**

**Extends Object**

CONSTANTS:

PAD:String

REFLECT:String

REPEAT:String

## Sprite

**Package: flash.display**

**Extends DisplayObjectContainer**

PROPERTIES:

buttonMode:Boolean

dropTarget:DisplayObject

graphics:Graphics

hitArea:Sprite

soundTransform:SoundTransform

useHandCursor:Boolean

METHODS:

Sprite()

startDrag():void

stopDrag():void

## StackFrame

**Package: flash.sampler**

**Extends Object**

PROPERTIES:

file:String

line:uint

name:String

METHOD:

toString():String

## StackOverflowError

**Package: flash.errors**

**Extends Error**

METHOD:

StackOverflowError():void

## Stage

**Package: flash.display**

**Extends DisplayObjectContainer**

PROPERTIES:

align:String

cacheAsBitmap:Boolean

displayState:String

focus:InteractiveObject

frameRate:Number

fullScreenHeight:uint

fullScreenSourceRect:Rectangle

fullScreenWidth:uint

height:Number

mouseChildren:Boolean

nativeWindow:NativeWindow

numChildren:int

quality:String

scaleMode:String

showDefaultContextMenu:Boolean

stageFocusRect:Boolean

stageHeight:int

stageWidth:int

tabChildren:Boolean

tabEnabled:Boolean

textSnapshot:TextSnapshot

width:Number

METHODS:

addChild():DisplayObject

addChildAt():DisplayObject

addEventListener():void

assignFocus():void

dispatchEvent():Boolean

hasEventListener():Boolean

invalidate():void

isFocusInaccessible():Boolean

removeChildAt():DisplayObject

setChildIndex():void

swapChildrenAt():void

willTrigger():Boolean

continued ➡

## StageAlign

**Package: flash.display**

**Extends Object**

CONSTANTS:

BOTTOM:String

BOTTOM_LEFT:String

BOTTOM_RIGHT:String

LEFT:String

RIGHT:String

TOP:String

TOP_LEFT:String

TOP_RIGHT:String

## StageDisplayState

**Package: flash.display**

**Extends Object**

CONSTANTS:

FULL_SCREEN:String

FULL_SCREEN_INTERACTIVE:String

NORMAL:String

## StageQuality

**Package: flash.display**

**Extends Object**

CONSTANTS:

BEST:String

HIGH:String

LOW:String

MEDIUM:String

## StageScaleMode

**Package: flash.display**

**Extends Object**

CONSTANTS:

EXACT_FIT:String

NO_BORDER:String

NO_SCALE:String

SHOW_ALL:String

## StaticText

**Package: flash.text**

**Extends DisplayObject**

PROPERTY:

text:String

## StatusEvent

**Package: flash.events**

**Extends Event**

PROPERTIES:
code:String
level:String

CONSTANT:
STATUS:String

METHODS:
clone():Event
StatusEvent()

## SWFVersion

**Package: flash.display**

**Extends Object**

CONSTANTS:
FLASH1:uint
FLASH2:uint
FLASH3:uint
FLASH4:uint
FLASH5:uint
FLASH6:uint
FLASH7:uint
FLASH8:uint
FLASH9:uint

## StyleSheet

**Package: flash.text**

**Extends EventDispatcher**

PROPERTY:
styleNames:Array

METHODS:
clear():void
getStyle():Object
parseCSS():void
setStyle():void
StyleSheet()
transform():TextFormat
toString():String

## SyncEvent

**Package: flash.events**

**Extends Event**

PROPERTY:
changeList:Array

CONSTANT:
SYNC:String

METHODS:
clone():Event
SyncEvent()
toString():String

continued ➡

# ActionScript
# Class Reference (continued)

## SyntaxError

**Package: Top Level**

**Extends Error**

**METHOD:**
SyntaxError()

## System

**Package: flash.system**

**Extends Object**

**PROPERTIES:**
ime:IME
totalMemory:uint
useCodePage:Boolean

**METHODS:**
exit():void
gc():void
pause():void
resume():void
setClipboard():void

## SystemTrayIcon

**(AIR only)**

**Package: flash.desktop**

**Extends InteractiveIcon**

**PROPERTIES:**
bitmaps:Array
height:int
menu:NativeMenu
tooltip:String
width:int

**CONSTANT:**
MAX_TIP_LENGTH:Number

## TabAlignment

**Package: flash.text.engine**

**Extends Object**

**CONSTANTS:**
CENTER:String
DECIMAL:String
END:String
START:String

## TextBaseline

**Package: flash.text.engine**

**Extends Object**

**Constants:**

ASCENT:String

DESCENT:String

IDEOGRAPHIC_BOTTOM:String

IDEOGRAPHIC_CENTER:String

IDEOGRAPHIC_TOP:String

ROMAN:String

USE_DOMINANT_BASELINE:String

## TextBlocK

**Package: flash.text.engine**

**Extends Object**

**Properties:**

applyNonLinearFontScaling:Boolean

baselineFontDescription:FontDescription

baselineFontSize:Number

baselineZero:String

bidiLevel:int

content:ContentElement

firstInvalidLine:TextLine

firstLine:TextLine

lastLine:TextLine

lineRotation:String

tabStops:Vector.<TabStop>

textJustifier:TextJustifier

textLineCreationResult:String

userData:*

**Methods:**

createTextLine():Text

Linedump():String

findNextAtomBoundary():int

findNextWordBoundary():int

findPreviousAtomBoundary():int

findPreviousWordBoundary():int

getTextLineAtCharIndex():TextLine

releaseLines():void

## TextColorType

**Package: flash.text**

**Extends Object**

**Constants:**

DARK_COLOR:String

LIGHT_COLOR:String

## TextDisplayMode

**Package: flash.text**

**Extends Object**

**Constants:**

CRT:String

DEFAULT:String

LCD:String

continued ➡

# ActionScript
# Class Reference (continued)

## TextElement

**Package: flash.text.engine**

**Extends ContentElement**

**PROPERTY:**
text:String

**METHOD:**
replaceText():void

## TextEvent

**Package: flash.events**

**Extends Event**

**PROPERTY:**
text:String

**CONSTANTS:**
LINK:String
TEXT_INPUT:String

**METHODS:**
clone():Event
TextEvent()
toString():String

## TextExtent

**Package: flash.text**

**Extends Object**

**PROPERTIES:**
ascent:Number
descent:Number

height:Number
textFieldHeight:Number
textFieldWidth:Number
width:Number

**Package: flash.text**

**Extends InteractiveObject**

PROPERTIES:

alwaysShowSelection:Boolean

antiAliasType:String

autoSize:String

background:Boolean

backgroundColor:uint

border:Boolean

borderColor:uint

bottomScrollV:int

caretIndex:int

condenseWhite:Boolean

contextMenu:NativeMenu

defaultTextFormat:TextFormat

displayAsPassword:Boolean

embedFonts:Boolean

gridFitType:String

htmlText:String

length:int

maxChars:int

maxScrollH:int

maxScrollV:int

mouseWheelEnabled:Boolean

multiline:Boolean

numLines:int

restrict:String

scrollH:int

scrollV:int

selectable:Boolean

selectionBeginIndex:int

selectionEndIndex:int

sharpness:Number

styleSheet:StyleSheet

text:String

textColor:uint

textHeight:Number

textWidth:Number

thickness:Number

type:String

useRichTextClipboard:Boolean

wordWrap:Boolean

METHODS:

appendText():void

getCharBoundaries():Rectangle

getCharIndexAtPoint():int

getFirstCharInParagraph():int

getImageReference():DisplayObject

getLineIndexAtPoint():int

getLineIndexOfChar():int

getLineLength():int

getLineMetrics():TextLineMetrics

getLineOffset():int

getLineText():String

getParagraphLength():int

getTextFormat():TextFormat

replaceSelectedText():void

replaceText():void

setSelection():void

setTextFormat():void

TextField()

continued →

# ActionScript
# Class Reference (continued)

## TextFieldAutoSize

**Package: flash.text**

**Extends Object**

**CONSTANTS:**

CENTER:String

LEFT:String

NONE:String

RIGHT:String

## TextFieldType

**Package: flash.text**

**Extends Object**

**CONSTANTS:**

DYNAMIC:String
INPUT:String

## TextFormat

**Package: flash.text**

**Extends Object**

**PROPERTIES:**

align:String

blockIndent:Object

bold:Object

bullet:Object

color:Object

font:String

indent:Object

italic:Object

kerning:Object

leading:Object

leftMargin:Object

letterSpacing:Object

rightMargin:Object

size:Object

tabStops:Array

target:String

underline:Object

url:String

**METHOD:**

TextFormat()

## TextFormatAlign

**Package: flash.text**

**Extends Object**

**CONSTANTS:**

CENTER:String

JUSTIFY:String

LEFT:String
RIGHT:String

## TextJustifier

**Package: flash.text.engine**

**Extends Object**

**PROPERTIES:**

lineJustification:String

locale:String

**METHODS:**

clone():TextJustifier
getJustifierForLocale():TextJustifier

## TextLine

**Package: flash.text.engine**

**Extends DisplayObjectContainer**

**PROPERTIES:**

ascent:Number

atomCount:int

descent:Number

hasGraphicElement:Boolean

mirrorRegions:Vector.
    <TextLineMirrorRegion>

nextLine:TextLine

previousLine:TextLine

rawTextLength:int

specifiedWidth:Number
textBlock:TextBlock

textBlockBeginIndex:int

textHeight:Number

textWidth:Number

unjustifiedTextWidth:Number

userData:*

validity:String

**CONSTANT:**

MAX_LINE_WIDTH:int

**METHODS:**

dump():String

flushAtomData():void

getAtomBidiLevel():int

getAtomBounds():Rectangle

getAtomCenter():Number

getAtomGraphic():DisplayObject

getAtomIndexAtCharIndex():int

getAtomIndexAtPoint():int

getAtomTextBlockBeginIndex():int

getAtomTextBlockEndIndex():int

getAtomTextRotation():String

getAtomWordBoundaryOnLeft():Boolean

getBaselinePosition():Number

getMirrorRegion():TextLineMirrorRegion

continued ➡

# ActionScript
# Class Reference (continued)

## TextLineCreationResult

**Package: flash.text.engine**

**Extends Object**

**CONSTANTS:**

COMPLETE:String

EMERGENCY:String

INSUFFICIENT_WIDTH:String

SUCCESS:String

## TextLineMirrorRegion

**Package: flash.text.engine**

**Extends Object**

**PROPERTIES:**

bounds:Rectangle

element:ContentElement

mirror:EventDispatcher

nextRegion:TextLineMirrorRegion

previousRegion:TextLineMirrorRegion

textLine:TextLine

## TextLineMetrics

**Package: flash.text**

**Extends Object**

**PROPERTIES:**

ascent:Number

descent:Number

height:Number

leading:Number

width:Number

x:Number

**METHOD:**

TextLineMetrics()

## TextLineValidity

**Package: flash.text.engine**

**Extends Object**

**CONSTANTS:**

INVALID:String

POSSIBLY_INVALID:String

STATIC:String

VALID:String

## TextRenderer

**Package: flash.text**

**Extends Object**

PROPERTIES:

displayMode:String

maxLevel:int

METHOD:

setAdvancedAntiAliasingTable():void

## TextSnapshot

**Package: flash.text**

**Extends Object**

PROPERTY:

charCount:int

METHODS:

findText():int

getSelected():Boolean

getSelectedText():String

getText():String

getTextRunInfo():Array

hitTestTextNearPos():Number

setSelectColor():void

setSelected():void

## TextRotation

**Package: flash.text.engine**

**Extends Object**

CONSTANTS:

AUTO:String

ROTATE_0:String

ROTATE_90:String

ROTATE_180:String

ROTATE_270:String

## Timer

**Package: flash.utils**

**Extends EventDispatcher**

PROPERTIES:

currentCount:int

delay:Number

repeatCount:int

running:Boolean

METHODS:

reset():void

start():void

stop():void

Timer()

continued ➡

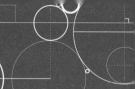
## TimerEvent

**Package: flash.events**

**Extends Event**

**CONSTANTS:**

TIMER:String

TIMER_COMPLETE:String

**METHODS:**

clone():Event

TimerEvent()

toString():String

updateAfterEvent():void

## Transform

**Package: flash.geom**

**Extends Object**

**PROPERTIES:**

colorTransform:ColorTransform

concatenatedColorTransform:ColorTransform

concatenatedMatrix:Matrix

matrix:Matrix

pixelBounds:Rectangle

## TriangleCulling

**Package: flash.display**

**Extends Object**

**CONSTANTS:**

NEGATIVE:String

NONE:String

POSITIVE:String

## TypeError

**Package: Top Level**

**Extends Error**

**METHOD:**

TypeError()

## TypographicCase

**Package: flash.text.engine**

**Extends Object**

**CONSTANTS:**

CAPS:String

CAPS_AND_SMALL_CAPS:String

DEFAULT:String

LOWERCASE:String

SMALL_CAPS:String

TITLE:String

UPPERCASE:String

## uint

**Package: Top Level**

**Extends Object**

**CONSTANTS:**

MAX_VALUE:uint

MIN_VALUE:uint

**METHODS:**

toExponential():String

toFixed():String

toPrecision():String

toString():String

uint()

valueOf():uint

## URLLoader

**Package: flash.net**

**Extends EventDispatcher**

**PROPERTIES:**

bytesLoaded:uint

bytesTotal:uint

data:data

Format:String

**METHODS:**

close():void

load():void

URLLoader()

## Updater

**(AIR only)**

**Package: flash.desktop**

**Extends Object**

**METHODS:**

update():void

Updater()

## URLLoaderDataFormat

**Package: flash.net**

**Extends Object**

**CONSTANTS:**

BINARY:String

TEXT:String

VARIABLES:String

## URIError

**Package: Top Level**

**Extends Error**

**METHOD:**

URIError()

continued ➡

# ActionScript
# Class Reference (continued)

## URLMonitor

**(AIR only)**

**Package: air.net**

**Extends ServiceMonitor**

**PROPERTIES:**
acceptableStatuses:Array
urlRequest:URLRequest

**METHODS:**
checkStatus():void
toString():String
URLMonitor()

## URLRequest

**Package: flash.net**

**Extends Object**

**PROPERTIES:**
authenticate:Boolean
cacheResponse:Boolean
contentType:String
data:Object
digest:String
followRedirects:Boolean
manageCookies:Boolean
method:String
requestHeaders:Array
url:String
useCache:Boolean
userAgent:String

**METHOD:**
URLRequest()

## URLRequestDefaults

**(AIR only)**

**Package: flash.net**

**Extends Object**

**PROPERTIES:**
authenticate:Boolean
cacheResponse:Boolean
followRedirects:Boolean
manageCookies:Boolean
useCache:Boolean
userAgent:String

**METHOD:**
setLoginCredentialsForHost():*

## URLRequestHeader

**Package: flash.net**

**Extends Object**

**PROPERTIES:**
name:String
value:String

**METHOD:**
URLRequestHeader()

## URLRequestMethod

**Package: flash.net**

**Extends Object**

### CONSTANTS:
```
DELETE:String
GET:String
HEAD:String
OPTIONS:String
POST:String
PUT:String
```

## URLVariables

**Package: flash.net**

**Extends Object**

### METHODS:
```
decode():void
toString():String
URLVariables():void
```

## URLStream

**Package: flash.net**

**Extends EventDispatcher**

**Implements IDataInput**

### PROPERTIES:
```
bytesAvailable:uint
connected:Boolean
endian:String
objectEncoding:uint
```

### METHODS:
```
close():void
load():void
readBoolean():Boolean
readByte():int
readBytes():void
readDouble():Number
readFloat():Number
readInt():int
readMultiByte():String
readObject():*
readShort():int
readUnsignedByte():uint
readUnsignedInt():uint
readUnsignedShort():uint
readUTF():String
readUTFBytes():String
```

## Utils3D

**Package: flash.geom**

**Extends Object**

### METHODS:
```
pointTowards():Matrix3D
projectVector():Vector3D
projectVectors():void
```

continued ➡

## Vector

**Package: Top Level**

**Extends Object**

**PROPERTIES:**

fixed:Boolean

length:uint

**METHODS:**

concat():Vector.<T>

every():Boolean

filter():Vector.<T>

forEach():void

indexOf():int

join():String

lastIndexOf():int

map():Vector.<T>

pop():T

push():uint

reverse():Vector.<T>

shift():T

slice():Vector.<T>

some():Boolean

sort():Vector.<T>

splice():Vector.<T>

toLocaleString():String

toString():String

unshift():uint

## Vector3D

**Package: flash.geom**

**Extends Object**

**PROPERTIES:**

length:Number

lengthSquared:Number

w:Number

x:Number

y:Number

z:Number

**CONSTANTS:**

X_AXIS:Vector3D

Y_AXIS:Vector3D

Z_AXIS:Vector3D

**METHODS:**

add():Vector3D

angleBetween():Number

clone():Vector3D

crossProduct():Vector3D

decrementBy():void

distance():Number

dotProduct():Number

equals():Boolean

incrementBy():void

nearEquals():Boolean

negate():void

normalize():Number

project():void

scaleBy():void

subtract():Vector3D

toString():String

## VerifyError

**Package: Top Level**

**Extends Error**

**METHOD:**

VerifyError():void

## Video

**Package: flash.media**

**Extends EventDispatcher**

**PROPERTIES:**

deblocking:int

smoothing:Boolean

videoHeight:int

videoWidth:int

**METHODS:**

attachCamera():void

attachNetStream():void

clear():void

Video():void

## XML

**Package: Top Level**

**Extends Object**

**PROPERTIES:**

ignoreComments:Boolean

ignoreProcessingInstructions:Boolean

ignoreWhitespace:Boolean

prettyIndent:int

prettyPrinting:Boolean

**METHODS:**

addNamespace():XML

appendChild():XML

attribute():XMLList

attributes():XMLList

child():XMLList

childIndex():int

children():XMLList

comments():XMLList

contains():Boolean

copy():XML

defaultSettings():Object

descendants():XMLList

elements():XMLList

hasComplexContent():Boolean

hasOwnProperty():Boolean

hasSimpleContent():Boolean

inScopeNamespaces():Array

insertChildAfter():*

insertChildBefore():*

length():int

localName():Object

name():Object

namespace():*

namespaceDeclarations():Array

nodeKind():String

normalize():XML

parent():*

prependChild():XML

processingInstructions():XMLList

propertyIsEnumerable():Boolean

removeNamespace():XML

replace():XML

setChildren():XML

continued ➡

## XML *(continued)*

```
setLocalName():void
setName():void
setNamespace():void
setSettings():void
settings():Object
text():XMLList
toString():String
toXMLString():String
valueOf():XML
XML()
```

## XMLDocument

**Package: flash.xml**

**Extends Object**

**PROPERTIES:**
```
docTypeDecl:Object
idMap:Object
ignoreWhite:Boolean
xmlDecl:Object
```
**METHODS:**
```
createElement():XMLNode
createTextNode():XMLNode
parseXML():void
toString():String
XMLDocument()
```

## XMLNode

**Package: flash.xml**

**Extends Object**

**PROPERTIES:**
```
attributes:Object
childNodes:Array
firstChild:XMLNode
lastChild:XMLNode
localName:String
namespaceURI:String
nextSibling:XMLNode
nodeName:String
nodeType:uint
nodeValue:String
```

```
parentNode:XMLNode
prefix:String
previousSibling:XMLNode
```
**METHODS:**
```
appendChild():void
cloneNode():XMLNode
getNamespaceForPrefix():String
getPrefixForNamespace():String
hasChildNodes():Boolean
insertBefore():void
removeNode():void
toString():String
XMLNode()
```

## XMLNodeType

**Package: flash.xml**

**Extends Object**

CONSTANTS:
```
ELEMENT_NODE:uint
TEXT_NODE:uint
```

## XMLSignatureValidator

**(AIR only)**

**Package: flash.security**

**Extends EventDispatcher**

PROPERTIES:
```
digestStatus:String
identityStatus:String
rcferencesStatus:String
referencesValidationSetting:String
revocationCheckSetting:String
signerCN:String
signerDN:String
signerExtendedKeyUsages:Array
signerTrustSettings:Array
uriDereferencer:URIDereferencer
useSystemTrustStore:Boolean
validityStatus:String
```

METHODS:
```
addCertificate():*
verify():void
XMLSignatureValidator()
```

## XMLSocket

**Package: flash.net**

**Extends EventDispatcher**

PROPERTY:
```
connected:Boolean
```

METHODS:
```
close():void
connect():void
send():void
XMLSocket()
```

# ActionScript Operators Reference

The following is a list of the operators in ActionScript 3.0:

## Basic Operators

The following table shows the operators used throughout the language in a variety of situations.

| OPERATOR | DESCRIPTION | EXAMPLE |
|---|---|---|
| = | Assignment; assigns the value on the right to the expression on the left | `var name:String = "Mal";` |
| . | Accesses properties or methods of objects or separates class names from package names | `mcBox1.scaleX = 42;` |
| () | Groups mathematical operators or invokes functions and methods | `this.gotoAndPlay(42);` |
| : | Declares data type | `var lastName:String;` |
| + | Concatenates strings | `var fullName:String = firstName + " " + lastName;` |

## Mathematical Operators

The following table describes the operators used in mathematical expressions:

| OPERATOR | DESCRIPTION | EXAMPLE |
|---|---|---|
| + | Performs addition | `var total:Number = num1 + num2;` |
| - | Performs subtraction | `var total:Number = num1 - num2;` |
| * | Performs multiplication | `var total:Number = num1 * num2;` |
| / | Performs division | `var total:Number = num1 / num2;` |
| % | Returns modulus, the remainder in a division problem | `var total:Number = num1 % num2;` |
| ++ | Increments the value by one | `i++;` |
| -- | Decrements the value by one | `i--;` |
| += | Adds the value to the right to the current value of the variable | `newTotal += num1; //same as`<br>`newTotal = newTotal + num1;` |
| -= | Subtracts the value to the right from the current value of the variable | `newTotal -= num1; //same as`<br>`newTotal = newTotal - num1;` |
| *= | Multiplies the value to the right by the current value | `newTotal *= num1; // same as`<br>`newTotal = newTotal * num1;` |
| /= | Divides the value to the right by the current value | `newTotal /= num1; // same as`<br>`newTotal = newTotal / num1;` |

## Comparison Operators

The following table summarizes the comparison operators that you can use in your scripts:

| OPERATOR | DESCRIPTION | EXAMPLE |
|----------|-------------|---------|
| < | Less than | `var isTrue:Boolean = num1 < num2;` |
| > | Greater than | `var isTrue:Boolean = num2 > num1;` |
| <= | Less than or equal to | `var isTrue:Boolean = num3 <= num4;` |
| >= | Greater than or equal to | `var isTrue:Boolean = num4 >= num3;` |
| != | Not equal to | `var isTrue:Boolean = num5 != num6;` |
| == | Equal to | `var isTrue:Boolean = num7 == num8;` |

## Boolean Operators

The following table summarizes the Boolean operators available in ActionScript 3.0:

| OPERATOR | DESCRIPTION | EXAMPLE |
|----------|-------------|---------|
| ! | Logical NOT; negates value | `if(!num1.isBoolean())` |
| \|\| | Logical OR | `if(num1 > num2 \|\| num3 < num4)` |
| && | Logical AND | `if(num5 <= num6 && num7 >= num8)` |

# Supported
# HTML Tags

**F**lash text input fields support a small subset of HTML for formatting. This formatting only works if the Format As HTML box is checked in the Properties panel or if the field's text is assigned to its `htmlText` property rather than its `text` property.

| TAG | DESCRIPTION |
|---|---|
| `<a>` | Anchor tag. Creates a hyperlink. Supports the `target` attribute, with possible values of `_self`, which references the current window and has no effect outside of frames-based sites; `_blank`, which opens the link in a new browser window; `_top` and `_parent`, both of which have no effects outside of frames-based sites. Also supports `href`, a required atttibute to specify the target page for the link. You can specify either a relative path, such as `"index.html"`; an absolute path, such as `"http://www.robhuddleston.com"`; or a reference to an ActionScript function, such as `"event:someText"`. When using `event`, Flash Player dispatches a `TextEvent` event; in this case, the event's `text` property would be set to `someText`. You can create a function to handle the event, just like any other event, and respond accordingly. |
| `<b>` | Bold tag. Renders the enclosed text in a bold typeface. If a bold typeface does not exist for the current font, the tag will have no effect. |
| `<br>` | Break tag. Inserts a line break. The field's `multiline` property must be set to `true` for this to work. |
| `<font>` | Font tag. Formats the enclosed text. Supported attributes include `color`, which takes a hexadecimal color value in the form #RRGGBB; `face`, which takes the name of one or more fonts in a comma-separated list to be used to display the text; and `size`, which can take either absolute pixel sizes such as 12 or 18 or relative sizes such as +1 or -3. |
| `<img>` | Image tag. Inserts the specified image into the field. JPG, GIF, PNG, SWF, and `MovieClips` can be inserted. Text will flow around the inserted image. The field must have its `multiline` property set to `true`. You need to specify the path to the image to be inserted via the tag's `src` property. You can use either a relative or absolute path. If referencing a `MovieClip`, you need to use its linkage identifier, set through the Properties dialog box in the library. `src` is the only required attribute. You can optionally include the width and height, each in pixels. You can use `align` for the horizontal alignment of the image within the field; valid values are `left` and `right` — `left` being the default. The space around the image can be controlled with the `hspace` and `vspace` attributes; the default for both is 8 pixels. You can control the embedded image via ActionScript by providing an ID, which then serves as an identifier for the `MovieClip` that Flash creates to hold the image. |
| `<i>` | Italic tag. Renders the text as italic if an italic typeface exists for the current font. |
| `<li>` | List item. Creates an item in a list. Flash Player does not recognize either the `<ol>` or `<ul>` tag, so all lists are unordered and bulleted. |
| `<p>` | Paragraph tag. Creates a paragraph within the text. The field's `multiline` property must be set to `true`. You can optionally include an `align` attribute to change the text's alignment within the paragraph to left, right, center, or justify or a `class` attribute to reference a CSS class selector to style the paragraph, as defined by a `flash.text.StyleSheet` object. |
| `<span>` | Span tag. Creates a span within the text, usually to apply a style via the tag's optional `class` attribute. Note that ID selectors do not work in Flash Player to apply styles. |
| `<textformat>` | The text format tag is not technically an HTML tag, but it is supported nonetheless. It supports as optional attributes `blockindent`, which indents the text from both margins by the specified number of points; `indent`, which indents the first line of text and accepts both positive and negative values; `leading`, to set the leading, or space, between lines of text, `leftmargin` and `rightmargin` to indent either side by the speficied number of points; and `tabstops`, with takes an array of non-negative integers. Note that `leading` is set as a number of pixels between lines and is not measured as baseline-to-baseline as in traditional graphic design applications or even HTML. Therefore, if you are using 12-pixel text and want to add a half line between each line, you should set your leading to 6, not 18. |
| `<u>` | Underline tag. Underlines the specified text. Should be used with extreme caution to avoid confusion with hyperlinks. |

## HTML Entities

Flash Player also supports a set of character entities that enable you to insert characters that would otherwise be illegal:

| ENTITY | DESCRIPTION |
|--------|-------------|
| &amp; | Ampersand, & |
| &lt; | Less than, < |
| &gt; | Greater than, > |
| &quot; | Double quotes, " |
| &apos; | Apostrophe or single quote, ' |

# INDEX

## SYMBOLS AND NUMBERS

## A

# INDEX

# INDEX

# INDEX

# INDEX

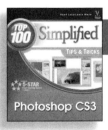

# ...all designed for visual learners—just like you!